IN THE
SHADOWS
OF ROMANCE

IN THE
SHADOWS
OF ROMANCE:
ROMANTIC TRAGIC DRAMA
IN GERMANY, ENGLAND,
AND FRANCE

◆JEFFREY N. COX◆

OHIO UNIVERSITY PRESS
ATHENS

Library of Congress Cataloging-in-Publication Data

Cox, Jeffrey N.
    In the shadows of romance.

    Bibliography: p.
    Includes index.
    1. European drama (Tragedy)—History and criticism.　2. Drama—18th
century—History and criticism.　3. Drama—19th century—History and
criticism.　4. Romanticism—Europe.　I. Title.　II. Title: Romantic tragic
drama in Germany, England and France.
PN1898.E85C68　1987　　　　　　809.2'512　　　　　　87-1585
ISBN 0-8214-0858-5

For My Parents
Always an Inspiration

TABLE OF CONTENTS

PREFACE

Théophile Gautier tells us that in the Paris of the romantics, "All thoughts of youth turned to the stage...."[1] This could, in fact, be said of virtually every major writer of the nineteenth century, young and old, from Wordsworth and Hugo, Goethe and Scott to Swinburne and Mallarmé, James and Zola. Very few romantic poets or novelists would be excluded from a list of writers who shared the dream of creating a great body of drama for their age that would rival the tragedies of the Greeks and of Shakespeare. In England, Coleridge, Wordsworth, Scott, Byron, Shelley, Landor, Beddoes, Lamb, and Hunt each wrote at least one play; Keats conceived his astounding poetic achievements as mere apprentice work that would one day "nerve me up to the writing of a few fine Plays"; even Blake wrote a fragmentary *Edward II* and composed a short dramatic vision in response to Byron's *Cain*. In Germany, a long line of distinguished authors sought to establish German culture on an equal footing with English and French cultures by creating a great national dramatic tradition; the list runs from Storm and Stress playwrights like Lenz and Klinger through such major figures as Goethe, Schiller, and Kleist and their contemporaries, Tieck and the Schlegels, to such diverse figures as Grabbe, Grillparzer, and Büchner. From Madame de Staël's *De l'Allemagne* to Stendhal's *Racine et Shakespeare* and Hugo's famous preface to *Cromwell*, romantic writers in France made the conquest of the stage a major plank in the platform of romanticism; Hugo, Vigny, Dumas, and Musset all worked for a romantic victory in the theater.

Elsewhere the story was the same. Manzoni called for an Italian national tragic drama that would reject the unities and embrace romanticism. The Spanish romantics, returning from exile in 1834, brought with them the new forms of the romantic drama to aid them in their struggle to banish from their stage the Frenchified neoclassical plays imposed by Bourbon rulers. Central figures in the Polish romantic movement—Mickiewicz, Slowacki, and Krasinski—sought to establish a national literary tradition by writing dramas in a romantic mold. We could continue to expand our list: Pushkin, Alfieri, Nerval, Tennyson, Browning, Balzac, Lamartine, Hölderlin....

We rarely read these plays today. Romantic drama appears to us as a collection of poeticized plays that cannot hold the stage, weak copies of Elizabethan masterpieces, and sword-rattling melodramas. There is perhaps no other period the drama of which pleases us so little as does that of the nineteenth century. We can read Greek drama and seventeenth-century sexual comedies, Roman farces and Renaissance masques, medieval mysteries and absurdist plays, all with pleasure. But we balk at Hugo's *Hernani,* Byron's *Cain,* and Schiller's *Wallenstein.* We find little to appreciate in these works that the romantics hoped would rival Aeschylus, Shakespeare, and Racine.

Yet, as paradoxical as it may seem, dramatizing was the central mode of the romantic imagination. In earlier years, the epic may have provided the vehicle for an encyclopaedic vision of a culture, and thus the *Iliad, The Divine Comedy,* and *Paradise Lost* may strike us as the central works of their day; but Goethe created the masterpiece of romanticism in dramatic form: *Faust.* We have come to realize the importance of the dramatic mode to the romantic lyrics and novels that do win our favor. Robert Langbaum, for example, has explored the ways in which the romantic lyric adopted and adapted dramatic features; Peter Brooks has revealed the melodramatic heart of the romantic novel. There is clearly a dramatic imagination behind the poems of a Byron or a Browning and the novels of a Balzac or a Dickens.

Our tendency to ignore the dramatic efforts of the romantics thus threatens our understanding of other romantic works and of romanticism as a whole. It also weakens our understanding of the development of modern drama. We continue to see the history of the nineteenth-century drama only in relation to the victory of naturalism in the later part of the century. Most of us are taught to trace the development of modern drama from the rather feeble theatrical efforts of writers like Lillo and Diderot through the works of Scribe, Robertson, and Pinero to the "rebirth" of the drama in the plays of Ibsen, Strindberg, Shaw, and Chekhov; there is no place in this "history" for the dramas of Goethe and Schiller, Shelley and Byron, Hugo and Musset. How, then, are we to understand the importance of romantic plays for writers like Ibsen and Strindberg or for later figures like Artaud and Brecht? While each year brings new, insightful studies on the romantic period and on the modern drama, we have yet to do justice to the huge corpus of dramatic work produced by the romantics. There have, certainly, been some excellent forays into the field. Individual plays and playwrights have inspired such fine books as Stuart Curran's *Shelley's "The Cenci": Scorpions Ringed with Fire,* Jean Gaudon's *Victor Hugo dramaturge,* and Ilse Graham's studies of Schiller, Kleist, and Goethe. The theatrical history of the nineteenth century has always seemed more intriguing than its drama and has thus attracted, among other experts, Allardyce Nicoll, Marvin Carlson, Maurice Descotes, and Michael Booth. Perhaps the most important works have been those that explore the range of dramatic efforts made by romantic writers within a particular national tradition, works like Charles Affron's *A Stage for Poets: Studies in the Theatre of Hugo and Musset,* Benjamin Bennett's *Modern Drama and German Classicism: Renaissance from Lessing to Brecht,* Joseph Donohue's *Dramatic Character in the English Romantic Age,* W. D. Howarth's *Sublime and Grotesque: A Study of French Romantic Drama,* Terry Otten's *The Deserted Stage: The Search for Dramatic Form in Nineteenth-Century England,* and Benno von Wiese's *Die deutsche Tragödie von Lessing bis Hebbel.* I am deeply indebted to these works and to those of other scholars of the romantic drama. Yet each of these studies has in one way or another limited its approach to the drama, most have hedged in their evaluation of it, and thus none has really provided the thorough reevaluation of romantic drama as a whole that I feel is needed.

There has, in fact, been only one major work that has treated in a serious and comprehensive manner the drama of the romantics in England and on the Continent: George Steiner's *The Death of Tragedy.*[2] In view of our century's dislike for nineteenth-century drama and Steiner's overarching thesis of decline, it comes as no surprise that this, the central study of romantic drama, comprises an attack upon it. Steiner offers a wealth of insights into the plays he discusses, but he is finally interested in demonstrating the failure of romantic drama and in indicting the contribution of romanticism to the deadening of Western man's tragic sense of life.

Steiner is not alone. Joseph Wood Krutch, Geoffrey Brereton, and many others exploring the tragic have doubted the ability of modern writers to create tragedy. And, of course, it is true that the romantics, who dreamed of combining the art of Shakespeare with that of Sophocles, wrote plays unlike those of either the Greeks or the Elizabethans. The question is whether the romantics' failure in the impossible task of revivifying past forms removes their dramas from the realm of the tragic. Since Steiner believes that there is only one model for tragedy, he must see the romantics as contributing to its demise. His definition of the tragic is normative. Like most students of tragedy, he establishes a set of criteria and rejects as nontragic any work that does not meet it. Such a normative definition tends to condemn change in a genre. If an author offers an innovative tragedy, he more likely than not will be seen as a contributor to the "death" of the form.

There are, of course, other critics who completely reject such restrictive definitions, arguing that each new play that calls itself tragic must alter our idea of the genre. Morris Weitz, for example, in his *Hamlet and the Philos-*

ophy of Literary Criticism, concludes that, "The concept of tragedy, thus, is *perennially debatable.*"[3] I hope to steer a middle course between the prescriptions of Steiner and the relativism of Weitz. The desire to write tragedy is present in every period of our literature; many artists have felt they were writing tragedies even if we do not agree that they succeeded. Each age has had to confront the issues central to this genre, issues such as the idea of the hero, the relationship between man and whatever lies beyond and above him, the fact of man's mortality. The need to face such issues persists. It is the form of tragedy that cannot last. In approaching the drama of any period, we need to recognize that writers can alter the form and even the vision of earlier tragedy without abandoning a commitment to the tragic. In the case of the romantics, we must accept the fact that they were unable to replicate classical or Renaissance drama, but at the same time we must seek to understand and to appreciate the transformation of the tragic which romantic writers wrought as they struggled to discover an equivalent to traditional tragedy for their own age. While modern critics have bemoaned the death of tragedy, nineteenth-century poets joined with Nietzsche in looking for its rebirth; and Nietzsche himself demonstrates the vitality of the romantic project of redefining the tragic. The romantic dramatists may have written when the structure and the vision of traditional drama were threatened as never before, but they sought to affirm in the collapse of traditional tragedy the heroic stature of man and the awe-inspiring nature of his fall that have always been associated with the tragic sense of life.

In part, then, my study seeks to answer Steiner's questioning of romantic drama. I have tried to offer the interpretive framework, the theatrical background, and the close readings of individual plays necessary to a thorough examination of the romantic drama in Germany, England, and France, the three countries that contributed most to the romantics' pursuit of the tragic. While I agree with Steiner that the romanticists did not write tragedies like those of Sophocles or Shakespeare or Racine, I hope to demonstrate that they were tragic dramas—that is, plays still in touch with a tragic sense of life that occupy the same place within the vision of romanticism that traditional tragedy held within earlier cultures.

This last point is important, for it seems to me that the attack upon romantic drama is also an assault upon romanticism. There is for us perhaps no greater sign of cultural weakness than the inability of a period to produce tragedy. Susan Sontag, in a piece entitled "The Death of Tragedy" included in *Against Interpretation,* has observed that "Modern discussions of the possibility of tragedy are not exercises in literary analysis; they are exercises in cultural diagnostics, more or less disguised." She sees works like Steiner's *Death of Tragedy* as elegies to the "lost potential of sensibility and attitude which the defunct form incarnated.''[4] Her discussion suggests that laments on the modern inability to create tragedy are less important as literary studies than they are as meditations on modern culture's inadequacies vis-à-vis traditional culture. Perhaps realizing that the epic has truly been lost as a possible form, we see tragedy as the greatest of literary modes. We are stingy with this word, *tragedy,* knowing that it is not merely a descriptive term but also a mark of praise. Only too well aware of the failings of the societies and cultures that have dominated the world since the birth of romanticism in the later eighteenth century, we are unwilling to believe that they could have produced tragedy. More specifically, as the many attempts to link tragedy with religious vision and practice suggest, we doubt that a secular, skeptical, and liberal culture provides the proper ground for a tragic tradition. Tragedy is the literary form that both exalts man as a hero and reveals him as a mere mortal, that both sets forth the grandeur of human culture and suggests its limitations as it confronts something beyond and perhaps greater than the human being. In denying its ability to create tragedy, our "diagnosis" of romantic culture would seem to be that it lacks a sense of its own limits, that it therefore cannot understand man's restricted lot, that it is incapable of confronting the evil in life, that it is, after all, too "romantic."

I cannot accept this "diagnosis" and would proffer a second opinion in the form of the following study. Romanticism did attempt to envision human life freed from the chains of oppression, ignorance, and violence—life remade by the imagination and love; but even at moments of visionary triumph, like that celebrated in Shelley's *Prometheus Unbound,* the romantic poets did not forget that man is subject to "death, and chance, and mutability." Their tragic dramas go further, to explore life dominated by such forces; that is, their dramas do test the limits and perhaps the collapse of their imaginative ideals, while trying to discover heroism in modern man's attempt to live in a world cut off from the God of tradition and denied a vision of an ideal future. While the romantics may have hoped to revive Shakespearean or Greek tragedy, what they did was to transform tragedy by exploring the dark side of their own poetic imaginings.

I have tried to indicate my intellectual debts to other scholars of the romantic drama above and in the notes and bibliography to this study; these debts are, of course, much deeper than any list or citation can indicate. How much more difficult is it then to detail more personal debts. The greatest of these is to Robert Langbaum, without whose wisdom and kindness this study would never have come into being. I also owe thanks to Paul Cantor, Frank Ryder, Robert Denommé, Alfred Turco, Jr., and Terry Otten, whose ideas and suggestions have shaped my work. My friends Phillip Swoboda and Wayne Terwilliger devoted more time and energy to helping me than anyone should have. Jerome Loving offered advice and aid at a key moment in my work. Holly Panich, Helen Gawthrop, and the rest of the staff of Ohio University Press have been most understanding and helpful. To my wife Amy, I would just like to say, "It is finally done."

I would also like to offer thanks for permission to quote from two essays which appear elsewhere and contain portions of this study. "Melodrama, Monodrama, and the Forms of Romantic Tragic Drama" appeared in *Within the Dramatic Spectrum: The University of Florida Department of Classics Comparative Drama Conference Papers,* vol. 6, edited by Kare-lisa V. Hartigan (New York: University Press of America, 1986), 20-34; this essay covers some of the material treated in chapter 2 of this study and glances at the readings of *The Cenci* and *Lorenzaccio* in chapters 6 and 8. "Romantic Redefinitions of the Tragic" appears in the volume on *Romantic Drama* in the *Comparative History of Literatures in European Languages;* the volume is edited by Gerald Gillespie and published by Akadémiai Kiadó for the International Comparative Literature Association; this essay outlines the definition of romantic tragic drama I offer here in chapter 1.

NOTE ON TRANSLATIONS

I HAVE PLACED translations of the French and German works I treat in the text of my study. I have used accessible, standard translations, as identified in the notes; where such translations were not available, I have provided my own. The original French and German passages for the plays under discussion are found in the notes; I provide translations alone for non-dramatic works. Both the original and translated title are provided for plays the first time they appear; the translated title, after that.

CHAPTER ONE
ROMANTICISM
AND TRAGEDY

Tragedy seems to demand a closed world, a world from which the hero cannot (or will not) escape, a world that has narrowed to the point where choice and fate name two facets of the same act. The unities of place, time, and action, often defended on the grounds of verisimilitude, work less to make the tragic world believable, than to shield it from the myriad possibilities of life that might lead away from tragedy. Even when the unities are violated, we usually experience a movement into an enclosed world. Othello leaves Venice behind to travel to Cyprus, but in doing so he journeys from the courtly Christian society that has witnessed his marriage to a primitive, claustrophobic land that provides the backdrop for murder and suicide. Hamlet, who escapes briefly from the hothouse of the Danish court to wander in the romance world of pirates, returns to the confines of Elsinore and so to certain death. Sophocles' Oedipus perhaps best reveals the tragic hero's fated affinity for a closed world. Because he seeks to avoid tragedy by fleeing his assumed parents and becoming a wanderer, he ironically returns to Thebes, the tragic place from which he cannot escape. The variations may be as many as the ways of genius, but tragedy always returns to a closed world at its climactic moments.

Many have argued that the romantic age must therefore be antitragic, for it seems to demand an open world.[1] Following upon the simultaneously liberating and destructive work of the Enlightenment, the vision of romanticism was forged during what R. R. Palmer has called "the age of democratic revolution," from 1760 to 1800;[2] it was further tempered by the tumultuous years of the early nineteenth century, marked by the Napoleonic Wars, Restoration and repression, and further revolution. This vision was shaped in particular in the fires of the French Revolution, perceived as enacting the previous century's attacks upon the hierarchies, immutable laws, and mythic repetitions that had defined traditional society. While we must avoid any simple equation of romanticism and revolution, romanticism arose within a period of political, social, economic, and cultural upheaval that resulted in a fundamental break with traditional society and with the literary forms like tragedy which it had supported. Born in this era, romanticism celebrated the liberated individual. It embraced new lands, remote times, and strange experiences. It delighted in new and open literary forms that sought to reflect a world of endless possibilities; one thinks of the unending travels of Byron's Don Juan, of the kaleidoscope of modes and moods in Schlegel's *Lucinde*, or of the encyclopaedic reach of Goethe's *Faust* and Hugo's *La Légende des siècles*.

Romanticism brought, after all, the rebirth of romance and thus of the quest that breaks out of the enclosed world of tragedy. This opposition between tragedy and romance had appeared as early as the Homeric epics: locked in combat between the city and the sea, the Greek and Trojan heroes can only seek a tragic death, but Homer's great antitragic figure, Odysseus, can leave behind the confines of the tragic world to make his life into a romance as a wanderer always moving on to new adventures, always able to avoid the identification with a single act or place that leads to tragedy. In adopting the romance, romanticism explored a potentially antitragic theme, that of personal change and development. From the growth of the poet's soul in Wordsworth's poetry to the evolution of Satan in Hugo's *Fin de Satan*, the romantics sought paths for the individual to follow out of or around limits. Such poems defeat tragic closure in pursuit of imaginative romance.

But what if this quest fails? What if man cannot reach the ideal he seeks? For Friedrich Hebbel, Greek tragedy could reach an ideal order—the Idea—by a straight path, and Shakespearean tragedy also achieved it, if by a "crooked line"; but modern plays, such as those of Goethe, found division within the ideal itself, "the dialectical problem in the Idea."[3] While romanticism seeks a world made new by the imagination, it begins with an awareness of what was lost in the collapse of an older order—whether it be the loss of the innocent state of nature imagined by Rousseau and Schiller, of the perfection of morals and art that Shelley found in ancient Greece, or of the hierarchical and organic "age of faith" admired by Novalis and Carlyle. The romantics may have celebrated the independent individual, but they were only too well aware that his new freedom brought with it the isolation and alienation of intense self-consciousness. Romanticism inherited the struggle of the Enlightenment to free man from religious, political, and ideological oppression; but the romantics also knew that this struggle had resulted in the Revolution and its literal and violent destruction of the way of life ruled by Monarch and Priest. What happens when man finds that he has destroyed the closed world of the traditional order, but that he is unable to break through to the open world of the romantic imagination? Is there not, in this moment between the fall of the order of the past and the creation of a new romantic order, an occasion for a peculiarly modern tragedy? Is there not a tragic drama lurking in the shadows of imaginative romance?

Certainly critics like George Steiner do not believe so. In *The Death of Tragedy*, Steiner goes beyond conventional complaints that the romantics as lyric poets were incapable of penning actable plays, to argue that romanticism was unable to present the closed and ordered world of tragedy. Steiner believes that from the Greeks through Shakespeare and Racine, the tragic was within the reach of the Western imagination. He contends that tragedy became impossible after rationalism and secular metaphysics undermined the world view that saw human life enclosed by a providential plan and a hierarchical social system. He argues that in tragedy, from the Greeks to Racine, "mortal actions are encompassed by forces which transcend man."[4] Steiner sees tragedy as revealing a divine realm. It possesses a plot that follows a providential script, whether that of the Greek oracles or that of the Christian God. A hierarchical social order defines the tragic hero, for it identifies as heroic those who occupy the summit of that order, it reveals the significance of their fall from such a height, and it ensures that this fall will have a public significance. Steiner argues that romantic drama lacks a sense of the divine, that it orders its plots only by drawing upon the moralistic melodrama, and that it sought tragedy not in the fall of great personages but in the private troubles of inward-turned individuals.[5]

However, the decisive blow to tragedy came for Steiner not with the loss of the traditional metaphysical or political orders but with romanticism's acceptance of what he sees as a Rousseauist, secular "redemptive mythology." He makes this point in noting that Schiller called his *Maid of Orleans* (*Jungfrau von Orleans*) "Eine romantische Tragödie":

and this is, I believe, the first time the antithetical terms "romanticism" and "tragedy" were conjoined. They cannot honestly go together. Romanticism substituted for the realness of hell which confronts Faustus, Macbeth, or Phèdre, the saving clause of timely redemption and the "compensating Heaven" of Rousseau.[6]

Such a "redemptive mythology," that enables the protagonist of romantic drama to experience a "remorse" that reconciles him with the cosmos and thus wins for him a "compensating Heaven" either in the next world or even on earth, cannot be tragic for Steiner: it evades the judgment that closes in on the tragic figure and allows him to escape the web of fate woven from his past actions and the punishment they should bring. Despite all of his insistence upon a divine order for the tragic world, it is destruction that for Steiner is essential to tragic closure, for "any realistic notion of tragic drama must start from the fact of catastrophe. Tragedies end badly."[7] The gods themselves may no longer dwell with us, but for Steiner it is the departure of punishing devils that signals the end of tragedy.

The apparent inconsistency in Steiner's attack upon romantic drama also surfaces in his treatment of Christian tragedy. Discussing *Samson Agonistes*, he calls Christian tragedy "a notion in itself paradoxical"; he finds Milton's play "in part a *commedia*," but he seems to accept it as a tragedy nonetheless.[8] Behind these hesitations lies an unresolved tension in Steiner's sense of the tragic. On the one hand, he feels tragedy must participate in a providential order upheld by the Greek or Christian, but not the romantic, world view. From this perspective, the romantics failed to produce tragedy because they abandoned the traditional Christian vision. On the other hand, Steiner deems a catastrophic climax essential to tragedy, a climax like that of *Antigone*, where the destruction brought down upon the guilty and the innocent alike suggests that whatever order the universe possesses may well be beyond man's ken. Given this sense of the tragic, he sees the romantics as merely hastening the death of tragedy by secularizing the redemptive vision with which Christianity had already weakened Western man's tragic sense. Peter Brooks points to the distance between Steiner's two views of tragedy:

The problem is not, as George Steiner would have it, that "the romantic vision of life is non-tragic," in that Romanticism promises a "compensating heaven" to "the guilt and sufferings of man." Steiner goes astray, I believe, in his argument that Christian (or Rousseauist) redemption is incompatible with tragedy. Some form of a reconciliation to the Sacred is probably indispensable to the tragic, and this is no less true for *King Lear* or *Phèdre* than it is for the *Oresteia* or the *Bacchae*. It is thus not the rise of Christianity that makes tragedy impossible, but rather its decline, entailing the loss of the last operative system of embracing sacred myth—as Steiner appears in other pages of his book to recognize.[9]

While Steiner's differing accounts of the death of tragedy may weaken his definition of the tragic, it is clear that his attack upon romantic drama rests upon his contention that romanticism, in abandoning the divine and redeeming man from demonic destruction, turned from the traditional vision of an enclosed, orderly universe. Before we can assess the merits of this critique of romantic drama, we need a firmer sense of traditional tragedy, that is of tragedy from Aeschylus to Racine.[10] I do not pretend to offer an absolute or all-inclusive definition of tragedy; in fact, such a definition would work against my argument, since I hope to demonstrate that the romantics created plays that were both recognizably tragic and significantly different from traditional tragedies. My goal has been to delineate the central and vital concerns to which all tragedies are related in some way and from which tragic artists draw perennial inspiration.

I
TRADITIONAL TRAGEDY AND THE ROMANTIC REDEFINITION OF THE TRAGIC

AS STEINER'S HANDLING of traditional tragedy may have already suggested, the tragic world is suspended between a vision of order and a fall into chaos, between the revelation of the divine and the destruction of man. Some such tension seems essential to our sense of the tragic—whether we define it as a struggle between fate and free will, an opposition between a revelation of the divine and the destruction of the hero, or a debate between "optimistic" and "pessimistic" interpretations of tragedy. Tragedy confronts the gaps that arise between the life of man and an extrahuman order, an enclosing order that might in different plays be conceived as the will of the gods, the power of fate, the providential plan of God, or even the natural rhythms of life and death. We can get a better sense of the concern of tragedy with the rifts between the human and whatever lies beyond man if we compare it to comedy. In comedy, whether the problem be confusion about appropriate mates as in Plautus or Shakespeare's romantic comedies, the imposition of a destructive law as in *The Merchant of Venice* and *Measure for Measure*, or the domination of society by fixated, "humourous" men as in Jonson and Molière, the questions raised concern the social order and can be solved in social terms. The resolution defines each character's place within the social sphere; and thus the end of comedy is usually marked by the marriage of appropriate social and sexual partners (e.g., *A Midsummer Night's Dream* or *The Way of the World*) and the expulsion of antisocial characters (e.g., *Volpone* or *The Misanthrope*). This resolution may gesture towards a cosmic order. We may feel, for example, that a larger Christian vision lies behind the pattern of Shakespeare's comedies. But there is rarely in comedy a suggestion of cosmic *dis*order. This is the province of tragedy.

In comedy, man opposes man within society. In tragedy, the fabric of human society is rent and the individual thus faces his world without the mediations of society. Tragedies typically begin with the recognition of the breakdown of the structures of everyday social life that would otherwise provide man with a secure sense of himself and his place in the scheme of things. There may be civil strife that thrusts the protagonist from society as in *Coriolanus*. Cultural and political upheaval may threaten man's sense of himself as in the *Bacchae* where Pentheus cannot be certain to which god he owes allegiance, or as in *Antony and Cleopatra*, where Antony is slowly dismembered by the tuggings of the rival claims of Egypt and Rome. Perhaps two opposing visions of order battle each other as in *Antigone*, or a confusion of values exists as in *Macbeth*, where "fair is foul." In *Hamlet, King Lear*, and countless Jacobean dramas, society finds itself dominated and thus undermined by usurpers, murderers, and adulterers. Human society may even directly challenge God's plan for man as in *Samson Agonistes* or Racine's *Athalie*. In each case, human existence has lost the clear, meaningful shape the gods or God grants it. Society, rather than mirroring a providential plan, lacks order—or, worse, embraces a demonic order of violence and perversity.

With society in disarray, the individual must confront alone the question of whether there is a final order for life. Prometheus bound to his rock, Hamlet drawn apart by the ghost, the exiled Orestes wrestling with the Furies—these are memorable images of man cut off from the companionship of his fellow man and threatened by messengers from an extrahuman and perhaps inhuman realm. We often conceive of tragedy as man's battle against the gods or fate, because tragedy questions the order that lies outside the stockade of rules and laws erected by society. The stakes in tragedy are always the highest. Othello, for example, may find himself involved in sexual and marital difficulties rather than in a war with heaven, but he realizes that more than domestic felicity is at stake; when he loses his love for Desdemona, he finds, "Chaos is come again" (III, iii, 92).[11]

The sense of cosmic disruption that we find in tragedy implies that, in fact, an absolute order exists to be disturbed—whether man can comprehend that order or not. Tragedy confronts chaos but is grounded in a vision of order. Prometheus challenges Zeus's rule, but never doubts that fate provides his destiny with an intelligible shape. Hamlet's tragedy—arising as it does from the loss of his rightful place in society, his filial ties to his parents, and perhaps even his reason—is defined in relation to a vision of order in which society, the family, and even the individual's character all possess a divinely sanctioned, hierarchical structure, an order in which "There's a divinity that shapes our ends, / Rough-hew them how we will" (V, ii, 10-11). Oedipus's murder of his father and his own marriage to his mother impress us as centrally tragic because they strike at the most fundamental human bonds. The very fact that we can talk of tragic figures transgressing laws, violating limits, and overturning taboos suggests the importance to tragedy of a sense of law, limit, or taboo. The questioning of traditional patterns of life threatens a fall into chaos only from the perspective of a valid enclosing order.

The presence of some extrahuman order is strongest in those works that end—*pace* Steiner—in reconciliation. In some tragedies, man rediscovers the connection between his life and the divine. In *Oedipus at Colonus,* for example, the gods welcome the former violator of their laws. In *Macbeth,* Malcolm is crowned the rightful, anointed king of Scotland, as the divine and human realms once again come into alignment. In other works, a new order is established to overcome the catastrophe facing man, as in the *Oresteia* where Athena persuades both men and gods to accept a new system of justice or in *The Cid* where a society of love and loyalty replaces the rule of harsh laws and violence.

There are, of course, plays in which the transcendent order is not embodied in human institutions, but rather implied by the very distance between human life and the divine plan. The tragic life of Samson Agonistes, for example, invokes the ideal pattern of Christ's life, of which Samson's is only a shadowy prototype. Again, Antony and Cleopatra's quest for immortal fame through *eros* can be placed in relation to the soon-to-be-granted revelation of the divine plan in which immortality will be won through *caritas*. Perhaps other Shakespeare plays, like *Othello* and *Lear,* belong here, too, with their final assertion of a social order of survivors who seem to lack the energy of the heroes and villains who have perished. In such plays, we might begin to feel that the resolution achieved at the end of the action is inadequate to the problems raised during it. In a play like Euripides' *Orestes,* the order mandated by the gods makes little sense from man's perspective. When Apollo descends at the end of that play to foreclose destruction and to enforce marriage between the warring parties, the order he establishes can only strike us as grotesque in view of the violence that threatened just moments before. We find tragedy here (and in some Jacobean plays) not in the moment when traditional order is threatened, but in the long aftermath following the collapse of this order, when man can no longer find a way to affirm a meaningful structure for life. There may be a wide variation in these tragedies—from plays that conclude with man in accord with his gods, through plays in which man has not yet won his way through to a life ordered in accordance with divine will, to works in which the order of the gods seems inadequate to the dilemmas of human life—but tragedy is always centrally concerned with the question of the final pattern for man's existence.

Tragedy may begin with the disruption of the order of things and end with its reassertion, but such a pattern is hardly a complete description of tragedy. If tragedy merely comprised a movement from confusion to revelation, it would be difficult to distinguish it from romances—like those of the grail quest or those found in Spenser's *Faerie Queen*—that move towards man's discovery of a world remade in the light of the divine and his integration into it. Tragedy, however, is concerned not only with the loss of order and its return, but also with the hero's attempt to create in the chaotic interim between these two moments his own vision of order based upon a sense of his own greatness, upon the shape and power he has given his own character.

While there are those critics who argue that the hero is not present in all tragedies and thus should not be considered part of the definition of tragedy,[12] the key tragedies of the Western tradition from Aeschylus's *Agamemnon* to Racine's *Phèdre* tell stories of extraordinary individuals who seek to impose their wills on their worlds. There is much truth in the commonplace that comedy is concerned with society, while tragedy explores the individual: in confronting the individual with the divine, tragedy raises questions not only about the order of the universe but also about the nature of the human character.

Of course, the traditional hero is not defined in isolated subjectivity. He has achieved a place at the summit of his society. He is, as Chaucer's Monk tells us, the man of high degree. While we should avoid the reification of this insight that would assert a necessary link between heroism and a particular class, it is true that the traditional hero requires both the dignity and the freedom granted only to the man who sits atop the social hierarchy. The heroic individual needs the fame granted him by society, for it provides him with proof of his heroism. Thus Achilles' heroic sense of himself is threatened when Briseis, the war spoil that manifests his fame, is taken from him; and Antony, sporting in Egypt, worries about what is said of him in the streets of Rome. Moreover, the hero also needs the independence from social controls that is possessed by those who rule. He is of society in that it reveres him, but also above it in that he seeks to escape from its restrictions. He is like Oedipus, who uses his position as king to assert his will over the objections of all those around him, or like Faustus, who has mastered human knowledge only to quest beyond it.

The hero also has a special relationship with the extrahuman forces of his world. Sitting at the summit of society and beginning even to move beyond it, the hero is in the frontlines of any conflict between the human and the divine. In plays like *Prometheus Bound* and *Doctor Faustus,* the hero himself challenges the gods in pursuing human freedom and power. In other works, the hero is responsible for severing the ties between his society and the divine order; for example, Oedipus unwittingly causes the plague Apollo rains down upon his city, and Lear divides and disrupts his kingdom. At times, the hero is not the cause of the confusion in his world, but the witness to it, the man who can—like Hamlet—best perceive the nature and source of his society's rot. Such figures may, again like Hamlet or like Marlowe's Tamburlaine, see themselves as the "scourge" of heaven, doing God's will. Whether he sees himself as God's messenger or the enemy of the gods, the hero believes that he knows the proper shape for his world. Whether he is the proud overreacher storming the heavens or the revenger attempting to restore single-handedly the moral balance of his world, he tries to bend the world to his will. Thus, when the gap between the human and the divine opens, it is the hero who asserts himself as the solution to the disorder. In the hero's eyes, the structures and rhythms of life that are disturbed in tragedy have in the past not only provided man with a secure order but also bound the extraordinary man within ordinary limits. With the old stability threatened, the hero, who feels he has mastered his world, glimpses the possibility of extending human power and vision. The closed world compromised, he would become the hero of a world no longer bound by such closures.

Whatever the hero's relationship to society or the gods, his heroism results from his absolute sense of himself, and his heroic task is to offer himself as the solution to his world's problems. The fame he wins from society and the contact or confrontation he has with the gods are rewards granted the hero; they identify but do not define him. Of course, the hero is recognized as such because he has accomplished extraordinary deeds— whether they be acts of prowess (Ajax or Coriolanus), of leadership (Agamemnon or Lear), or of intellect (Oedipus or Faustus). However, as the range of heroic deeds suggests, heroism does not rest in a particular action but in the ability to act with greatness. The hero is the man who has found within himself the power to free himself from the limits that define and restrict other men.

The hero resists any external force that would shape him and insists that he is self-defining. For example, Othello has, before the opening of his play, left behind the secure position that was his as a man of "royal siege" to establish himself as a hero in his "unhoused free condition" (I, ii, 21– 28). Prometheus will not allow himself to be shaped by Zeus's will. Faustus will not accept the traditional limits set on man's knowledge. The revenger, like Hamlet or Tourneur's Vindici, cannot abide society's tolerance of crime nor obey God's injunction against murder. Each of these heroic figures places himself above or beyond the bounds recognized by ordinary men. Heroic men insist they live in what Hegel calls "absolute independence" and thus can assert a total unity between who they are and what they do; for neither identity nor action is to be shaped by anything outside the hero's own character: ". . . this heroic type of *personality* persists in immediate unity with all that he may will, act, and accomplish."[13] The monumental quality of the hero arises from his sense that he determines absolutely who he is and what he does.

There may be moments in which the hero loses control, but he always works to reestablish it. In the moment of self-recognition that many have felt to be a key to the definition of the hero, the heroic figure—whether he be Oedipus at Colonus offering a summary of his life or Othello at Cyprus trying to impress his sense of his fall upon the memory of his society—not only admits that he has violated some law or limit but also asserts that he possesses a final knowledge of his actions and thus control over them. Again, while there is a movement in the development of tragedy towards increasing subjectivity and thus towards a division between self and act, the traditional hero—whether he be the awesomely self-possessed Agamemnon or the inwardly-troubled Hamlet—finally achieves the "immediate unity" between his character and his actions that we gesture towards in the phrase "character is fate."

The hero, then, is the man who has hoped to free himself from all restrictions in order to exalt his own human power, to pursue his own sense of what man is. He appears great in relation to other men because he has granted his own character an absolute status and thus given it intensity, integrity, and even a sense of inevitability. Having discovered a final shape for his own character, he tries to impose that shape upon his disordered world. Confronting the threat of chaos, the hero will become, like Nietzsche's superman, "the meaning of the earth." He adopts the role of Faustus's magician who "is a Demi-God, / Here tire my braines to get a Deity" (I, i, 89–90).[14] Much of the grandeur of tragedy rests in the fact that the hero, finding that the suprahuman plan for his world is in doubt, offers himself as a superhuman source of meaning.

At the height of his power, the traditional hero appears capable of granting a new significance to his world. His absolute conception of his character enables him to act with such resolution that his deeds take on the aura of destiny. His acts, though freely willed, appear necessary. He seems to have tapped some power that, once freed from the restrictions placed on it in the past, enables him to remake the world. Achilles on the battlefield, Coriolanus in his wrath, Faustus in his incantations, and even Phèdre in her passion, all take on such an elemental force that they seem ready to sweep aside anything that lies in their paths. The hero may conceive of the power he possesses as coming from the gods or arising from within, but in either case his magnificence and his pride lie in his conviction that he is the locus of an absolute power. And in this power there seems proof that man can be supreme in the world, that man can escape the limitations of the past to create a world open to the values and the order of the heroic human character.

Yet this heroic drive to recreate the world in one's own image also results in destruction. While the hero has claimed to free man from past limitations, he has, in fact, substituted the order of his own character for the threatened extrahuman order. He may have moved beyond the closed world of the past, but he has sought to enclose life within the order he finds in his own absolute sense of self. He thus brings destruction upon himself and upon those around him. In granting his character an absolute shape, the hero must destroy something quintessentially human within himself. He is forced to narrow his character, severing from his self-conception anything inconsistent with his heroic ideal. Euripides' Hippolytus and Pentheus, for example, both try to define themselves apart from powerful internal forces that finally return to destroy them.

Having narrowed his character so as to give it the order he seeks, the hero then pushes his capabilities so far beyond the normal limits of man that he begins to appear inhuman and approaches a world not of heroic value but of the criminal, the mad, and the demonic. The madness of Ajax and Lear, the destructive passions of Othello and Phèdre, the supernatural alliances of Faustus and Macbeth, all signal the point at which the exceptional and the extraordinary become the unnatural and the abnormal. Moreover, in pursuing the independent power that exalts him, the hero fails to recognize or to value those ties of love and loyalty that link him to others—as tragedy's woeful list of patricides, betrayers, and incestuous lovers attests. The heroic pride that finds an absolute in the hero's character may affirm man's power, but it destroys something essentially human for the sake of self. The tragic hero learns the truth of the insight Macbeth ignores: "I dare do all that may become a man; / Who dares do more is none" (I, vii, 46–47).

The hero's attempt to mold the world to his will also violates the extrahuman order that, though challenged, still structures his world. When the hero transgresses against the limits of his own humanity, he becomes subject to the external forces the temporary obscurity of which encouraged him to make his stand. The overreacher who storms heaven only to be hurled into the depths, the tyrant who asserts his total authority only to become a martyr to man's creaturely state, the man who has risen to the summit of his society only to be brought low by the wheel of fortune— each of these key tragic patterns provides an image of man's subjugation to an extrahuman force at the very moment when he was about to shatter all the chains of human existence. The hero having failed to order the world, the divine returns—perhaps to punish as in *Doctor Faustus* or to heal as in the *Oresteia,* to enforce the rule of fate as in *Romeo and Juliet* or to reveal God's plan as in *Samson Agonistes.* None of these resolutions is more tragic than the others. They all partake of the tragic, for they explore the relationship between the human and the divine.

For the richness of tragedy does not lie in the assertion of a particular world order or in the total affirmation of the hero; as Northrop Frye has pointed out, a work that focuses upon the destruction of man by a force beyond his control is ironic, not tragic, and a play in which the hero is capable of freely bending the world to his will is a romance.[15] The richness of tragedy depends rather upon its simultaneous intimation that there exists an order beyond man—perhaps even beyond his understanding—and its suggestion that man possesses a power, an irreducible strength of character that cannot easily be contained within the limits the gods set for him. Tragedy looks to both the new order the hero would usher in and the closed world the gods defend. Out of the disorder and destruction that attend the confrontation between the hero and the gods arises an expanded sense both of man's potential and of the extrahuman order that limits it.

Traditional tragedy, then, originates in a vision of a closed world and returns to it, but it also presents a moment when a rift between the human and the extrahuman offers the heroic individual the opportunity and the task of opening his world to the power he has discovered in himself. Steiner argues that the romantics could no longer write such tragedies, for they presented neither men whose heroism takes them so far beyond ordinary limits that they must be destroyed nor an order outside of man capable of enforcing meaningful limits. While Steiner does provide us with a sense of what was lost to the tragic dramatist in the movement from traditional culture to that of the romantic age, he does not see that the romantics sought to recover the tragic by grounding it in the very fact of that loss. While traditional tragedy explored the conflicts between the heroes and the gods, romantic tragic drama discovered a new tragic tension between the would-be hero's struggle to forge an autonomous, humane order for life and his fear that existence without the gods is chaotic and meaningless.

Clearly, the romantics could not reproduce Greek or Elizabethan drama, but such a failure is not the issue; for the romantics were not interested in reviving past forms of tragedy but in recovering the tragic vision. Because the romantic playwrights often imitated the formal features of traditional tragedy, we are misled into asking ourselves whether the romantics could write tragedies exactly like those of Sophocles and Shakespeare. We should instead ask ourselves whether the romantics preserved the tragic vision. Neoclassical tragedy had already fought an unsuccessful rearguard action against the decline of traditional tragic forms. The insistence on the unities worked to keep the world of tragedy closed. The doctrine of poetic justice asserted an absolute order for the tragic world even as the sense of life that supported such an order was being challenged. The titanic figures of the heroic drama invoked the rhetoric and stance of an older heroism in an increasingly unheroic world. The eighteenth century—which remade so many literary forms in the image of its own satiric, didactic, and loco-descriptive genius—was unable to impress its vision on tragedy, perhaps because tragedy more than any other form except the epic was "protected" by the rules and by classical precedent from innovation. While the literary theoreticians of the eighteenth century began to suggest a new sense of tragedy, its dramatists for the most part sought to maintain the form of tragedy rather than to renew its vision. Those playwrights, like Lillo or Diderot, who departed from the traditional form, ushered in the melodrama and the bourgeois *drame,* not a new tragic drama. This latter task fell to the romantics.

We will never arrive at an adequate sense of romantic tragic drama if we focus upon formal issues. The romantics did not write one type of play, but rather engaged a disparate set of dramatic forms. They borrowed from every conceivable precursor, from the Greeks, from Shakespeare and his contemporaries, from Calderón, and even from Racine. The plots of romantic drama were drawn from extremely diverse sources, from Greek myth and current life, national history and heroic romance. The romanticists—Hugo is a prominent example—wrote in both verse and prose. They experimented with historical realism and with visionary dream plays, as Byron's corpus attests. Some playwrights drew heavily upon the conventions of the contemporary theater, while others sought to reform it, and still another group shunned it altogether. Goethe's plays alone suggest the teeming variety of romantic drama, for his career embraced every dramatic tendency of the age, from the Storm and Stress problem play to the monodrama, from the "Shakespearean" *Götz von Berlichingen* to *Iphigenia in Tauris (Iphigenie auf Tauris)* and its romantic classicism. He recapitulated all of these modes in his masterpiece *Faust.* There is a sense in which the romantic drama attempts to incorporate all past and present dramatic forms, to experiment with every embodiment of the tragic vision. It is as if the romantic dramatist had a vision but lacked a style and thus was forced, not unlike nineteenth-century architects, to attempt every conceivable style. While in the next chapter I will turn to the romantics' search for a dramatic and theatrical form, it is clear that what makes all of these plays romantic tragic dramas is not their form; it is their shared tragic vision.

We thus err if we define romantic tragic drama as a simple rejection of neoclassical form—primarily the unities, but also the strictures of decorum on style and subject matter and the insistence on "moral" tragedy embodied in the doctrine of poetic justice. In France, where neoclassicism dominated the literary tradition, the debate over the rules can seem all-consuming. From François Guizot's assertion that Shakespeare and not Voltaire provided the model for modern French drama (1821), through

Stendhal's attack on the rules in *Racine et Shakespeare* (1823), to Hugo's "Preface" to *Cromwell* (1827) and the "battle" of *Hernani* (1830), the French romantics expended a great deal of energy in ridiculing the rules. Elsewhere similar assaults were launched. In Germany, Lessing had long before held that the only important unity was that of action; and his praise of Shakespeare, when seconded by Hamaan and Herder, led to the Shakespeare-mania of the Storm and Stress playwrights and those who followed them. In Italy, Manzoni challenged neoclassicism in his preface to *Carmagnola* (1820) and in his *Letter on the Unities* (1823). If the furor over the rules was tamer in England than on the continent, it was largely because the neoclassical tradition was less well entrenched, with Shakespeare always looming over the theater as the great counterexample to the efficacy of the unities.

While much ink was spilled over such formal issues, we mistake the impetus behind the romantic campaign to rediscover the tragic if we focus too narrowly upon such matters. As the case of a Lessing or a Samuel Johnson demonstrates, the unities had been successfully challenged well before the romantics came to write their plays. The romantics were not merely trying to replace one set of formal features with another. They protested against the idea that any set of formal rules defines the tragic. They sought to replace a definition of the form of tragedy with a definition of the tragic vision. This movement from form to vision, a part of the larger romantic attempt to redefine the genres and the hierarchy of genres, is revealed not only in demands for the end of generic distinctions—as in Gerstenberg's call, "Away with the classification of the drama"—but also in attempts, like that of J. S. Mill, to define genres in relation to the central emotion each expresses, or, as in the case of A. W. Schlegel, to discuss comedy and tragedy in relation to the "tone of mind" that lies behind them.[16] As the comments on tragedy by writers like Hegel, Schopenhauer, Shelley, and Hugo suggest, the romantics also sought to replace the moral emphasis of the doctrine of poetic justice with what Raymond Williams, in discussing Hegel's theory, has called "a metaphysic of tragedy." [17] For the romantics, the tragic was no longer identified with a particular aesthetic form, but rather with a vision or philosophy of life.

We can see this divorce between vision and form as one more example of what was lost with the passing of the closed world that underwrote the traditional literary types. However, we can also see this quest for a modern tragic vision as part of the project of romanticism as a whole as defined by Robert Langbaum:

Thus, the nineteenth century accepts the iconoclastic contribution of the eighteenth. It starts with the acknowledgment that the past of official tradition is dead. But it seeks beneath the ruins of official tradition an enduring truth, inherent in the nature of life itself, which can be embodied in a new tradition, a new Mythus.[18]

The romantic dramatist searches through the "ruins" of past tragic forms for the true tragic vision, for the tragedy inherent in the nature of modern life.

However, the romantic tragedian does not discover the new Mythus called for by Carlyle, the vision of a new imaginative order. This Mythus is, as Langbaum notes, the creation of the central works of romanticism. But romantic tragic drama arises in the moment between the loss of traditional culture and the creation of this new Mythus, between the collapse of the closed world and man's entry into an open world. We can perhaps see more clearly this relationship between romantic tragic drama and the key visionary works of romanticism if we glance at two quite different plays by Shelley. Shelley's *Prometheus Unbound* is one of the essential testaments to the romantic Mythus. After completing the third act of his great visionary drama, Shelley turned to write *The Cenci;* and in the dedication to that play, he pointed to the distance between his celebrations of the imagination and his tragic drama:

Those writings which I have hitherto published, have been little else than visions which impersonate my own apprehensions of the beautiful and the just . . . . they are dreams of what ought to be, or may be. The drama which I now present to you is a sad reality.[19]

This "sad reality" defines the plight of the man whose life is neither structured by providential and hierarchical orders nor organized by a new humanistic order of beauty and justice, vision and love. The romantic tragic protagonist can be neither a hero of traditional myth nor a member of the "visionary company" that creates the romantic Mythus. He is instead a man who must struggle to become heroic in opposition to the "sad reality" of his unheroic and unimaginative world. While *Prometheus Unbound* announces an imaginative triumph, *The Cenci* explores man's attempt to lead a heroic life in a world that defeats vision.

Traditional tragedy, resting upon a valid order, explores the chaos of its temporary eclipse and the heroic attempt to set it right, before returning to a vision of that order. Romantic tragic drama, as Shelley's comment on its "sad reality" suggests, begins in the chaotic world that follows the collapse of traditional order and explores the protagonist's struggle to break through to a world remade in the light of an imaginative ideal, a struggle which fails as the protagonist embraces the limited self and not the imagination, violence and not vision. Romantic drama redefines the terms of tragedy, but the dynamics of the tragic remain the same. Just as traditional tragedy explored the threats that challenged traditional culture, so does romantic tragic drama reveal the nightmare that haunts the imagination's "dreams of what ought to be." That is, romantic tragic drama portrays the failure of romanticism's own central literary mode—the visionary quest romance.

II
ROMANTIC TRAGIC DRAMA: THE SELF, REVOLT, AND HISTORY

ROMANTIC TRAGIC DRAMA arose, like the rest of romanticism, in response to the perceived collapse of traditional providential and hierarchical order. While Nietzsche did not preach the death of God until late in the nineteenth century, Steiner is certainly correct in contending that theistic tragedy was already moribund when the romantics first began to write at the close of the eighteenth century. The romantics wrote when it was no longer possible to present the divine directly on stage, when the gods no longer provided the framework and plot for tragedy. While for Steiner this development marks the end of tragedy, the romantics found tragedy in man's loss of the divine and in his continuing attempt to make sense of a chaotic world from which the gods have fled.

This point is perhaps made most emphatically in those romantic plays that still ostensibly engage a theistic world view. Byron's *Cain,* for example, retells the Bible story and would thus seem to contradict our sense that the romantics could no longer dramatize the divine. However, Byron's revisionist play focuses not upon the divine, but upon Cain's sense of loss in being kept from Paradise and thus from direct contact with God. Cain desperately wants to discover a divine plan for life, but Jehovah's rule appears to him as oppression, not order. He longs for the divine presence, but like Goethe's Faust meets only a demonic messenger. The God invoked by Shelley's Count Cenci, the cosmological order sought by Schiller's Wallenstein, and the vague sense of fate embraced by Hugo's Hernani are all revealed as, at best, weak echoes of an earlier theistic vision and, at worst, emblems of an oppressive world, Blakean Nobodaddies.

With the loss of a providential plan, the hierarchical organization of society also ceases to provide a meaningful structure for human life. Not only the gods are lost, but also the heroic sense of life supported by the social organization of traditional tragedy. The romantic protagonist is not, like the figures of traditional tragedy, a hero by virtue of his lofty place in society and the fame it grants to him. The romantic character must struggle to create himself as a hero in opposition to an unheroic world. Many romantic plays explore explicitly a contrast between a traditional, heroic society and the modern, unheroic age. Schiller and Goethe were especially concerned with dramatizing the change in the hero's relationship to his society.[20] Goethe portrayed in his *Götz von Berlichingen* the moment when the feudal society of heroes gave way to a modern, bourgeois world lacking a heroic sense of life. In *The Robbers (Die Räuber),* Schiller has Karl Moor revolt against a world that he feels has lost touch with the grandeur of the past. Moor's protest originates in his sense of the distance between his "puny age" and the time when the world was filled with heroes like those described by Plutarch. We find a similar longing for a heroic past throughout romantic drama. We hear Moor's call for Plutarchan heroics echoed by Musset's Lorenzaccio. Like Goethe's Götz, Byron's Marino Faliero finds himself at a pivotal moment in his society's history when the structures that have supported his heroic self-image begin to collapse. The romantic protagonist does not find himself as a hero within society, but— like Hugo's Hernani—as an outcast in revolt.

We can agree with Steiner and others that the romantic protagonist is not a great personage at the center of his world who comes into conflict with the gods. However, we must still respect romantic man's attempt to become heroic. We must not confuse the romantic would-be hero with the modern antihero or "unheroic" hero (though, as the discussion of Kleist in chapter 9 suggests, there are glimpses of such a modern tragicomic figure in romantic plays). In an important sense, the romantic protagonist wants to live in the world of traditional drama; for then he would, in fact, be a hero and human existence would again possess the rich, powerful order found in traditional tragedy. But this attempt to emulate the heroes of the past merely emphasizes the distance between them and the romantic protagonist, as can be seen in the case of Hugo's Cromwell. Cromwell appears as a self-made man who not only has defined himself in opposition to the hierarchical order that structured English society in the past but has destroyed it as well. Through strength of will, he creates himself as the greatest man in his world. Yet Hugo's Cromwell is obsessed by one desire: to become King. An absolute ruler in fact, he wants the hierarchical and even providential role that marked the hero in the past. He finds that, as a romantic rebel, he will never attain the heroic status defined by the traditional order, an order he, ironically, destroyed. The play ends with Cromwell triumphant but still musing, "When will I be King?"(V, xiv).[21]

The romantic protagonist finds himself seeking heroism in an unheroic world and order in the midst of chaos. Though he lacks the absolute sense of self granted the traditional hero, his heroism lies in his continuing struggle to become heroic, to forge a meaningful order for his own life and for the modern world. This project has two important aspects or phases. Cut off from objective systems of order, the romantic protagonist must first turn inward to discover an inner vision within which he is heroic and his world meaningful. He must then turn outward to act in an attempt to realize this vision. In view of his relationship to his society, this action can only take the form of a revolt waged in the name of his inner ideal.

This project arises in response to the collapse of traditional order, but it must be judged in relation to romanticism's quest for the open order of the imagination.[22] Romantic tragic drama engages the twin themes of selfhood and revolt which are central to romanticism as a whole. They are already present in the writings of Rousseau, "father" of romanticism and author of both the *Confessions* and *The Social Contract;* and they continued to be central concerns in Blake's visionary epics, Wordsworth's lyric autobiography, Schiller's essays, Goethe's *Faust,* the French poets' "social romanticism" and elsewhere. Romantic art was, after all, born in an age of revolutionary individualism, an age that experienced the isolation brought on by the disappearance and even the "death" of the divine, that felt the old ties of mutual family and community obligations threatened by the greedy atomism of the capitalist marketplace, that saw nature in retreat before technology and industry. Romanticism begins with the isolated, alienated individual, because he is the "given" of the post providential world it portrayed. It feels the lure of revolution as a political apocalypse that might usher in a new paradisiacal era in which man would be at peace with himself and the world.

In its key works, romanticism offered an ideal resolution to the difficulties of modern selfhood and the dangers of revolt. Romantic art cries out again and again against the isolation and alienation threatening man. We can hear this protest in Blake's "London" with its images of division and oppression and in Schiller's *On The Aesthetic Education of Man In A Series of Letters* with its assertion that "Selfishness has established its system in the very bosom of our exquisitely refined society." These issues echo in Michelet's history of the French Revolution with its account of the interplay between egotism and fraternity during the greatest political event of the era and in Wordsworth's *Prelude* with its exploration of the relationship between self-consciousness and nature.[23] We have come to understand that romanticism explores the self only in pursuit of what Geoffrey Hartman has called "anti-self-consciousness," usually a breakthrough into an imaginative realm where the divisions within the self and between the self and the external world are healed.[24] We have learned to uncover in romantic poetry a tripartite movement into and out of the self, a movement like that in Blake's myth from innocence through experience to an "organized" innocence. Again, Kleist sets forth a similar pattern in his essay "On the Puppet Theater," which traces the path of consciousness as it falls from the innocent grace possessed by the puppet into the self-consciousness of man only to expand and to transcend such awareness in the infinite consciousness of a god.[25] For us, romanticism is in large part a project to discover for the individual an identity—an indivisible, harmonious selfhood—that not only unites all of his faculties but also links him to other men and to the world around him.

Romanticism was, of course, also in part a cultural response to the revolutionary events of the day that marked every nation in Europe and that found their exemplary expression in the French Revolution. Shelley called the Revolution the "master theme" of the age;[26] Blake tried to work out the dynamics of that "master theme" in his so-called "Orc Cycle"; Wordsworth saw the Revolution as a vital moment in the growth of his poetic soul; in *Hermann and Dorothea* and elsewhere, Goethe sought a response to what he saw as the dangers of the Revolution; Hölderlin sang the glories of the revolutionary age in poems like his "Hymn to Freedom" and "Hymn to Mankind"; and the French romantics even suggested that romanticism be equated with revolution. While these writers adopt different postures vis-à-vis revolution and the Revolution, they all recognize that revolt defines their age. The Revolution awakened the hope for a world community freed from the dead hand of the past and the grasp of the egoistic self; but it also demonstrated the violent dangers attending this attempt to remake human life, dangers the romantics hoped could be overcome by an imaginative "transvaluation" of man, nature, and society. M. H. Abrams has argued that the poets turned from the destruction of political revolution to a vision of imaginative reformation.[27] It is the visionary Los and not the revolutionary Orc who redeems man's fall in Blake's myth. It is the organic metamorphoses of "Neptunism" that Goethe embraces, not the violent and revolutionary changes of "Vulcanism." Michelet, in examining the Revolution itself, insisted that the ideals of that "holy period" were love and sympathetic community, not violence and egotism. Shelley offered a non-violent "beau ideal" of the French Revolution in *The Revolt of Islam;* and he set forth perhaps the most memorable treatment of an ideal victory over tyranny in *Prometheus Unbound,* where imagination renews the world as Prometheus comes together with Asia in love.[28]

In its movement to the self and then to revolt, romantic drama offers the tragic version of this central romantic pattern. The world of romantic tragic drama is not that of the new visionary Mythus, but of the "sad reality" of history. It does not celebrate what Blake called the "Real Man, the Imagination," but rather portrays man's heroic attempt to shoulder the burdens of a limited selfhood. When the romantics transformed the drama into visionary poetry, as in *Prometheus Unbound,* they depicted the movement from this trapped world to one freed by the imagination; when Goethe tried, as we will see in chapter 4, to reconnect tragic drama with imaginative romance, he hoped to demonstrate that individual tragedies are a part of the larger quest of all mankind. However, in those plays that accept the limits of the drama and the theater, the romantics set forth the tragedy that occurs when the imaginative quest fails and man finds himself torn between the siren songs of the self and the call to revolutionary violence.

The inward turn of the romantic protagonist is perhaps the most familiar feature of these plays, but it has rarely been understood. It is the common view that the romantic dramatists replaced tragic myths with psychology, providential plots with character analysis; and that in doing so, they offered a one-sided and reductive treatment of the drama. While romantic writers and critics did stress the importance of character in the drama,[29] it should be clear that this focus upon the individual partakes of romanticism's exploration of the self and the consciousness of self. Romantic drama did not set out merely to depict the inner depths of single characters; this was, in fact, the technique of a rival contemporary form—the monodrama. Like romantic poetry, romantic tragic drama takes the individual as its starting point. It does present solitary protagonists like Manfred and Lorenzaccio, but it does so because their isolation from social and familial ties defines their brand of heroism and shapes their fate. Isolation, alienation, sickly subjectivity—these are problems confronted by romantic drama, not the parameters of its form.

In turning inward to find a vision of order with which to confront the chaos of his world, the romantic protagonist seems similar to the traditional hero. However, the hero faces a temporary break in a universal order, while the romantic would-be hero confronts the pervasive disarray of postprovidential life. Moreover, the hero possesses an absolute sense of himself, while romantic man initially has only an alienated, divisive self-consciousness. When the romantic protagonist turns inward, he discovers a chaos of passion and thought, spiritual longings and physical appetites. Neither providence nor society provides him with the means to structure the complexities of the self. He has no map to chart out the regions of the intellect, the will and the appetites, nor a role to shape his personality. The hierarchies of the inner life have collapsed with those of the outer world.

Denied the absolute heroism of the past, the protagonist of romantic tragic drama also cannot attain an imaginative "anti-self-consciousness." He must, like the quester of romanticism's lyric and narrative poetry, contend with the dangers of isolated selfhood, but he does not discover a visionary redemption from them. Instead, the romantic protagonist attempts to create a heroic mode of self-consciousness. That is, he seeks to grant his own subjectivity the absolute status that the traditional hero possessed by virtue of his position within objective systems of order. As Hegel notes, the romantic character strives for "the formal greatness of character and power of the personal life which is able to ride out everything that negates it."[30] Whether he is Byron's Manfred struggling to be true to his divided nature as "half dust, half deity" or Kleist's Homburg pursuing an ideal in his wish-fulfilling dreams or Hugo's Hernani claiming to mold the tumultuous passions within him into a "force that drives on," the romantic protagonist strains to transform his inner life into a powerful identity—not Kleist's "infinite" consciousness nor Blake's "organized" innocence which have been purged of self-consciousness, but an absolute selfhood. Hegel describes such characters as "free artists of themselves";[31] that is, denied imaginative vision and thus a world remade, the romantic tragic protagonist must be an artist of his own selfhood rather than a creator of a new world. He is like Schiller's "sentimental" artist. Possessing neither the "naive" unity of character of the traditional hero nor the imaginative unity of the visionary quester, he embraces an internal, self-conscious ideal of himself and his world.[32] His artful identity gestures beyond the alienation and isolation of the present to a fuller humanity, but it does not reach the visionary point where the imagination transcends the distinction between art and reality.

As a "free artist" of himself, the romantic protagonist may not become a visionary redeemer like Blake's Los or Shelley's Prometheus, but the artful shape of his identity—which grants his selfhood a more than subjective status—does enable him to escape some of the more debilitating modes of self-consciousness. Dangers arise when the romantic protagonist grapples with his inner life, for he may become lost in an inward gaze. Endlessly fixated upon the self, torn between this thought and that desire, he may become a romantic Hamlet, incapable of action and—in Goethe's words—"without the strength of nerve which forms a hero."[33] Or his struggle to know the self may lead him to betray his full humanity and to accept a reductive sense of himself. Schiller portrays men and women who, in order to control the self, identify themselves with only a portion of their full potential.[34] As Schiller's Franz Moor suggests, the isolated and alienated intellect poses a special danger, for romantic man is tempted to adopt a destructive mode of analytic consciousness that defines itself by severing all the ties that link the individual to others. He may then become an intellectual nay-sayer, a demonic spirit of negativity like Byron's Lucifer and Goethe's Mephistopheles. He may further discover that a dependence upon the analytic intellect leaves the individual unprepared to defend himself against his baser desires. Seeking to submit his self and his world to an intellectual idea, he may find himself, in fact, under the sway of an unconscious will. Shelley's *The Cenci* investigates all of these dangers of what he calls "self-anatomy"; his play will give me an opportunity in chapter 6 to examine the romantic tragedy of selfhood and the romantic protagonist's struggle to create a heroic self-consciousness that defeats at least the more nightmarish aspects of modern selfhood.

The creation of a heroic mode of self-consciousness is only the first step for the romantic protagonist. Once he has completed his journey into the interior of the self, he must then turn outward in order to body forth his self-conception and to remake his world. This outward turn is in part a flight from the self. Action offers relief from the burdens of the inner life. But it is also an attempt to liberate the present from the grip of the past. Brandishing the ideal he has discovered in his turn inward, the romantic protagonist hopes to impose that ideal on the future of his world. To do so, he must revolt.

From the rebellion of Schiller's Robber to that of the bandit Hernani, from the metaphysical plaint of Byron's Cain to the social protest of Dumas's Antony, from the conspiracy of Schiller's Fiesco to the revolution planned in Musset's *Lorenzaccio,* revolt dominates the action of romantic tragic drama. While the difficulties of subjectivity lie at the heart of the characterization of romantic drama, revolt shapes its plot. Romantic drama, arising from the ashes of traditional tragedy, can no longer draw its plots from myth. Instead, romantic man must plot his own life. He does not live in a mythic world where the fates chart his rise and fall. Rather, he lives in historical time, where the future seems uncharted, ready to be shaped by the human will. Revolt thrusts man into history and reveals itself as the paradigmatic attempt on man's part to shape his own life, to create an ideal future. As Camus suggests in *The Rebel*—a work which often reads as if it were a commentary on romantic drama—revolt is the only mode of action open to man in a postprovidential world:

If in a world where things are held sacred the problem of rebellion does not arise, it is because no real problems are to be found in such a world, all the answers having been given simultaneously. Metaphysic is replaced by myth. There are no more questions, only eternal answers and commentaries. . . . The rebel is a man who is on the point of accepting or rejecting the sacred and determined on laying claim to a human situation in which all the answers are human. . . . From this moment every question, every word, is an act of rebellion while in the sacred world every word is an act of grace. It would be possible to demonstrate in this manner that only two possible worlds can exist for the human mind: the sacred (or, to speak in Christian terms, the world of grace) and the world of rebellion. The disappearance of one is equivalent to the appearance of the other. . . .[35]

The romantic rebel asks with Camus: "Is it possible to find a rule of conduct outside the realm of religion and its absolute values? That is the question raised by rebellion."[36] Without traditional myth or new Mythus, the romantic protagonist finds his rule of conduct in the order he has given to his own self. He projects that order into the future in an attempt to shape history to the human will and a humane conception of life. His glory and his claim to heroic stature lie in his assertion of his inner ideal against the chaos of a world without God, against the oppression of a powerful but illegitimate political order, against a society that debases the spirit and exalts materialism. As Camus states, revolt is a demand for order:

Rebellion is born of the spectacle of irrationality, confronted with an unjust and incomprehensible condition. But its blind impulse is to demand order in the midst of chaos, and unity in the very heart of the ephemeral. It protests, it demands, it insists that the outrage be brought to an end, and that what has up to now been built upon shifting sands should henceforth be founded on rock. Its preoccupation is to transform. But to transform is to act, and to act will be, tomorrow, to kill. . . .[37]

This revolt in the name of order is, however, caught in a tragic dilemma. If the future seems open to a heroic ideal, it is in the unheroic present that the protagonist must act. Seeking to forge the future, he must adopt the debased means of the present and thus betray the ideal end for which he fights. As Camus suggests, revolt seeks transformation but brings destruction. Revolt, waged in the absence of a divine plan, falls into violence when it seeks to coerce history to follow a humane path. The French Revolution was, of course, the great historical exemplum of this tragic impasse. In his fascinating attempt to explain and to justify the violence of the Revolution, Hugo wrote in *Ninety-Three* of the link between violence and the ideal:

Great things are being planned. What the Revolution is doing at this moment is mysterious. Behind its visible work there is a work invisible. One conceals the other. The visible work is cruel, the invisible work is sublime. At this moment I can see everything very clearly. It is strangely beautiful. It was necessary to make use of the materials of the past. Hence this extraordinary '93. Under a scaffolding of barbarism, a temple of civilization is building.[38]

While Hugo puts a hopeful construction on this tension between the barbaric present and an ideal future, romantic tragic drama—including the plays of Hugo—finds that the violence of the present, the violence that arises when a revolt for the future must use the "materials of the past," compromises the "sublime work" which the rebel would undertake. Romantic drama explores the central difficulty of modern revolt, with its dream of completely transforming human life: how can man change the world until he has severed himself from the past to be born again in the light of the future ideal he pursues; but how can man change while he still lives in the present world that is unilluminated by that ideal? The romantic protagonist's solution to this dilemma—his choice of the violence of the present as the means to create the future—must be measured against the visionary solution of works like *Prometheus Unbound.* The fully imaginative man like Prometheus purges himself of the selfhood that ties him to the past and abjures the violence of the present in order to greet the world with love and vision. The protagonist of romantic tragic drama, however, has only the heroic selfhood he has created in emulation of the great men of the past and the violence of the revolt he must wage against the oppression of the present.

It is an interesting fact about the criticism of romantic tragic drama that, just as the introspection of its protagonists is seen as a weak imitation of Hamlet, so the historical emphasis of these plays has struck many as a feeble attempt to pit Shakespearean historical drama against neoclassical tragedy, and the violence of romantic drama has appeared as mere Gothic theatricality. It should be clear, however, that the problem of historical violence is important to romanticism as the literature of a revolutionary age. The murders, rebellions, executions, and suicides that fill the romantic stage are not merely a concession to a thrill-seeking audience. Romantic tragic drama draws upon the gruesome stage business of its day to depict the historical violence that defines the world of experience between innocence and vision.

It is important to note that this is not the ritual violence of mythic sacrifice and expiation, but the historical violence of unique acts of revolt. The historical ground for romantic violence has led some critics to deny it tragic status: if violence arises from a historical mistake and not from a fated action, presumably it is avoidable and thus not tragic.[39] However, it is the very historical nature of the violence these plays depict that makes it tragic. Historical violence has no ultimate significance as part of a divine plan. Violence cannot be purgative in romantic drama as it can be, say, in the plays of Shakespeare. Violence in traditional tragedy can contribute to a larger pattern of order. In romantic tragic drama, man's turn to violence can only compromise the order he would create. Mircea Eliade, in discussing the differences between traditional cultures and modern, historical culture, points out the distance between the traditional structuring of history through repeated mythic patterns and the modern confrontation with the "terror of history," a terror before a temporal succession composed of perhaps meaningless acts, that leaves man open to violence without explanation, destruction without salvation.[40] Romantic drama arose with the modern historical sense, the sense that history involves not only the past but a continuum running from the long ago through the present and into the distant future, the sense that this historical continuum might not follow a divine order and that the task of granting significance to history might fall to man himself. While the historical basis of these plays is often seen as a rather trivial affair to be dismissed with a few comments on local color, the involvement of romantic tragic drama with historical revolt evidences its confrontation with both the glory that attends man's attempt to make history and the terror that accompanies his recognition that the creation of the future entails the destruction of the present. This dual view of revolutionary man's place in history shapes the tragedy of revolt that we find, for example, in Schiller's plays (chapter 3), in Byron's historical dramas (chapter 5), and preeminently in Musset's *Lorenzaccio* (chapter 8).

The double task of the romantic protagonist offers him opportunities to prove himself to be a hero, but also provides occasions that invite tragic destruction. We can agree with Steiner that the romantics were barred from writing tragedies of the closed world and yet realize that they forged a new mode of tragic drama by depicting the travails of the extraordinary individual as he plumbs the ever-deepening recesses of the self and hurls himself into the rush of history. The romantic tragedy of the open world portrays modern, revolutionary man's heroic attempt to order the chaos of the liberated self and to shape history freed from divine control. He meets his tragedy when his rage for order leads him to betray the possibilities of an imaginative consciousness and a visionary future for the confines of the self and the violence of the present. That is, the romantic dramatists discovered a romantic tragic vision that is the negative counterpart of visionary romance. But before we can explore that tragic vision, we must first glance at the romantics' search for an appropriate dramatic form within which to present it.

CHAPTER TWO
THE FORM OF ROMANTIC
TRAGIC DRAMA

While Steiner has argued that the romantics contributed to the death of Western man's tragic sense, conventional histories of the drama have contended that the romantic playwrights found themselves unable to embody their poetic visions within the limits of theatrical practice. The romantics, it is felt, had a choice between crafting unstageable "closet" dramas and producing sensational but senseless popular entertainments.[1] This standard account of the relationship of romanticism to the stage does justice to neither romantic drama nor the nineteenth-century theater.

Recent histories of nineteenth-century theater have sought to displace this older view; Michael Booth speaks for these revisionists when he states, "I still believe, contrary to generally received opinion, that drama did not so much 'decline' in the nineteenth century as transform its character in response to significant cultural, social, economic, and theatrical changes."[2] Proponents of the nineteenth-century theater point to its great actors—to Kemble, Siddons, and Kean, Talma, Lemaître, and Dorval, Iffland, Jagemann, and Devrient. They discuss the innovations in scene painting, set design, and lighting produced by an age that offered dioramas, equestrian extravaganzas, and naval battles. These scholars largely agree with the traditional negative evaluation of the literary drama of the day, seeing it as committed to the past and isolated from the stage; however, they argue for the theatrical vitality and historical importance of such popular forms as the pantomime, the spectacular extravaganza, the *vaudeville,* the burletta, and the melodrama. We have learned a great deal from such scholars about nineteenth-century theatrical practice, and, more important, about the form and vision of the popular drama. These studies do justice to the nineteenth-century theater.

They do not, however, do justice to the plays of the great romantic poets. When one looks at the dramatic works of the English writers alone, it is easy—though not entirely fair—to characterize the romantics as hopelessly untheatrical; but it is not so easy to divorce romanticism from the stage when one looks to Goethe, Schiller, Hugo, and Dumas. It seems to me that scholars belittle romantic drama not so much because it failed to capture the stage or to produce intriguing plays (it could do both), but because it does not fit within either the orthodox or revisionist accounts of dramatic history. Both camps see the same goal for nineteenth-century drama and theater: realism. The older view, lamenting the "decline" of the literary drama during the nineteenth century, leaps from neoclassicism over romanticism to see realism as the true form of modern drama; for them, the drama is "reborn" through the efforts of Ibsen, Strindberg, Shaw, and Chekhov. The newer view merely makes this overall scheme more believable by demonstrating how popular writers like Coleman, Morton, Kotzebue, and Scribe prepared the way for Pinero, Dumas fils, and Zola who in turn influenced the great realists of the end of the century. From these critics, we receive a fuller view of the theatrical landscape of the nineteenth century, but we still have the old historical vision of a slow march towards the triumph of realism. We have a dramatic history in which Iffland, Kotzebue, Pixérécourt, Scribe, Dibdin, and Robertson have a place, but Goethe and Schiller, Byron and Shelley, Hugo and Musset do not.

These standard histories trace only one line of development within the nineteenth-century drama, and, as a result, they distort our view of both romantic plays and of later dramas, even realistic and naturalistic ones. Theater historians have demonstrated that the drama did not have to wait for Zola, Ibsen, or Shaw for a workable, naturalistic style. Naturalistic *theater* was inaugurated much earlier by writers of melodrama and the well-made play. Late nineteenth-century naturalism did not so much introduce new stage practices as yoke techniques developed earlier in the popular drama to a new vision. In the case of Zola, naturalism was an appropriation of melodramatic techniques to serve an ironic vision opposed to the easy moralism of much melodrama. Here is the key to Zola's naturalistic drama: it is melodrama without the morality.

If the plays of Ibsen or Strindberg impress us more than those of Zola, it is not because they drew upon the bourgeois drama of Scribe rather than the melodrama of Pixérécourt and his followers; it is because they infused Scribe's eminently theatrical form with a vision that owes much to romantic drama. Ibsen, for example, is often seen as the great naturalist, as the creator of a modern realistic drama that eschews heroism and high tragedy. He is seen to be everything the romantics supposedly were not: a realist, a practical man of the theater, an innovator. In fact, Ibsen was deeply influenced by romantic drama, as his early work through *Brand* and *Peer Gynt* demonstrates. He went on to create in his middle period works that were not merely naturalistic in the style of Zola or Scribe, but that rather placed the heroic and tragic vision of romantic drama within the confines of a realistic stage technique. In his late plays, Ibsen once again broke through these confines to create in characters like Solness and Borkman the inheritors of the tragic heroism of Faust and Wallenstein. Naturalism as a technique has served the theater well, but it is only when a playwright like Ibsen has infused naturalism with the vision of romantic tragic drama that it achieves the status of great literature. We will not understand the development of the drama since the decline of neoclassicism if we continue to ignore the contributions of romanticism to the modern drama.

But what of the complaints that the romantics were incapable of finding an appropriate and stageable form for their tragic vision? We have already seen that the romantic redefinition of the tragic centered upon vision not form, but such an emphasis obviously did not free playwrights from the need to find a style to body forth their content. The romantics' constant experimentation as they attempted virtually every dramatic style from Greek tragedy to melodrama indicates their difficulties in arriving at such a form. These difficulties were deepened by the nature of their vision, for it embraced a strikingly new version of the tragic that opened a gulf between romantic drama and the tragic tradition. The struggle of romanticism with such issues as selfhood and revolt forced it to rework all the artistic forms available to it. Illuminating the innovations of the romantic lyric, Josephine Miles has argued that the "idea which gave life to this romantic mode was the idea of the spirit's narrative, the individual's lyrical story, half articulated and half heard."[3] Ronald Paulson has written of the French Revolution and its impact on the visual arts that it

tests our basic assumption that an unprecedented event can be defined only in terms of the known, in terms of models already at hand. An experience hitherto unknown is inevitably assimilated by analogy to areas of experience felt to be already understood, but the movement toward the familiar is contested by a less predictable movement from the familiar to the unfamiliar in which the figurative elements are modified by confrontation with the historical referent as well as with each other.[4]

Like the lyric and painting, drama was transformed by a confrontation with a new history of both personal and political life.

Romanticism's search for dramatic form naturally turned in two directions: towards the dramatic tradition, or what Geoffrey Hartman calls the "reserve" of forms, "acknowledged works of art which guarantee, even when they do not directly influence, the paper in circulation";[5] and towards the theatrical practices of the day. Paulson can again be helpful, for he defines a similar choice facing painters who sought to represent the Revolution: confronted with the startling events of the Revolution, an artist could seek to order these events through "imagery-from-above," that is, traditional images, models, and icons such as the Roman ones used by the revolutionaries themselves; or he could work with the images that arose from "below," that is, from the subculture or counterculture of the mob that spoke through revolutionary songs and the "great angers and great joys" of Hébert's *Père Duchesne.*[6]

We might, then, think of the prospective romantic playwright as possessing many sources of inspiration. He could look back to a grand tradition that included Sophocles, Shakespeare, and Racine. He could look to a stage teeming with vital new forms. However, the romantics found the "reserve" of tragic forms almost exhausted and the popular theater, often serving both a state censor and the crowd, unable to become a vehicle for their unconventional vision. Moreover, they faced the widening split between a mass popular culture and a "high" or literary culture, a split in striking contrast to the ties between folk and literary cultures that, for example, supported Shakespeare's theater. Despite these problems, the key romantic playwrights rejected neither the tradition nor the theater. Instead, they sought to revise as well as revive traditional tragic forms, while working to reform the theater of their day.

I
ROMANTIC DRAMA AND THE DRAMATIC TRADITION

DESPITE THE CONTINUED presence of both neoclassical and baroque traditions on the late eighteenth-century stage, despite the development of newer styles like the Gothic tragedy, the *drame,* and the historical play, the romantics felt that they confronted the twilight of the tragic tradition; they dreamed of a new dawn. There had not been a great tragedy written since Calderón and Racine. Voltaire was the most important tragedian the early eighteenth century had to offer; and outside of France, neoclassical tragedy found its exponents in less powerful dramatists like Addison and Gottsched. Shakespeare had yet to become a real presence on the French or German stage, and even in London his plays were performed only in heavily edited versions. If plays like Walpole's *Mysterious Mother,* Diderot's *Fils*

Naturel, and Home's *Douglas* broke with a strict neoclassical model to adumbrate certain features of romantic drama, they did not as yet constitute a new tradition. As Schlegel's, Shelley's, and Stendhal's reactions to the literary drama of the day indicate, the romantics felt that the "great tradition" of drama had been lost. They felt the need to leap over their immediate precursors to engage the masterworks of more distant eras.[7]

When one thinks of the romantics' precursors, it is usually Shakespeare who comes to mind. He did, of course, have an important place in the hearts of playwrights, theater audiences, and the reading public in this age of Bardolatry. During the eighteenth century, he had become the most performed playwright on the English stage, and his works remained at the heart of the repertoire of Drury Lane and Covent Garden. Shakespeare's reception in Germany was spurred by the appreciations of Lessing, Hamann, and Herder; his works became available to readers in much of their original force through the translations of A. W. Schlegel. France was slower to accept the great English playwright, but a series of translator/adaptors from Le Tourneur and Ducis to Vigny introduced his plays to the French public. This enthusiasm for Shakespeare sometimes extended to his contemporaries, as the interest of Lamb, Beddoes, and Tieck in Elizabethan and Jacobean drama demonstrates.[8]

To many, the romantics' debt to their great precursor was excessive, making their plays little more than attempts to revive Elizabethan poetic tragedy.[9] However, Shakespeare was only one of many models adopted by the romantics. The German romanticists rediscovered Calderón, to whom Shelley was drawn as well. While most romantics railed against neoclassicism, it could still attract Byron, Goethe, and Schiller. Greek drama itself inspired Hölderlin and Shelley. It should not surprise us that the romantics explored the possibilities of every tragic form available to them, for the arts in the late eighteenth and early nineteenth centuries were marked by revivals of earlier styles. An artist might adopt different styles for different projects; different artists might treat the same theme in strikingly different styles. As Robert Rosenblum has said of late eighteenth-century painting, "a one-to-one correlation of style and subject was as frequently the exception as the rule."[10] Rosenblum has shown how artists like Vien, Greuze, and David could share a moralizing theme while working within quite different styles; a parallel phenomenon was that artists like English architect John Nash worked in a myriad of styles from the neoclassical to the Gothic, from the Italianate to the Old English and even the Chinese.[11] Similarly, we find Byron moving from the Gothic to the neoclassical as he turns from *Manfred* to his history plays. Goethe wrote both Shakespearean plays

(Götz) and classicizing ones *(Iphigenia in Tauris)*. A theme like revolt might be presented in neoclassical form by Goethe *(The Natural Daughter; Die natürliche Tochter)*, in a strictly Greek form by Shelley *(Hellas)*, and in the form of a chronicle play by Grabbe *(Napoleon or the Hundred Days; Napoleon oder die hundert Tage)*.

There is, then, no single historical style from which the romantic artists sought inspiration; but there is a pattern to their responses to the past. The turn to earlier dramatic forms seems to have had a double impetus. First, there is little doubt that the romantic playwrights were unhappy both with those plays that remained committed to a neoclassical ethic and with the popular drama with its reliance upon spectacle, music, and pantomime; and thus they felt the need to revolt against the contemporary drama. Second, while much has been learned by studying the romantics' anxiety in face of the influence of the poetic tradition, we need to see that part of that anxiety lay in the fear of losing touch with this tradition. This fear particularly marks the playwrights. If the poets sought to disguise their debts to their precursors, the models adopted by the dramatists were often painfully clear. A few writers even attempted a direct recreation of earlier dramatic styles, just as some artists worked within what Rosenblum calls the "Neoclassic Archeologic."[12] Beddoes's imitations of Elizabethan and Jacobean drama come immediately to mind; Hölderlin's continuing revisions of his tragedy on Empedocles represent a struggle to recreate Greek tragedy in its original splendor. We might also note here the extraordinary effort the romantics devoted to translating earlier works, with Schlegel and Vigny turning to Shakespeare; Schlegel and Shelley to Calderón; and Hölderlin to Sophocles.

Of course, the romantics usually appealed to the past to sanction a new departure of their own; imitation served innovation. Goethe looked to Shakespeare for a justification of the chronicle style of *Götz*. A number of playwrights followed new developments in the Shakespeare criticism of the Schlegels, Coleridge, Hazlitt, and others to find in Elizabethan plays a model for a new brand of psychological drama, in which character would take precedence over action. Again, Tieck found in Calderón what he believed to be a mixture of narrative and lyric elements within the drama, a combination he offered in his *Life and Death of Saint Genoveva (Leben und Tod der heiligen Genoveva)* and *Kaiser Oktavius*. Shelley argued that his astonishing alterations of the Prometheus myth followed the Greek tragedians' own revisionary approach to their subject matter.

Romantic dramatists link imitation and innovation through a revisionary approach in which the earlier work is emulated only in order to show the distance between its vision and their own. We will explore this revisionism in detail in discussing Shelley's use of Shakespeare in *The Cenci* and

Goethe's turn to the Greeks in *Iphigenia in Tauris;* but we can sense immediately the importance of this tactic for romantic playwrights if we note that Byron turns to the Bible in *Cain* only to find the first murderer heroic, that Shelley adopts a Greek model in *Prometheus Unbound* only to alter its conclusion, that Goethe retells the Faust story only to save the traditionally damned magician, and that writers from Schiller to Hugo put robbers on stage only to discover their nobility.

The complexities of this revisionary turn to the past can be seen in its relation to "classical" forms, a relation of particular interest since we often see the romantic drama as utterly opposed to the classical tradition. Our understanding of the romantics' use of classical forms has been hindered by our tendency to speak of a number of romanticisms while assuming that there is a single, coherent classicism—there should be a solitary temple that offers refuge from the lush jungles of the nineteenth century. However, the late eighteenth and early nineteenth centuries saw a number of rival classicisms, with the romantics often using one classical precedent to oppose another.[13]

When the romantics began to write, neoclassical tragedy still represented the official literary drama for many theatergoers and critics. In Germany, Gottsched had tried to establish a neoclassical tradition against which the playwrights of the Storm and Stress revolted; in England, plays in the Augustan mode continued to be written long into the nineteenth century, as the career of Thomas Noon Talfourd demonstrates. But it was in France that neoclassicism remained strongest, in part because it received support from the pre-Revolutionary monarchy, Napoleon, the Restoration, and—with a twist—from the Revolution itself. Most of these plays are of little interest today. Most arose from a spirit of cultural conservatism that stood against romantic innovations. Neoclassical tragedy could appear as a strictly conservative form, not only because it maintained the unities and decorum against the onslaught of formal experimentation, but also because in its treatment of kings and noble heroes and its portrayal of a world lifted far above the struggles of the people, it could appear as a denial in formal terms that the age was one of revolt.

Neoclassicism also had its revolutionary side, however. David had demonstrated in his *Oath of the Horatii* and *Lictors Returning to Brutus the Bodies of his Sons* that a classical style could serve patriotic, revolutionary themes. A Roman setting, a severe style opposed to the elegance of the rococo, and a moralizing strain set against what was perceived as aristocratic flippancy—these were the marks of David's revolutionary classicism. Republican Paris wanted dramatic equivalents to David's great paintings. One was found in Voltaire's *Brutus,* which was revived at the Comédie Française (renamed the Théâtre de la Nation) during November of 1791. While

Voltaire's play, dealing with the defeat of the Tarquins and Brutus's order to execute his sons for collaborating with the tyrant, strikes us as a defense of a limited monarchy against the tyranny of both the king and the crowd, revolutionary audiences found contemporary echoes in it, with Brutus seeming a prototype for Mirabeau, for example. At the close of the second performance, a tableau was struck in imitation of David's painting, suggesting the links between the revolutionary interpretation of this neoclassical play and David's work.[14]

Revolutionary neoclassicism was not limited to revivals. Marie-Joseph Chénier, a friend of David's and his collaborator on the revolutionary fêtes, presented a series of plays in the neoclassical mode that offered a political message in response to the developments of the Revolution. The most important of these was his first success, *Charles IX*, which was produced on November 4, 1789, after being blocked by the censors for over a year. This play was the first clearly political tragedy staged under the Revolution, and it continued to be offered throughout the revolutionary years. Other French playwrights—including Ronsin and Légouvé—followed Chénier's example in writing neoclassical, often Roman plays that had a clear relevance to the events of the day. Alfieri's plays on the two Brutuses offer further examples of neoclassical plays on Roman subjects that take up what were, at least in their context, revolutionary themes. The first play was dedicated to George Washington and the second to the Italian people of the future; both were published during 1789 in Paris where the playwright had come in 1785 "to write loftily of liberty."[15]

It is, however, neither conservative neoclassicism's rearguard defense of tradition nor revolutionary classicism's espousal of a Roman model of revolt that is central to romanticism's turn to the classics. For the romantics desired not the Latinate classicism of the Age of Louis XIV and the Augustans, but a Hellenic classicism that sought inspiration from the Greeks themselves. We can see the importance of the Greeks for the romantics in Goethe's *Iphigenia in Tauris*, Schiller's *Bride of Messina (Die Braut von Messina)*, Hölderlin's *Death of Empedokles (Der Tod des Empedokles)*, Kleist's *Penthesilea*, Shelley's *Hellas*, and Swinburne's *Atalanta in Calydon*. The adoption of Greek precursors is part of the romantics' search for their roots in ancient, primal sources. The Greek influence serves a function similar to those of the Bible, folk ballads, or Ossian; for all were seen to provide an inspiration from periods of early "pure" art. Even the turn of the Revolution to a "Roman" art can be seen as an attempt to get to a forceful, moral classicism that had preceded the "false" classicism of the aristocratic rococo. Romanticism sought to remake art from the ground up, and one way to do this was to return through historical styles to ever earlier precedents.

This development is perhaps clearer in late eighteenth-century classical painting, where the turn against rococo classicism led beyond Roman and even Athenian inspirations to "Etruscan" and primitive Greek sources; in Flaxman, in the "primitifs" who seceded from David's studio, and even in David himself, we see an attempt to recapture what was felt to be the earliest classical art—the line drawings of recently unearthed Greek pottery. While the changes within the drama were not so clearly drawn, we can still see this quest for an original classicism. Shelley, for example, had little affection for neoclassical form or Roman subject matter. His translations demonstrate his interest in Greek drama, and his classicizing plays, *Prometheus Unbound* and *Hellas,* both derive from Greek models. It is important that they turned to Aeschylus who was seen as the exemplar of the original, most primitive form of Greek drama. During the late eighteenth century, as the first translations of Aeschylus's works appeared in French in 1770 and in English in 1777, he was championed in opposition to the later Sophocles and Euripides.[16]

Of course, Shelley embraces Aeschylus only to revise him. While noting in his preface to *Prometheus Unbound* the debt of imitation that every artist owes to nature, to the "spirit" of his age, and to the masterworks of the past, he still maintains the artist's right to alter his model and thus to create anew. He explicitly rejects an "Archeologic" art in refusing to resurrect the lost plays of Aeschylus's trilogy—a task he does contemplate. He also rejects Aeschylus' vision. Not only does Shelley alter the outcome of the Greek trilogy by staging the defeat of Jupiter, but he also takes his play beyond the formal limits of his Greek model as his final act explodes into a visionary lyricism. In his preface to *Hellas,* Shelley engages another aspect of the romantic artist's use of classical form. While this play is studiously Greek in its form, observing the unities and imitating choral odes, he notes his dependence upon "newspaper erudition" in treating the Greek struggle for freedom.[17] He thus recognizes the tension that Paulson discusses between his formal model and the historical material he tries to incorporate within it. Shelley's prefaces and his dramatic practice outline the revisionism that is the hallmark of the romantic adoption of classical and other traditional forms.

We find a similar revisionary use of classical models in the quite different plays of Byron and Goethe. Byron's tastes were shaped less by Greece than by French and English neoclassicism and by the romantic classicism of Alfieri. In his three historical plays, *Marino Faliero, The Two Foscari,* and *Sardanapalus,* he sought a "regular" British drama to replace the imitations of Shakespeare that he felt were ruining England's theater. Still, the romantic content of the plays subtly revises the classical form, finally bursting forth at the close of *Sardanapalus,* where the court-dominated world of neoclassical tragedy is consumed in flames as Sardanapalus envisions a world remade.

Goethe was also interested in French neoclassical models, as his translations of Voltaire's *Mahomet* and *Tancred* and his own classicistic *Natural Daughter* suggest. However, Goethe's work evidences a quest through all the various forms of classicism, from the Latin love elegy in *Roman Elegies* to the epic in the fragmentary "Achilleis" and *Hermann and Dorethea,* from the epigrams of the *Xenia* to the drama in *Iphigenia in Tauris.* Then there is the attempt to recreate Greek culture and Greek tragedy in the second part of *Faust;* but here, as in the earlier *Iphigenia,* at the very moment when Goethe seems to have returned to Greek art in the most immediate way, he transforms and transcends his precursors: in *Faust,* he literally transforms the scene and the style of the play from ancient Greece to medieval Germany, before celebrating the birth of Euphorion/Byron and hence of modern poetry. Goethe thus provides a program for romantic classicism as an art that uses classical form as a means of stylistic rigor and a sign of self-control, but that also sees the need to move beyond these conventional forms to encounter the issues of the modern, romantic age.

Faust recalls us to our larger theme: the romantics' use of the entire dramatic tradition. For Goethe's masterpiece engages Shakespeare, Voltaire, the drama of the Storm and Stress, and Calderón as well as the Greeks. Byron's corpus also suggests the range of romantic inspiration. He called *Cain* and *Heaven and Earth* mysteries, forging a link to medieval drama. *Manfred,* despite Byron's disclaimers, descends from Marlowe's *Doctor Faustus* and *Faust. Manfred* also owes something to the contemporary monodrama, while *Werner* draws upon the melodrama, two key contemporary forms to which we will turn shortly. Any part of the tradition may be revived to serve the aims of the revisionary artist.

The romantics' revival of earlier dramatic forms can be seen in part as an attempt to fill the "reserve" of forms with neglected or undervalued works. If official neoclassicism seemed sterile, one found one's tradition in Shakespeare or Calderón. If Euripides and even Sophocles seemed too closely tied to their French imitators, then Aeschylus could still inspire innovators. Interestingly, where formal experimentation had gone a great distance and had still failed to create a "reserve" of great works, playwrights even returned to the neoclassical tradition; we can see such a development in Goethe's and Schiller's interest in French neoclassicism after the excesses of the Storm and Stress and, to a lesser extent, in Byron's espousal of Augustan forms after what he saw as the victory of sensationalism on the London stage. In each case, a romantic playwright finds a precursor through whom he hopes a vital tradition can be recreated. In each case, the precursor is used not only as a model but as a justification or guarantee of new creation.

This revisionism is the formal counterpart of the romantic reworking of the tragic vision. One way in which the romantics demonstrated their transvaluation of traditional tragedy was to emulate traditional forms only to transform and to transcend them under the pressure of their explorations of self and revolt. This emulation made sense, since a number of earlier dramatic works would seem to have offered models for treating these romantic themes. The titanic individualism of Macbeth or Edmund would seem to suggest a way to portray the romantic protagonist as he asserts his newly strengthened individualism. The inward-turned Hamlet would seem to be a prototype for romantic man's journeys through self-consciousness. The resistance of a Prometheus or the assassination of a Caesar would seem to provide parallels to the acts of a revolutionary age.

However, as Frederick Antal has argued, we should not "exaggerate the significance of formal similarities between the styles of different periods to the extent of using them for purposes of definition," since the styles will vary formally to some extent and will certainly take on different meanings in changing cultural contexts.[18] Within the milieu of romanticism, the imitation of earlier forms is never mere reduplication; as the revolutionary interpretation of Voltaire's *Brutus* or the romantic reinterpretation of Shakespeare suggests, even older works were redefined by formal and thematic revisionism. Prometheus might appear as the model rebel, but Shelley had to break with the traditional resolution of the myth to stage a visionary revolt. Brutus might be the perfect revolutionary, but the tragedy of Musset's Lorenzaccio is defined by his failure to be a Brutus. Hamlet or Macbeth might be prototypes for romantic subjectivism, but it is exactly the distance between Shakespeare's titans and romantic figures like Lorenzaccio or Wallenstein that measures the depth of the latter's tragic fall. All of this suggests that traditional forms are imitated and revised in order to demonstrate that romantic tragic drama is tragic in large part because life no longer operates within the rhythms of traditional tragedy. Imitation serves romanticism's tragic vision.

II

MONODRAMA AND MELODRAMA

THE LITERARY DRAMA may have been in disarray in the later years of the eighteenth century as dramatists hunted through the tradition for inspiration, but the popular theater was thriving as never before. More people could see more plays than during any previous period: in London, Covent Garden was enlarged to hold over 3000 people, while the capacity of Drury Lane reached 3611; in London and Paris, new "minor," popular theaters arose despite government controls; in Germany, there was a proliferation of "national" theaters. The improvements in stage machinery such as traps, the development of controlled gas lighting and limelight, the trends in scene painting and set construction, and many other technical innovations increased the theater's command of spectacle and realism. Great actors from Kemble to Bernhardt, from Talma to Irving provided the stage with much of its energy and excitement.[19] We may question the literary quality of nineteenth-century drama but not the vitality of the theater of the period.

The growth of the theaters helped ignite an explosion of new dramatic forms. Drawing upon such earlier forms as the *commedia dell'arte* and the pantomimes offered at eighteenth-century fairs, the popular drama responded to the massive social and political changes that marked the period and, more immediately, to the loosening of state controls upon the stage, by offering a wealth of new dramatic genres. Hybrid forms needed new names, and thus we hear of the melodrama, the burletta, and the *vaudeville.* Playbills of the period announced harlequinades, heroic pantomimes, aquatic battles, dioramas, and equestrian spectacles. A play like Lewis's *One O'Clock; or The Knight and the Wood Daemon* was labeled a "Grand Musical Romance," while his *Timour the Tartar* was called a "Grand Romantic Melo-Drama in Two Acts." With changing audiences demanding new types of drama and with technical innovations opening the way to new theatrical styles, the stage became a laboratory in which dramatists, directors, actors, and craftsmen experimented in the hope of discovering the perfect entertainment.

Historians of the theater and the drama have taught us more and more about this immensely vital popular theater. What has not been fully understood is the response to that theater of the great romantic poets. Both traditional and revisionist historians have contended that the romantics ignored the changes in the nineteenth-century stage and thus rendered themselves unable to write for it.

Certainly, some romantic playwrights reacted violently against the popular theater, particularly the melodrama, and at times their dislike turned them against the stage as such. Ludwig Tieck, for example, while intensely interested in the theater (he not only wrote plays, but was also an active drama critic, a promoter of Elizabethan plays and Spanish and German Baroque drama, the editor of the works of Lenz and Kleist, and at one time the *dramaturg* of the Dresden theater), reveals in his dramas his total contempt for the theatrical practices of his day. His *Puss in Boots (Der gestiefelte Kater,* 1797), a rather delightful Aristophanic handling of the fairy tale, has a prologue which attacks the popular melodramatists Kotzebue and Iffland and the audiences who applauded them. The play itself is remarkable mainly for its frontal assault on the naturalistic style of the domestic melodrama: it is a play-within-a-play, with an audience on stage, speeches by the author, a mixture of genres, and the total disruption of dramatic illusion that marks "romantic irony" in the drama.

The dramas of Tieck, and of those writers like Brentano, Arnim, and Eichendorff who reflect his influence, can be seen merely as exercises in an antitheatrical prejudice. However, they also embraced what Renato Poggioli has defined as a typical response of artists to modern mass art: the formation of an avant-garde.[20] Poggioli sees the avant-garde coming into being when a failure of established culture coincides with the rise of mass popular culture. Seeing the high culture of the past as moribund and the popular taste of the day as debased, the artist strives to create art for the future. Poggioli himself notes the ways in which the romantic circles at Jena and Heidelberg offer a foretaste of later, explicitly avant-garde movements. We find similar responses elsewhere. For example, Byron, who was interested in reforming the stage, turned against it when he became aware of the failure of his *Marino Faliero* in London: he wrote *Cain,* which rejects the limits of the theater, to explore the vastness of space and the abyss of time. Musset, after his first play failed, turned his back on the theater to write the "armchair" plays of his *Un Spectacle dans un fauteuil.* Hugo, again after a setback in the theater, stopped writing for the stage, creating instead his *Théâtre en Liberté.* This rejection of the stage for the broader spaces of an imaginary theater can be seen as a failure to come to grips with the practicalities of the drama; but it also makes a grand experimental gesture, presaging Wagner's search for the total art work of the future or the constant challenge to our idea of the theater made by the twentieth-century drama. And, in fact, experimenters like Tieck, Lenz, and Musset have been seen as forerunners of Pirandello, Brecht, and the absurdists.

Still, as the theatrical historians point out, such experiments did not provide romanticism with a drama for its own time. Fortunately, such glances to the future were not the only romantic response to the theater of the day. In fact, romantic playwrights often drew directly upon the forms popular

on the contemporary stage. Byron may have leapt beyond the stage in
Cain, but he also penned a melodrama, *Werner,* which became quite successful later in the century through the acting skills of Macready.[21] Kleist's
early work *The Feud of the Schroffensteins (Die Familie Schroffenstein)*
reflected the German public's delight in *Ritterdrama,* plays of knightly exploits. The prose plays of Hugo owe much to the melodrama, and those of
Dumas often were melodramas.

The romantic adoption of popular forms need not have been merely a
plea for applause, for they suggested approaches to the key romantic
themes of selfhood and revolt. For example, pantomime and music, so essential to the popular drama, provided new means for bodying forth internal emotional states. The settings of the Gothic drama, with their castles
and dungeons, have struck many as emblems of the darker side of the
mind. Revolutionary Paris staged plays that directly represented revolutionary events such as the death of Marat, the King's flight to Varennes, and
the Vendée revolt. Other dramas went beyond historical reportage to stage
republican fantasies. The most famous of these is Sylvain Maréchal's *Judgment Day for Kings (Le Jugement dernier des rois;* Théâtre de la République, 1793), in which European sans-culottes maroon their former heads of
state on an island whose volcano obligingly erupts to put an end to the tyrants' lives. Faced with death, these noble figures all vow to become revolutionaries, the Pope claiming he will marry and Catherine of Russia
voicing her desire to join the Jacobin Club. But it is too late, and they are
swallowed up in a fiery finale for which the Committee of Public Safety
provided the gunpowder—an indication of how important the government, at war and in need of such supplies, considered this propaganda
play to be. London also witnessed plays inspired by the Revolution, with
works like John Dent's *The Bastille* (Royal Circus, 1789) offering fictional-
ized accounts of events in France, and others like Sheridan's *Pizarro*
(Drury Lane, 1799) presenting allegories of revolutionary history—in
Sheridan's case a veiled attack upon Napoleon. The burlesque might have
provided another means for dealing with current political events, as Shelley's *Swellfoot the Tyrant* suggests; Booth discusses the social commentary
made by the Regency harlequinade.[22]

Two contemporary forms had particular importance for the development of romantic drama: the monodrama and the melodrama. These key
popular forms arose alongside of romantic tragic drama and confronted
the same social, political, and cultural changes. We can see, for example, a
concern with the problems of selfhood and violence in the initial scene of
Thomas Holcroft's *A Tale of Mystery* (Covent Garden, 1802), the first English melodrama so called and an adaptation of a play by Pixérécourt, the
"father" of French melodrama:

Selina:	I almost dread to tell you. Count Romaldi is coming.
Stephano:	Romaldi!
Selina:	I shudder, when I recollect the selfishness of his views, and the violence of his character.
Stephano:	Add, the wickedness of his heart. (Act I)[23]

Monodramas such as Southey's *Lucretia,* where the assaulted matron urges revolt, and Lewis's *The Captive,* where a wife imprisoned by a tyrannical husband slowly goes mad, indicate the ability of that form to explore extreme emotional states while touching upon conventional images of oppression and revolution.

The monodrama and the melodrama existed not only as discrete "forms" of drama, but also as "modes" within other dramatic kinds, to adopt a distinction set forth by Ralph Cohen.[24] There were not only pure monodramas with single characters exploring a series of emotional states and pure melodramas with morally defined characters waging a struggle against a spectacular backdrop; there were also other types of plays that invoked a monodramatic or melodramatic mode. The tendency towards soliloquies and lyric interludes in tragedy and towards domestic moralism in comedy, pantomime, and even farce suggest such modal influences. It is as "modes" that the monodrama and the melodrama were incorporated within and then reinterpreted by the romantic drama.

As the presence of monodramatic and melodramatic elements in very different kinds of plays suggests, these two forms embodied basic tendencies in the drama of the day. From the perspective of the romantic dramatists, however, they embraced reductive tendencies. Hegel made this point when he argued that contemporary plays threatened to dismember the drama into its constituent parts:

. . . the poet is for this reason compelled to devote the full strength of his presentation to the psychological analysis of character, and to make the course of the situation a mere instrument of such characterization. Or, as an alternative, he admits a too extensive field for the display of the material aspect of historical or ethical conditions; and, under the pressure of such material, he attempts to keep attention alive through interest in the series of events evolved. To this class of composition we may assign a host of our more recent theatrical pieces, which rather aim at theatrical effect than claim to be poetry. They do not so much seek to affect us as genuine poetical productions as to reach our emotions generally as men and women; or they aim on the one hand simply at recreation, and on the other at the moral education of public taste. . . .[25]

Hegel joins many romantic theorists in considering the drama as the central literary form that mediates between the lyric and the epic and sees the drama of his day being pulled towards lyric characterization on the one hand and epic or novelistic extension of plot on the other.[26] Hegel's dramatist is offered a choice between the monodrama with its focus upon the immediate presentation of the passions of a single character and the melodrama with its spectacular and entertaining plot that enforces an absolute, if simple, moral.

While such plays at first appear to provide a means of portraying the self and staging the violence of history, the romantics could not adopt them unchanged if they were to create a central dramatic form to present a modern tragic vision. Romanticism's use of the monodrama and the melodrama defines its stance towards the popular theater. It is neither an avant-garde rejection of the popular theater nor a slavish acceptance of popular taste that is central to romantic drama. Romantic playwrights did not despise their prospective audience, but they did hope to adapt popular forms like the monodrama and the melodrama as part of a larger tragic structure and thus to engage their audience in tragedy's broader vision.

Both the monodrama and the melodrama have eighteenth-century roots. The monodrama appears to be a creation of Rousseau. In 1762, he began work on a piece entitled *Pygmalion,* a play for one actor and musical accompaniment; short speeches alternate with passages of music that reinforce the emotional impact of the text. *Pygmalion* was performed successfully in Paris in 1772 and sparked interest throughout Europe in the monodrama. Interestingly enough, Rousseau defended *Pygmalion* in an essay on the opera by claiming that it represented the only type of "mélodrame" or "music-drama" suitable to the French stage. He thus coined the term that later came to be applied to the popular dramatic spectaculars that were anything but monodramatic. In that the monodrama and the melodrama have a common ancestor in Rousseau, *Pygmalion* stands in its own small way as a watershed in the history of modern drama.[27]

A. Dwight Culler has suggested as a definition of monodrama Tennyson's reported description of *Maud; a Monodrama* as "a drama where successive phases of passion in one person take the place of successive persons."[28] *Pygmalion* and its progeny in Germany and England (both Goethe and "Monk" Lewis were among Rousseau's imitators)[29] do for the most part place a single character on stage in a situation capable of evoking a series of extreme emotional responses. A wide range of emotions is usually depicted, and the character moves rapidly from feeling to feeling. The monodrama uses both language and music to express these emotional states. Drawing upon the spectacular stage devices of other contemporary forms, the monodramatist marshaled all the resources of the theater to accomplish one goal: the direct and immediate communication of passion.

The monodrama could apparently have quite an impact. Lewis tells us that his own monodrama, *The Captive,* affected the audience so powerfully that the piece had to be withdrawn: "Terror threw them into fits," and several people actually fainted in hysterics.[30] One reason for the impact of the monodrama was that it restricted itself, as Hegel notes, to the analysis of character, subordinating plot to characterization. It thus displayed character directly, without any mediating pattern of judgment embodied in plot. Culler makes the important observation that the monodrama differs from the dramatic monologue in that there is no ironic tension between sympathy and judgment in the monodramatic display of passion as there is in the monologue's investigation of character.[31] The monodramatic character affects us deeply because we are given no framework—no plot—within which to judge him; there is no standard in the work other than his feelings, and thus we are completely absorbed in them. We are presented with highly theatrical passions, nothing more.

Before examining the use the romantics made of the monodrama, I want to make it clear that the monodrama is not the same thing as the so-called "closet drama," though at times critics use these terms interchangeably. There are plays that are close relatives of the monodrama that are also closet dramas—*Manfred,* for example. But there are other plays—Hugo's *Cromwell* is an example—that are closet plays without being monodramas. In fact, Hugo's play is a closet drama for the very reasons that it is not a monodrama; that is, it cannot be easily performed because it has a huge cast and adopts a "novelistic" approach to its subject matter. The monodrama, although it began in Rousseau's attempt to reform opera and the stage, never turned against the theater of the day. The category of closet drama, however, includes by definition only those works not performed. The closet drama is a contingent category, for it measures the ever changing distance between a dramatist's aspirations and theatrical realities. Many romantic works that were published as closet dramas—Shelley's *The Cenci* or Musset's plays, for example—later met with some theatrical success. In a few cases, the closet drama represented not an armchair drama but bold dramatic experiment. In any event, it was not the same thing as the monodrama. The monodrama was a theatrical form of the late eighteenth and early nineteenth centuries. The closet drama sought the theater of the future.

The romantics were interested in the monodrama as a means for staging extreme states of consciousness; they worked to transform it into a tragedy of the self. In England, for example, we find a group of plays—including Wordsworth's *Borderers,* Lamb's *John Woodvil,* and Byron's *Manfred*—that possess monodramatic traits yet seek tragedy in the close analysis of character. Undoubtedly the most ambitious project of this kind was Joanna

Baillie's *A Series of Plays: In Which it is Attempted to Delineate the Stronger Passions of the Mind: Each Passion Being the Subject of A Tragedy and A Comedy.* Seeking to unveil "the human mind under the dominion of those strong and fixed passions, which seemingly unprovoked by outward circumstances, will from small beginnings brood within the breast till all the better dispositions, all the fair gifts of nature are borne down before them,"[32] Baillie's plays are clearly the sisters of the contemporary monodrama; their concentration upon a single character, largely internalized action, and pervasive use of the soliloquy all suggest the monodramatic mode. Of course, Baillie alters the monodramatic portrayal of "the successive phases of passion in one person"; for she presents her protagonist progressing through the phases of a single passion, detailing such passions "not only with their bold and prominent features, but also with those minute and delicate traits which distinguish them in an infant, growing, and repressed state. . . ."[33] The progress of this single passion provides her with a plot. She translates the lyric emphasis of the monodrama into the idiom of tragic drama by finding in extreme passion the badge of the hero and in the inevitable growth of that passion an equivalent to fate.

Most romantic playwrights went even further in subordinating the monodrama to a larger tragic form. As Culler notes, there were few pure monodramas, its importance being "as a stylistic element which enters into other forms."[34] As a reductive dramatic form, the monodrama was used by the romantics to portray a reductive mode of existence—an entrapment in the self. The monodramatic portrayal of passion free from judgment offered the romantics a style for putting on stage an individual totally absorbed in his selfhood and for making the audience feel the inward pull of the self. While there are certainly exceptions, we can say for the most part that a character in a romantic play presented monodramatically has succumbed to the dangerous attractions of the self.

Because of its very immediacy, the monodrama could stage but not analyze self-consciousness. Romantic plays draw upon the monodrama, but they must move beyond it; Goethe's *Faust,* for example, begins as a monodrama only to shatter the limits of that form in exploring Faust's larger quest. As we will see most clearly in discussing *The Cenci,* the romantic playwright uses monodramatic devices to portray the ravages of "self-anatomy," placing these devices within a larger dramatic form capable of judging the fall into the self.

The rise of the monodrama is clearly linked to broader changes in the critical definition of the drama: from drama as an imitation of an action to drama as a presentation of character. This transformation is perhaps most familiar in that movement within Shakespeare criticism—from Maurice Morgann's *Essay on the Dramatic Character of John Falstaff* (1777) to A.

C. Bradley's *Shakespearian Tragedy* (1904)—which focuses upon Shakespeare's ability to create powerful individuals and to portray their inner lives; it is summed up in Browning's pronouncement in the preface to *Strafford* (1837) that drama should offer "Action in Character, rather than Character in Action."[35] In this context, the monodrama is part of the attempt to redefine literary forms in relation to the romantic concern with subjectivity, with consciousness.

Still, the monodrama, with its presentation of characters freed from any external judgment, indicates again the loss of traditional patterns of judgment fixed in mythic plots and enforced by poetic justice. Incorporating a monodramatic style in his work, the romantic dramatist might find himself creating an egotistical monster who escapes the ability of the play to judge him; the playwright could, however, have found a pattern of judgment, had he wanted it, in the monodrama's antithesis—the melodrama.

The melodrama's origins are not so clear as the monodrama's, despite Rousseau's introduction of the term. One point is certain: the melodrama represented the popular theater's central mode of serious drama. While some critics have attempted to see the melodrama as a degenerate offshoot of some branch of the literary drama,[36] it arose as the culmination of various developments in the popular theater throughout Europe. The French dramatist René-Charles Guilbert de Pixérécourt is often cited as the "father" of melodrama. His use of the term to define his enormously popular plays did fix its meaning, and he created what might be called the "classic" melodramatic form; but there were earlier writers—Kotzebue, Iffland, Coleman, and Morton, for example—who worked within a melodramatic mode. Like them, Pixérécourt drew upon a broad range of eighteenth-century forms: on English Gothic plays and French convent dramas like Monvel's *Les Victimes Cloîtrées* (translated and transformed by Lewis as *Venomi; or the Novice of St. Mark's)*, on the *comédie larmoyant* and sentimental tragedies like Lillo's *London Merchant,* on the German "terror" dramas and the heroic pantomime. The popular theaters that had sprung up at fair grounds and in music halls were denied the right to present the classics, and thus they turned to pantomime, spectacle, and music, creating an alternative to the drama of the word jealously protected by the state-supported theaters of Paris and London. This alternative was shaped into the burletta, the extravaganza, and the *vaudeville;* it continued to draw upon the harlequinade. But melodrama was the popular rival to tragedy.

The melodrama achieved immense popularity, dominating the stage in Germany, France, and England. While we remember Goethe and Schiller as the great German playwrights of their day, the two most popular were the melodramatists August Wilhelm Iffland and August von Kotzebue. Kotzebue's amazing success is suggested by his most famous play *Men-*

schenbass und Reue (1787), which not only became a German favorite, but also had record runs in Paris and Madrid; under the title of *The Stranger,* it filled theaters in London and New York. Kotzebue's works furnished a major part of the repertoire of every theater in Germany. In his role as actor/ director, Iffland himself put on three works by Kotzebue to every one of his own. Even at Weimar, six hundred performances of Kotzebue were given under Goethe's direction; eighty-seven of Kotzebue's plays were given, compared to thirty-one of Iffland's, nineteen of Goethe's, eighteen of Schiller's, and eight of Shakespeare's. Kotzebue's international reputation was also immense. When an English theatergoer at the turn of the century spoke of the German drama, he was most likely referring to the plays of Kotzebue; ten of the nineteen plays included in Benjamin Thompson's *German Theater* (1800) were by Kotzebue, while Goethe was represented by a single play.[37]

Pixérécourt was to France what Kotzebue was to Germany; as Armand Charlemagne said in his *Mélodrame aux boulevards,* "Monsieur Kotzebue is the Pixérécourt of Germany just as Monsieur Pixérécourt is the French Kotzebue." Thrilling audiences year after year, Pixérécourt's many plays achieved some thirty thousand performances in France alone between 1797 and 1834. Known as the "Shakespeare of the Boulevard," and the "Corneille of the melodrama," he was often followed by respectful crowds of admirers. Such important critics and writers as Geoffroy, Jules Janin, Charles Nodier, and Théophile Gautier wrote in admiration of his melodramas. His plays were performed in England, Germany, Italy, Holland, Russia, and Portugal.[38]

England did not have a comparably dominant melodramatist but Holcroft, Pocock, Dibdin, Dimond, and many others supplied the theaters with successful melodramas. Many of these plays were translations or adaptations of German and French plays. At least seventeen of Pixérécourt's plays were performed on the English stage, some in more than one version.[39] There was a rage for Kotzebue in the last years of the eighteenth century, and his plays provided many successes for the London stage, including Sheridan's *Pizarro,* an adaptation of Kotzebue's *Rollas Tod.* The ease with which these German and French plays were translated into the English theater suggests the degree to which the melodrama embodied the theatrical language of the day. Images, characters, plots, and entire plays were "borrowed" by one melodramatist from another. We thus can find Holcroft adapting Pixérécourt, Pixérécourt himself drawing upon Kotzebue, and Kotzebue—at least according to Coleridge—imitating earlier English writers.[40]

The melodrama was from the first censured by men of letters for emphasizing spectacle over substance, confusing genres, and offering a simple-minded morality. Today, we are perhaps not so quick to dismiss this immensely popular form, as a number of scholars have defended it against earlier attacks. We see it as a key to the taste and vision of nineteenth-century theater audiences. For surely, the melodrama's success originated in its themes as well as its form. Music, spectacle, and special effects were essential to the melodrama, but so was its enactment of the victory of virtue over vice that provided a moral certainty audiences craved.

It is no coincidence that the tumultuous final decade of the eighteenth century witnessed the birth of the melodrama, nor that its "father," Pixérécourt, fought against the Revolutionary government in Paris, then for it, before barely escaping the Terror to create the dramatic form most popular with the audiences that had experienced with him the violent upheavals of the Revolution. Melodrama represents a popular response to the excitement and anxiety generated as traditional social and cultural orders were challenged by revolutions in America, France, and elsewhere. Peter Brooks argues persuasively for this point, locating the rise of melodrama specifically in the French Revolution's destruction of an aristocratic cultural order and the literary types it had supported:

[Melodrama] comes into being in a world where the traditional imperatives of truth and ethics have been violently thrown into question, yet where the promulgation of truth and ethics, their instauration as a way of life, is of immediate, daily, political concern. . . . We may legitimately claim that the melodrama becomes the principal mode for uncovering, demonstrating, and making operative the essential moral universe in a post-sacred era.[41]

As Brooks notes, this link between the melodrama and the Revolution had already been made by Pixérécourt's friend and best critic, Charles Nodier, who wrote in his introduction to Pixérécourt's *Théâtre Choisi:*

This much is certain, that given the circumstances within which it appeared, the melodrama was necessary. The entire populace had enacted in the streets and public squares the greatest drama in history. Everyone had been an actor in this bloody play, everyone had been a soldier, or a revolutionary, or an exile. These solemn spectators, who had inhaled the scent of powder and blood, needed emotions analogous to those from which the return of order had severed them. They needed conspiracies, dungeons, scaffolds, battlefields, powder and blood; the unmerited misfortunes of the great and famous, the insidious maneuvers of the traitors, the perilous self-sacrifice of good men.[42]

Nodier reads the melodrama as an allegory of the Revolution. He sees the melodrama's striking features—its violent plots, dungeon-like settings, and black and white characters—as signs of the realities of France under the

Terror. For him, the violence that filled the streets of Paris is displaced upon the melodramatic stage.

Nodier also locates melodrama's moralism in its response to the Revolution, contending that these plays teach "the morality of the Revolution": "virtue is never without reward, crime is never without punishment."[43] While we tend to find melodramatic moralizing a completely superficial version of poetic justice, Nodier suggests that melodrama can only discover a conventional ethical vision in the midst of violence. Melodramatic characters may finally appear in black and white terms, but the world of melodrama is initially a morally murky one. The lightning flash of violence is required to illuminate each man's moral complexion.

If we glance at *Coelina or the Child of Mystery (Coelina ou l'enfant du mystère;* this is the play Holcroft translated as *A Tale of Mystery),* an early and typical work by Pixérécourt, we find that only the machinations of the evil Truguelin finally reveal the identity and the innocence of Coelina's mute father. Had there been no villainy, virtue would not have been known, the mystery of the title would never have been unraveled. Pixérécourt's conventional sense of morality offers a surprising justification for violence. Violence and virtue are secret sharers in a plot that moves towards a total clarification of each man's place in a moral order. The age of the Revolution and its Terror appeared to destroy traditional morality, but Pixérécourt's corpus asserts that this violence directed against the moral order actually helps to clarify it.

We must not oversimplify the melodrama. It could, for example, appeal to the audiences of both London's "patent" theaters and the new working class theaters of the East End. Characters ranged from the moral absolutes of Pixérécourt to the repentant sinners of Kotzebue and the villain-heroes of the Gothic drama. Stories were drawn from history, the Bible, novels, and the news; a play might be set in medieval Europe or the South Seas. Still, the melodramas of the early nineteenth century shared Pixérécourt's commitment to an absolute moral vision revealed through violence and made impressive through spectacular effects.[44] Some melodramas apparently question the traditional political order, with a class struggle simmering beneath the surface of Pocock's *Miller and His Men* (Covent Garden, 1813) and hints of the abuses of slavery in John Fawcett's *Obi; or Three-Fingered Jack* (Haymarket, 1800); but such plays did not question conventional morality. Even Kotzebue, who was often accused of subverting the morality of his audiences because he granted sympathy to women whose virtue had slipped, still ended his plays with morality triumphant.

Hegel's analysis of Kotzebue's plays provides one of the strongest statements of the commitment of melodrama to what Hegel calls the "triumph of ordinary morality."[45] Kotzebue's men and women stray from the path of virtue only to be called back to the moral fold by sentiment and shame. While this flirtation with vice was felt to be a realistic touch, there is something insincere in their moral regeneration, this bow to convention. His villains abjure their passions, while his fallen women unlock their hearts of gold. As Hegel puts it, we are not asked to judge whether these characters are good or bad; rather it is a "question of pardon and the promise of moral improvement, and we are therefore confronted with the possibility of spiritual conversion and surrender of the self."[46] "Let the heart break and change its views"—that is the motto of Kotzebuean melodrama according to Hegel. Having indulged their passions, Kotzebue's characters are then willing to sacrifice their identities if only society will pardon them. As Kotzebue's plays suggest, the turn to ordinary morality—to domestic virtue, sexual continence, and family ties—continued to mark even the most daring popular works, a point made again by *The Second Mrs. Tanqueray* as late as 1893.

While the melodrama was the dominant dramatic form during the early nineteenth century, we must not equate the romantic drama with it, as many critics from Nodier to the present have done.[47] Pixérécourt himself never made such a mistake. He despised the drama of the French romantics, for it failed to provide the "religious and providential ideas" he found central to melodrama. He spoke of the romantic drama as "dangerous, immoral, destitute of interest and truth."[48] Like the monodrama, the melodrama could enter the romantic drama only as a stylistic element within a larger thematic and dramatic context. The melodrama offered the powerful providential plots missing from the monodrama, but its vision stood in opposition to that of the major romantic playwrights. To begin with, even if the melodrama arose, as Nodier claims, in response to the French Revolution, these plays sought to deny the historical nature of the conflicts presented. The violence necessary to unveil the eternal but hidden moral order of the melodrama is not part of a unique historical moment, but a recurring episode in the continuing revelation of virtue; thus Nodier can assert that the melodramatist's morality is eternal, found in all philosophies, all religions.[49] Situated in every possible historical era and in every possible locale—Pixérécourt's plays, for example, range from Robinson Crusoe's island to the mines of Poland—the melodrama still rejects the historical to offer itself as a modern myth of morality victorious through violence. The melodrama, born of historical change, denied the historicity that lies at the heart of romantic tragic drama.

The romantic playwrights also found themselves opposed to the increasing domesticity of the melodrama. In its Gothic incarnation or in the absolutist spectacles of Pixérécourt, the melodrama could inspire a Byron or a Hugo, for these works played for the same metaphysical stakes as the romantic drama. However, the melodrama drifted increasingly from the demonic to the domestic (there were, of course, other types of melodrama, like the English "nautical" variation, best represented by Jerrold's *Black-Eyed Susan* of 1829), thus revealing its inherent commitment to "ordinary morality." One indication of this trend is that this popular genre turned increasingly from public to private virtues. Monvel's *Victimes Cloitrées*, mentioned above, is one candidate for the honor of being the first melodrama and was translated by "Monk" Lewis; interestingly, it still stages a struggle between public and private obligations, as a republican official seeks to persuade a young friend to dedicate his services to the nation rather than give up to private despair and enter a cloister. Later plays, like Buckstone's *Luke the Laborer* (Adelphi, 1826) and Jerrold's *Rent Day* (Drury Lane, 1830), recognize class conflict but offer private, not political, solutions. In the latter play, which at first seems to confront the problem of absentee landlords, the landlord is revealed as a force of order; it is the local steward who is corrupt, and he is punished as the hero discovers the money to pay his rent. Everything is settled at an individual level, and it is the moral character of the heroes and villains, not the social class of landlord and renters, that determines the vision of the play; as Robertson Davies has said, in such plays "poetic justice is preferred to protest."[50]

The romantics did adopt many of the spectacular techniques of the melodrama. On occasion they used apparently melodramatic plots. But the melodramatic elements within romantic plays represent a pitfall facing the protagonist, not the vision that he and his play struggle towards. Romantic dramatists use melodramatic techniques to portray the failure of the rebel to plot history according to a humane ideal. When that rebel finds he must commit violence, he at least hopes to prove himself heroic and to forge in violence a sign of an ideal future. But his nightmare is that his actions will merely form part of a melodramatic pattern, that the terror to which he commits himself will merely reconfirm traditional order. There is tragedy in this gap between his dream and his nightmare. We will see this interplay between tragedy and melodrama in Hugo's *Hernani* and Dumas's *Antony*. More powerfully, Musset's *Lorenzaccio* places Lorenzo's struggle to create himself as a heroic rebel within a melodramatic pattern in which historical violence appears as merely part of a cyclical reaffirmation of the oppressive order against which he fights. While the monodrama provided the romantics with the means of theatricalizing the self, the melodrama enabled them to stage the tragedy of revolt, to depict the failure of the heroic attempt to change the world.

It should now be clear that the romantic drama cannot be reduced to either the monodrama or the melodrama. It drew upon both, only to incorporate them into a new tragic drama. Significantly, these limited forms were used to set forth the restricted modes of existence in which the romantic protagonist can entrap himself. Just as the romantic protagonist is caught between the lures of the inner world and the call to revolt, so is the romantic drama positioned between two reductive versions of the drama, one that demands unmediated sympathy for the individual and the other that imposes violently an unquestioned judgment. In an interesting way, the romantics discovered tragedy when their protagonists fell from an ideal state into the world of either the monodrama or the melodrama, from visionary romance into the nineteenth-century theater. Their search for a form, which led them to define their plays against traditional tragedy and to find a new tragic drama within the confines of the contemporary stage, thus mirrors their transformation of the tragic vision. As we turn now to the drama of Germany, England, and France, and to the plays of writers like Schiller and Goethe, Byron and Shelley, Hugo and Musset, we need to consider the varying ways in which the romantics sought—successfully and unsuccessfully—to redefine the tragic and to renew the stage.

CHAPTER THREE
SCHILLER AND THE
IMPORTANCE OF
GERMAN ROMANTIC
DRAMA

Goethe's *Faust*, the most famous product of German romanticism, was completed in 1831, after English romanticism had exhausted its initial energies and the French romantics had established themselves as their country's leading literary movement. But German romantic drama had arisen much earlier, as early as Goethe's *Götz von Berlichingen* (1773) and Schiller's *The Robbers* (1781). These dramas already linked the inward-seeking individual with revolt and thus outlined the basic themes and shape of romantic drama. These two plays in particular, and the German drama of the late eighteenth century in general, had a significant impact upon English and French literature and helped to spur the creation of romantic drama throughout Europe.

In England the last decade of the eighteenth century was a period of intense interest in things Germanic. Henry Mackensie's paper before the Royal Society of Edinburgh on April 12, 1788, did much to spark England's interest in the German drama. Evidence of this interest includes Benjamin Thompson's *The German Theatre* (1801), containing plays by Goethe, Schiller, Kotzebue, and Iffland; and the work of William Taylor, perhaps the most enthusiastic of the Germanists, who began translating German poetry in 1790 and continued to produce a string of translations of and articles on German literature that culminated in his *Historic Survey of German Poetry* (1828-1830). More famous writers also joined the ranks of German translators. *Götz* found a translator in Sir Walter Scott, Lewis adapted Schiller's *Kabale und Liebe* as *The Minister;* and Coleridge translated *Wallenstein*. While *The Robbers* did not find such a prominent translator, it did become a romantic touchstone, the reading of which had an important place in the development of Wordsworth and Coleridge, and later of Byron and Shelley.[1]

The German influence seeped into France at a slower rate, but seemed to have a more profound effect—in part, perhaps, because the German drama reinforced tendencies in the native English drama while it represented a new and liberating model for French playwrights. While *The Robbers* was an early favorite in France, it first reached the stage only in a melodramatic adaptation by Lamartellière (1792). While there continued to be translations of German works, it was a long time before German plays had a significant impact upon French literary drama. Constant's translation of *Wallenstein* and Madame de Staël's *De l'Allemagne* mark important steps in the French assimilation of the German theater, but it was not until the French romantics seized the stage in the late 1820s that we see this influence inspiring major new works. These romantic writers invoked the names of Goethe and Schiller along with that of Shakespeare in their attempts to storm the bastions of neoclassicism. The importance of *Faust* is revealed not only in Delacroix's magnificent illustrations for the play and Nerval's translation of it, but in the latter's own plays and in dramas by Musset and Gautier. We see the examples of Schiller's influence in Hugo's *Hernani* and in Musset's *Lorenzaccio*. Musset, in fact, once wrote that he would be either a Shakespeare or a Schiller or write nothing at all. One indication of the importance of the German theater to the romantic drama in both England and France is that the opponents of the plays of the romanticists often referred to the romantic drama as the "German school" of theater.[2]

German romantic drama is central to romantic drama as a whole, and the works of Schiller are central to Germany's dramatic efforts. Goethe may be the greatest romantic poet, but his plays offer variants of the dominant pattern of romantic tragic drama, as we will see in the next chapter. Schiller was the first dramatist to explore deeply and systematically the tensions of modern man's rebellion and its links to his attempt to create himself as an individual. From his first play, *The Robbers,* written in the rebellious mood of the Storm and Stress, to his unfinished *Demetrius,* which treats of the usurper of the Russian throne, Schiller's investigation of revolt, of the struggle for the ideal, and of the individual cut off from his ties to traditional society marks him as the prototypical romantic dramatist to whom writers like Wordsworth, Coleridge, Hugo, and Musset could turn for inspiration.

I
THE QUEST FOR A "ROMANTIC CLASSIC"

WHEN THE GERMAN romantics turned to the drama, they faced a different situation from that of their counterparts in France and England. For Germany in the late eighteenth century still lacked an established dramatic tradition. The Baroque period, which brought great drama to Spain and England, left no major works for the German theater. In France, neoclassicism partially supplanted and partially transformed the Baroque to create the masterworks of Corneille and Racine. German neoclassicism brought only the sterile experiments of Gottsched. The Enlightenment furnished the first German dramatist of international stature, but Lessing was a single playwright, not a tradition; and his plays both contributed to the rise of the melodrama and sparked attempts to create a German literary drama.[3] When the German romantics came to write their plays, they had no tradition to draw on, no precursors to show them the way or against whom to define themselves.

There were both advantages and disadvantages in this situation. The German writers did not have to struggle against an entrenched neoclassical tradition as did the French romantics, nor did they have to compete with the memory of Shakespeare. They thus had a freer hand to create a modern dramatic tradition to replace traditional tragedy. However, they also wrote for theaters which had few established masterworks in their repertoires and were as a result all too easily dominated by the popular melodrama. The melodramatic *Familienstücke* of Kotzebue and Iffland—which like our soap operas convinced audiences they were naturalistic despite contrived plots, incoherent characters, sentimentality, and rigid moralism—threatened to become Germany's dramatic tradition. The Comédie Française, while a stronghold of neoclassicism, had at least preserved a French audience for verse drama; even if audiences there hissed the poetic innovations of a writer like Hugo, they could still comprehend them. In Germany, where the actors had never been trained to perform verse plays nor the audience to listen to them, the new playwrights had to remake the theater and its audience as well as write plays for them. Goethe's stylized productions at Weimar, the "atmospheric" theatrical techniques of romantic directors, even the turn of Goethe and Schiller from prose to poetry, all need to be understood at least in part as attempts to move the theater away from the supposed naturalism of the melodrama. Schiller spoke for the literary figures of the day in declaring "war" against naturalism in his essay on the chorus, included with *The Bride of Messina* (1803).

This rejection of the popular drama could become a revolt against the theater itself, as we have noticed in the case of Tieck. However, the goal of Schiller and the other major playwrights of his day was to create a body of German plays comparable to the masterworks of England and France and capable of holding the stage. Lacking a literary tradition upon which to build and faced by a hostile popular form that tempted some to reject the stage entirely, romantic writers like Goethe and Schiller deserve all the more credit for creating the "classics" of the German drama.

The verbal paradox of this romantic achievement has sometimes led critics to isolate these "classic" works—especially those of Goethe and Schiller—from the romantic movement. There is in German literary history a tendency to divide what we call the romantic period into a series of smaller, disparate movements. The line of great German drama—stretching from Storm and Stress playwrights like Lenz and Klinger, through the great trio of Goethe, Schiller, and Kleist, on to later writers like Grabbe, Grillparzer, and Büchner—is broken into several opposed developments. We find in the literary histories that the Storm and Stress movement was followed by a quite different romantic movement, which found itself opposed by the Weimar classicism of Goethe and Schiller. A second wave of romanticism followed, perhaps a return to classicism with Grillparzer as well, and then a preview of the twentieth century with Büchner. The results of such classifying schemes prove to be a bit puzzling. We are told that Goethe, for instance, began as a Storm and Stress writer, flirted with romanticism, and then became the leading classicist of his day; it is recognized, however, that he returned to some aspects of romanticism in later works, particularly *Faust*. Romanticism in Germany is reduced to small circles of writers gathering in Jena or Heidelberg. Kleist and Hölderlin, certainly key figures, seem to belong in none of these limited groups and are instead lauded as a proto-modern and a reborn Greek. When romanticism becomes a minor ripple in intellectual history, when Weimar classicism can be defined only as a ten-year period in the lives of a few men, when key figures escape such reductive division, then we can begin to doubt this entire schematization.

French and English writers have, of course, always viewed these authors as part of European romanticism, and the best critics of German literature have agreed with them.[4] Goethe and Schiller were certainly seen as romantics by their contemporaries elsewhere in Europe, as their influence on romantic drama suggests. Even within Germany, the "romanticists" at Jena did not see themselves in opposition to the "classicists" at Weimar, especially not in their shared quest for a German dramatic tradition. A striking collaboration between the two groups reveals much about their common dramatic project. In 1802, Goethe produced two plays by the Schlegel brothers, the leaders of the Jena romantic circle. A. W. Schlegel's *Ion* was derived from Euripides, while Friedrich Schlegel's *Alarcos* merged a classical notion of fate with material taken from Spanish romance and techniques derived from Calderón. Both were staged by Goethe in the stylized manner he felt to be the mark of classical works; he even used masks for *Ion*. Friedrich Schlegel later revealed the common dream behind this collaboration between "romanticists" and "classicists" and this combination of Greek and modern inspiration: "The purpose of *Alarcos* must be clear to everybody: it is intended to be a tragedy, in the ancient sense of the word, but with a romantic subject and form."[5] The struggle to forge a modern "classic," to create a German tragedy that merged the best of the ancient and the modern or romantic was also central to the plays of Schiller and Kleist, Hölderlin and Grillparzer. The fact that in some cases the authors succeeded so well that their works have come to be called "classics" should not obscure for us their status as romantic works. Friedrich Schlegel called romanticism "an endlessly developing classicism."[6] German romanticism in the theater was the continuing search for a dramatic form that would possess the stature of classical works while treating modern, romantic themes.

This "romantic classic" could not be produced by the melodramatic theater nor the antitheatrical drama of a Tieck; nor did the academic exercises of the Schlegels hold much promise. Yet, despite the tensions between romantic aspirations and theatrical realities, several writers—Goethe, Kleist, and above all Schiller—did create a modern tragic drama capable of holding the stage. While Kleist's plays were not popular during his lifetime, Goethe and Schiller did manage to form the basis of a German dramatic tradition. One indication of their success is that their plays could spark popular theatrical fashions. Goethe's *Götz von Berlichingen* inspired a whole series of popular plays called *Ritterdrama,* plays of chivalry set in the heroic age of German knights and filled with kidnappings, trials by ordeal, and secret tribunals. Schiller's *The Bride of Messina* and Goethe's urgings lay behind the composition of Zacharias Werner's *Der 24. Februar* (1809), the first of the so-called "fate dramas" that were to remain popular until the 1820s, after Grillparzer had written as his first successful play a fate tragedy, *Die Ahnfrau.*[7]

Schiller himself, however, is the key figure in German romanticism's attempt to create a theatrical tradition. Schiller represents a watershed in the development of German drama because in him all of the various native and foreign strains within the German theater find expression. He revived the Greek chorus in *The Bride of Messina;* found in Shakespeare the inspiration for formal freedom, historical tragedy, psychological portraiture, and much else; drew upon Calderón in writing the *Maid of Orleans* and *Wilhelm Tell;* and admired the French ability to construct a taut play. He also turned to native German traditions. The spirit of the German Baroque hovers over many of his plays. Gottsched's brand of neoclassicism had failed, but Schiller, with Goethe and the other major figures of the day, struggled to create a new, broader German classicism. Lessing was a direct influence on early works like *Love and Intrigue.*

We should not assume, however, that Schiller learned merely from past masters or that his plays are pastiches of moribund literary models. As Bruford points out, Schiller was a man of the contemporary theater:

But the contemporary appeal of Schiller was not due so much to what he had learnt from Shakespeare, the Greeks and the French as to his power of expressing the thought and emotions of his German public in a form adapted to their theater in his own time, and the general tendency throughout the century had always been towards the same kind of higher synthesis which he finally achieved of artistic and cultural elements derived from many classes of society.[8]

Schiller never turned against the stage as did the romantic circles and, at times, even Goethe.[9] He drew upon the devices of the popular theater, and that means even upon the melodrama. It is ironic that Schiller is accused of being overly theatrical by the same critics who chastise other romantics for lacking any feeling for the stage. Schiller's well-developed theatrical sense is essential to his success. He had the ability to put other dramatic types, even the melodrama, to his own uses. His works can, of course, be reduced to pure melodrama; that is what Lamartellière did when he adapted *The Robbers* for the Paris stage. But Schiller himself uses melodramatic devices only to engage his audience in what Bruford calls the "higher synthesis" of his dramatic art. Grillparzer, deeply influenced by Schiller, understood his predecessor's relation to the popular theater:

He did not come down to the level of the people. He placed himself on a level where it is possible for the people to come up to him, and the amplitude of expression which some criticize in him is in fact the bridge by which travellers from all grades of culture can reach his heights.[10]

Schiller, drawing upon world drama, German tradition, and the contemporary stage, managed to please while creating the "romantic classics" so eagerly sought. He thus became, as Friedrich Schlegel called him, "the true founder of our drama."[11]

II
THE ACHIEVEMENT OF SCHILLER

THE PLAYS OF writers like Tieck fail as satisfying dramatic works because they cannot surmount a problem that faced the romantic dramatist, a problem that Hegel defined for us in the last chapter: the loss of the heart of drama as it is torn now towards the epic, now towards the lyric. In other words, the drama was on the verge of becoming pure monodrama, mere melodrama, or some loose mixture of the two. The search for a solution to this situation can be seen in the two popular literary forms discussed above. The *Ritterdrama* confronted this split into epic and lyric elements by seeing in formless epic plots a reflection of history and in characters bursting lyrically from their dramatic context an espousal of freedom. The fate dramas found unity in a mechanistic fate that reduced characters to pawns, judgment to nemesis.

But it was Schiller who created a truly satisfying reintegration of plot, character, and judgment or theme. Not that his plays have escaped attack for failing to blend these elements into a whole. The incidents in *Don Carlos* and the *Wallenstein* trilogy are seen to be too complex to be integrated into a single plot. The use of a traditional form for *Maria Stuart* may seem to obscure its treatment of romantic themes. Characters like Karl Moor in *The Robbers* and the Marquis of Posa in *Don Carlos* are felt to dominate their plays unduly. And ideas and ideals, the heart of Schiller's plays, strike many as extraneous or disruptive.

Schiller was aware of the dissolution that threatened his plays. He came to regard his early expansive efforts with misgiving.[12] After writing *Don Carlos,* the work which more than any other seems to tear itself apart, he did not complete another drama for ten years, but rather sought to prepare himself for new creation through historical and philosophical studies. When he returned to the drama with the *Wallenstein* trilogy, his chief concern was to create a tragic drama that would be unified, not sprawling like his earlier plays. In letter after letter to Goethe, Schiller speaks of the intractable bulk of the source material for *Wallenstein.*[13] Schiller realized that he did not possess, as the Greeks and Shakespeare had possessed, preexistent stories from which to create his plays. He did not have a tragic myth or a providential plot to provide a backbone for the drama. He had to create a tragic shape for his historical material; and thus we find him saying of *Wallenstein* that through his work "the subject had *changed* into a purely tragic story" (my emphasis).[14] Schiller explored more fully than any other playwright of the period the formal problems that faced the romantic playwright. He demonstrated more profoundly than any of his contemporaries that a new ground for tragedy could be discovered in the very possibility that traditional tragedy might no longer be possible. While Schiller did not always succeed in his struggle with the dissolution of the dramatic center that threatened the drama of his day, while we may feel that his plays no longer appeal to us so strongly as do *The Cenci, Lorenzaccio,* or Kleist's *Prince Friedrich,* his dramas can still provide us, and did in fact provide many of his contemporaries, with a model of romantic tragic drama.

Schiller's plays arise with the rest of romantic drama from the recognition of the loss of past dramatic modes. It is thus not surprising that the central fact of his plays is their concern with revolt, with the loss or rejection of the past. One reason for the enormous international success of his first play, *The Robbers,* was that it portrayed modern man in revolt. It gave voice to the revolutionary cries of the day, and such cries resound not only throughout Schiller's theater but also in the plays of Wordsworth and Byron, Hugo and Musset.

Goethe's Faust argues that in the beginning was the deed. Schiller's characters find that deed to be revolt. The first time that we meet the hero of *The Robbers,* Karl Moor, he announces his revulsion for his world: "I hate this age of puny scribblers, when I can pick up my Plutarch and read of great men" (I, ii).[15] Many romantic heroes took up this cry; we will hear it again—down to the reference to Plutarch—in the mouth of Musset's Lorenzaccio. Moor rages against an age of compromising lackeys and hypocritical social climbers, an age that seeks to "smother healthy nature with their ridiculous conventions." He feels that society and its laws have entrapped and weakened him: "The law has cramped the flight of eagles to a snail's pace. The law never yet made a great man, but freedom will breed a giant, a colossus" (I, ii).[16] This rejection of the present, the demand for freedom, the quest for heroic stature—these are central to Schiller's protagonists, virtually all of whom are defined by revolt. Fiesco leads a revolt against the Genoese tyrants. Don Carlos and the Marquis of Posa dream of a free Netherlands and a free Europe. Wallenstein plots insurrection against the Emperor. Johanna and Tell find themselves swept up in struggles of national liberation. All of these characters follow Moor in rejecting the limits of their age.

However, the revolt of the Schillerian protagonist cannot be adequately defined as social protest. While the rebellion of many Storm and Stress figures centers on class struggle, Schiller's characters revolt because they find themselves unable to discover their full humanity within the confines of their world.[17] In his characters' quest for a full humanity, Schiller treats the key romantic theme of selfhood. When they discover that their world will not allow them to mature and thus become all that they might be, these figures turn inward to discover in their own self-conception an eagle-like identity to oppose the snail's role offered them by society. Their revolt begins in personal frustration. Schiller places Don Carlos in a paradigmatic situation. As his play opens, Don Carlos has come of age only to have his bride taken by his father and his place in royal councils taken by Alba. He has been denied the wife and the work that would have marked his movement into adulthood and a full life. Again, Karl Moor comes to revolt against his society only when he has been denied the normal avenues to maturity, when his brother has cut him off from his father, his patrimony, and his fiancée. Even an older, ostensibly mature figure like Wallenstein lives with the fear that his powers will be taken from him as he struggles in a world ruled by a paternalistic Emperor. Always lurking in Wallenstein's mind are the events at Regensberg, where, years before the opening of the play, the Emperor removed him from his command. It is against such a curtailment of his field of action that he fights.

For these characters, the world is a place of frustrations, of limitations that prevent them from fulfilling themselves. It is interesting to note that some of Schiller's plays have been seen as *Bildungs-dramas,* for the Schillerian protagonist seems to be the victim of a frustrated development.[18] Any process of *Bildung* that he undergoes will be one he forges in the fire of rebellion. If Schiller's characters (even some of his older ones) strike us as adolescents crying out against a world they do not find pleasing, it is because the structure of their world denies them the maturity of full human development.

The personal frustration that lies behind the revolt of the Schillerian protagonist suggests both a link between the individual's quest for self-definition and revolt, and a tension between his private motive for revolt and the public or political form that it takes. While Karl Moor tries to present himself as a Robin Hood of revolt, he becomes a robber because of private, not public, wrongs. While the Marquis of Posa embraces the cause of freedom and Wallenstein proclaims himself to be an apostle of peace, their acts seem to reflect a desire for personal power. In *Fiesco,* the tension between personal and political motives determines the course of the tragic action; for Fiesco moves towards his doom when he allows his personal desires to take precedence over his political commitment to the creation of a Genoese republic. Even in *Wilhelm Tell,* where the revolution is successful, there is a tension between the protagonist's self-definition and his public role.[19]

Frustrated in his personal development, the Schillerian protagonist seeks an outlet for private complaints in ostensibly political acts; but the gap between his thwarted selfhood and the grand public role he adopts points at the bad faith, the self-falsification, that taints his actions. He attempts to leap out of the difficulties of selfhood by taking on a political role that partially disguises his inner turmoil, but he can do so only at the expense of his hopes for a full individual development and of his respect for the individuality of others. Schiller's treatment of the problems of selfhood and of self-betrayal touches upon the tragedy of the self that we will explore most fully in discussing English romantic drama. His portrait of the revolutionary who dons a public role to escape the limits on his personal life looks ahead to the rebels of French romantic drama. Most important, he demonstrates that these two key facets of romantic drama are intimately linked as aspects of romantic man's struggle to create for himself a fully human identity within a humane society.

Where do Schiller's characters discover an image of the full humanity they seek? Moor's opening statement, quoted above, is suggestive, for it indicates that his model is the hero of past literature. Moor attributes his difficulties to his birth in the age of scribblers rather than in the heroic age described by Plutarch. He expands upon this opposition until it becomes clear that he sees the past as a time when men lived tragic lives and the present as a day in which they only write tragedies:

Pah! An age of eunuchs, fit for nothing but chewing over the deeds of bygone days, mutilating the heroes of old with their learned interpretations and mocking them with their tragedies. (I, ii)[20]

These may appear as odd sentiments to put into the mouth of your hero as you attempt your first tragedy, but they serve Schiller well by contrasting Moor's characterization with the portrayal of past heroes. A typical romantic protagonist, Moor wants to be a hero in a world without heroes.

Moor's desire to be a hero and his fear that this is no longer possible are comparable to the hope and fear of his creator, for Schiller sought to create tragic dramas to rival the classics of the past, and yet he remained uncertain of his ability to do so. The distance between the present and the past is of concern not only to Schiller's characters; it occupies him in major poems ("The Gods of Greece," "Ideals and Life") and in seminal essays *(On The Aesthetic Education of Man in A Series of Letters, Naive and Sentimental Poetry)*. In his plays, Schiller depicted men and women confronting the issue that was central to him and that he felt was central to his culture: the sense that modern life is a divided and diminished version of the past and the need to reintegrate and enrich it. This sharing of concerns between creator and creature—which has nothing to do with arguments over whether certain characters speak for Schiller—results in a rather odd situation in his plays; for the characters are seeking within their plays the same type of unity that their creator is trying to achieve in writing his dramas. His protagonists battle for a full humanity that would simultaneously make them the type of full character that Schiller seeks to construct in opposition to the fragmented, lyric figures of his age. The difficulties within the play echo the playwright's difficulties in writing the play.

Schiller's protagonists may revolt against the present and they may do so with an eye to the heroic past, but they rebel to create the future. The orientation towards the future that marks Schiller's theater is clear already in *The Robbers,* where Schiller creates a parallel between the rebellion of Karl Moor and that of his brother Franz in order to reveal the difference between the revolt of the traditional villain and the revolutionary leap into the future of the romantic idealist.

Karl and Franz reveal two sides of the same revolt, one that looks backward; the other, forward. Both rebel against society, the faults of which they condemn in strikingly similar terms (see I, i; I, ii). Both see revolt as a means of opening up new opportunities in a world that would deny them. Both find that revolt leads to isolation. Still, Franz is a villain and Karl is "a remarkable and important personage, abundantly endowed with the power of becoming either a Brutus or a Catiline."[21] Karl, to a much greater extent than Franz, is the prototype of the Schillerian protagonist, for Schiller continued to be concerned with the revolt of the idealist, while he came to view villains as a weakness in a play.[22] Franz is in many ways a quite traditional villain, as the debts his characterization owes to Shakespeare's Richard and Edmund suggest. His revolt is purely personal. He wishes to invert, and thus to pervert, the order of nature and society so that he may rise to the top.

Karl, however, does not wish to climb the social hierarchy. His revolt may originate in private dissatisfaction, but it does not remain merely personal. Karl attempts to place his personal complaints within a political program. He revolts not to pervert his world, but to convert it in the name of an ideal society. Franz wishes to change his place in the world by moving upward. Karl hopes to change his world by moving forward. Even though his is not a historical play, Karl—like later Schiller protagonists drawn from history's chronicles—seeks to establish himself as a hero within the historical realm by breaking with the past to create the future.

It is this historical dimension that enables Karl Moor's revolt—unlike Franz's—to become a potentially positive force. Revolt no longer means the inversion of a static order, but rather the creation of a new order. Thus, Schiller's characters argue for a link between revolt and the advent of a new golden age. Karl Moor feels certain he can build in Germany a great republic: "Give me an army of fellows like me to command, and I'll turn Germany into a republic that will make Rome and Sparta look like nunneries" (I, i).[23] The Marquis of Posa, in his famous interview with King Philip, sets forth a vision of an enlightened Europe, blessed with freedom of thought. Wallenstein, who might otherwise appear as a villainous outlaw plotting against the sovereign, sees himself as a great peacemaker and as the harbinger of a new paradisiacal era. Such revolutionary visions can be seen as positive, for they challenge not a hierarchical order seen to be an earthly reflection of divine order as in traditional tragedy, but rather a static social order seen to limit and corrupt man.

The commitment to an ideal vision of the future marks the heroic nature in Schiller's plays, for that commitment involves the attempt to discover the full humanity possessed by heroes in the past.[24] Moreover, in a sense, the ideal replaces the divine in Schiller's dramas. In traditional tragedy, contact with the divine often both identifies one as a hero and brings about one's destruction. Oedipus proves himself in solving the riddle of the Sphinx and is destroyed by the revelation of an oracle he presumes to understand. Macbeth, after he listens to the witches, becomes more than a soldier fighting for a king, but his dependence upon their guidance also contributes to his downfall. The divine marks a man as a hero and destroys him when he presumes too much on the basis of this distinction. As a romantic, Schiller began to write plays wholly bereft of the divine. While *The Maid of Orleans* and *The Bride of Messina* represent an attempt to recapture the power of traditional providential drama, the central Schillerian situation is one in which man finds himself without divine guidance, without any contact with a providential realm. Instead he has an ideal: a human construct, an idea created in the recognition of the loss of a divinely ordered world and in the hope for a humanely ordered one. Cut off from the divine and trapped within an unheroic society, modern man can fashion an ideal to replace the divine and thus prove himself heroic. Still, there is an important difference between this heroic idealism and the heroism of the past. The traditional hero is chosen as much as he chooses; he is a hero. The romantic protagonist wills his heroism in choosing the ideal; he will become a hero.

The Schillerian protagonist's espousal of an ideal sets him in opposition to present reality; hence, his revolt. However, he must act within the present unheroic world if he is to work for the ideal future he envisions. The extreme hesitation that marks so many of Schiller's protagonists—Karl Moor wavering between commitment to his outlaw band and revulsion against it, Fiesco playing with revolt, and most strikingly Wallenstein forever attempting to put off decision—indicates their desire to keep their commitment to the ideal free from the taint of action in the debased reality of the present. But they must act if they are not to be ineffectual; and when they do, they betray the future to the present. Schiller seizes here upon one of the key dilemmas of romantic tragic drama. Historical action—the attempt to make the future by acting in the present—betrays the ideal shape man would give to history; for action forces man to adopt means that, insofar as they are available in the limited reality of the present, are defined by their distance from an ideal end. Shelley's Beatrice committing patricide in her attempt to eradicate wrong, Byron's Marino Faliero stooping to a plebian revolt that plots violence against his noble friends, Musset's Lorenzaccio involving himself in murder and a hopeless rebellion to liberate Florence—all of these figures discover the same tragic impasse that confronts Schiller's idealists.

This conflict between an ideal end and the debased means of the historical present provides Schiller with a substitute for the traditional tragic confrontation between man and the divine. In traditional tragedy, man's attempt to overleap the gap between himself and the gods brings his destruction. Similarly, the distance between man and his ideal defines Schiller's tragic vision; the hero's attempt to actualize his ideal results in a contradiction resolved only in death. Fiesco, for example, finds that his rebellion in the name of a Genoese republic involves him in an accumulation of personal power that contaminates his commitment to an ideal society. He betrays the revolution and is killed by Verrina, the virtuous republican. Again, as Schiller himself explained in his comments on *Don Carlos,* the Marquis of Posa compromises his ideal vision of a free Europe by attempting to realize the ideal immediately through the power of Philip II.[25]

Schiller's strategic use of the ideal solves another problem facing the modern tragedian. As the case of Tieck suggests, many of Schiller's contemporaries wrote plays in which the theme expressed through set speeches floated free of the plot. By defining his theme through man's relation to a future ideal, Schiller grounds the disjunction of plot and theme in the tragic dilemma of his plays. He can no longer write plays in which plot reveals the divine order. But he can write dramas in which an ideal order is envisioned, even as the quest for that ideal is defeated within the tragic action. He has again discovered a tragic situation—the destruction of the idealist—in the difficulties facing the modern dramatist.

Schiller came to realize that the greatest of these difficulties was presented by plot. As he worked to wrest a tragic drama from the historical material for *Wallenstein,* he wrote to Goethe of the importance of plot:

I find that the more I reflect upon my own doings, and upon the manner in which the Greeks treated tragedy, that the whole *cardo dei* of Art lies in inventing a poetic story. The modern writer beats wearily and anxiously about coincidences and secondary matters, and—in his endeavor to follow reality—burdens himself with things that are empty and of no importance, and in doing this runs in danger of losing sight of that deep-seated truth which in reality contains all that is poetical. What he wishes is perfectly to imitate an actual case, and he does not consider that poetical representation can never coincide with reality, for the very reason that it is absolutely true.[26]

The naturalist fails to create true poetry because he gives himself up to the chaos of reality. Life is not art. History, the subject matter of Schiller's drama, has no plot. The poetic dramatist needs a "poetic story" that will reveal the truth that lies hidden in reality. As another of Schiller's letters makes clear, he means by "poetic story" something close to legend or myth:

I have during these last days been occupying myself a good deal in finding a subject for a tragedy in the style of *Oedipus Rex,* and one that will afford the same advantages to the poet. These advantages are inestimable, to mention but one, that the most involved action—such as altogether resists the form of tragedy—may be taken as the foundation, inasmuch as this action has, of course, already happened, and consequently falls wholly beyond the domain of tragedy.[27]

The Greeks did not face the problem that Schiller had in writing *Wallenstein*. A myth establishes the events which form the basis of *Oedipus Rex,* and they can thus be imagined as occurring before the play begins, the drama then lying in what Schiller calls "only a tragic analysis." The myth has, as it were, already predigested reality, releasing from it the truth which art seeks; the poet can thus create a drama of pure poetry. Schiller longs for such a myth and its advantages, since *Wallenstein* presented a "most involved action" but no "poetic story" to control it.[28]

While Schiller once attempted a modern equivalent of *Oedipus Rex* (in *The Bride of Messina*), he usually seems aware that he, as a modern writer, will never find the type of mythic drama written by Sophocles. In the letter quoted above, he wrote, "But I fear that the *Oedipus* is its own genus, and there is no second species of it; and least of all would one be able to find a 'pendent' to it in less fabulous times."[29] It was not fabulous myth but history which formed the core of his subject matter. He did not have a poetic story, but had to create one. Once again, he solved his problem by posing it for his characters. He discovered the shape of his plots in his characters' efforts to give shape to their lives. If history has no plot, his characters try to give it one, and it is their struggle to control history and their failure to do so that comprise the action of Schiller's tragic dramas.

The attempt to shape history is, of course, the project of the revolutionary; we see again why revolt is so central to Schiller's dramas. The Schillerian protagonist's attempt to make his own future is his glory; it is also his pride. He believes that he knows the shape of the future, and he tries to realize it in the present. Whether his vision is right or wrong, he finds that he cannot bend history to fit his image of it. The Marquis of Posa seeks to control the actions of everyone around him, for he feels certain that he alone knows the direction history must take. Yet he destroys every life that he touches and plays into the hands of the very forces he opposes. Wallenstein peers into the future, seeking to map it, trying to be certain that his acts have the force of historical necessity. He finds that his efforts are futile, that events have caught up with his dreams. The Schillerian protagonist longs to mold history, to create the future as a triumphal play that will reveal him as a hero of humanity. But he finds himself trapped within the history he would tame.

The loss of a hierarchical vision and its replacement with a sense of history and an ideal of progress have signaled for critics like Steiner the death of tragedy. Schiller, however, shows that this new sense of history—the idea of man's struggle to make his own history that was explored by a line of thinkers from Vico to Marx—provides a field for both heroic action and tragic destruction. Once man posits for himself the realm of history free from providential control, he seems to have discovered a field for the exercise of human freedom. But history, freed from the hand of providence, is unlikely to be controlled by the individual. Tragedy can arise within history for it provides a ground for a struggle between freedom and necessity, between dreams of the future and present realities, between the power of the independent individual and the force of all the other human wills and material forces that also shape the historical process. History invites a heroic expression of man's freedom, but it also embodies the tragic limits upon that freedom.

Another limit lies in the self-conception of the protagonist. Believing the future is in his grasp, he elevates his self-image as a model for the individual and society. However, his sense of self, grounded in the limited present, is only a partial humanity, as Schiller suggests through his much discussed technique of characterization.[30] Many of the figures in his plays seem to be parts of characters, not whole ones. They have accepted their present, partial humanity over their potential development in the future. Franz Moor is an example of a character who embodies a single dominant human attribute. In him, Schiller depicted the intellect and the will freed from all ties to tradition, to society, and to others. This portrait of the lethal power of the isolated intellect was to have an impact upon Wordsworth and Coleridge. In the plays of Byron, Shelley, and Musset we will see similar analyses of the destructive intellect. In Schiller's drama, Franz has betrayed all other aspects of his humanity to the force of his mind. In the preface to the play, Schiller describes Franz as a "monster," "who has gone so far. . .as to quicken his understanding at the expense of his soul."[31] But the intellect is not the only faculty that man can embrace in opposition to a fuller identity. Several of Schiller's characters—among them Karl Moor and the Marquis of Posa—are seized by an enthusiasm that Schiller sees as a type of fanaticism.[32] In the *Bride of Messina*, the destructive power of fixated passion is made clear.

The Schillerian protagonist has two goals: a reformed society and a full development of his own powers. He believes these goals to be connected. He hopes to prove himself a hero and to discover his full humanity in a revolt aimed at creating an ideal society. This connection, however, reveals the paradox that defeats him. He can achieve heroic identity only within that ideal society. In that he lives in the play's present and not in a society of the future, his present persona must be in some sense false or limited. Confronted by this distance from his future ideal, he can fall into two traps. Either he can lose his sense of his unique identity in his public role (Karl feels that his role as robber falsifies his own sense of himself; Tell's personal struggles become something quite different in the public eye); or he can allow some aspect of his unperfected selfhood to contaminate his public task (Fiesco and the Marquis of Posa both allow their pursuit of personal power to undermine their pursuit of freedom). Either he loses his sense of self, or he elevates it. In both cases, the protagonist makes the mistake of accepting a time-bound and limited role in the place of the open potentiality of the future for which he is supposedly struggling.

The revolt of the Schillerian protagonist, then, is an attempt to plot history as a heroic romance in which the fragmentation of modern life is overcome and the rebel is revealed as a hero. Once again, Schiller has his protagonist try to accomplish within his world what his creator is trying to accomplish in his play: both try to tame history. There is, however, an ironic tension between Schiller's achievement and that of his protagonists. One key to Schiller's dramas is the conflict between the play his characters would write for themselves and the one that Schiller does, in fact, write. They discover that they have provided themselves with self-aggrandizing scenarios, the rejection of which constitutes Schiller's plot. This attempt on the part of Schiller's characters to write their own plays is central to the project of the romantic protagonist who wants to be, in Hegel's phrase, the free artist of his self.[33] The role playing and disguises found throughout French romantic drama, the attempt of Shelley's Beatrice to combat the horrible reality of her situation with a myth of her own innocence, the struggle between Kleist's Prince Friedrich and his Emperor to plot their lives—all of these reflect the same conflict that Schiller charts between the drama an individual would write for himself and the greater drama in which he finds himself caught.

Already in his first play, *The Robbers,* there is a tension between the play Karl Moor would live and the script Schiller writes for him. Karl wants to see his life as a heroic struggle against injustice. While he becomes a rebel out of personal frustration more than anything else, he envisions himself as a heroic liberator. When he is forced to admit that he leads men who are more robber than rebel, he insists on the difference between his own motives and their acts. A paradigmatic case is reported by Ratzmann (II, iii).

Moor, having stopped a richly laden carriage, murders a villainous lawyer and then turns to his men: "I have done my part!...plundering is your business" ("ich habe das Meine getan!...das Plündern ist eure Sache"). When, by the third act, he has been forced to see the criminal under his own noble guise, he decides to return home to battle his brother; for even if his own revolt is questionable, that of his brother is clearly evil. Karl tries to write the end of life as a heroic melodrama in which he, the embodiment of good in disguise, fights against the evil Franz to free his father and win the innocent girl pledged to him. He has almost succeeded in this task—defeating his brother, finding his father, and winning back his fiancée—when the robber band reminds him of his pledge to remain with them. They demand that he sacrifice the girl that would bind him to others in favor of the outlawry that sets him apart (V, ii). Moor honors his commitment. He kills the girl in recognition of the fact that his revolt has irrevocably cut him off from all that he has been in the past. He has failed in his attempt to plot his revolt as a story of personal and social redemption.

Moor still tries to provide his life with a noble ending. Having made good his pledge to the robbers, he rejects the life of an outlaw and vows to sacrifice himself to the moral order. The man who once demanded an army of liberation made up of men like himself now argues that *two men such as I would destroy the whole moral order of creation* (V, ii).[34] His statement might appear to be a tragic recognition of his responsibility for the violence that he has committed in the pursuit of his vision. But it seems to be one last attempt to write a noble part for himself. As he goes off to give himself up, the robbers exclaim, "Let him go! These are fantasies of greatness. He will stake his life on empty admiration." And as he contemplates handing himself over to a poor man who might profit from the reward, Moor muses, "I might be admired for it" (V, ii).[35] He is still playing a part. However, *The Robbers* is not the drama of moral sacrifice he would now write. It is instead Schiller's tragic drama of the distance between man's dream of the ideal and the reality of his attempts to achieve that dream. Moor's life is tragic because it can be neither the heroic romance nor the noble tragedy he envisions it to be; it is instead Schiller's tale of the tragic waste of a potentially heroic individual.

This juxtaposition of the protagonist's final sense of himself and that of the dramatist and the viewer—so different from the classic tragic recognition that brings the character's self-conception in line with the destiny enforced by his play—can also be found at the close of Shelley's *The Cenci* and Kleist's *Prince Friedrich;* Hugo's *Hernani* ends with a variation on the concluding tension of *The Robbers* itself. In his later plays, Schiller deepened his treatment of this tension by grounding it in the conflict between free will and determinism, in the collision between man's attempt to shape history and the autonomous movement of historical events. Nowhere did Schiller explore man's problematic place in history more profoundly than in the *Wallenstein* trilogy—a judgment supported by Coleridge's decision to translate the play, suggesting that he grasped its significance as a new kind of tragic drama. So the best way to summarize Schiller's achievement is with a brief discussion of these three central plays.

The trilogy opens with *Wallenstein's Camp (Wallensteins Lager)*, a prologue that depicts the activity in the general's camp. We do not see Wallenstein nor the other central characters, but rather hear of them through the comments of various minor figures, soldiers and the like. This dramatic prelude is often likened to a chorus that establishes the background to the action, telling us who will be involved and what the stakes will be. It does more than that, though, for *Wallenstein's Camp* defines the world of the play through a set of especially modern concerns. Although set during the Thirty Years' War, the play depicts the world of modern romantic problems. It is divided, strife-ridden, alienated man who is presented in this prologue. We learn that the camp houses international mercenaries uprooted from the life of the past when the world seemed steady and whole, and allegiances were clear. This army pledges itself to no country, to no belief, only to Wallenstein himself. He appears to them as the only one capable of giving shape to their turbulent world, of giving unity to their diminished lives.[36] This prologue establishes the situation that we have seen to be basic to Schiller's thought and to his plays: modern life (here, life after the Reformation and the decline of the feudal age) is a fall into alienation and division, and someone needs to make it whole again. Wallenstein enters not just as a general of a military camp, but as a hope for the future.

There is another purpose behind this short play. I noted earlier that Schiller used the devices of the popular stage to draw his audiences into his tragedies. Surely, this is one function of *Wallenstein's Camp*. With its lively action, stirring music, low-life characters, and realistic details, it was certain to please audiences raised in the "naturalism" of Iffland and Kotzebue. In a sense, the trilogy presents a hierarchy of dramatic forms, with *Wallenstein's Camp* offering a sprawling and spectacular entertainment, *The Piccolomini* presenting a drama of sentiment and intrigue, and *The Death of Wallenstein (Wallensteins Tod)* moving into the realm of high tragedy. The final play of the trilogy can achieve the tragic summit because the earlier plays have served to outline the action; the first two plays provide the "poetic story," leaving only the "tragic analysis" for the final play. Schiller has overcome the loss of myth through the unique structure of his trilogy.

The camp prepares us for Wallenstein, but we do not meet him immediately. The second part of the trilogy opens with a sense of haste and urgency, as character after character rushes on stage to tell us of his plans. We discover that this will be a play of plots: the plot of Illo and Terzy and their confederates to force Wallenstein's hand; the plot of Octavio to trap Wallenstein; and most important, the master plot of Wallenstein. Each character is seeking to shape the future, to place the flow of events under human control. Above all, Wallenstein, finding himself in personal command of the Emperor's army, has the opportunity to throw off the bonds of allegiance that tie him to his sovereign and to the past. He contemplates breaking with the Emperor and his war against the Swedes to make instead a pact with the enemy that would enable him to transform Germany into a unified and peaceful land. Wallenstein stands at a moment when he feels he has the power to make the future. He has a dream of peace and a desire to prove himself a hero by achieving it.[37]

Only one character remains aloof from this project to plot the future, Max Piccolomini. He is what Schiller and Goethe called a "beautiful soul," an individual for whom the divisions of modern life do not really exist. Max still lives in innocence, before the fall into modern life that splits the ideal from the real, thought from action, individual emotion from universal truth. He embodies the ideal he espouses, and his spirit can find expression in every act he performs or word he utters. Free from the problems that Schiller's tragic protagonists must solve, Max represents an ideal of free and beautiful humanity, but he is an innocent, living outside the modern historical world. He cannot continue to live in this world if he is to avoid compromising himself. He is finally faced with a choice: to side with Wallenstein and break his pledge to the Emperor or to betray the general he has always revered. Max cannot choose either of these alternatives without violating his ideal sense of what is right. Thus, in the last part of the trilogy, we are told that he has ridden to his death, essentially committing suicide in an engagement with the Swedes but thus avoiding a fight with either the Emperor or his idol, Wallenstein.

Max may be a "beautiful soul," but Wallenstein is the grander figure. Max embraces the ideal wholeheartedly. He is, in a real sense, not made for this world. Wallenstein attempts the more difficult task of making the ideal real. He does not wish to step outside history as does Max. Rather, he wishes to control it. However, he is not one to commit himself recklessly. Men like Illo and Terzy rush into action, caring little if their means debase the end for which they fight. Wallenstein will not act unless he can find a mode of action that will preserve him from any hint of compromise. He hesitates to act upon his dream of the future because he wishes to preserve the freedom of the dream, the integrity of his will, and the full potential of his humanity. He knows that to act is to be committed to something outside the self and thus to limit one's will, even in a sense to lose one's self.

Schiller thus presents us with what is in many ways an incredible portrait: Wallenstein, the great man of action, forever procrastinating; the romantic Hamlet as general.

What Wallenstein seeks is a moment in which his free acts take on the force of historical necessity, in which his will has become one with the movement of history. He seeks in his relation to history an equivalent to the merger between free will and fate that Schiller admired in classic tragedy. Wallenstein longs for an oracle. His prayers would be answered if he could, like Macbeth, meet prophetic witches. He does not, however, live in the age of providential plots, of fated actions. Schiller has created a magnificent symbol of this fact in his much criticized use of astrology in the play.[38] Wallenstein seeks through the science of the stars to discover the plot of history so that he can match his actions to the shape of the future. We see him puzzling over astrological signs and then drawing a curtain over them. Schiller has been seen in this moment as attempting to use the machinery of fate and then losing his nerve. In fact, he has defined Wallenstein's predicament exactly. Wallenstein wants the knowledge revealed through oracles and prophecy, but he lives in the modern age where man is denied divine guidance and must chart his own course. In the final play of the trilogy, at the moment when Wallenstein and his astrologer believe they have finally found the conjunction of the stars that will enable him to act, he discovers that the actions of other men—of the Emperor and Octavio, of Illo and Terzy—have already produced a situation in which his actions are constrained. In seeking providential assurances, he has allowed history to move past him. In attempting to preserve his free humanity until the moment in which he might seize the future, he has lost control of the present. He must act, but in doing so he ensures that he must die.

Interestingly, the final play of the trilogy presents Wallenstein as the hero he has longed to be, but he has achieved that heroism only because he faces death. The infinite potential of the future having been narrowed, he can now become the heroic man of action, free from hesitation. The romance of a nation remade having failed, he can now live out a tragedy, finally committing himself heroically to present action, challenging his inevitable destiny like Macbeth or Richard. His defeat is assured, for he has been lured into the present struggle where others, less visionary than he, rule. He will be succeeded not by a noble idealist like Max, but by the petty plotter Octavio.

Schiller's *Wallenstein* offers the tragedy of historical man who seeks in himself the pattern of the future only to find that history cannot be determined by any plan that man seeks to impose on it. History replaces divine fate as man's nemesis, and man's prideful stand against the gods is supplanted by his proud affirmation of the self's ideals as a guide to the future.

Schiller's dramas prove more convincingly than those of any other dramatist of the period that the romantic turn to historical drama was not a weak imitation of Shakespeare nor a merely theatrical delight in local color and spectacular action. Man's life in history offered a new ground for tragedy that touched upon key problems for romanticism and for modern culture in general. For Schiller, historical tragedy also offered a means of resolving his formal difficulties. He knew that modern characters were likely to be divided, fragmented figures. By creating his protagonists as rebels caught between the limits of the present and the dream of a future heroic identity, he made their inner divisions and alienation part of their tragic situation. He understood the tendency of romantic dramatists to split their theme off from their plot, to have the theme expressed in lyric interludes rather than enforced in the closure of the plot. By identifying his theme with the future ideals of his characters, he provided an explanation for this split in the nature of historical time. Most important, Schiller confronted the difficulty the modern playwright has in discovering a plot to organize his material into a tragedy. Schiller offered the paradoxical and profound solution that the tragic shape of historical drama is found in man's inability to shape history. With each difficulty he faced in creating modern tragic drama, Schiller solved the problem by "theatricalizing" it, that is by posing it for his characters. If he has difficulties in creating full, rounded characters, then he makes his characters struggle for total humanity. If the modern dramatist lacks usable poetic stories, he depicts man fighting to plot his life. This theatricalization solved the formal problems of Schiller's theater by reintegrating the key issues of romanticism with the dramatic mode and thus with the stage.

Schiller's drama lies at the heart of the romantic drama of Germany and Europe and thus provides an outline for the romantic tragic vision. Schiller was not only the most important figure in the creation of a German tragic tradition. In many ways he created the modern sense of the tragedy of history; he forged a new type of tragic hero in the rebel in pursuit of a future ideal. His successes were such that later playwrights like Ibsen and Brecht still turned to him in their efforts to stage the travails of the modern idealist and the twists of history. Schiller's success lay in large part in the fact that he overcame the formal difficulties that plagued other German romantics. He bridged the gap between the literary drama and the stage to create dramatic "classics" for Germany. And by doing so, he provided playwrights throughout Europe with a model. While we find English plays that probe more deeply into the self and French plays more centrally concerned with the issue of revolt, it is unlikely that any of these plays would have taken the shape they did had their authors not had the inspiration and the example of Schiller's theater.

CHAPTER FOUR
GOETHE AND
ROMANTIC DRAMA:
VARIATIONS ON A
THEME

Goethe's plays explode a number of the commonplaces used to denigrate romantic drama. Goethe was, for example, no isolated poet penning plays in the closet. He was, as the director of the stage at Weimar, a man of the theater. He did not pander to the public's taste for the Gothic, heaping wild excess upon violent improbability and justifying it all by an appeal to Shakespeare; while he was accused of excess for his Shakespearean *Götz von Berlichingen,* he also turned to the Greeks and Racine to write works like *Iphigenia in Tauris* and *Torquato Tasso.* Nor are his dramas minor pieces within his entire corpus, of interest only to specialists. His *Faust* is perhaps the greatest work of the romantic period.

Yet, despite Goethe's unique place among romantic playwrights, students of romantic drama seem uncomfortable with his plays. His dramatic style, particularly in the supposedly "classical" plays like *Iphigenia,* has discouraged critics from linking his dramas to *The Cenci, Hernani, Remorse,* or *Lorenzaccio.* His rejection of the inwardness of "Wertherism" and his stand against the French Revolution seem to place him at odds with the attempt of romantic dramatists to discover heroism in the inward turn to the self and the outward turn to revolt. Goethe's place in the romantic struggle to discover a modern tragic form has been further complicated by the widely held view that his vision necessitates an "avoidance" of the tragic. Considerable effort has been spent arguing that the greatest romantic was capable of producing only "partial or arrested tragedy."[1]

Given this uneasiness about Goethe's plays, we still cannot doubt their importance to the romantic effort in the drama. While his influence was less important than Schiller's, Goethe's dramas helped to spur romantic drama throughout Europe. As we have seen, his *Götz* was with Schiller's *Robbers* one of the main inspirations of romantic playwrights in England and France. The impact of *Faust* on the imagination of writers like Byron, Shelley, Nerval, and Gautier is well known. If a play like *Iphigenia* rejects some formal features found in many romantic dramas, it is only to pursue the quest for a "romantic classic" discussed in the preceding chapter. Most important, Goethe's plays do explore the central themes of romantic drama—selfhood and revolt. Götz, the rebellious knight, and Egmont, the fighter for Netherland's freedom, take their place beside Hernani and the Marquis of Posa. Iphigenia is a sister to Beatrice Cenci in her attempt to preserve an innocent humanity in a world of barbaric experience. Tasso is as clearly involved in a tragic struggle with his inner life as any other figure the drama of the age produced.

Still, there is no denying that there is something different about Goethe's plays, and this difference can be mistaken for an avoidance of the tragic. Baldly put, Goethe reconnects romantic tragic drama with imaginative romance. His plays do trace the pattern of romantic tragic drama that we find, for example, in Schiller; but they also move beyond this pattern to see it as a moment in a grander human romance. There is in Goethe's work (and not only in his dramatic work) a "progressive universal" quality, first praised by Friedrich Schlegel.[2] Goethe seems to want to encompass as much of his total vision as possible within a single work. Shelley, for example, needed both *Prometheus Unbound* and *The Cenci* to promulgate his ideal vision on the one hand and to portray life's "sad reality" on the other. Schiller explored in his *On the Aesthetic Education of Mankind* a path beyond self-consciousness and revolt that is blocked to the protagonists of his tragic dramas. Musset set forth in his comedies an aesthetic resolution of the problems that defeat Lorenzaccio.[3] Each of these writers places his vision of an imaginative ideal and his nightmare of tragic defeat in different works; Goethe yokes them together, granting Egmont, for example, a vision of the future at the moment he is defeated and leading Faust through various tragedies to a role in a larger undivine comedy. While I do not have the space here to treat Goethe's dramatic corpus in detail—in a sense, one can write a book about romantic drama or *Faust,* but not both—I do want to demonstrate through brief discussions of *Egmont, Iphigenia,* and *Faust,* first, that Goethe did engage the basic pattern of romantic tragic drama and, second, that the peculiar shape he gives to his plays results from his attempts to rediscover imaginative romance beyond tragedy. To see this as an avoidance of tragedy is to deny the tragic writer a vision of an order arising from the wisdom that tragedy supposedly grants.

I
EGMONT: THE PATTERN OF ROMANTIC DRAMA

GOETHE'S *EGMONT* MOVES to the rhythms of romantic historical drama. As in the plays of Schiller, Byron, or Musset, *Egmont* chronicles the tragic dilemma of a man caught in the transition from a traditionally ordered society to the chaos of modern historical life. Like Schiller's *Don Carlos* and *Wallenstein,* Goethe's play is set during the stormy passage from the medieval to the modern world. Like Karl Moor, Egmont looks to the past as an ideal age of free heroism, firm loyalties, and an organic system of rights and obligations; thus, Egmont finds himself as out of step with his own times as Musset's Lorenzaccio and Byron's Faliero are with theirs.

However, while most romantic dramas depict the struggles of romantic man, Goethe's play pits a more traditional figure against the modern perplexities of selfhood and revolt. As Hegel noted, the early works of both Goethe and Schiller juxtaposed the "lost self-sufficiency" of heroic man against the "prevailing conditions of modern times."[4] *Egmont* thus engages the central themes of romantic drama from a different perspective than do other works. They generally presuppose man's "fall" into modern life. *Egmont* traces this fall and, in keeping with Goethe's pursuit of a total vision, it also gestures towards a heroic paradise regained.

Before his play opens, Egmont has established himself as a hero. From the archers of Brussels in the first scene, who laud the noble Egmont, to Clara, who idolizes her lover, the play presents witness after witness to Egmont's heroic stature; they offer a choral portrait of the protagonist, foreshadowing Schiller's technique in *Wallenstein's Camp.* As the "Victor at St. Quentin" and the "hero of Gravelines" ("Überwinder bei St. Quintin!"; "Dem Helden von Gravelingen!"; I, i),[5] Egmont yearns for the recent, simpler past in which he could prove himself a hero by serving his people and his ruler in battle against the French. He believes in a social order where he owes allegiance to king and emperor, but where his own privileges and independence are assured by his status as a Knight of the Golden Fleece. Within such a society, "the protection of life and property depends on the isolated energy and courage of each individual by himself, who is compelled to look after his own security and that of everything which belongs to him," and thus that society is, in Hegel's terms, heroic.[6]

However, Egmont's society is changing, and these changes constrain his proud spirit. Like Wallenstein, Egmont has earned the appellation of hero; but, again like Wallenstein, his heroism seems to lie only in the past. Critics have wondered at the gap between what we hear about Egmont's heroic actions and what we see of this surprisingly passive figure.[7] Still, this apparently troublesome tension in Egmont's characterization is central to Goethe's purpose. Egmont is a heroic figure quite different from would-be heroes like Moor, but Egmont's world is rapidly moving towards Moor's puny age. Moor dreams of a new heroic age. Egmont tries to perpetuate one. They share a heroic opposition to a world of stultifying limits.

This opposition to society defines the tension in Egmont's character, for the hero is a social concept. An individual is established as a hero not only through his actions, but also through his society's reactions. His heroism is bound up in the fame he wins. The tensions between the individual's assertion of his heroic stature and society's response to him comprise a central theme in Western literature. Achilles finds his heroic identity threatened not by any defeat, but by his society's removal of the objective badge of his heroism—his spoil of war, Briseis. The chivalric knight sets forth alone, but he always returns to court where he tells his tale to establish his fame. We see Shakespeare's exploration of the often tense link between heroic act and public fame in Antony's concern for his repute at Rome, the debate between Cassio and Iago on reputation, Prince Hal's soliloquy on public image, and Coriolanus's struggle with his mother-city of Rome. Society looks to the hero as its defender and saviour, but that man, to know that he is a hero, needs to see himself reflected in the praise of his society.

Goethe's *Egmont,* like the rest of romantic drama, moves away from a heroic world towards the society perfectly captured in Stendhal's *Red and Black,* where Julian Sorel while alone in a cave dreams that he is another Napoleon only to discover that he must falsify his heroic self-conception in trying to find his way in society. Egmont, like the earlier Götz, is an epic figure who has strayed into the world of the bourgeois novel, defined by laws, limits, and lackeys. This distance between the hero's self-definition and his society's failure to ratify that identity (one version of the Goethean theme of the tensions between the extraordinary individual and society, presented differently in *Werther* and *Tasso*) forces Egmont into the role of a rebel and lures him into an inward-turned alienation.

Egmont experiences the dislocation of a man who has outlived his era. The first scene of his play depicts the public turmoil that marks the present, as old rights and rituals are replaced by new, oppressive rules. Given this volatile situation, Orange, an ally of Egmont and like him a favorite of the people, urges a temporary retreat. Egmont, however, eschews patience and retreat. He demands that he live immediately, proclaiming, "Shall I deny myself enjoying the present moment, in order to make sure of the moment to come?" (II, ii).[8] He will be a hero now, not merely in the past or in some hazy future.

Egmont insists that as a knight he can remain both a loyal subject of the king and a defender of the people. His opponent, Alba, has a different view. He has arranged the situation so that Egmont will be cast in the role of rebel and thus arrested as an enemy of the state. Egmont's fall from heroic defender of the people to outlaw is mirrored in the public's changing reactions to him, charted in the crowd scenes. In the first crowd scene (I, i), the people proclaim Egmont their protector. In the opening scene of the second act, Egmont is still able to control the crowd, but finds himself losing touch with their rebellious demands. In the next crowd scene (IV, i), the agitator Vansen voices his cynical yet correct criticism of Egmont's behavior and debunks the public's devotion to its hero by showing that the people would not fight to save him. In the final crowd scene (V, i), the people who once raised Egmont's name in joyous toasts are now afraid to speak it even in a whisper. Egmont is by then imprisoned, cut off from the people whose adulation once ratified his heroic identity. But even were he free, he would find himself in a society no longer capable of supporting his independent heroism.

Egmont's new isolation suggests a movement into the self.[9] Initially, Egmont appears to be almost a natural force. Unlike Orange who views life as a chess game of closely considered moves or Machiavelli who, according to Margaret, is more a man of reflection than of deeds, Egmont seeks to sink himself in spontaneous action to free himself from the worrying self. Machiavelli defends Egmont from the charge of frivolity, even when he acts on his immediate emotions: "It seems to me that in everything he does he acts according to his conscience" (I, ii).[10] Such a merger between desire and duty, feeling and conscience, links Egmont to Schiller's Max, the "beautiful soul" who possesses a prelapsarian inner unity. However, while Max dies rather than allow a fallen society to shape him, Egmont finds himself unable to escape the fall into self-consciousness.

The changes in Egmont's world lure man to reflection. In his first major scene, he battles against the reflective character of the new "Spanish" way of life:

Being cheerful, taking things lightly, living fast is what makes my happiness; and I have no intention of exchanging it for the safety of a tomb. Not one drop of blood in my veins has any sympathy for the Spanish way of life, I have not the slightest wish to fit my steps to the new, cautious tune they are dancing at court. (II, ii)[11]

Still, the very fact that he must reject this enervating sense of self indicates how open he is to its allure.

Egmont wants to avoid self-consciousness in an objective sense of self, grounded in immediate action and the praise it earns him. However, his chosen status as a "public man" (Orange reminds him, "We are not private men"; "Wir sing nicht einzelne Menschen"; II, ii) makes him vulnerable to changes in the social order. His dialogues with his secretary and with Orange dramatize his attempts to fend off the realization that these changes make necessary reflection and even a retreat into the self. He still hopes to escape from the worries that Orange urges him to confront:

That others' thoughts can have such influence on us! It would never have occurred to me; and this man infects me with his anxiety.—Away!—It is a foreign drop in my blood. Kind Nature, cast it out of me! And these furrows of thought on my brow—yes, I know there is still one ever ready to soothe them away. (II, ii)[12]

Dependent upon the reactions of others, he is open to their influence upon his sense of himself. In an anxious time, he can thus be made to feel the anxiety of self-consciousness. While he hopes to escape this "foreign" contamination in the arms of Clara, his mistress, Egmont admits in his next scene with her that a gap has opened between his public persona and his inner self, between the Egmont who must act cautiously in the political arena and the Egmont who would find his old spontaneity in the caresses of his love (III, ii). Still, despite or perhaps because of his new worries, Egmont continues in the next act to pursue his public career in the hopes of escaping the self and preserving his status as a hero of the people.

In returning to the public realm, Egmont meets the man who symbolizes the changes Spain brings to the Netherlands, the Duke of Alba, the new military governor. Standing opposed to Egmont and his delight in immediate pleasure, Alba is the master of the modern reflective sense of self. He prides himself on his ability to think through his actions, to avoid spontaneous pleasure: "I rejoice only over things that have been accomplished—and not too readily over those; for something always remains to be considered and provided against" (IV, ii).[13] If it were not for his supreme self-control, Alba might find himself lost in an inward balancing act of worry and resolution. When, for example, he finds that Orange has avoided his trap, Alba reveals that "I had long considered everything maturely, thought even of this contingency, determined what should be done in this event too; and now that it is to be done, I can scarcely keep my mind from being unsettled once again by all the pros and cons" (IV, ii).[14] Alba, the great general and courtier, is threatened by paralyzing reflexiveness. He needs all of his immense will to commit himself in action.

Egmont is no match for this man who is ushering in an order where the Count has no place. Imprisoned by Alba, Egmont, perhaps for the first time, finds himself wholly wrapped up in his own self: "Though still I stand upright, I shudder inwardly" (V, ii).[15] "Care" (Faust's "Sorge") can now seize him: "0 care, care, which begins the assassin's work before its time, desist!—Since when is Egmont alone, so wholly alone in this world? It is doubt that makes you helpless, it is not fate" (V, ii).[16] The threat he has been fleeing is not some adverse fate but a doubting self.

Egmont does not die doubting, however; he is freed from the self by an unexpected supporter: Alba's son, Ferdinand, who reveals that Egmont has always been his hero. Seeing himself in the loving admiration that Ferdinand bears for him, Egmont can be restored to his former self-conception and thus face death as a hero:

Young friend, whom, by a strange fate, I gain and lose at once, you who feel the anguish of death for me, who mourn for me, *look upon me* in these moments; you do not lose me. If my life was a *mirror in which you liked to see yourself,* let my death be even such to you. . . . *I live for you,* and have lived enough for myself. (V, iv; my emphasis)[17]

Realizing that we live not in self-reflection but for others and through others, Egmont can say when Ferdinand leaves, "Through him I am freed from cares and griefs, from fear and every anxious thought" (V, iv).[18] He wins free of the self and thus can give voice to a final hopeful vision.

Egmont's vision of Clara as Freedom has suggested to some a movement away from tragedy in the concluding moments of the play. I do not find here an "avoidance" of tragedy, but rather, as I suggested before, a movement towards a completion of Goethe's vision. Goethe strives in each play for the totality of vision that can be found in *Oedipus at Colonus* and preeminently in the *Oresteia,* Goethe's favorite among the Greek plays. Goethe explores the possibility that a play, while charting the destruction of the romantic protagonist, can still affirm man's continuing quest for the ideal, a quest that the protagonist tried to complete too precipitously. *Egmont* turns in its final moments from the destruction of the protagonist to a hope for mankind's future. Such a turn does not "arrest" the tragedy of Egmont; he still dies, with his dreams unfulfilled, his heroic identity threatened. Goethe preserves the integrity of Egmont's tragic career while placing it within a larger pattern that looks to the future for an order more nearly complete than either the protagonist's vision or the limited society he opposed. By placing the tragedy of the individual within the quest romance of mankind, Goethe discovers a romantic counterpart to the totality of vision found in the *Oresteia.*

This double perspective also completes Goethe's treatment of the hero in a changing society. Egmont has lost a society supportive of his heroic identity, but the finale of the play suggests that there will exist a future society capable of appreciating him. This double perspective is maintained by the controversial "operatic" vision of Freedom with which the play closes.[19] Through this vision, Egmont comes to understand that his own defeat and death will help free the Provinces. He is given a glimpse of the society of the future which will praise him, and he can thus die—or as he says, sacrifice himself—heroically. Most romantic protagonists die confronted with the gap between the desire to be a hero and the failure to create a society which would recognize them as such; Wallenstein's death ushers in a society ruled by plotters, Beatrice Cenci is executed by a society that affirms the tyrannical spirit of her father, and Lorenzaccio finds that his struggles have engendered a social order even more despicable than the one he opposed. Egmont, however, is granted a vision of his future apotheosis. He sees the complete pattern of his heroic fate—from public hero to isolated hero to future hero. This glimpse of the future moves us out of Egmont's time and towards Goethe's and our own. Egmont's tragic end can be in the audience's present both a warning and a sign: a warning against the petty yet oppressive limits that destroyed Egmont and a sign that we, insofar as we are made to empathize with Egmont, may be the posterity that will create a new order capable of appreciating such men. The audience in the theater replaces the supportive society that Egmont has lost in the course of his fall.

This reconciliation of Egmont with future society mutes the tragic impact of the play for many, though it does so no more than the reconciliation with the divine granted to Orestes or Job. As we have seen in Schiller's plays, man's relationship to the gods is replaced by his relation to an ideal in history, and a complete tragic pattern—such as that found in the *Oresteia* and sought by Goethe—can portray not only a break between man and god or man and his ideal but also a renewal of the bonds between them. Others object to the "operatic" finale to this history play, with its vision and stirring music. Yet, interestingly, the operatic nature of this final scene both completes and preserves the tragic pattern. Goethe's dramatic technique makes it quite clear that the final scene is a vision: Egmont is for an instant lifted out of the historical realm—the realm of his tragedy—into that of visionary romance. Goethe does not want to deny that within the historical moment that defines the action of his play there has been a tragedy—not only for Egmont, but also for Clara and perhaps for Ferdinand and others. This final vision, set off from the rest of *Egmont* by its style, does not "arrest" that tragedy; but it does resolve the thematic crux of the play—the relationship between the hero and his society.

We can get a firmer grip on this resolution if we turn for a moment to Goethe's comments on Egmont's daimonic quality, found in *Poetry and*

Truth. Goethe, stressing the daimonic individual's ability to attract others to him, talks of Egmont's "gift" of "winning favour of the people, and which, while it inspired a princess with a silent, and a young child of nature with an avowed, passion, won for him the sympathy of a shrewd statesman, and even the loving admiration of the son of his greatest adversary." When he describes the daimonic man in detail, he again emphasizes his power over others: ". . . a tremendous energy seems seated in them; and they exercise a wonderful power over all creatures, and even over the elements. . . ."[20] The daimonic is, in at least one of its aspects, a type of heroic charisma, like that of Napoleon or, in a way, Byron. It wins for such figures the praise the hero needs.

However, as we have seen, this reliance upon a publicly affirmed identity has dangers. It was towards such dangers that I believe Goethe was gesturing when he wrote that the daimonic element in *Egmont* "is in play on both sides, and in conflict with which the lovely falls while the hated triumphs."[21] By suggesting a division within the daimonic, Goethe cannot mean that there is a daimonic individual opposed to Egmont; Alba hardly fits the bill. Rather, Goethe defines the tragic aspect of the daimonic figure here: if his power lies in his ability to attract others, his power is in a real sense out of his hands and he is at the mercy of others. The daimonic is at play on both sides, for it deserts Egmont when his society changes, leaving him without followers.[22]

If the closing scene of *Egmont* is not fully successful, it is not then because it avoids tragedy; rather, it is because Egmont is not fully involved in the problems which the final scene seeks to resolve. He has established his heroic identity before the fall into modern life, and his story lies in the resistance to that fall. He is thus an unconvincing vehicle for man's redemption from that fall. In his later plays, Goethe presented characters more fully involved in the changed world that destroys Egmont and thus resolved the tensions of the double-ending *Egmont*. In *Iphigenia,* the inward-turned, titanic protagonist finds that a new human order can be built only upon the ruins of the heroic past; she acquires her vision of order in tragic loss. And Faust learns that meaning can be given to man's life only by the individual who—unlike Egmont—has come to terms with Care, with self-consciousness and the difficulties of modern life.

VARIATION I: *IPHIGENIA'S* "DEVILISH" CLASSICISM

IPHIGENIA WOULD SEEM to have little in common with *Egmont*, since *Iphigenia* returns to a classical mode in apparent opposition to romantic drama. Yet Schiller was certainly correct in seeing the play as "astonishingly modern and un-Greek."[23] In January of 1802, Goethe sent a copy of *Iphigenia in Tauris* to Schiller, asking that he look into revising it for production. Goethe notes that he had just reread the play and found it "devilishly humane." This statement is often taken to indicate some displeasure on Goethe's part with a work of his earlier years.[24] Schiller, however, certainly did not take this phrase as indicative of a flaw in the drama. He replied to Goethe, "I shall now reread the *Iphigenia* with a proper regard for its new destination, and listen to every word from the stage and with the public. That which you call humane in it will stand this test especially well and I should advise you not to leave out any of it."[25] As Schiller realized, Goethe was drawing attention to a key feature, one it shares with many romantic works: the attempt to rework theocentric art in a devilish fashion— in the light, that is, of humanistic revelation. *Iphigenia* stands as a model for the relationship between romantic drama and classical forms discussed in chapter 2.

Blake argued that Milton was of the devil's party. In Shelley's hand, Jupiter, the king of the gods, became a figure of evil. Hugo worked out of the salvation of Satan. All of these poets wrote works that were devilishly humane in that they subvert providential myths for humanistic purposes. When Nietzsche used Zarathrustra, the prophet of a theistic system of morality, to preach the Superman who is beyond good and evil, he was working within a long tradition of romantic inversion. In *Iphigenia,* Goethe uses a Greek form with its gods and sense of fate to chart the development of a modern, romantic vision in which man moves from a theistic culture to attempt to shape his own life. Goethe offers the devilish humanism of a romantic classicism. The search for a modern classic meets here with romantic revisionism.[26]

Iphigenia thus need not be opposed to *Egmont,* for it approaches the same key themes, with even its classical form "devilishly" defining that approach. While *Egmont* turns to Shakespeare to discover a romantic alternative to neoclassical drama, *Iphigenia* challenges the neoclassicists on their home turf, presenting in generalized or "mythic" terms the same tragic configuration that is grounded in specific, historical events in *Egmont:* modern man's sense of loss at the collapse of traditional heroic and theocentric culture. However, while in the earlier play Goethe envisions a prelapsarian age free from the taints of self-consciousness and rebellion, in *Iphigenia* the "fall" into selfhood and revolt has occurred long ago and it has implicated man's heroism in inwardness and violence.

In the first act, Iphigenia tells Thoas the story of her great ancestor Tantalus, of how he was admitted to the councils of the gods because of his wisdom only to be cast down for having dared to aspire to such heights:

> But gods should not
> Associate with men as with their peers.
> The race of mortals is too weak by far
> Not to grow dizzy at unwonted heights.
> Ignoble he was not, nor yet a traitor;
> But too great for a slave, and for a fellow
> Of the great Thunderer a mere mortal man.
> Thus his crime too was human and their judgment
> Severe. (I, iii, 315–23)[27]

We are being told here the story of a fall, of the first disobedience of the Tantalid line and of the curse that was its fruit, though Goethe again works a devilish transformation of the traditional story. Tantalus's fall is not seen as a just punishment for a sin against a perfect God, but rather as the natural result of a confusion of the human and divine realms, what Hölderlin called the "monstrous and terrible in the coupling of god and man."[28]

This reading of Tantalus's fall can be supported and expanded by Goethe's comments in his autobiography on Tantalus and others like him:

. . . the Titanic, gigantic, heaven-storming character afforded no suitable material for my poetic art. It better suited me to represent that peaceful, plastic, and always patient, opposition, which, recognising the superior power, still presumes to claim equality. And yet the bolder members of the race, Tantalus, Ixion, Sisyphus, were also my saints. Admitted to the society of the gods, they would not deport themselves submissively enough but, by their haughty bearing as guests, provoked the anger of their host and patron, and drew upon themselves a sorrowful banishment.[29]

Goethe finds the violent revolt of the Titans who stormed heaven, like that of Satan, unpoetical.[30] He replaces the satanic rebels with two other groups within what he sees as a "vast opposition" to the gods. There are those like Tantalus who pridefully challenge the gods; they are cast down by Zeus. Then, there are those like Prometheus who recognize the gods while asserting for themselves a separate but equal power. Prometheus claims equality with the Olympians as a creator, in fact, man's creator. In the lyric monologue that Goethe has him speak, Prometheus announces his independence from Zeus:

My earth you must perforce
Leave standing yet
And this my hut that you did not erect
And my own hearth
Whose radiant fire
Excites your envy.
. . . .

I sit here, forming mankind
After my image,
A race to resemble me:
To weep and to suffer,
To enjoy life and to feel delight,
And never to heed you,
Even as I![31]

Prometheus offers himself as a model for man to follow in his relationship with the powerful but inhumane gods: leave to them their heavenly realms, but ignore them and cultivate life here on earth. Together, Prometheus and Tantalus define the two sides of the romantic project to create a fully human life, one turning his back on the gods and the other confronting the gods defiantly. The human "crime" of Tantalus can now be understood. Tantalus, a Faustian rebel, wants to know the divine at first hand. He attempts to live on the heights. But man was made in Prometheus's image for an earthy life. In seeking to scale the heights, Tantalus finds himself cast into a demonic underworld.

In the "Parzenlied" that closes the fourth act (IV, v, 1726–66), Goethe offers a generalizing account of Tantalus's fate, suggesting that his destiny is that of all men. While some readers find Goethe finally hitting an appropriately Greek note in this passage, he is again working an inversion; for he is not so much summoning up the spirit of Greek tragedy to celebrate it as summing up a vision of life that is soon to pass away. Life under the gods is revealed as a trap. Man is invited to join the gods at golden tables on "cliffs and on clouds" ("Auf Klippen und Wolken"; IV, v, 1734), but this invitation is merely a prelude to discord and to man's imprisonment in a hellish underworld, "the depths of the dark" ("In nächtliche Tiefen"; IV, v, 1740). It is striking that in both the "Parzenlied" and in Iphigenia's account of Tantalus's life, we hear only of the heights and depths. There is no mention of the middle ground cultivated by Prometheus. Tantalus and those like him betray the earth for the heights, and thus his inheritors see themselves as exiles on earth, like the "old one, the exile" ("Der Alte, die Lieder"; IV, v, 1764), who listens to the Parcae's song.

In exile, the Tantalids and, more broadly, the entire Greek nation have adopted Tantalus's mode of heroic struggle. Orestes recalls the Greeks as heroes and his life in Greece as one of "mighty deeds" ("grossen Taten"; II, i, esp. 666–79). To Iphigenia, the Greeks are godlike heroes, her father Agamemnon, "göttergleichen Agamemnon" (I, i, 46), among them. The key to Greek heroism lies in this titanic assertion of equality with the gods. But Iphigenia knows the heroic claim to be "göttergleichen" leads to destruction. It is she who tells Thoas in a passage already quoted, "aber *Götter* sollten nicht / Mit Menschen wie mit ihres*gleichen* wandeln" (my emphasis). The continuing Greek quest for godlike stature is an attempt to provide meaning for man's life in exile, but it also reenacts the fall of Tantalus and necessarily involves man in a life of violence.

When Iphigenia recounts the history of her family, we find that their heroic pursuit has resulted in horror after horror: Pelops's murder of his father-in-law, Atreus and Thyestes' assassination of their half-brother, their mother's suicide, Thyestes' adultery with Atreus's wife, Atreus's murder of his own son, Thyestes' feast upon his children. Blind to the barrier between themselves and the gods, the Tantalids become blind to the bonds that form human society. Marriage and family ties give way to the horrible intimacy of rape, murder, and cannibalism. The history of Iphigenia's family is marked by two significant traits: brutal violence and a deceit that arises from an inward-turned deviousness.[32] Greek heroism—unlike that of Egmont—is implicated in rebellion and self-consciousness. The Tantalids may be Greeks, but they suffer a romantic agony.

Iphigenia and her brother Orestes inherit the Tantalid's cursed heroism. The first two acts serve to define their life of exile—and by mythic generalization, man's. Nearly the victim of her father's violence, Iphigenia escapes to live a hidden life on Tauris. Despite attempts to turn her into a "beautiful soul" or a serene, Winckelmannian Greek, a violent strain of protest runs through her account of her exile on Tauris, an exile which she, together with such romantic exiles as Cain or the Ancient Mariner, finds to be death-in-life, a "second death" ("zweiten Tode"; I, i, 53).[33] Orestes, the murderer of their mother, arrives in Tauris disguised and plotting violence; and as his madness attests, he has become lost in the inward gaze of his guilt-ridden consciousness.

However, Orestes finds himself unable to persist in the lie his friend Pylades has used to mask their identities. He reveals himself to Iphigenia: "A stranger, wily and accustomed to / Deceit, may for another stranger weave / A web of lies to trip him; between *us* / Let there be truth" (III, i, 1078–81).[34] Such truth telling possesses great virtue in *Iphigenia,* for the pattern of the Tantalid curse has been deceit issuing in violence. By revealing his identity Orestes breaks with the cursed past.

But he is not ready to face the future. Orestes is a fatalist who believes the cruel gods of the "Parzenlied" rule over man. His first words on stage ("It is the path of death that we are treading"; II, i, 561)[35] indicate his belief that his is a life damned to destruction. Thus, when Iphigenia reveals herself to him and he realizes that his sister has been ordered to sacrifice him, he despairs. The furies, emblems of the cursed heritage he believes controls his life, seize him; he collapses, possessed by a vision in which Tantalus, the "peer of gods" ("Göttergleiche") still suffers:

> What is it? The peer of gods is in pain?
> Alas! The all-too-powerful ones
> Have riveted horrible torments
> To that hero's breast with iron chains. (III, ii, 1306–9)[36]

Orestes cannot imagine the gods' forgiving man's claim to equality with them. Believing in the gods' inevitable dominion, he can see life only as a horrible exile; if "the olden race of Tantalus" has its "joys," they are only to be found "on the further side of night" (III, ii, 1298–99).[37]

Orestes is freed from his nightmare only by Iphigenia. Through her, he sees his dream not as a call to restful death but as a putting to rest of the dead. Late in the last act, Orestes tells us that his fantasy had been the work of his inner Furies and that Iphigenia has rescued him: "I / Have been healed at your touch; in your embrace / The evil seized upon me with its claws / For the last time" (V, vi, 2119–22).[38] Orestes has always lived in the world of the "Parzenlied," certain that man's place, once he is thrown from the heights, lies only in the depths. Awakened to present reality, Orestes now envisions a life that ignores the mountaintops and Hades to find the middle ground—the plains of earth—enough:

> The curse is lifting; my heart tells me so.
> To Tartarus pass the Eumenides,
> I hear their going, and they close behind them
> The doors of bronze with far-reaching thunder.
> The earth exhales refreshing fragrance and
> Invites me to its plains for full pursuit
> Of life's delights and high accomplishment. (III, iii, 1358–64)[39]

Orestes and Iphigenia, having opened their arms to each other and closed the doors on the past, are now ready to create a human life on earth in the present. They have moved out from the self-involved solitude that is the other side of Tantalid frenzy. However, having freed themselves from a life structured by the gods' curse, they still must give meaning to their freedom.[40]

The danger facing the newly liberated will is the temptation to squander its freedom. Pylades and Thoas step forth to offer comforting plots for Iphigenia's and Orestes' future. Pylades is essentially a melodramatist. Usually mistaken as a model friend and a realist, Pylades in fact appears as an evil counselor whose belief that the gods "are . . . preparing / Some way and means of glad escape for us" (II, i, 602–3)[41] enables him to justify deceit and violence against the Tauridians. He would have Iphigenia and Orestes use Tantalid cunning and violence, not with their ancestors' tragic sense of transgression, but rather with the naive faith of a melodramatist who justifies human crime as part of a divine plan. Orestes describes Pylades as another Kotzebue: "With rare skill you entwine the gods' devices / And your own wishes neatly into one" (II, i, 740–41.)[42]

Where Pylades would write a melodrama for Iphigenia, Thoas wants her to play a comic role. He tempts her with marriage and a secure life in Tauris. By joining the rather bourgeois Tauridian world,[43] Iphigenia would leave behind her family's heroism to take part in a domestic comedy where people live happily ever after because they ignore the strenuous tasks man must accomplish to create a free and meaningful life. Where Pylades would have Iphigenia still follow the now meaningless forms of the past, Thoas wants her to reject the past completely. Iphigenia, however, must transform her heritage if she is to shape the future.

Asking, "Shall I beseech the goddess for a marvel?/ Is there no strength in my soul's inner depths" (V, iii, 1884–85),[44] Iphigenia turns from dependence upon the gods to belief in her own humanity. Abjuring the violence that has been man's lot under the god's curse, she places her faith in trust among men and reveals to Thoas the plot to steal the statue. Had Goethe faithfully followed Euripides, he would have had the goddess Diana descend at this point to resolve the conflict. It is not, however, divine intervention that prevents the eruption of violence between Greeks and Tauridians; it is Iphigenia's humane vision and Orestes' interpretation of that vision, both the creation of words, man's sole tool for building his world, as Iphigenia knows ("I have only words"; "Ich habe nichts als Worte"; V, iii, 1863).

The point of contention between the Greeks and the Tauridians is the statue of Diana that Apollo ordered Orestes to return to Greece. Touched by Iphigenia's vision of a trusting humanity, Orestes reinterprets the oracle, perceiving "the error which a god / Cast like a veil about our heads when he / Bade us set out upon our journey here" (V, vi, 2108–10).[45] When he demanded that Orestes undertake another violent and deceitful mission to win his freedom from the furies, Apollo sought to involve him in fresh crimes and thus to prolong the Tantalid curse. Orestes now finds a human content in the oracle. Iphigenia's love and trust have opened life to the future. While Apollo promised to cure Orestes after he returned the statue of his sister Diana, Orestes has in fact already been cured by his own sister. Of course, her humanism must leave behind the old heroism of the Tantalids:

"Men's highest glory, violence and cunning, / Are by the truth of this exalted soul / Now put to shame" (V, vi, 2142–44).[46] However, Orestes finds that she reveals to man his own divinity and a new heroism. Iphigenia, whom Orestes sees as a sacred statue (V, vi, 2127), becomes the goddess of a humanistic religion and she, not an immortal god, can "give back all things" ("gibst du uns alles wieder"; V, vi, 2134), redeeming man from his fall.

The final vision is given to Iphigenia. Thoas agrees to let the Greeks go, but remains angry. She asks for his blessing, evoking a humanized world in which man's exile will be at an end:

> 0 do not banish us. A friendly guest-right
> Must rule between us: that way
> We are not cut off forever. For you are
> As dear to me as ever was my father
> And this impression is fixed in my soul.
> And if the least among your people ever
> Brings to my ear the cadence of the voice
> I am so used to hear from you, or if
> I see the poorest man dressed in your manner,
> I shall receive him like a god, I shall
> Myself prepare a couch for him, myself
> Invite him to a seat beside the fire,
> Inquiring news of you and your fate. (V, vi, 2153–65)[47]

Iphigenia redeems Tantalus's banishment by the gods when she forges a bond between human guest and human host. Iphigenia prevents Thoas from imitating the gods and continuing their curse on man, by urging him to create in forgiveness a "guest-right." This human institution will put an end to the exile the gods willed for man: all earth will be a home for man, and even the least of men will be treated like gods.

We hear in this passage Goethe's final transformation of the term "godlike" ("göttergleich") and thus the final twist of his "devilishly humane" revision of his theistic predecessors. The gods invited Tantalus to associate with them as if he were their equal ("wie mit ihresgleichen"), only to banish him for having the audacity to do so. The "göttergleichen Agamemnon" tried, like the rest of his cursed family, to prove his heroic worth through acts of destruction and deceit. In the course of the play, Iphigenia rejects the prideful, heroic striving of the past when she argues that the gods truly live in the human soul and that man becomes godlike when he treats his fellow men as if they were gods. The devilish pattern of the play is revealed as a progressive internalization and humanization of the divine. Iphigenia offers herself as the model of a new humane heroism that renounces the mountain tops of pride and the depths of cunning violence to forge a human kingdom of trust and truth. When, in her final speech, she depicts a world of hearth and home, we recall Goethe's Prometheus who also built a home and a fire to create a life on earth apart from the gods. Iphigenia passes through the romantic titanism of her heritage to an equally romantic vision of the earth remade through the human imagination—the power of the words which are her only resource—and through human love.

Iphigenia tries to capture not only the tragic story of man's entrapment in the self and in historical violence, but also the larger romantic myth of a world remade. The play thus departs from the pattern of romantic tragic drama that Goethe engaged in *Egmont*, a point we can see more clearly if we return to Schiller's historical dramas and his quest for an equivalent to tragic fate in the workings of history. A fated, mythic action is a closed circle; the end is in the beginning and often an oracle predetermines the final catastrophe. A linear historical action, insofar as it is potentially open to acts of the will, resists the imposition of fate and thus requires a new tragic configuration. The problem in writing historical tragedy, as Schiller well knew, is that the author must avoid portraying the tragic catastrophe as the result of merely willful error on the part of totally self-defined individuals; yet, in restricting their scope of action to give the plot the force of necessity, he must not reduce his characters to puppets. Tragedy apparently cannot occur if the will is either totally free or totally constrained.

Schiller's profound solution to these difficulties was to pit the free will of historical man against the structure of historical time. Where the Greeks found tragedy in the mythic conflict between the individual and fate, Schiller discovers it in the existential tensions between the acts the individual must perform in the present and the future end toward which his acts are directed. Historical man may have a freer will than mythic man, but as the gap between present and future suggests, he cannot leap out of time to perform exemplary heroic actions. His acts are time bound and thus their meaning is relative—viewed now in the context of an antagonistic present, now from the perspective of an ideal future.

Egmont, though close to Schillerian historical drama in many ways, already reaches beyond the confines of the history play in its operatic finale. In *Iphigenia,* Goethe seems to have rejected history completely to return to the Greek world of myth. However, he does not seek to revive the tragedy of fate, as Schiller once tried to do in *The Bride of Messina.* He invokes the ancient world of the "Parzenlied" and the Tantalid curse only to chart man's movement from a life understood through myth to a life lived in history. *Iphigenia* enacts within its mythic and apparently classical form the birth of modern, historical—that is, romantic—culture.

An understanding of this movement has a bearing upon our sense of *Iph-igenia's* alleged "avoidance" of tragedy. Since the play ends in triumph, it has struck many as untragic.[48] However, we must remember that this victory is won only at the cost of traditional heroism and theism. When Iphigenia leads the cast of the play to reject the fateful past to create freely the future, she divorces them from the patterns of cyclical action (the repetition of the curse, the ritual sacrifice of strangers in Tauris) that have defined Greek and Tauridian life. This rejection of repetition is clearly a gain in freedom. Still, man knew the significance of his actions under the gods, whether he was a priest or a proud usurper of the gods' rights. Freedom within history offers no such certainty.

Goethe gives us a clear measure of the impact of the shift from myth to history in his treatment of the oracle. Within the fated world of myth, the oracle had a clear meaning. By reinterpreting the oracle, Orestes, Iphigenia, and Thoas take a crucial step forward into a world shaped by man's will, but they undermine the oracle's clarity. It no longer commands a physical deed but offers a spiritual message. And a doubt remains: how can man know that his interpretation is correct, that it will not in turn be rejected tomorrow by a new understanding that reveals him to be as barbaric as those he sought to correct? In the future that opens up at the end of *Iphigenia,* man may find that while there is sanctity even in a cursed life, freedom may carry the curse of meaninglessness.

The questioning that attends the close of *Iphigenia* suggests that there is no "avoidance" of tragedy here. The play engages not only the vision needed to create a new humane society but also the tragic loss felt at the destruction of a valued past—the triumph and tragedy of romanticism itself. Goethe provides both tragedy and vision, but without the awkwardness of *Egmont's* double ending. Unlike Egmont, Iphigenia is fully involved in the dangers of self and violence. She can thus help man defeat them; and it is important that she does so through an increased internalization that relocates the gods and their power within the human soul and through a transformation or sublimation of violent revolt into a revisionism that can contribute to human growth and cultural evolution. In this play, Goethe moves closer to his goal of presenting in a single action both the fall from a world of myth and man's quest for redemption in human and historical terms. In a sense, Goethe creates a myth of history: an archetypal account of man's transition from a mythic to a historical life and an assessment of the gains and losses experienced in any movement from one cultural configuration to another.

We may react to Goethe's myth of history in two ways. We may accept it as the final vision of the play, feeling triumph in the slow internalization of the divine, in the humanistic polemic against the barbarity of a theocentric world, and in the bravura reinterpretation of the oracle as a revelation of man's self-defined divinity. However, we may also find this myth of history contradictory, a piece of artistic sleight of hand. If we recall the concern of the play with truth telling and thus accurate language, if we note that Iphigenia herself admits she has only words to work with, or if we dwell upon Goethe's devilish play with classical forms, then we might conclude that the play's final vision is to be seen as a self-conscious illusion.[49]

As I hope my discussion suggests, I cannot see *Iphigenia* as either Goethe's blueprint for a humanist's utopia or an exercise in reflexive artificiality. I find in the play's conclusion the same tension we hear in Wordsworth's great line from "Resolution and Independence": "By our own spirits are we deified." Wordsworth both proclaims the power of the imaginative poet and worries over his lack of authority when he speaks only for himself and from his own humanity rather than for a divine muse. Wordsworth's poet deifies himself just as man will create himself as a god in Iphigenia's world of the "guest-right." But in that we, mere mortals, are deified only by ourselves, questions arise about the reality of this deification. There *is* a sense in which Iphigenia creates a work of art, an illusion, in the final moments of her play. Her heroism is that of an artist, for it is through imaginative vision and critical interpretation that the humanistic compact of the play is hammered out. But if the vision of the play is bound up in imaginative illusion, this does not render it *mere* illusion. The maturity of *Iphigenia's* conclusion is that it celebrates the power of the imagination to envision a fully human life even as it recognizes the precariousness of the imagination as a source of meaning. The play's vision is not undermined by being an artistic construct. Its human truth lies in the very fact that it is a creation of the imagination, the power in man that enables him to reach truth through beauty. *Iphigenia,* for all of its classicist trappings, takes its place at the center of romanticism's exploration of imaginative art, and here we can see one more devilish twist in Goethe's play. Art, imaginative illusion, is revealed as the vehicle for humanistic culture. Historical, romantic man discovers in this mythic play that in modern life art replaces myth, human illusion creates the meaning once sought from the gods. If *Iphigenia* is a play about art, it is a celebration of art that remains tragically aware of what is at risk when art must take the place of religion in human life.

VARIATION II: *FAUST'S* VISIONARY FORMS DRAMATIC

GOETHE USES THE traditional study scene with which he opens the main body of *Faust* to set forth a prototypically romantic encounter: a solitary man bemoans the gap between his inner life and the world around him. We meet Faust as an isolated, alienated rebel, forced to confront the perplexities surrounding the modern attempt to know the self. While the most famous formulation of his inner struggle—"Two souls, alas, are dwelling in my breast" ("Zwei Seelen wohnen, ach! in meiner Brust"; 1: 1112)[50]—occurs later, Faust tells us in his opening monologue that for him the world is a "dungeon" in which he is "entombed"; despite the striving he feels within himself—his "spirit's anxious surge"—he is frustrated in his attempt to come into contact with the external world, finding himself "Shut out from Nature's teeming throng" (1: 398–414).[51] This Faustian ode on dejection also gives voice to his rebellion against established patterns for coming to know the world, as he denounces philosophy, jurisprudence, medicine, and above all theology as the building blocks of man's mental prison. Like the Faustian Manfred who finds that "knowledge is sorrow" or like any of the rebels from Götz to Lorenzo who feel the oppressive weight of their society and culture, Goethe's titan severs all contact with the order given life in the past to pursue another type of knowledge, a new order, in magic. This turn to magic—which we see also in Manfred, Wallenstein, and Hugo's Cromwell—represents both a revolt against custom and a dream of an immediate, total knowledge of the world that would overcome man's isolation:

> So I resorted to Magic's art,
> To see if by spirit mouth and might
> Many a secret may come to light;
> So I need toil no longer so,
> Propounding what I do not know;
> So I perceive the inmost force
> That bonds the very universe,
> View all enactment's seed and spring,
> And quit my verbiage-mongering. (1: 377–85)[52]

Faust's flight from language-bound consciousness towards an immediate contact with the world is made clearer when he later translates the opening of the Gospel according to John, replacing the traditional translation of *Logos* as "word" with, first, "thought," and then "power," before finally hitting upon "deed." In magic, Faust seeks a set of words that are deeds, a language that acts directly upon the world rather than merely reflecting it in an isolated consciousness. That is, Faust wants the visionary language of Coleridge's primary imagination, where the divine decree, "Let there be light," is an accomplished deed and not just a speech act. Faust desires the imaginative word granted to Shelley's Prometheus:

> Language is a perpetual Orphic song,
> Which rules with Daedal harmony a throng
> Of thoughts and forms, which else senseless and shapeless were.[53]

If Faust found such power in magic, there would be no tragedy; he would possess that vision granted the angels in the "Prologue in Heaven." While Goethe's play ends in vision, he makes it clear at the outset that Faust's life will transpire in a world denied the imaginative breakthrough celebrated in *Prometheus Unbound* and in the angels' hymn to creation that Shelley so admired.

Faust, of course, still hopes for such a breakthrough as he turns to the sign of the Macrocosm. At first, the emblem seems to heal the inner division that Faust feels and to connect him with the external world, as it "calms the tumult in my breast" and "Makes Nature's powers about me manifest" (1: 435, 438).[54] However, the sign of the Macrocosm—that "glorious show! Yet but a show, alas!" ("Welch Schauspiel! Aber ach! ein Schauspiel nur!"; 1: 454)—only provokes contemplation in Faust, providing him with an image of a unified life but not an experience of it.[55] The sign propels him back into reflection not forward into action. He thus turns to the Earth Spirit, "emboldened now to venture forth, / To bear the bliss, the sorrow of this earth" (1: 464–65).[56]

The Earth Spirit, however, rebuffs Faust who finds that he cannot bear the presence of the terrifying entity and the experience of change—of the "tides of living, in doing's storm. . . A changeful plaiting, / Fiery begetting" (1: 501, 506–7)—it incarnates.[57] We can see Faust's situation more clearly if we compare it to a similar moment in Keats's *Hyperion*. In the final section of that fragment, Apollo is granted a vision by Mnemosyne which, like that of the Earth Spirit, is of "Creations and destroyings," of both the beauty and the destruction of the earthly life. However, while Faust turns from this revelation, Apollo finds that "Knowledge enormous makes a God of me," that his vision of reality enables him to "Die into life."[58] Keats's poem breaks off with Apollo's triumphant embrace of human life in all of its immediacy, all its splendor and misery. Goethe's drama begins in the recognition that Faust cannot easily regain this relationship to life, lost in the fall into modern divisiveness.

Like the dialogists in Kleist's essay on the marionette theater, Faust finds
that the paradise of innocence and immediacy is "locked and bolted and
the Cherub is behind us. We must make a journey around the world, to see
if the back door had perhaps been left open." For Kleist, man will regain
Eden only when consciousness has "traversed the infinite"; "we would
have to eat of the tree of knowledge a second time to fall back into the
state of innocence."[59] Faust cannot regain innocence directly; he cannot
swallow life in a single draught as can Keats's Apollo. He must experience
life bit by bit, from the small world of a girl's love to the great world of historical activity, from the classical past to the romantic present. The Earth
Spirit, the spirit of an immediate apprehension of life, is not the proper
companion for Faust; he must instead journey through life with the spirit
of mediation—Mephistopheles.

Where the Earth Spirit affirms everything—creation *and* destruction—
Mephistopheles, the "spirit which eternally denies," would negate everything. For Mephisto, the mortal nature of material creation—the fact that it
comes into being and passes away—renders it valueless: "for all that which
is wrought / Deserves that it should come to naught" (1: 1338–40).[60]
Mephisto is the appropriate companion for Faust because self-conscious
man can perceive the world only in a mediate, ironic way.

Mephistopheles also presents a new temptation, the possibility of another fall. Despairing upon finding Paradise sealed off by the flaming
swords of the cherubim, man may elevate his own selfhood as the only
source of value or he may seek to escape the self in feverish pursuit of sensual pleasure. Mephistopheles, who combines an ironic intellect with an
appetite for gross sensuality, is the messenger of a romantic hell in which
the isolated self can escape itself only by denying its full humanity in animal pleasures. Byron's Cain and Musset's Lorenzo face similar satanic temptations; Shelley's Count Cenci stands with Mephisto as a portrait of the
secret alliance between the ironic, anatomizing intellect and uncontrolled
desire.

While Mephistopheles clearly embraces negation, he is not thereby a
completely negative figure and certainly not a conventional figure of evil.
For he is part of the process through which man must pass in searching for
the back door to paradise; he is the principle of the negative in the dialectic of man's development. As he puts it, he is "Part of that force which
would / Do evil, and does ever good" (1: 1335–36).[61] He works for an ultimate good, because he reveals to man the mediate nature of all of the partial goods he encounters. The Lord tells us in the "Prologue in Heaven"
that man too readily abandons his quest, and thus Mephistopheles exists to
goad man on to the fulfillment of his nature (1: 340–43). Man must, the

Lord tells us, err in striving for this goal (1: 317), but only through this effort can he "traverse the infinite" and come to know finally the truth and beauty of creation.

The "Pact Scene" brings to a climax what has come to be known as the "Scholar's Tragedy," the first of several tragedies through which Faust must pass. Despairing once more, Faust curses life; and above all he curses faith, hope, and patience, those virtues that would nourish his belief in life, his vision of the future, and his ability to endure man's mediate lot (1: 1573–78, 1583–1606). Like the curse uttered by Shelley's Prometheus, this rebellious condemnation of life, arising from the frustrated self, brings about a fall, a destruction of the world in which man has lost faith. An invisible Chorus of Spirits tells Faust, "You have destroyed it / The beautiful world" and orders him to "See it rewon, / In your own breast re-erect it!" (1: 1608–9, 1620–21).[62] This climactic moment reenacts man's fall from immediate contact with the "beautiful world" and announces Faust's task: he must rebuild within his own consciousness all he has lost; he must internalize the world of experience in its entirety in order to return to the paradise he has destroyed. There is both a challenge and a risk here: the key romantic challenge to discover within the self a vision of meaning which can reintegrate man with the world; and the risk that he will be satisfied with the self's illusions and not truly reenvision life.

Both this challenge and this risk are embodied in the pact and wager into which Faust and Mephistopheles enter, though neither fully understands their bargain. Mephisto interprets this pact in his monologue later in the same scene (1: 1851–67). Believing only in the isolated intellect and earthly dissipation, Mephisto is certain that Faust has abandoned the first to pursue the second. He understands that Faust's striving soul will not be satisfied with any single experience ("Fate has endowed him with a forward-driving / Impetuousness that reaches past all sights"; 1: 1856–57)[63]; so Mephisto plans to make him despair of all experience. Mephistopheles intends to win Faust by forcing him to deal in the degraded and trivial until he finds himself unable to satisfy his titanic striving, thus becoming another Tantalus, seeking any relief: "Through dissipation I will drag him, / Through shallow insignificance . . . And for his parched incontinence / Have food and drink suspended at lip level; / In vain will he be yearning for relief" (1: 1860–61, 1863–65).[64]

To many, Mephistopheles seems to be working against the terms of the wager. If Faust loses the bet when he finds a moment of fulfillment, why does Mephisto present him with only moments of frustration? We must remember that, for Mephisto, there is no such thing as fulfillment, not even a partial or momentary satisfaction. He waits for Faust to despair of experience and to ask for oblivion—the only fair moment for Mephisto, as he makes clear when, thinking the wager won, he philosophizes over Faust's dead body:

> All over and pure nothing—just the same!
> What has this constant doing ever brought
> But what is done to rake away to naught?
> So it is over! How to read this clause?
> All over is as good as never was,
> And yet it whirls about as if it were.
> The Ever-empty is what I prefer. (2: V, 11597–603)[65]

Mephisto believes he has defeated Faust by turning him against earthly joys to embrace "The final moment, worthless, stale, and void" ("Den letzten, schlechten, leeren Augenblick"; 2: V, 11589). A true son of Chaos, he cannot understand Faust's quest.

Faust has a deeper and growing understanding of the pact, but he, too, fails to offer a convincing interpretation of the agreement at the time of its making. Faust enters the pact for a specific reason: deprived the vision of the Earth Spirit, he finds life in the isolated self to be torture. Mephisto thinks that Faust desires oblivion, but Faust makes it clear that what he truly wants is to obliterate the self:

> And what to all of mankind is apportioned
> I mean to savor in my own self's core,
> Grasp with my mind both highest and most low,
> Weigh down my spirit with their weal and woe,
> And thus my selfhood to their own distend,
> And be, as they are, shattered in the end. (1: 1770–75)[66]

Mephisto correctly believes that Faust wants to escape, but he thinks Faust wants to escape life in nothingness, while in fact he wants to escape the self by plunging into life.

Faust connects himself with one of the key values of the play in committing himself to an encounter with all of life; but at this point he is making the purely tragic decision to pursue the limited, the mediate, and even the demonic after having failed to achieve the absolute and immediate. Faust thus stands with figures like Byron's Cain, Shelley's Beatrice, and Musset's Lorenzo in the paradigmatic position of the romantic tragic protagonist: unable to reach an imaginative appreciation of the world, he must struggle to improvise a meaningful life for himself, while believing that life can never attain the perfection he seeks.

Goethe stages Faust's initial tragic confrontation with the fact of self-consciousness as a monodrama, that key contemporary theatrical form Goethe helped import onto the German stage. As in a monodrama, the opening scenes of *Faust* are dominated by its protagonist and they chart the often rapid fluctuation of his moods. The other characters appear mainly to draw forth or externalize his internal questionings. Of course, Goethe is using the monodrama as a limited form within the much larger drama of the completed *Faust*. He adopts it because it is completely appropriate to his investigation of Faust's isolation in consciousness: one indication that Faust is tragically barred from the visionary movement out of the self is that he must live this monodrama. Goethe begins his play with one pole of romantic thought, the isolated self, and one pole of romantic drama, the monodrama—though he already moves away from monodramatic monologue in the "Scholar's Tragedy" offering a series of dialogues that finally pair Faust with Mephistopheles who delights in ironic debate and serves as Faust's interlocutor-for-life. Goethe will in the course of the play not only traverse the world, from heaven through earth to hell, but also survey the dramatic possibilities open to the romantic playwright, from the monodrama to the melodrama, from the historical pageantry of Faust's encounters with the Emperor to the romantic classicism of the "Helena Act."

When Faust allies himself with Mephisto to enter the realm of earthly experience, he encounters another tragic dilemma; for Faust has not really turned from his quest for the infinite, but rather will now demand that the mediate and finite reveal to him all the beauty and value that he previously sought in an absolute. Like the poet of Shelley's *Alastor,* Keats's Endymion, or E. T. A. Hoffman's Don Juan, Faust demands that a mortal woman provide him with a transcendent experience in love. Fresh from the tragedy of self, Faust must now undergo the tragedy of human love, the "Gretchen Tragedy." Goethe again touches upon a central pattern in romantic tragic drama. From Manfred longing for Astarte to Hernani seeking a heroic love in the arms of Dona Sol, from Don Carlos's desire for Elizabeth to Lorenzo's fascination with innocent girls, the romantic protagonist seeks— usually with destructive consequences—for a perfect partner in whose arms he can escape the isolation of his selfhood and prove himself the grand figure he wants to be.

From the first moment he sees Gretchen, with his claim that he will never forget his initial glimpse of her (1: 2614), Faust speaks in absolutes. He argues that his desire for the girl is really an expression of his passion for the infinite, and thus he demands that we "call this blaze that leaves me breathless, / Eternal, infinite—yes! deathless!" (1: 3064–65).[67] It is particularly Gretchen's innocence that has for the fallen Faust a "holy worth" ("heil'gen Wert"; 1: 3102–5). Like Egmont fleeing to his Clara, Faust hopes to find with Gretchen an escape from his own baffled selfhood. He hopes "To give one's whole self, and to feel / An ecstasy that must endure forever!" (1: 3191–92).[68]

Faust seeks in Gretchen the ideal beauty he beheld in the mirror of the "Witch's Kitchen." In seeing a "form from heaven above" that makes him wonder "Can earthly beauty so amaze?" (1: 2429, 2437),[69] Faust has had his first glimpse of the "eternal feminine"—the ideal not-self—that is the object of his quest. Granted this vision, Faust will not be satisfied with any limited incarnation. Faust finds his love for Gretchen tainted by his sense of the distance between his earthly love and his vision. His love is no more immediate than the knowledge granted to him: Mephistopheles, the spirit of mediation, acts as the go-between in Faust's affair.

Thus their love hardly follows the ideal course Faust imagines for it. Shortly after his grand protestations of love, Faust comes to understand, in the "Forest and Cave" scene, both the glory of his love for Gretchen and its ultimately flawed nature. Faust first celebrates the beauties of nature and, by extension, of the natural, innocent love he believes the Earth Spirit has granted him ("You gave me splendored Nature for my kingdom"); taught "to know my brothers / In leafy stillness, in the air and water," Faust sees the natural world as almost a Wordsworthian friend to man. Moreover, in loving something outside the self, he is granted a revelation of the "secret deep-laid miracles" "of my own breast" (1: 3217–27, 3232–34).[70] He delights here in everything that he can gain by binding his striving soul to earthly life. However, he also recognizes that such experience can never be perfect. Nature may provide a virtual heaven on earth, but it is—insofar as it is on earth—not heaven:

> Ah, nothing perfect is vouchsafed to man,
> I sense it now. Unto this ecstasy
> That makes me near and nearer to the gods,
> You joined me that companion, whom already
> I cannot miss, though, chill and insolent,
> He does debase me to myself, makes naught
> Your gifts with but the vapor of a word.
> He fans within my breast a raging fire
> For that fair image with his busy spite.
> Thus reel I from desire to fulfillment,
> And in fulfillment languish for desire. (1: 3240–50)[71]

In this passage, Faust signals his increasing understanding that his bond with Mephisto is an emblem of the fact that he can have only a partial relationship with the perfect and infinite. The Earth Spirit has granted Faust access to the beauties of nature; but in turning from him and telling him to seek a spirit closer to his own selfhood (1: 512–13), he has condemned Faust to partnership with Mephisto. Faust senses that Mephisto, by revealing the limited nature of all earthly joys, hopes to convince Faust that they are all insignificant and thus to throw him back upon his own selfhood ("He does debase me to myself"). Mephisto, as is appropriate for a romantic devil, wants to keep Faust trapped in a debilitating mode of self-consciousness.

While Goethe has Faust speak in general terms in "Forest and Cave," the understanding he achieves has as immediate impact upon his relationship with Gretchen. He now sees himself as a demonic "fatal man" who must bring tragic destruction down upon her: "Am I not the fugitive, the homeless rover, / The man-beast void of goal or bliss" (1: 3348–49).[72] What makes Faust destructive is that he roves the world in search of something he does not believe the world can grant— "celestial graces" from an innocent girl "All in domestic cares enfurled," "Encompassed by the little world" (1: 3345, 3351–55).[73] Faust has acted as if his love lifted them to a transcendent plane above the cares of mankind. In fact, Gretchen is very much part of the bourgeois world that Goethe richly evokes. Faust has tried to believe they can live a perfect romance, when in fact she lives in a society that moves to the rhythms of the melodrama.

The basic situation of the "Gretchen Tragedy"—a middle-class girl seduced by an aristocrat who leaves her pregnant, driving her to commit infanticide for which she is imprisoned by a harshly moralistic society—had parallels in both actual occurrences and the Storm and Stress drama.[74] But it also follows a melodramatic configuration: the corruption of the innocent by the evil nobleman, the turn to violence, the scenes of repentance, and the enforcement of the traditional moral code. Gretchen inhabits a world of neighborly gossip (the scene "At the Well"), a world dominated by the church and its morality ("By the City Wall" and "Cathedral"). Their love is tragic, because while Faust insists they live on passion's heights searching for the infinite, Gretchen finds she must return to a society that follows the melodramatic pattern of excess issuing in moral judgment. Just as the staging of Faust's pursuit of knowledge as a monodrama indicated his tragic failure to break out of the self, so the ensnaring of Gretchen in the melodrama imposed by her society signals her (and Faust's) tragic inability to discover a transcendent love.

The first part of *Faust* has the type of double ending familiar to us from *Egmont*. On the one hand, there is the tragic fall into selfhood and violence that links Faust with Mephisto and drags Faust and Gretchen from love's intoxications through the violence of the deaths of her mother and brother to her imprisonment and society's condemnation of her sin. On the other hand, there is a visionary leap out of the tragic present, for a voice "from above" announces that Gretchen is redeemed (1: 4611). Faust's love has failed, but Goethe's play never loses sight of the "Prologue in Heaven's" sublime vision of creation caught in "love's enchanting fetters" ("der Liebe holden Schranken"; 1: 347). This double ending suggests that the first part is, in a sense, complete in itself, as Schelling suggested in arguing we could predict on the basis of *Faust. A Fragment* (1790) that the finished work would both pursue Faust's tragedy and grant him a final vision.[75] However, the implications of this ending are not yet explicit. *Faust's* long, complex second part works out the movement from the tragic nadir of Gretchen's death to a fulfillment of the visionary celebration hinted at here in her redemption. The intricacies of Faust's second part cannot be unraveled here, but I do want to suggest how Goethe wins vision out of tragedy just as Faust wins redemption out of his erring quest.

The first four acts of the second part of *Faust* trace Faust's search, as he moves through the realms of politics and art, for a way out of the self, for an act to perform that would bring him into contact with his world. In the first and fourth acts, Goethe recreates in more universal terms the late medieval world of *Götz von Berlichingen*.[76] We find ourselves once again at the crucial historical moment in which the old order has passed away and no new order of equal worth has arisen. The Imperial Court faces chaotic change in the rebellion of the Rival Emperor of Act IV. Within this world, the young Emperor struggles like Götz or Egmont to discover an appropriate social and political role; as we might expect, he sees this struggle as an attempt to prove himself a hero.[77] The tragic irony of his situation is that he can find a field of action only in revolution and war, and victory only in Mephisto's violent magic. The Emperor, hoping to prove himself great through acts of violence, instead finds that his pact with Mephisto betrays him into a limited, constrained position. Like Faust's, his dreams of glory bring him into conflict with the mediate nature of human life.[78]

Faust, who plays a secondary role during the Emperor's struggles, is once again dominant in the second and third acts where the political strife of the present is left behind in Faust's search through the past for a cultural ideal. From the birth of Greek culture in the East through the triumphs of classical art, the creation of medieval poetry, and the birth of the modern poetic spirit in Euphorion/Byron, Goethe surveys the arduous growth of human culture. In a sense, he presents here a deepened and more nearly universal account of the quest in *Iphigenia in Tauris* for an ideal merger of the classical with the romantic. However, while an ideal is presented in the union of Helena and Faust, it is not with their marriage that this movement concludes, but rather with the death of Euphorion. Moreover, the cultural compact between past and present, imaged in Goethe's use of the form of Greek tragedy, dissolves as the chorus loses its classical function to mourn the death of Euphorion before departing from the world of art back into the chaos of nature that art can only temporarily organize.[79] This section celebrates man's cultural achievements, but also reminds us they are not absolutes; they are art, artifices, not revelations. Like Iphigenia's vision of human life, they are creations of the godlike man, not the Creation of God. While man will continue to create "afresh new anthems" ("erfrischet neue Lieder"; 2: III, 9935), his triumphs will always be partial ones.

Mephistopheles' aid is as important in the Helena-Euphorion sections as it is in the seduction of Gretchen or the battle with the Rival Emperor, which indicates the limited nature of man's cultural attainments. In the "Helena Act," Mephisto takes on a very suggestive role; as Phorcyas, he acts as a stage manager throughout Goethe's exploration of classical, medieval, and modern culture and thus gives an ironic twist to the recreation of Greek tragedy, the evocation of medieval poetry, the survey of the pastoral, and the operatic treatment of the Euphorion story. Throughout this section, we seem to be granted a vision of the ideal; but we are, in fact, watching a stage show put on by Mephisto/Phorcyas. The ironic tension between the affirmations of Faust, Helena, and Euphorion and the stage tricks of Mephistopheles brings to a climax the key opposition in *Faust* between imaginative vision and the theater. From the "Prologue in the Theater" through the "Walpurgisnacht" of the first part and the carnival masque and "Rape of Helena" of the second part to the staging of the "Helena Act" itself, Goethe has grounded his tragic drama in the distance between vision and the stage. He reveals this distance in the contrast between the vision of the Earth Spirit and the monodrama of Faust's entrapment in the self, between the vision of the ideal woman in the witch's mirror and the melodrama of Gretchen's destruction by Faust, between Faust's enchantment by the vision of Helena in "The Rape" and the fact that "It's your work, this ghostly mask, you dunce!" ("Machst du's doch selbst, das Fratzengeisterspiel!"; 2: I, 6546). Constantly demanding the visionary ideal, Faust finds himself in the midst of the merely theatrical. He wants to grasp the absolute directly, as he tries to grasp Helena in his own play; but questing for an ultimate creative act, Faust finds himself merely acting. Faust's tragedy is that in trying to write for himself a heroic part in a grand pursuit of the ideal he turns life into a puppet play managed by Mephisto.

There is, however, in this interplay of vision and theater a suggestion of a third alternative—human life lived in a natural world. Having alienated himself from nature and his fellow man in the isolation of his selfhood, Faust has tried to regain contact with life through the magic—the stagecraft—of Mephistopheles. But Faust has still not committed himself to human life; he has sought only images and myths of the ideal, not the cares of his fellow men. He has thus shut himself off from a fully human existence and condemned himself to a life of playacting that—no matter how brilliant or beautiful—is not a life of human action.

Faust's final act recapitulates his tragic history and resolves his situation. The story of Philemon and Baucis reiterates the central pattern of romantic tragic drama: insofar as it is involved in the self and the self's violent struggle with all that is external to it, the pursuit of the ideal leads inevitably to destruction. Of course, this pattern is worked out in Faustian terms, as Faust, impatient for the perfection of his ideal community, turns to Mephistopheles again and adopts a violent means to achieve his ideal end, bringing destruction to the aged couple. However, this time, Faust understands what he has done and takes responsibility for it. He is thus ready for his confrontation with "Care," the care that Egmont fled at the end of his play and that Faust has been fleeing throughout his.

"Care" arrives at Faust's palace just as he desires a break with Mephisto and his magic, just as he seeks to "die into life," to enter fully into man's common experience:

> I have not fought my way to freedom yet.
> Could I but clear my path at every turning
> Of Spells, all magic utterly unlearning;
> Were I but Man, with Nature for my frame,
> The name of human would be worth the claim. (2: V, 11403–7)[80]

Though he faces "Care" alone, undefended by magic, he is not defeated by her; he does not despair of the striving he embraces. But he does admit "Care" into his consciousness; "Care" recognizes his ability to resist her, but she still blinds him. Yet, significantly, this blinding that marks Faust as part of the limited, human world he has sought to escape also grants him a second sight into the heart of the human predicament, as he makes clear in his last speech. There he explains that he will no longer exert his energy to pursue some abstract ideal. He now hopes to build a human community: "I'd open room to live for millions / Not safely, but in free resilience. . . . A land of Eden sheltered here within, / Let tempest rage outside unto the rim" (2: V, 11563–64, 11569–70).[81] He knows man cannot live "safely," free from the sorrows of life; but if he puts aside egotism to work with his fellow man, he can build a human Eden. Faust wins his way here to freedom and life—freedom from Mephisto and life with his fellow man—for he finally comes to understand that his fellow spirit is neither the Earth

Spirit with his total vision nor Mephisto with his demonic parodies of human life; rather, his place is to stand "free among free people" ("Auf freiem Grund mit freiem Volke stehn"; V, 11580). Like Iphigenia and Orestes, he turns from both dreams of the ideal heights and nightmares of hell to seek human life on the plains of earth.

Of course, Faust does not just "die into life"; he dies. He has accepted his lot as a mortal man, and thus his long life comes to an end. Mephisto stands ready to seize his prey, but Faust has already won his way free of him. In fact, Mephisto has helped Faust to his final triumph, for it is through his experience of the shadowy world of Mephistophelean magic that Faust finally comes to appreciate life. Faust can be "saved" by the hosts of angels, for led on by a love for the other he has not fully understood, he has continued to strive until he has found that the path out of the self lies in the community of men.

Still, Faust dies. The conclusion of *Faust* does not avoid tragedy. It rather accepts the tragic and celebrates the joy that can be won through that acceptance. Just as Faust confronts "Care," so does the play *Faust* confront the final fact of man's life: life *is* limited—and not just by human failing or the self's errors, but finally by death; no matter how far man strives, how far he develops his culture, he will still be subject to what Shelley calls "death and chance and mutability."[82] Goethe recognizes that from the perspective of the individual, life is a series of tragic involvements in the limited means of this world. But he sees these tragedies as contributing to the larger life of the human community as it pursues the never completed development of humanity. Thomas Mann saw this open-ended nature of *Faust*'s vision, saying that "of its own nature it might have gone on forever."[83] Goethe, however, offers his famous close:

> All in transition
> Is but reflection;
> What is deficient
> Here becomes action;
> Human discernment
> Here is passed by;
> Woman Eternal
> Draw us on high. (2: V, 12104–11)[84]

A "Chorus Mysticus" voices here a visionary pronouncement grounded in tragedy. The "eternal feminine"—the desire and love for the other and not just the self—will lead man forever higher, but each individual must live "in transition," in the lower world of mediation. There is hope here and joy, but also the recognition that man can never achieve the perfect world he can imagine, that there will always be a gap between vision and "human discernment."

Goethe accomplishes brilliantly here the juxtaposition of vision and tragedy that he sought in earlier plays. His tragedy, which has surveyed so many different dramatic types, moves in the end into a visionary mode. Whatever the surface similarities, this is not the mode of the "Walpurgisnacht" or of the "Helena Act," which were finally shadowy reflections of life staged by Mephisto. This is vision enacted or, to adapt a phrase from Blake, a "visionary form dramatic." Goethe leaves behind the stage world Mephisto controls to create a grander theater capable of including all of human life. For some, this may be a retreat to a mental theater. For Goethe, it is a transformation of the theater into a vehicle not only for tragedy but also for the celebration of life.

What sets *Faust* apart from other romantic dramas is its encyclopaedic quality, its attempt to include both romanticism's dreams and its nightmares. In *Faust,* the tragic sense of life finds a place in a larger medley of imaginative responses to human life; and both Greek and modern tragic forms are located within a larger visionary dramatic form. *Faust* insists that tragedy—at least, tragedy conceived as a plunge into destruction and chaos—provides a limited version of life. Tragedy, which along with epic has always stood at the summit of the hierarchy of literary forms, is here subordinated to a visionary mode, lyric in intensity though presented dramatically, that rejects the limits of the theater—the theater of monodrama and melodrama, and of Greek tragedy for that matter—in order to envision the drama of life itself. Harold Bloom has written of romanticism's visionary quest poems that their "fulfillment is never the poem itself, but the poem that is made possible by the apocalypse of the imagination."[85] If we amend this to say that the goal is the life that lies beyond and outside of poetry, then I think we have an accurate statement about *Faust.* The final moments of *Faust* with their ironic invocation of Christian vision create an imaginative apocalypse that shatters the limits of the theater and of tragedy to return us from art to life. *Faust,* like its protagonist, leaves behind the theater of self and violence in order to "die into life," a life remade by the imagination and love.

While Schiller provides us with a model of romantic tragic drama, Goethe's plays indicate how the romantic tragic sense of life reconnects with romanticism's key mode, the visionary quest romance. Goethe suggests that tragedy is part of the existential reality of man's quest for the ideal, that in some sense it is necessary to this visionary pursuit. Of course, most of romantic tragic drama does not seek to bridge the gap between the tragic drama of self-absorbed, revolutionary man and the romance of his redemption, between the stage and vision. In the plays of Byron, Shelley, Hugo, and Musset, there is no apocalyptic breakthrough like the one celebrated in *Faust,* and thus man remains trapped in the self and violence. The protagonists of these plays must live in a world filled with tragic destruction but denied the light of love and imagination granted to the blind Faust.

CHAPTER FIVE
BERTRAM, BYRON, AND
ENGLISH ROMANTIC
DRAMA

In the penultimate chapter of his *Biographia Literaria,* Coleridge draws attention to the crusade embarked upon by Drury Lane's governing committee to eliminate from its stage the melodramas and extravaganzas that had come to dominate it.[1] They hoped to return the theater to the traditional repertoire of English classics—Coleridge mentions Shakespeare, Jonson, Otway, and the "expurgated muses" of Restoration comedy; but they also sought to promote new plays of high calibre. The committee members, among them Lord Byron, solicited plays from a number of established writers, notably from Scott and from Coleridge himself. One of the first fruits of this hopeful nurturing of contemporary serious drama was the production in 1816 of the Reverend Charles Robert Maturin's *Bertram.*

The play was an enormous success. Scott admired it greatly. He had sent it to Byron for consideration when asked to submit something of his own. Byron, having by his own account studied the five hundred plays in the possession of Drury Lane and found them all wanting, welcomed Maturin's play and appeared deeply impressed by it. With Edmund Kean in the title role, *Bertram* was the hit of the season; it had what was then a considerable run of twenty-two performances and was long remembered as one of Kean's best parts. Well received by the critics (even Hazlitt called it a success), the play also pleased the reading public, going through seven printings in its first year of publication.[2] It appeared to fulfill the committee's hopes for the revitalization of the theater.

Today, *Bertram* is remembered only as the object of Coleridge's scathing attack in the *Biographia Literaria.* The play has suffered the fate of much of romantic drama. Met with extravagant hopes, it strikes us as extravagant nonsense. We cannot imagine how it could please audiences and earn the respect of such gifted writers as Scott and Byron. Still, *Bertram* looms large in the theater of the day, and we cannot afford to ignore it. It owed much to the popular theater, particularly the Gothic melodrama, but also the contemporary monodrama. However, it owed even more to the attempts of a number of literary figures to transform the melodrama and the monodrama into tragedy. *Bertram* stands between the plays of the popular stage and the tragic dramas of the romantic poets, and thus not only sums up much that was occurring in the British theater but gestures towards the innovations and insights found in the plays of Byron and Shelley, the best dramatic works of the English romantic movement.

I
GOTHIC MELODRAMA, MONODRAMATIC PSYCHOLOGY, AND THE PURSUIT OF THE TRAGIC

WHATEVER OUR FINAL opinion of the popular melodramas, farces, pantomimes, and burlettas that filled London's theaters during the romantic period, the litterati of the day lamented the decline of the "legitimate" drama. For example, in his theatrical "diary," John Genest—who found the melodrama "an unjustifiable species of the drama" with its "mixture of dialogue and dumb show"—constantly decries the drama's condition.[3] We hear accounts of the decline of tragedy and comedy in prologues to many plays of the period; even a melodramatic work like James Boaden's *Secret Tribunal* (London, 1795) was preceded by a speech detailing tragedy's retreat before the demand for spectacular effects. By the time Bulwer-Lytton's Select Committee examined the status of the drama and the theater in 1832, it was found that "a considerable decline, both in the Literature of the Stage, and the taste of the Public for Theatrical Performances, is generally conceded."[4] Today, theater historians may praise the melodrama as a popular predecessor of realistic, prose drama; then, critics and poets hoped to revive the greatness of poetic tragedy.

Both generations of romantic writers sought to reform the stage and to renew England's dramatic glory. The first generation—Wordsworth, Coleridge, Southey, and Scott along with Lewis, Baillie, Godwin, and others—sought to seize the stage between 1795 and 1805; in the years following the delayed but successful staging of Coleridge's *Remorse* in 1813, the second generation—not only Byron, Shelley, and Keats, but also Maturin, Cornwall, and Beddoes—wrote a number of interesting plays in their bid to revive the poetic drama. Theater historians generally dismiss these plays as academic efforts divorced from theatrical realities. Literary scholars turn from the few romantic theatrical successes, seeing their value compromised by the inclusion of popular techniques. However, the most interesting of these plays are neither closet dramas nor potboilers, but attempts to discover tragedy within popular theatrical modes. There were certainly British playwrights who resembled Tieck in his rejection of the stage, but there were others who sought in the melodrama and monodrama the means to stage their key themes of selfhood and revolt.

While the first English play to be labeled a melodrama—Thomas Holcroft's adaptation of Pixérécourt, *A Tale of Mystery*—was performed in 1802, writers like George Coleman the Younger, Thomas Morton, James Boaden, and Holcroft himself had written earlier plays that are clearly in a melodramatic vein; Holcroft's identification of his play thus signals less melodrama's birth than its flourishing maturity. As in Germany, the melodrama—with its absolute morality, mixture of humor and seriousness, and spectacular stage effects—provided a popular substitute for tragedy. These plays could thrill an audience with fear of the violent and the unknown and fill them with pity for a distressed heroine, while providing a simplified moral vision that avoided the tense ambiguities of tragedy.

As the melodramas that pleased English audiences became increasingly domestic, they moved farther away from the heroic and tragic vision sought by the romantics; but before 1820—the year that witnessed W. T. Moncrieff's *The Lear of the Private Life* and, thus, according to Gilbert Cross, the arrival of the domestic drama[5]—English melodrama was largely of the Gothic variety. Given Gothicism's many links with romanticism, these melodramas offered more to prospective romantic tragedians than did, for example, the trivializing social plays of Kotzebue to German writers. The English poets not only borrowed many Gothic trappings—the "Gothic gallery" of *Manfred*, the forbidding castle of Petralla in *The Cenci*, or the robber band of *The Borderers*. They also felt in the underlying plot of Gothic drama the rhythms of revolt; and they found in the increasingly sympathetic villain-hero an adumbration of their own tragic protagonists.

Gothic drama has been traced back through the later eighteenth century to plays like Home's *Douglas* (1756), but its theatrical triumph came during the two decades bracketing the turn of the century when popular writers like Coleman the Younger joined with literary figures like William Godwin in exploring and exploiting Gothic conventions. Bertrand Evans lists thirty-five Gothic plays for the years between the Fall of the Bastille and 1800, and another thirty-two through 1810; he identifies only twenty-five before 1789. In part, the success of the Gothic novel spurred its stage counterpart. In 1794, London saw the first of many stage adaptations from Ann Radcliffe's novels; Lewis's *The Monk* was dramatized several times in the years following its publication in 1796. Foreign influences also contributed to the development of the Gothic after 1789, with the first English translation of *The Robbers* in 1792 supplying the native Gothic tradition with a literary ally and Boaden's *Secret Tribunal* of 1795 bringing the *Femgericht* of Goethe's *Götz* to the English stage. The popular triumph of "Monk" Lewis's *The Castle Spectre*—with forty-three performances in 1797 and continuing popularity for many years—perhaps marks a high point in the appeal of the Gothic drama.[6]

The Gothic drama flourished, then, in the years immediately following the French Revolution and the Terror—not that these plays dealt directly with revolutionary events. There had been plays that put revolutionary history on stage; John Dent's *The Bastille* (Royal Circus, 1789), for example, has the people of Paris successfully rehearse their uprising. But the mood of the authorities and audiences changed as Britain entered into its long struggle with France. Drury Lane closed on January 24, 1793 in memory of the executed Louis XVI. Genest notes the anti-French feeling of a number of plays of the period, including George Watson's *England Preserved* (Covent Garden, 1795) which he felt was offered "for the sake of introducing patriotic sentiments and invective against the French" and Sheridan's enormously successful *Pizarro* (Drury Lane, 1799) which Genest saw as having as its goal "to reprobate the principles of the French Revolution."[7] Pro-French and revolutionary sentiments were discovered and denounced even in harmless, nonpolitical plays. The attitude of the theatrical authorities can perhaps be glimpsed in the much later comments of George Coleman the Younger, who was made Examiner of plays in 1824; even at this late date, he opposed as inflammatory plays "so allusive to the times as to be applied to the existing moment," particularly those plays "which are built upon conspiracies, and attempts to revolutionize a state" and "pourtray the disaffected as gallant heroes and hapless lovers."[8]

In this atmosphere, the Gothic drama appears as a vehicle for exploring, however obscurely at times, revolutionary sentiments and the rhythms of revolt. The Gothic could appear quite anti-aristocratic. For the most part, Gothic plays involve the attempt of a young hero and heroine—who, if not of the people, represent essentially middle-class domestic values—to escape from a crumbling castle ruled by a demonic aristocrat. Villains were usually chosen from the ranks of the nobility or from the hierarchy of the Catholic Church, while peasants, servants, and other members of the lower orders tended to oppose them. Such class divisions were suggested even in plays where romance conventions dictated that the hero and heroine have noble origins. In Lewis's *Castle Spectre*,[9] for example, the heroine,

Angela, is the daughter of an earl, and the hero, Percy, is an earl; she, however, has been raised by a peasant family and he disguises himself as a peasant in order to woo her in the name of true love rather than rank. Lewis still provides an evil aristocrat who traps Angela in his castle—Osmond, who has murdered her mother and sought to assassinate her father, his brother.

In plays like this one, the Gothic drama charts an escape from the ruins of an aristocratic past symbolized by the crumbling battlements of the villain's stronghold; and in that this escape is usually accomplished with the help of a comic rustic of some sort (Angela and Percy are aided by servants, a fool, and a comic friar), these plays could be seen to embrace a democratic ethos of natural equality. At times, direct statements of humanitarian and democratic sentiments were introduced into these plays, as was the case in *The Castle Spectre* where Osmond's black henchman attacks slavery (I, ii). Lewis, in fact, offered the printed version of the play at least in part to dispel rumors that he had dramatized radically democratic ideas; that he felt a need to vindicate himself suggests that Gothic plays were seen as touching upon revolutionary themes. Coleridge makes the point even more explicit when, in attacking *Bertram,* he attacks the entire genre as the "modern Jacobinical drama."[10]

This is not to say that the Gothic drama was truly revolutionary; even in the working class theaters that cropped up later in the nineteenth century, the melodrama remained escapist rather than inflammatory. If radical values creep in at the social level, they have no place in the moral and metaphysical vision of these plays. Thus, while the Gothic pattern of the young and sometimes lowly fighting free from an older, aristocratic generation could be used by Shelley in *The Cenci* or Byron in *Werner* to chart the tragedy of revolt, the most important contribution of the Gothic to the romantic drama came in characterization.[11]

Characterization is not one of melodrama's strong points, as our tendency to speak of its characters as "black" or "white" suggests. Melodrama presents its conflicts through situation rather than character. The cast of the average melodrama fills out a series of stereotypes—the hero and heroine, the villain, the comic man, the old rustic. Not only were these figures typed morally, but even their speech and dress became conventionalized.[12] Such stylized plays offered little to the English romantics with their interest in psychological states and their attempt to stage man's struggles with self-consciousness. The Gothic drama, however, began to develop a more complex, inwardly divided figure in the villain-hero, who was destined to enter the romantic drama and become the Byronic hero.

There were Gothic plays that were strictly melodramatic in that they enforced a traditional moral code through the triumph of the hero and heroine over their evil enemy. *The Mysteries of the Castle* (Andrews and Reynolds; Covent Garden, 1795) pits a thoroughly evil Count Montoni—who has married his wife under false pretenses and now intends to kill her—against her true love, Carlos. Boaden's *Fountainville Forest* (Covent Garden, 1794) ends with Nemours, a Parisian official, arriving like a *deus ex machina* to put an end to an evil Marquis' plots and to restore the formerly disgraced hero to society; as good and evil are sorted out, Nemours speaks of a "secret Providence" that is controlling the action (Act V).[13]

However, even in these conventional plays, we can see hints of the tensions that could enter into Gothic characterization. In *Mysteries of the Castle,* the evil Count has some of the moments of remorse that came to mark the villain-hero, moments when into "an injur'd husband's breast, resisted pity will at times intrude—fear, too, appals, and dread remorse" (II, i). In Boaden's play, good and evil again mix, since the villain at first appears as a savior and the hero acquires some villainous traits; for he has been forced to become a robber after ruining himself in Paris and finally finds himself trapped into aiding the vicious Marquis. While the characters in these plays are reduced to moral absolutes at the conclusion, in the course of the action their mixture of good and evil begins to liberate them from melodramatic moralism.

To the extent that the villain-hero usurps the interest and sympathy of the audience, we begin to sense the ambivalence in the Gothic drama's treatment of these powerful, audacious lords. For they seem to represent not only an aristocratic past against which the hero and heroine struggle, but also a new freedom of the self that threatens any moral order, traditional or bourgeois. Jean Starobinski has written of the late eighteenth-century libertines—Mozart's Don Juan, Laclos's Valmont, Sade's voluptuaries—as being libertarian proponents of unlimited freedom at the same time that they are self-destructive upholders of an outmoded life of pleasure.[14] This odd infusion of revolutionary energy into a decadent aristocrat—which can be seen in so early a figure as Richardson's Lovelace—is a key to the Gothic villain-hero. Using his inherited feudal power in his attempts upon the virtue of the heroine, the Gothic villain-hero is clearly evil; but in that he comes to recognize and to lament his evil—as the Gothic drama's increasing emphasis upon his remorse demands—he comes to see himself as pursuing his own destruction along with that of his victim. Moreover, no matter how destructive and even self-destructive he is, the villain-hero is the only source of energy in his collapsing world. The passivity of the official hero has often been noted; in Lewis's *Castle Spectre,* for example, Percy for the most part sits helplessly by, unable to control the action. Osmond, however, reveals his heroic power when, confronted by what he believes to be the ghost of his brother, he proclaims, "Hell and fiends! I'll follow him, though lightnings blast me!" (II,i). Like Don Juan before the Commendatore's statue, he is ready to battle even the dead.

It was the presentation of heroic virtues in vice-ridden figures that struck contemporaries as the "revolutionary" aspect of Gothic drama. These figures may not be political revolutionaries—they may in fact be the opponents of social change—but they do suggest the revolutionary possibility of creating an identity independent of social mores, "beyond good and evil." The "age of the democratic revolution" was also the age of more individual rebellions; it fathered both Saint-Just and Sade. Audiences seem to have been both enthralled by and fearful of the powerful, free individuality of the Gothic villain-hero. To some, his appeal was clearly a threat. When Coleridge attacked these plays as Jacobinical, it was their tendency to make villains attractive that bothered him. J. G. Holman, in the preface to his melodramatic transformation of Schiller's *Robbers* into *The Red Cross Knights* (Haymarket, 1799), notes that the licenser of plays had prohibited the production of Schiller's drama since the "grandeur of his [Moor's] character renders him more likely to excite imitation than abhorrence"; Holman agrees that this "junction of sublime virtue with consummate depravity, though it may be found in nature, should never be dragged into view:—the heroism dazzles the mind, and renders it blind to the atrocity."[15]

Within the schema of the Gothic melodrama, the amoral individuality of the aristocratic villain-hero must lose out to the domestic virtue of the hero and heroine. But a sense of loss accompanies the destruction of the villain-hero, for it was his energy that illumined his world and his personality that energized the audience. His self-sufficiency, his attempt to assert his independent selfhood, even his egotism, all link him to the traditional tragic hero's quest for the summit of his world; critics have recognized the near-tragic stature of Gothic figures by comparing them to the "satanic" heroes of Elizabethan and Jacobean drama.[16] In that their energy must be discarded to usher in the new order symbolized by the union of the hero and heroine, we approach a tragic lament for human potential destroyed in order to rediscover security and providential certainty.

Still, as long as the Gothic villain-hero remained the vicious opponent of social change, he stood at a distance from the romantic protagonist with his proclamation of revolt. In a sense, what the romantics did was to redefine aristocratic pride, heroic energy, and self-conscious remorse as attributes of revolutionary figures rather than their opponents. Byron literally transformed aristocrats into rebels, having Marino Faliero revolt against the society he nominally rules and Sardanapalus rebel against his nation's traditions. Maturin's Bertram is a member of the nobility, but he has joined a

Schillerian robber band. Even in Shelley's *The Cenci,* where the Count can seem one more villain-hero, the true heroine is the noble yet rebellious Beatrice who shares with her father his energy and his temptation to pursue the self beyond moral and social constraints.

We can see the attempt to create a tragic figure from the Gothic villain in the plays of Lewis. In *The Castle Spectre,* Lewis's first substantial play, Osmond already has considerable complexity and appeal. At times, he seems merely a figure of evil, marked by his actions and appearance as a villain; Angela, for example, comments upon his "strange demeanour": "in that gloomy brow is written a volume of villainy" (I, ii). For us, however, Osmond holds a great deal of interest, since he is both the most vital and the most self-conscious character in the play. We have already noted his heroic stand in the face of the unknown. We are also able to witness his anguished and aware remorse. His first appearance, "with arms folded, and his eyes bent upon the ground" (stage direction, II, i), manifests his inner turmoil. And while his first speech announces his titanic egotism—"I will not sacrifice my happiness to hers!"—it also informs us that his villainy has arisen from thwarted love. Lewis demands sympathy for Osmond in all of his villainy, before sending him to his death amid his brother's pleas for repentance.

Still, Osmond is a villain, defined in moral terms. In *Alfonso, King of Castille* (Covent Garden, 1802), one of his two efforts at tragedy, Lewis grounded his characters in a tension between their passions and morality:

. . . *sublimity* of characters is seldom (if ever) produced, except by the *un*amiable passions when employed in the service of virtue; and it was to illustrate the above opinion, that I sketched Orsino. ("Preface," xiv)[17]

Lewis rejects completely the arguments of Coleridge, Coleman, and Holman against the depiction of divided characters. Lewis mentions in this regard Orsino, the former right-hand man to Alfonso whose death has long ago been ordered by the King on the basis of forged evidence but who has, in fact, been saved by Amelrosa, the King's daughter. Lewis sees Orsino as a disinterested servant of the state (he finally kills his son to prevent him from killing Alfonso, though this scene was dropped in performance as too horrible) whose pride, aristocratic reserve, and stubborn silence left him open to attacks by his enemies. Orsino's character is thus "unamiable" but he serves virtue.

It is not Orsino who holds our attention in the play, however; it is his son Caesario, who believes Alfonso has succeeded in killing his father and thus plots revenge. Caesario is a Gothic villain-hero as rebel. His revolt, like that of the romantic protagonist, originates in an ideal vision, in this case a vision of his father, seen by Caesario as a "hero / A demi-god" (III, ii). Armed with an ideal, Caesario is willing to perform any deed to enact his revenge. He has allowed Otilla, who loves him, to poison her husband, only to betray her by marrying the King's daughter. When Amelrosa learns of his plot, she begs him to save the King, but his hatred for Alfonso outweighs his love for the daughter:

> Dearly, fiercely love her!
> But not so fiercely as I loathe this king—
> Hatred of him cherished from youth is now
> My second nature . . .
> . . . .
> To cease to hate him, I must cease to breathe! (II, i)

We will see such struggles between love and hate again in Maturin's *Bertram* and Byron's *Cain;* the victory of violence over love signals the rebel's loss of his ideal end in adopting a contaminated means to accomplish it.

Caesario—who feels there is something rotten in the state of Castille and that he was born to set it right—must die because unlike his father he has adopted self and violence over service to others. But his death approaches tragedy in its needless destruction of needed talents. Caesario has an energy, a heroic charisma we admire. This energy is revealed within the play by his ability to attract women; it is also celebrated by Orsino, who echoes Lewis's preface in arguing that Caesario's passions could have been put in the service of virtue had he had a proper education ("Preface," p. xv; V, iv). In this play, Lewis took the Gothic as close to the tragic as he could manage; the transformation of the traditional villain into a hero, the aristocratic lord of the manor into a noble rebel, would be taken even further by that later master of the Gothic, Maturin.

The quest for the tragic in the hero's personality pursued by the Gothic playwrights is even more central to another group of plays written around the turn of the century that seek to discover tragedy in monodramatic character study. These "psychological" tragedies met with only minimal success in the theater, when they were staged at all. Wordsworth's interesting attempt to merge Schiller, Shakespeare, the Gothic, and psychology in *The Borderers* was not even published until 1842, and Lamb failed to have his *John Woodvil* (1801) staged; but Godwin's *Antonio* appeared at Drury Lane in 1800, Lewis's monodrama entitled *The Captive* was given at Covent Garden in 1803, and Coleridge's important play *Osorio* was finally performed as the revised *Remorse* in 1813.

Joanna Baillie's series of plays on the passions, mentioned in chapter 2, represents the most concerted attempt to ground tragedy in psychology and thus to wrest the tragic from the monodramatic. This pursuit of a psychological tragedy is well illustrated by her *Orra* (1812),[18] a play possessing many Gothic features—a villain motivated by love, a band of robbers, a haunted castle, a vaguely medieval setting—but seeking a tragic catastrophe in an analysis of fear. Orra, the young ward of Count Hughobert whose passion for ghostly stories has turned her normally vivacious temperament to melancholy, is sought in marriage by the Count's son, by the heroic Theobald, and by Rudigere, the villain. The Count imprisons her in a castle supposedly haunted by a huntsman murdered by their common ancestor; he hopes she will choose his son over such a fearful imprisonment, meant to work upon her susceptible nature. He has, however, unwittingly left her in the hands of Rudigere who plots to terrify her into marrying him. Theobald, her true love, learns that the ghostly visitations troubling the castle are in fact a ruse of noble robbers seeking to prevent discovery. He dresses himself as the dead huntsman, believing that Orra has received a message telling her of his plan to rescue her in this guise. But she has no chance to read his note and is driven mad by fear when Theobald appears as the ghost. Baillie's climax, while involving the plots of the various characters, rests upon Orra's psychology—her initial delight in being frightened, her half-terrified attraction to the supernatural, and her final inability to confront what she believes to be a messenger from another world.

Baillie, like the major romantics, sought to explore the self. But in creating psychological tragedy, she still maintained the link between the tragic and the moral; she argued that her plays would educate the audience to recognize wickedness in its early stages, before its growth to an all-consuming passion.[19] However, a conflict arises between her psychological portraiture and her moral preachings, between the sympathy extended to the man of passion as we come to understand his inner life and the judgment that she wanted to pass upon him. That is, she had to confront the same difficulty that Gothic dramatists did when they empathized with their villain-heroes. She tried to resolve this tension in a formula: "... it is the passion and not the man which is held up to our execration."[20]

Yet, as the text of her most successful play *De Monfort* (Drury Lane, 1800) attests, this tension gave her more difficulty than her theoretical remarks would indicate. In this tragedy of hatred, Baillie at first works to establish our sympathy for De Monfort. He may be proud, egotistical, and even monomaniacal; but every other character, including his saintly sister, assures us of his noble nature. We extend our sympathy to him even as he becomes obsessed with his hatred for Rezenvelt, who loves his sister. However, once De Monfort has killed Rezenvelt, Baillie seems uncertain whether to continue urging sympathy for her protagonist or to force us to condemn him for his evil action. She tries to have it both ways. She allows him to appear grand in his last scene when he is led offstage in chains.[21] The final scenes, however, offer moralizing comments on the murder. Still uncertain where to let the final emphasis lie, Baillie gives the sister the final speech: she excuses De Monfort for his "one dire deed" and extols his "record of as noble worth, / As e'er enrich'd the sculptur'd pedestal." But Baillie hedges again, adding a note that these lines represent "the partial sentiments of an affectionate sister" and not her own (V, vi & n.).[22] Baillie's commitment to moral tragedy runs afoul of her technique of sympathetic portrayal, as she vacillates between sympathy and judgment.

Such tentative resolutions of the problems facing romantic tragic drama as those found in *De Monfort* or in the ambiguous villain-heroes of the Gothic drama are typical of the plays written around the turn of the century. Seeking tragedy in psychological struggle or in the personal revolt of the Gothic villain-hero, dramatists were still unwilling or unable to break with the moralizing tendency that marked not only the melodrama but virtually every dramatic form of the period. The revolt of the villain-hero cannot become the heart of tragedy until he is truly a hero. The sympathy granted to psychologically complex figures cannot earn our respect for their heroism and their destruction until their ambiguous relation to judgment is clarified, as this relation is clarified in figures like Beatrice Cenci and Lorenzaccio. Maturin's *Bertram* is an interesting and even important play, for it does with simple but compelling force what these earlier plays had done with hesitation and uncertainty.

II
MATURIN AND COLERIDGE: IDENTITY AND MORALITY

READING *BERTRAM* TODAY, all we notice are its weaknesses. Its faults are as glaring as its wild-eyed namesake. Set on the Italian seacoast beloved by Gothic writers, the play indulges in the requisite castles, monks, and robbers. It offers a generous selection from the contemporary dramatic menu of sex and violence, opening with a shipwreck and moving on to adultery, murder, infanticide, and suicide. The cast includes a mysterious villain-hero and a female lead who can be depended upon to weep and to go mad. To dismiss this Gothic smash hit as the product of a popular fad would be comforting, but Maturin's use of verse and his habit of making learned allusions reveal the pretensions of the piece. *Bertram* sought the label of tragedy and as such it was received and praised by both the audience and the critics. Perhaps the key to *Bertram*'s success was that Maturin, more clearly than Lewis or Baillie, offered the age its own brand of hero, a hero who lives beyond moral judgment, defining himself in isolation and revolt.

Significantly, Coleridge's discussion of *Bertram* in chapter 23 of his *Biographia Literaria* revolves around the appeal of the hero. He argues that Bertram should be understood as a descendant of a line of dramatic figures stretching back through Schiller's Karl Moor to the protagonists of the Don Juan plays, especially that of Shadwell. He feels that these figures all impress us through their assertion of the self's independence even when they are faced by great obstacles. While they may act basely, we accept them as heroic when their individuality and intelligence seek to triumph over the limits set by nature, society, and religion. Coleridge suggests that the dangerous appeal these figures exert over us is dramatized through the influence they have over women. He imagines the response of a member of an audience watching the immoral Don Juan conquer woman after woman:

There is no danger (thinks the spectator or reader) of *my* becoming such a monster of iniquity as *Don Juan*! *I* never shall be an atheist! *I* shall never disallow all distinction between right and wrong! *I* have not the least inclination to be so outrageous a drawcansir in my love affairs! But to possess such a power of captivating and enchanting the affections of the other sex!—to be capable of inspiring in a charming and even virtuous woman, a love so deep, and so entirely personal to *me*!—that even my worst vices (if I *were* vicious), even my cruelty and perfidy (if I *were* cruel and perfidious), could not eradicate the passion! to be so loved for my *own self,* that even with a distinct knowledge of my character, she yet died to save me! this sir, takes hold of two sides of our nature, the better and the worse. For the heroic disinterestedness, to which love can transport a woman, can not be contemplated without an honourable emotion of reverence towards womanhood: and, on the other hand, it is among the miseries, and abides in the dark groundwork of our nature, to crave an outward confirmation of that *something* within us, which is our *very self,* that something, not *made up* of our qualities and relations, but itself the supporter and substantial basis of all these. Love *me,* and not my qualities, may be vicious and an insane wish, but it is not a wish wholly without a meaning.[23]

Coleridge is clearly describing here the tension between judgment and sympathy that we have found in the Gothic drama and in the plays of Baillie. He sees our reaction to Don Juan and Bertram—we reject their vices, yet identify with their naked assertion of selfhood—in much the same way as Robert Langbaum views the response elicited by Browning's nobleman in "My Last Duchess": "We suspend moral judgment because we prefer to participate in the duke's power and freedom, in his hard core of character fiercely loyal to itself."[24] Characters like Don Juan and Bertram evoke a divided reaction from the audience, because we condemn their acts while delighting in the strong independence of a selfhood affirmed against all limits.

Even though he thoroughly understood the tension between sympathy and judgment and put it to use in his own poems, Coleridge still insists that the drama bring judgment upon characters; and he finds here the central difference between the traditional portrayal of Don Juan and the portrayal of Bertram. While the Don Juan plays present an appealing villain, they work finally to demonstrate the hollowness of that appeal. Don Juan is seen at last as devilish and is appropriately assigned to hell at the conclusion of the play, the plot thus revealing God's judgment.[25] *Bertram,* however, arouses our admiration for its titanic protagonist but fails to subordinate him to a moral vision. In fact, Maturin's play offers Bertram repeated opportunities to assert his selfhood apart from any moral order.[26] For Coleridge, *Bertram* thus takes its place within the "modern Jacobinical drama" which "consists in the confusion and subversion of the natural order of things."[27]

The ambiguities surrounding the Gothic villain-hero are clarified in the light of the tension between sympathy and judgment found in *Bertram.* Joanna Baillie's struggle to find a formula to account for both the empathy granted the protagonist and the final affirmation of a moral vision—"it is the passion and not the man which is held up to our execration"—is explored further in Coleridge's statement of the demand made by a character like Bertram—"love *me,* and not my qualities." The tension surrounding the portrait of the amoral self was clearly central to the romantic conception of the tragic, as Hazlitt's discussion of tragedy in relation to egotism and "disinterestedness" and Shelley's belief that tragedy defeats the "principle of self" through "self-knowledge" attest.[28] Coleridge tells us much about *Bertram* and its exploration of these issues, but his very insights should lead us to qualify his attack upon the play.

Bertram opens with a shipwreck that a disgusted Coleridge compares with the third act of Shadwell's Don Juan play *The Libertine,* where there is also a spectacular storm. He notes that Shadwell places his play clearly within a providential framework, with heaven above and hell below, and thus he "not only prepared us for the supernatural but also accustomed us to the prodigious." Shadwell's storm, unnatural in its savagery, is intelligible as a manifestation of a providential realm. As for *Bertram*:

But what is there to account for the prodigy of the tempest at *Bertram's* shipwreck? It is a mere supernatural effect, without even a hint of any supernatural agency; a prodigy, without any circumstance mentioned that is prodigious; and a miracle introduced without a ground, and ending without a result.[29]

In objecting to this prodigious opening that lacks a providential significance, Coleridge voices here, over a century before *The Death of Tragedy,* a central motif in Steiner's attack upon romantic drama.

A more sympathetic reading of the play, however, reveals that this scene honestly depicts the universe of *Bertram;* for in this as in all romantic plays, man must live without divine guidance. Shadwell's Don Juan lives in a world with a moral and divine order that even he recognizes in his violation of it. No such certainty exists in *Bertram,* as the opening scene makes clear. A prior and several monks are watching the storm. One suggests that it has a demonic origin: "Oh holy prior, this is no earthly storm. / The strife of fiends is on the battling clouds, / The glare of hell is in these sulphorous lightnings." The prior, who voices the thoughts of his clerical author throughout the play, rejects this view: "Peace, peace—thou rash and unadvised man; / Oh! add not to this night of nature's horrors / The darker shadowing of thy wicked fears" (I, i).[30] The shipwreck and storm do not provide providential revelation but rather provoke human interpretation. Maturin signals here the shift from a providential to a human framework that we have already seen in the humanistic interpretation of the oracle in Goethe's *Iphigenia;* we will encounter a similar moment in the reaction of Byron's Cain to the sacrifices he and Abel make at the close of their play. Maturin dramatizes this shift through the prior, the man of religion who learns to admire the powerfully demonic humanity of Bertram.

Bertram, an outcast and an outlaw, experiences the loss of an ordered world more deeply than any other character in the play, his career prior to the play's opening having charted the course of this "fall." Once "The darling of his liege and of his land" (II, i), Bertram has stood at the summit of his society, beloved by all, including Imogine. However, he has fallen from grace. While the cause of this downfall is never made clear, his enemy St. Aldobrand claims that Bertram, "the coiled serpent" (IV, ii), attempted to usurp his sovereign's power. This hint of satanic revolt is entirely appropriate to Bertram, for he was cast out from a heaven of position, power, and love and has taken on by the opening of the play a "fiend-like glory" (IV, i). Rejected by society, he has turned against it to become a pirate and a robber. While the presence of a Schillerian robber band suggests that Maturin wanted to ally his protagonist's personal revolt with some broader opposition to society, the play focuses upon Bertram's attempt to exalt his own selfhood, an attempt described by the admiring prior:

High-hearted man, sublime even in thy guilt,
Whose passions are thy crimes, whose angel-sin
Is pride that rivals the star-bright apostate's.—
Wild admiration thrills me to behold
An evil strength, so above earthly pitch—
Descending angels only could reclaim thee. . . . (III, ii)

Maturin does not offer the subtle analysis of the self that we find in Byron and Shelley, Musset and Kleist. Bertram's isolation, his journey into the depths of the self are givens in the play, much as they are with Lewis's Caesario.[31] Maturin instead focuses upon Bertram's attempt to reconnect with his world. Upon his return to his native land at the beginning of the play, two paths present themselves to him, for Bertram has returned not only to pursue his hatred of St. Aldobrand, but also to press his love for Imogine. While we may feel that the egotistical Bertram should be incapable of love, Coleridge has already suggested the link between the assertion of self and the need for love: "Love *me* and not my qualities, may be a vicious and insane wish, but it is not a wish wholly without meaning."

Much of romantic drama serves to define the meaning of this vicious wish. As we have seen in the plays of Goethe and Schiller, when the romantic protagonist finds himself cut off from society, he loses the traditional badge of the hero: fame. The romantic would-be-hero, cast out and thus at best infamous, seeks compensation for this loss of fame in an asocial and perhaps unholy love. If he can find a woman who will love his very self, then she will have confirmed his heroic sense of himself, even as everyone else condemns him. This search for a society of two, perhaps clearer in French romantic drama, can also be seen in the Gothic villain-hero's need to make a love conquest, in De Monfort's monomaniacal demands upon his sister's love, and in Manfred's incestuous desire for Astarte.

Bertram pursues fulfillment through love spasmodically. He insists that Imogine prove her love. Even though she has married St. Aldobrand, she assures Bertram of her love and finally gives herself to him. Imogine's love is seen as a potentially redemptive power; when near her, Bertram seems ready to reject his role as violent rebel: "I'll gaze no more— / That fair, that pale, dear cheek, these helpless arms, / If I look longer they will make me human" (II, iii). Still, the very violence of his love suggests that it is hatred for her husband as much as love for her that drives Bertram; and at the very moment when he seems ready to give up his hatred for Aldobrand (IV, i), he learns of his rival's plot to arrest him and thus returns to violence as his guarantee of freedom.

While Coleridge emphasizes Bertram's demand that he be loved, the power of Maturin's play lies in his protagonist's pursuit of hatred as a means of self-assertion. In love, the self is ratified by another. In hatred, the self affirms itself by destroying another. Love puts the self in debt to another. In hatred, the self rules supreme. Maturin portrays rather boldly the intuition, central to plays as different as Wordsworth's *Borderers,* Shelley's *Cenci,* and Kleist's *Penthesilea,* that the isolated self often prefers hatred to love as the means of bringing itself into contact with the world.

Bertram describes two visions that outline the appeal hatred has for him. In the first, he imagines that he and his enemy Aldobrand are lost at sea together, "With but one plank between us and destruction" (II, i). Then, having killed Aldobrand, Bertram is surprised to find this final confrontation disturbed by other men:

> I am amazed to see ye living men,
> I deemed that when I struck the final blow
> Mankind expired, and we were left alone,
> The corse and I were left alone together,
> The only tenants of a blasted world
> Dispeopled for my punishment, and changed
> Into a penal orb of desolation. (V, ii)

Bertram is possessed by an apocalyptic dream of an encounter between self and other in which he proves his power through destruction. The fact that his dream entails his own punishment only reveals how strong his drive is to demonstrate his ascendancy.

Although he envisions his own punishment, Bertram does not experience remorse for his deeds, the remorse usually felt by the Gothic villain-hero; and this fact perhaps turned the author of *Remorse* against Maturin's play. *Bertram* echoes and inverts the earlier work in a number of ways. In both plays, a man returns from exile to claim his love and to deal with the man who has injured him. But Coleridge's mysterious stranger, Alvar, is handled far differently from Bertram. We learn that he and his brother Ordonio love the same woman and that Ordonio has, as a result, tried to have Alvar killed. Still, Alvar returns not seeking revenge, but hoping to awaken remorse in Ordonio. While Alvar may appear at first with all the mystery of a Gothic villain-hero, we soon learn that he is a truly virtuous man. He has not committed some foul deed in the past; rather he has been the victim of his brother's plots. He has not become an outcast and a robber. He has been a freedom fighter. Most important, it is not he who is an inward-turned egotist, but Ordonio, whom Alvar describes as a "blind self-worshipper" (V, i, 157).[32]

Bertram is both robber and rebel, a criminal and a victim, even a devil and an angel; Alvar and Ordonio divide these roles between them. Clearly disapproving of Maturin's "Jacobinical" mixture of virtue and vice,[33] Coleridge tries in his own play to segregate good from evil qualities without reducing his characters to stereotypes of innocence and depravity.

Coleridge takes pains to portray Alvar as a free-thinker and a rebel. During his years of exile, Alvar journeyed to "The Belgic states: there joined the better cause" (I, i, 75). His freethinking has led Teresa to reject Catholicism: "She hath no faith in Holy Church, 'tis true: / Her lover schooled her in some newer nonsense" (II, i, 35–36). He at times seems to embody all the good that can be won by freeing the intellect from traditional beliefs; he contrasts strongly with figures like Schiller's Franz Moor and Shelley's Count Cenci. However, there are suggestions that his skeptical view of life leads him to distrust the bonds that tie mankind together. He appears a bit too anxious to discover that Teresa has betrayed their love to marry Ordonio, when in fact she has remained true to him. Coleridge traces in Alvar the movement of the isolated intellect from skepticism to faith in love; that is, Alvar follows the path, rejected by Bertram, out of the self through love. Ordonio follows the other path of hateful destruction. Ordonio, plotting to kill his brother, heaps violent act upon violent act until he himself becomes a victim in the final scene. In his last moments of life, he finally acknowledges his misdeeds and asks for forgiveness. His repentance has led some critics to see him as a villain-hero like Bertram, a mixed character. There is, however, a difference. Bertram claims our sympathy while he acts out his evil deeds. Coleridge grants Ordonio sympathy only when he renounces evil. Coleridge was not trying to portray the mixture of good and evil, but rather to depict the growth away from evil to remorse.

By isolating Bertram's roles as noble rebel and vicious criminal in two different characters, Coleridge can develop a moral pattern defined by Alvar in the final speech of the play:

> In these strange dread events
> Just Heaven instructs us with an awful voice,
> That Conscience rules us e'en against our choice.
> Our inward Monitress to guide or warn,
> If listened to; but if repelled with scorn,
> At length as dire Remorse, she reappears,
> Works in our guilty hopes and selfish fears!
> Still bids, Remember! and still cries, Too late!
> And while she scares us, goads us to our fate. (V, i, 286–94)

The inward turn of the self can lead us to act with virtue if we listen to our "inward Monitress," conscience. But if we turn merely to the isolated self's fears and desires, we cut ourselves off from all that is good within us and leave ourselves open to the ravages of remorse. While Coleridge grounds his characterizations in psychological insights, it is clear that he wants these insights to yield moral judgment, not amoral sympathy. Psychology is put into the service of poetic justice.

Maturin seems intent upon dismissing the movement towards remorse that lies at the heart not only of the older poet's play but of the Gothic tradition as a whole; in a sense, this makes *Bertram* a more radically romantic play than *Remorse*. Throughout the final scenes, Bertram refuses to beg mercy from man or God. As if engaged in a debate with Coleridge, Maturin has Bertram proclaim: "Cease, triflers, would you have *me* feel remorse? / Leave me alone—nor cell, nor chain, nor dungeon, / Speaks to the murderer with the voice of solitude" (V, iii). Finally, Bertram commits suicide, crying, "Bertram hath but one fatal foe on earth— / And *he is here*." He stabs himself and then with a burst of wild exultation proclaims, "I died no felon death— / A warrior's weapon freed a warrior's soul" (V, iii). Bertram tries to establish himself as a romantic Othello. In suicide, he struggles to give a final shape to his identity, breaking completely free of the traditional pattern of moral judgment. There is no Alvar to stand over Bertram's body. Maturin gives Bertram the last word. In a sense, he discovers the heroic stature that is the goal of all romantic protagonists. When he has no options left, when he is faced with either capture and compromise or death, he finds the moment in which his defiance can be heroic. That Bertram could discover his heroism only in isolation and revolt and that he could affirm it only through destruction, both of his enemy and of himself—here lies Maturin's tragic conception. To be a hero in his world, Bertram must commit crimes. To win sympathy as a sublime figure, he must violate moral judgment.

Maturin's *Bertram* depicts a world in which, the providential and hierarchical orders having collapsed, man looks within to discover some pattern of meaning to espouse in opposition to his world. Maturin did not succumb to the lure of the monodrama. His play centers upon a single passionate individual, but he portrays not merely Bertram's emotional responses but also his relationships, defined through the dynamics of love and hate. Nor did he merely write another melodrama, for he departed from its moralizing tendency to give the portrait of his protagonist tension if not complexity. Maturin pushed further the process, begun by writers like Lewis and Baillie, of discovering tragedy behind the devices of the monodrama and the melodrama by playing the sympathy generated by an emotionally intriguing character against the type of moral judgment enforced in a melodramatic plot. He thus found a way to stage successfully some of the central themes of romantic tragic drama.

III
BYRON AND TRAGEDY: MYSTERIES AND HISTORIES

THE FACT THAT a play like *Bertram* can loom so large in a discussion of English romantic drama is one indication of the failure of the British romantics to discover a workable dramatic form. Of the major romantic poets, only Coleridge had a stage success, and *Remorse* finally turns away from some of the more radical aspects of the romantic vision. No one accomplished in England what Schiller did in Germany and Hugo in France: the creation of a workable dramatic form that could embody key ideas of the romantic movement and also be susceptible to successful imitation.

Still, there seemed a moment when the romantics might have captured the stage, a moment when Kean's acting was at its height and when a number of verse tragedies—Milman's *Fazio* (Covent Garden, 1818), Sheil's *Evadne* (Covent Garden, 1819), and *Bertram,* amongst others—were successfully staged. And there seemed to be a poet with all of the necessary qualifications: Byron. Always interested in acting and an avid theatergoer, he also gained experience as a "man of the theater" when he served on the Subcommittee of Management for Drury Lane. An active supporter of contemporary dramatists like Coleridge, Maturin, Baillie, Milman, and Sotheby, he was also well versed in the masterpieces of the drama; and unlike many of his contemporaries, he had catholic tastes, grasping the virtues of the neoclassicists as well as the Elizabethans, of Alfieri as well as Goethe. Yet only one of Byron's plays, *Marino Faliero,* was staged during his lifetime and that had only a limited success; his plays became popular only after his death and then in an altered form.[34] We will never know what Byron might have accomplished had he been given encouragement by the London audiences. What we do know is that he wrote a series of intriguing plays.

Byron did seek to adapt popular stage forms. In *Manfred*—a play which comes close to being a monodrama by delineating the inner development of Manfred, the other characters serving mainly as sounding-boards to his self-analysis—Byron follows Baillie, Coleridge, and others to find tragedy in the inner struggles of his hero. The melodramatic *Werner*—replete with a gloomy castle, storms, a mysterious murder, and a robber band—moves from the Gothic towards the tragic when it shifts its interest from the struggle between the evil Strahlheim and the essentially good Werner to the story of Werner's son, who has all the attributes of a hero but finds himself, like Karl Moor, in an age no longer open to heroic exploits. Having murdered Strahlheim to protect his father, he has become the leader of a band of noble robbers who have in peace no outlet for their energies. Engaging our sympathy for his powerful personality even as we reject his actions, he argues that the murder and the energy it expressed have moved him beyond ordinary morality, a position he takes as he answers his father's recriminations:

> If *you* condemn me, yet
> Remember *who* hath taught me once too often
> To listen to him! *Who* proclaim'd to me
> That *there were crimes* made venial by the occasion?
> That passion was our nature? . . . .
> . . . .
>
> Is it strange
> That I should *act* what you could *think*? We have done
> With right and wrong: and now must only ponder
> Upon effects, not causes. (V, i, 439–43, 452–55)[35]

He strides off at the end, leaving his love dead and his parents aghast and denouncing morality as "half-humanity, / Selfish remorse" (V, ii, 36–37). By grounding the vaguely medieval settings of the Gothic drama in the historical realities of the Thirty Years' War, Byron hopes to discover the tragedy of historical revolt outlined earlier by Schiller. In turning the hero of the first part of the play into the villain of the second, he explores further the tensions surrounding the Gothic villain-hero. Most interestingly, he creates a hero who, like Bertram, rejects remorse as a check upon his energy. While *Werner* is marred by a number of faults, it does suggest Byron's involvement in the attempt, like that of Lewis or Maturin, to convert the Gothic to the tragic.

Byron's plays also engage a wide variety of traditional dramatic types, from the medieval mystery play to the neoclassical palace tragedy. It has become conventional to divide this diverse collection of dramatic experiments into two major groups: the "history" plays (*Marino Faliero, The Two Foscari,* and *Sardanapalus)* and the "metaphysical" or "mystery" plays (*Manfred, Cain, Heaven and Earth, The Deformed Transformed*). This division provides an important insight into Byron's plays. We have noted that romantic tragic drama confronts man's fall from a traditional providential and hierarchical order. The importance of the Fall to Byron's work has long been noted.[36] I would suggest that in his "mysteries" Byron sought tragedy in the fall from a providential order and in his "histories" he explored the tragic collapse of a hierarchical social order.

Byron's two completed "metaphysical" plays, *Manfred* and *Cain,* have each as protagonist a man struggling to find order and meaning without divine guidance. The loss of providential order is portrayed boldly in *Cain,* a revisionary Biblical drama that prompted, among other replies, a pious play on the same subject.[37] Set in the "Land without Paradise," soon after the Fall, *Cain* explores the loss not only of Paradise, but also of an immediate relationship with the divine. Cain longs for God, but he never meets the absconded Jehovah whose rule appears to him as oppression. Rather, Cain meets with demonic negation in the figure of Lucifer. Like Cain, Manfred quests for the divine and with as little success. We meet Manfred near the end of his search. His opening monologue, like that of Faust, reveals that his pursuit of some final knowledge of the world has not opened up for him some harmonious vision. Rather, he finds, "The Tree of Knowledge is not that of Life" (I, i, 12). "Sorrow is Knowledge" (I, i, 10), for it does not reveal an ordered world, organized into an intelligible hierarchy with the angels above and the beasts below. Life presents itself as a battle between conflicting forces, and man is the battleground, torn between his higher and lower natures: "Half dust, half deity, alike unfit / To sink or soar, with our mix'd essence make/ A conflict of elements" (I, ii, 40–42). Manfred continues throughout the play to solicit supernatural guidance in the hopes of resolving the conflict within man, but he uncovers no higher order. Like Cain, he meets not a divine being who would fulfill man, but demonic creatures who would reduce him. He finds that his true role is to struggle to preserve the fullness and complexity of his divided humanity, a humanity which Byron defines in *Cain* as "fiery dust."[38]

Byron's characters, making the inward turn common to so many romantic protagonists, explore a rich humanity that refuses to be reduced to either the moral equations of *Remorse* or the mere egotism of Bertram. The inward quest is extremely clear in the monodramatic *Manfred.* Having turned from man in an unsuccessful quest for the divine, Manfred now journeys into himself: ". . . . in my heart / There is a vigil, and these eyes but close / To look within" (I, i, 5–7).

Manfred, however, is scarcely happy in the isolation of his selfhood. His quest for the divine was in itself a pursuit of an ultimate Other that would solace him. He also sought a human counterpart, a Shelleyan "epipsyche." In the tale he tells to the Witch of the Alps, Manfred reveals that he has in the past destroyed Astarte, a woman whom he loved and who was like an echo of his own selfhood (II, ii, 49–149). Byron uses the motif of the double to define the need of the isolated self for another in whom he is reflected and by whose love his identity is ratified. But by linking the image of the double to the theme of incest, Byron makes criminal and destructive this desire for an epipsyche. In *Manfred,* the love that in plays like *Hernani* and even *Bertram* offers to liberate and to fulfill the isolated self appears instead unnatural. Manfred is trapped in his solitude and thus longs for "Oblivion, self-oblivion!" (I, i, 144). But he refuses to flee from the burden of his self-consciousness into the arms of the various supernatural forces he meets that ask for man's subjugation. Like Bertram, but in a far more subtle and complex way, Manfred rejects various limiting ties to something outside himself and thus moves towards the affirmation of his pure selfhood.

Cain also espouses the isolated self, but the alternatives presented to him are perhaps even clearer. He rejects his parents' traditional theology of fear that affirms that the world must be good since God made it, because he cannot believe that a world defined by the Fall is justly ordered: "He is all-powerful, must all-good, too, follow?" (I, i, 77). He rebels against his parents' basic tenet, "Content thee with what *is*" (I, i, 45), and thus would seem to be a ready recruit for Lucifer, the archetypal rebel.

Lucifer argues that there are two paths open to man in the world of the Fall: "Choose betwixt love and knowledge—since there is / No other choice: your sire hath chosen already: His worship is but fear" (I, i, 426–28). In the contrast between the loving seraphim and the knowing cherubim (I, i, 418–19), Byron defines the options available to Cain and to his fellows like Bertram. Adah urges Cain to embrace love. She understands that Cain's discontent arises from the loss of the simple, yet harmonious and meaningful life of Paradise. She has seen him turn away from her in the pursuit of knowledge that he hopes will lead him back to such a life. She has tried to believe that his quest "Would have composed thy mind into the calm / Of a contented Knowledge" (III, i, 49–50); but she realizes that his quest, like Manfred's, has only made Cain more distracted and alienated. She argues that it is love that can restore all that was lost in the Fall:

> Why wilt thou always mourn for Paradise?
> Can we not make another?....
>   Here, or
> Where'er thou wilt: where're thou art, I feel not
> The want of this so much regretted Eden. (III, i. 37–40)

Adah feels certain that love can bind each man to another, freeing all from entrapment in the self and creating Paradise on earth. She finds the fulfillment of Eden in her love for Cain and urges him to realize that her love for him fulfills him: "Love us, then, my Cain! / And love thyself for our sakes, for we love thee" (III, i, 147–48).

While Cain is not barred from the solution of love like Manfred,[39] he does not adopt it. He cannot abjure the path of knowledge. At first, Adah sounds like Goethe's Iphigenia, arguing for a human community in a humanized world. But Adah dreams of a return to Paradise, not a struggle to build within the confines of the world a humanistic utopia. To Cain, Adah's vision of love can only appear as a desire for a Beulah-land of innocence in which man would hide from the truths of the world of fallen experience. It is Lucifer who most completely endorses the alternative quest for knowledge. He sees himself as the principle of intellectual spirit in revolt against Jehovah's material creation. Where Adah would turn away from the self's knowledge, Lucifer attempts to extend it. Where Adah seeks the unity of love, Lucifer envisions a vast and alien cosmos torn by a war between two opposing forces. The isolation of the self and the divisiveness of the analytic intellect are to him tools in his war against an oppressive God.

Lucifer clarifies the link between the turn to the self and the need for violence. Having cut himself off from all others, he can define himself only through opposition. His identity lies in the battle he wages against Jehovah. His Manichean vision of cosmic war elevates his selfhood by pitting it against the ultimate Other. In his final speech, he urges Cain to embrace the isolation of the self and to create a private universe of the mind opposed to God's creation:

> Think and endure,—and form an inner world
> In your own bosom—where the outward fails;
> So shall you nearer be the spiritual
> Nature, and war triumphant with your own. (II, ii, 463–66)

"Form an inner world. . . . where the outward fails"—this is the task and the temptation of the romantic protagonist. Byron ascertains the loss involved in the inward turn merely asserted by writers like Maturin. Cain realizes that Lucifer's extreme self-glorification is as reductive of man's complex humanity as is his parents' abnegation before Jehovah. Lucifer embodies key romantic problems, but he does not discover the solution found by, for example, Shelley's Prometheus. Lucifer would not free man from a limited and divisive selfhood, but lure him into a heightened awareness of his isolation.[40] Lucifer's rejection of the material world is not so much a heroic proclamation of the powers of reason, as it is a self-condemnation to eternal alienation. The fact that Lucifer, as one of the knowing cherubim, cannot love reveals him as a being wholly locked within the self. The other can never be a subject bound to him in love, but only an object he opposes in the violent attempt to assert his selfhood.

While Cain is attracted to Lucifer's doctrine of the self and to Adah's faith in love, he realizes that they both would force him to reject one side of his nature. The cherubim and the seraphim may be able to divide knowledge and love between them, but Cain must embrace the contradiction that is man's lot as both spirit and clay. Yet Cain is clearly torn by the unbearable tension of this division. He makes a final attempt to discover a resolution and in doing so meets his tragic fate.

Just as Manfred challenges the realm of the supernatural to reveal to him some solution to his quest, so Cain demands that God unveil his order to man. When Cain accompanies Abel to perform a sacrifice to Jehovah, he calls upon God to demonstrate his sovereignty. His prayer (III, i, 245–79) pleads for an epiphany, a manifestation of God's order on earth. God's apparent response in the form of a whirlwind does not, however, settle Cain's doubts. While Abel regards the destruction of Cain's sacrificial altar as a mark of divine displeasure, Cain feels the scattering of the fruit to be appropriate to his sacrifice. God has not revealed himself. There is merely an event open to human interpretation, an event like the storm in *Bertram* or the oracle in Goethe's *Iphigenia*. Cain thus moves to provoke Jehovah further, destroying the second altar himself. He would incur God's wrath and his own death if these would reveal to him a divine presence in the world.

Yet it is Abel who dies, and at Cain's hands. While Cain sought to affirm life in striking Abel when he claims to love God more than life, Cain instead brings death into the world. He longed to create a Paradise and has instead brought about a "second fall" through murder.[41] He is now condemned to the isolation from which he has struggled to escape. He is branded as an outcast and must bear the burden of his separateness and of his crime without hope or solace. Ironically, he finally achieves a fixed identity and discovers an order for his world, but it is the negative identity of the first murderer and the diminished order of an oppressive God. Unable to maintain the essential human tensions within himself, Cain finds that the only resolution of them is a tragic reduction of man's life.

For Byron, man is always divided against himself; to deny this division is to reduce man and embrace some form of "cant," some limited vision of human life. Cain succumbs to the temptation to attempt to heal this division and ushers in a fallen history, described in the play by Lucifer (II, ii, 219–28, 327–37), that will be dominated by the cant of an oppressive theology. Manfred lives at the other end of that history, and yet he still affirms the power, independence, and complexity of man. He will not subordinate himself to any of the supernatural powers he encounters, and in the final act he rejects the Christianity of the Abbot as well. Just as Bertram refused to stoop to remorse, so Manfred rejects any attempt to impose a moral reading on his life: "The *mind* which is immortal makes itself / Requital for its good or evil thoughts, / Is its own origin of ill and end" (III, iv, 129–31). He turns back the demons who have come to drag him off to hell, claiming a human and natural death, not one ruled by supernatural powers that would limit man:

> I have not been thy dupe, nor am thy prey—
> But was my own destroyer, and will be
> My own hereafter.—Back, ye baffled fiends!—
> The hand of death is on me— but not yours! (III, iv, 138–41)

Having freed himself from the demons' grip and thus from the control of any superhuman force, he now asks for the human hand of the Abbot, proclaiming, "Old man! 'tis not so difficult to die" (III, iv, 151). Manfred dies a martyr to man's independence and self-sufficiency. Unlike the heroes of visionary romance, he does not break out of his limited world to resolve the contradictions that confront him. Yet, unlike Cain, neither does he seek a final, reductive resolution of these conflicts. Rather he heroically affirms his humanity in all of its confused complexity.

Byron uses an open, experimental form in his "metaphysical" plays, capable of moving the action from Manfred's Gothic chamber to the Alps or from "The Land without Paradise" to "The Abyss of Space." This sweep is wholly appropriate to these dramas, in which Byron wishes to examine the loss of a providential order for human life. He adopts the quite different form of neoclassicism and the unities in his "history" plays, where he investigates the collapse of a hierarchical order within society.

While the very titles of *Cain* and *Manfred* suggest their focus upon the isolated individual, *Marino Faliero, Doge of Venice* dramatizes the conflicts that arise between private identity and social role. Byron's play does not merely rehearse some abstract and tired tension between personal passions and public duties; rather, it suggests the way in which social changes impinge upon and sometimes destroy individuals. Unlike Manfred or Cain, Marino Faliero has established himself as a traditional hero, for he has risen to the summit of his society, proving himself in battle and as a servant of the state. Where Manfred and Cain turn inward, the doge has always proved himself in action. And, unlike them, he identifies himself with his objective role in society, with his honor. Venetian society has offered him a framework within which to construct a heroic identity.

However, when Byron's play begins, the doge's heroic days already lie in the past. His society is changing. Byron offers in this play, as Goethe did in *Egmont* and Schiller did in so many plays, a dynamic historical society, not the fixed and immutable society associated with the neoclassical form he adopts. The traditional hero can base his identity on external, social actions because his society is stable. The doge has tried to fix his heroic identity in his commitment to Venice, but his Venice is changeable. We discover in the first scene of the play that Venice does not really possess the hierarchical order that supported the traditional monarch and hero. The doge, "Prince of the Republic," is a constitutional ruler whose position at the apex of his society does not carry with it commensurate power. Faliero has taken office only to find himself in the control of a party of selfish aristocrats. He realizes that in fact the "hundred-handed senate rules, / Making the people nothing, and the prince / A pageant" (I, ii, 269–71). He has climbed to the top of his city's government only to find that the social ladder has been pulled out from under him.

Two incidents demonstrate the power of the aristocratic party: first, the honor of the doge's wife has been sullied by a young nobleman, but the aristocratic tribunal of the Forty grants the culprit the lightest of sentences; second, a commoner, Israel Bertuccio, has been assaulted by a noble, but the plebian cannot win redress from the patrician. This society does not possess a functioning hierarchy in which every man has a place and a purpose. The aristocrats have usurped the power of the doge and the freedom of the people.

The doge realizes that the disruption and corruption of the social order have robbed him of his identity: "Our private wrongs have sprung from public vices" (III, ii, 154). He thus turns to the people and allies himself to a revolt against the aristocratic government. Like Schiller's protagonists or Musset's Lorenzo, the doge hopes that a popular revolution will reestablish his city as a free society capable of supporting his heroic honor; his goal is to "free Venice, and avenge my wrongs" (I, ii, 316). Finding Venice in the control of "this monster of a state, / This mockery of a government, this spectre" (III, ii, 165-66), he and his fellow rebels plot to kill the aristocrats in order to recreate Venice as an ideal constitutional monarchy:

> We will renew the times of truth and justice,
> Condensing in a fair free commonwealth
> Not rash equality but equal rights,
> Proportion'd like the columns to the temple,
> Giving and taking strength reciprocal,
> And making firm the whole with grace and beauty,
> So that no part could be removed without
> Infringement of the general symmetry. (III, ii, 168–75)

The turn to violent revolt in the pursuit of an ideal is beset with particular contradictions for Byron's doge. Faliero is willing to exterminate the entire aristocratic party to recreate Venice as the ideal state that, in granting him fame, gave an objective basis to his identity. However, the identity he fights to protect is bound up with the very nobles he must kill. He is, after all, an aristocrat himself; the men to be killed have been his friends. They have debased him by placing him in a symbolic position without real power; but the doge realizes that the destruction of the aristocracy will destroy a part of himself: "Each stab to them will seem my suicide" (III, ii, 472). If he does not act, he loses his honor, his identity; if he does act, he destroys a part of that identity—a contradiction that wrests from him a continuing lament over his involvement in the revolt: the rebellion seems to "quench a glorious life" and to force him to "dwindle to the thing I now must be" (III, i, 106–7).

The revolt itself is caught in a further contradiction. As in Blake's "Orc cycle," the rebels come to resemble the aristocrats they hate. The aristocracy has created a state that practices violence upon its people and allows the powerful to delight in corruption. The rebels are clearly correct in their desire to overthrow such a government, but the means they adopt involve them in the very evils they would correct. They find that the nobles have become "mere machines," operating a government that has become abstract, alienating, and inhumane. But the revolt also demands allegiance to an abstract ideal and the severing of human ties:

> Such ties are not
> For those who are call'd to the high destinies
> Which purify corrupted commonwealths;
> We must forget all feelings save *one,*
> We must resign all passions save our purpose. . . . (II, ii, 84–88)

The oppressive aristocrat meets his double in the fanatic rebel.

The rebellion founders on this contradiction, for one of the rebels refuses to betray his personal ties: he warns a noble friend of the coming uprising, enabling the aristocracy to crush the revolt. The plebian leaders are put to death, as is the doge. But not before he prophesies the total destruction of Venice. The play seems to suggest that there is no way to heal the wound society suffered when it lost its organic, hierarchical unity. Once that order is disturbed by self-interest and violence, these become the only means for social change. Man becomes trapped in a class war without resolution, a repeated cycle of oppression and violent revolt ending only with total destruction. Byron, the aristocrat with liberal leanings, is finally unwilling to believe that any class can save society. There is only the individual, bearing testimony to a humane vision of society. Thus, in a sense, Marino Faliero finally joins Manfred; for like Byron's Gothic hero, the doge affirms values that cannot be realized in this world. He can only preserve his vision of the ideal and confront honestly life's divisiveness and violence. As Manfred is a martyr to a vision of a humanized world, so—even as he foresees that the future will bring only destruction—the doge dies for a humane society.

The pursuit of an ideal state is also central to Byron's *Sardanapalus.* The strictly formal structure of that play mirrors the rigid Assyrian society that refuses to be liberated by its ruler's humanizing vision. Abjuring the violence that has been the hallmark of Assyrian rule, Sardanapalus has sought to inaugurate an era of peace and love: "I thought to have made my realm a paradise, / And every moon an epoch of new pleasures" (IV, i, 517–18). Where Manfred destroys his love, where Cain finds love a limiting expression of his complex identity, and where Marino Faliero has his love tainted by a corrupt society, Sardanapalus renounces hate to remake his world through love. He gives full voice to a Byronic view of the ideal society based upon an aristocratic self-confidence and delight in pleasure yet free from the oppressive rule of both Faliero's Venice and Byron's England. But Sardanapalus finally dies for a vision that seems to have little hope of ever becoming a reality. He finds that he, too, must turn to violence to defend his vision of peace. Bothered by this contradiction, he is happier when he realizes that his is a lost cause. He ceases the slaughter of his enemies and instead decides to immolate himself to provide the future with a martyr of love. He finally breaks free from the constraints of his world as the play shatters its neoclassical fetters in a grand romantic finale that inspired Delacroix's painting. While his death thus offers "a light / To lesson ages" (V, i, 440–41), Byron's play provides little hope that man will heed its teachings.

Byron's fear and hatred of "cant" prevent him from endorsing any final plan for society or the interests of any class. He may envision an ideal society, but he is unhappy with all of the means available to realize that vision. This unwillingness to endorse any group within society, rather typical of the nineteenth-century English intellectual,[42] lies at the heart of the tragic world of Byron's political plays. Since no achievable plan for society can finally be correct, there can be no movement towards its true regeneration. The only potentially heroic political stance man can adopt is that of the martyr who allows himself to be destroyed even as he pays homage to an impossible ideal of peace and love.

The political plays embody, I believe, a tragic version of the Byronic "mobility" that Bloom finds central to the achievement of *Don Juan*. Bloom suggests that in his satiric epic, Byron's narrator balances the contraries that plague Manfred and Cain, for his mobility enables him to endorse now one principle, now another, both with equal sincerity and neither with finality. However, this mobility, which Bloom sees as "Byron's social version of the Romantic 'Imagination,'"[43] can work only for the spectator. It can be the stance of *Don Juan*'s sophisticated narrator. But in the drama, man must act; he must commit himself. And as soon as he acts, he limits his mobility. Cain, striving to be true to his dual nature, finally acts and brings about destruction and a reduction of man. Marino Faliero tries to reform society, but action involves him in the very processes he rejects. Even Sardanapalus finds that he must use violence to defend his vision of peace. Given the idea of mobility and its impossibility for the dramatic character, death and in particular suicide become the only ways for the protagonist to assert a vision that avoids "cant," the opposite of mobility. Byron's plays reveal the tragedies of the life of action, the tragedies of a life lived without clear divine guidance, where man's ideals are not only his sole hope but also his downfall; for in a relativistic, mobile world, any ideal can become cant, any commitment can become fanaticism, any man can descend from idealism to murder.

Byron's dramatic achievement is considerable. We can perhaps best gauge that accomplishment by remembering that the new type of hero sought by the Gothic playwrights and Joanna Baillie, by Maturin as well as Wordsworth, came to be known as the Byronic hero. Byron provided his age with a portrait of man trapped in a world of uncertainty and division but still able to make a heroic stand, of man lost in a world without systems of order but still able to assert his own essential worth and strength. The story of English romantic drama is to a large extent that of the search for such a heroic figure and for a theater in which to present him. Perfecting that hero's portrait, Byron did not, of course, create a central dramatic form for the English stage. Perhaps the corruption of the patent theaters in England doomed any attempt to spark a romantic revival. Perhaps the English romantics were too distant from their people and their country. There was no Paris or Weimar for the English romantics, but rather seclusion in the country or exile. Whatever the reason for Byron's failure to reform the stage, there can be no doubt that he left a dramatic corpus of a worth we have yet to recognize. Only one other English play of the period rises to the level of Byron's work: Shelley's *The Cenci*.

CHAPTER SIX
SHELLEY'S *THE CENCI*: THE TRAGEDY OF "SELF-ANATOMY"

Of all the plays written by the English romantics, Shelley's *The Cenci* remains the most impressive. *The Cenci* is today the sole English drama of the early nineteenth century to command anything like universal critical respect. It had already received some recognition, and notoriety, during Shelley's lifetime. While its treatment of incest kept *The Cenci* from being performed, it sold quite well, and was the only one of Shelley's works to achieve a second authorized printing before his death. To such readers as Byron, Hunt, Beddoes, and perhaps even Wordsworth, *The Cenci* appeared to be the finest dramatic work of the age.[1] *The Cenci* continued to acquire admirers until it became a commonplace of Victorian Shelley criticism to compare the piece to Shakespeare's greatest plays; this enthusiasm finally brought about a private performance of the drama by the Shelley Society in 1886. *The Cenci* continues to be performed today and has come to be surrounded by a large body of distinguished criticism.[2]

Still, there has been some hesitation among both admirers and detractors of Shelley to view *The Cenci* as a success for romantic drama as a whole. Those who remain skeptical of *The Cenci*'s quality as a tragic drama usually agree with Allardyce Nicoll in regarding Shelley as "entirely a closet playwright, temperamentally unsuited to be a dramatist and ignorant of contemporary theatrical practice." Nicoll argues that Shelley, alienated from the stage, became "so occupied with the Elizabethan theatre that he echoes and reechoes mechanically the phraseology and the situations of Shakespearian days." Nicoll claims that *The Cenci* can be appreciated only by "Shelley enthusiasts"; and even such enthusiasts tend to treat the play apart from the drama of its day, as a lone masterpiece that portrays ideas peculiar to Shelley in the guise of an Elizabethan imitation.[3]

Such objections are not convincing. We may feel that Shelley had a lyric temperament, but in writing key works he returned time and again to dramatic forms. In fact, apart from Byron, Shelley evidences the broadest interest in working with the drama of all the English romantics. The range of dramatic types with which he experimented is almost as great as Byron's. In *Prometheus Unbound*, he reworked Greek tragedy to create a masterpiece of the romantic lyrical and metaphysical drama. While *Prometheus* departs formally from its Greek prototype, Shelley returned in *Hellas* to a classical model to write a play that observes the unities and uses the traditional device of a series of messengers to report what is occurring offstage. Shelley also worked on a Shakespearean drama entitled *Charles I*, contemplated a tragedy about Tasso, and left fragments of a dramatic romance. His experimentation extended even to the burlesque (*Oedipus Tyrannus or Swellfoot the Tyrant*) and the masque (*The Mask of Anarchy*). He also worked on translations of Euripides, Calderón, and Goethe.

It is usually assumed that Shelley's apparent aversion to attending London's theaters left him ignorant of the contemporary drama.[4] While his knowledge of the popular theater was limited, Shelley was well aware of the situation of the literary drama. His analysis of the place of drama in culture, set forth in his *Defence of Poetry*, enabled him to understand what the romantic drama had lost in relation to that of the Greeks and the Elizabethans. He noted the collapse of neoclassical tragedy, which left its adherents writing imitations of imitations; and he lamented the rise of the popular melodrama, which pleased ever-increasing crowds with moralizing tales of trivial domestic woes.[5] Shelley was also aware of the spate of poetic dramas that appeared after the success of *Remorse* and included plays such as *Fazio* and *Bertram*, discussed in the last chapter. His letters place *The Cenci* within the context of these romantic tragic dramas. Contemplating a tragedy about Tasso, Shelley wrote to Peacock that it would have "better morality than Fazio & better poetry than Bertram"; a year later, at work on *The Cenci*, he again wrote to Peacock, claiming that his new play was "certainly not inferior to any of the modern plays that have been acted, with the exception of *Remorse*...."[6]

Shelley had even witnessed one of these triumphs of the poetic drama, Milman's *Fazio*, at Covent Garden in 1818. Shelley enjoyed the production, being particularly impressed with Eliza O'Neill as Bianca; both Mary Shelley and Peacock tell us that Miss O'Neill was "always in his thoughts" when Shelley wrote the part of Beatrice Cenci. In seeking to arrange for the production of his play, Shelley sought not only to have her play Beatrice, but also to have Kean take the part of Count Cenci.[7] *The Cenci* hardly reveals its author's ignorance of the theatrical conditions of his day; rather it was written for the London stage and its leading performers. Composed as Shelley's contribution to the attempted revival of the English stage, *The Cenci* was, he felt, "singularly fitted for the stage."[8]

We will never know whether or not Shelley's play was "fitted for the stage" of the early nineteenth century, since it did not, in any event, fit the period's idea of morality in the theater. What is certain is that Shelley's play tackles the same set of issues that we have discovered in works like *Bertram* and *Remorse*. For *The Cenci* offers the period's most complex dramatization of the romantic protagonist's turn to the interior in the wake of the collapse of social and cosmic order. As we examine Shelley's use in *The Cenci* of his own ideas and ideals, his echoes of Shakespeare, and his adaptations of contemporary theatrical devices, we will discover that they are all subordinated to his attempt to clarify the tragedy of man's turn to the self when faced with the loss of the divine.

I
CULTURE AND ANARCHY: SOCIETY AND "THE PRINCIPLE OF SELF"

IT MAY SEEM odd to assert that *The Cenci* confronts the loss of a traditional cultural order, for Shelley's play takes place within the rigid and devoutly Catholic society of Renaissance Italy. How can a play that insists upon the power of a dominating father, a restrictive social and legal system, and a dogmatic religion fit within my model for romantic drama? The answer lies in a key Shelleyan idea: any oppressive institution, in that it is oppressive, cannot be an instrument of order, but is rather a destructive force. Within *The Cenci*, the family, the social hierarchy, and religion do not organize life meaningfully, but rather shackle it. Where many romantic dramas depict a world bereft of traditional order, Shelley's drama reveals the bankruptcy of that order when it stood in all of its oppressive strength.

Shelley's *The Mask of Anarchy*, composed in response to the "Peterloo" massacre at about the same time he was at work on *The Cenci*, can clarify this point.[9] Shelley envisions a procession of figures representing various powerful individuals and institutions in English society. He depicts them as forces of oppression responsible for the slaughter at St. Peter's Field. At the end of the procession, rides their leader:

> Last came Anarchy: he rode
> On a white horse, splashed with blood;

He was pale even to the lips,
Like Death in the Apocalypse.

And he wore a kingly crown;
And in his grasp a sceptre shone;
On his brow this mark I saw—
"I AM GOD, AND KING, AND LAW!" (30–37)[10]

Shelley argues that the law, the state, and religion—for all their system and structure—really serve anarchy, for they destroy human life.[11] In *The Cenci*, all figures—father, lord, Pope, and God—who appear as "monarchs" in some realm prove themselves to be "anarchs" in their oppressive misrule.

Shelley's dismissal of such seemingly objective institutions does not mean that his play celebrates the subjective individual. *Bertram* may extol the solitary egoist, but the plays of the major romantics suggest the dangers of the isolated and independent self. *Cain*, for example, rejects the destructive solipsism of Lucifer. *Remorse* insists that the villainous protagonist be understood within a moral framework. *The Cenci* evinces Shelley's awareness of the destructive potential of the alienated self: the oppressive forces of anarchy are projections of that selfhood.

At one point in *The Defence of Poetry*, Shelley somewhat gnomically proclaims that "poetry and the principle of self, of which money is the visible incarnation, are the God and Mammon of the world."[12] Shelley suggests that an objective social institution—here, money—manifests the "principle of self." Shelley is not drawing only upon conventional associations between greed or selfishness and money. This "principle of self" is opposed to poetry and thus to the visionary imagination. Where visionary poetry reveals a life of liberation and love, the principle of self creates institutions, like money, that objectify the self's struggle with the other and thus enslave man to a life of oppression. Money, not unlike Pound's "usura," becomes an emblem of man's perversion of life through his creation of a false order and a corrupted language.[13] Man must choose between Mammon and God—between the oppressive institutions, the hypocritical language, and the violence of the self's attempt to obliterate the other, and the liberation, the poetry, and the communion of the visionary imagination.[14]

The involvement of the Cenci family with a destructive mode of selfhood is revealed in the second act of Shelley's play by Orsino, a priest who would be Beatrice's lover:

... 'tis a trick of this same family
To analyse their own and other minds.

> Such self-anatomy shall teach the will
> Dangerous secrets: for it tempts our powers,
> Knowing what must be thought, and may be done,
> Into the depth of darkest purposes.... (II, ii, 108–13)

Typifying the misreadings of this passage and of the play as a whole, Carlos Baker suggests that Shelley here provides himself with an excuse to indulge in characterization through soliloquy because he could not truly dramatize his creations.[15] In fact, "self-anatomy" is not merely an aspect of Shelley's dramaturgy, but the quality in relation to which all of the characters of the play are defined. We have noted the importance of the protagonist's inward turn in plays like *Bertram, Remorse*, and *Manfred*. *The Cenci* explores further the temptations of the interior life that can lure one into a distorted, destructive, and even demonic relationship with others. Although man has already eaten of the apple of self-knowledge, each figure in *The Cenci* is tempted to take another bite, to analyze the self further. This preoccupation with the self threatens to destroy the bonds that tie the individual to the external world, leaving him isolated. When this inward turn occurs under the aegis of the dissecting intellect, the individual's isolation from the bonds of love and communion becomes all the more certain—as we have already seen in the case of Byron's Lucifer.

Shelley's Orsino suggests a danger beyond isolation in the analytic self. As the analyzing mind divorces the individual from external bonds, it removes all checks upon his behavior. Whereas the individual who defines himself through a social role or through any other mode of relation with the external world must accommodate his identity to the external world, the isolated individual begins to explore more and more of his interior desires and is tempted to act upon them. Orsino argues that the analytic intellect finds itself attracted to the "dangerous secrets" that lie within the self and "teaches" the will to act in an attempt to fulfill them. He suggests that an alliance exists between analysis and destructive desire, between the mind in isolation and the self's dream of bending the world to its every whim, no matter how perverse. Self-anatomy frees the mind from external limits, but at the same time binds the will to the self's basest drives—"the depth of darkest purposes." Musset's Lorenzaccio, who claims that "I would corrupt my mother if it occurred to my brain to do so," recognizes the connections between the analytic intellect and uncontrolled desire, as does Goethe in *Faust*, which tells in part the story of an alienated intellectual who craves sensual pleasure. The mind that murders to dissect and the cravings that drive one to "reel. . .from desire to fulfillment, / And in fulfillment languish for desire"—these are the demonic counterparts of imagination and love.[16]

Their world shares with the Cenci this commitment to the principle of self, as we might expect from Shelley's link between social institutions and the self. The Italian Renaissance setting of the play provided Shelley with the theatrical opportunity to portray social institutions at their most oppressive. Settings such as the Cenci palace, the castle of Petralla, and the prisons of Rome stand as emblems of the power of oppressive social structures—much like the castles and dungeons of the Gothic drama; moreover, their claustrophobic atmosphere suggests man's isolation from meaningful contact with others. Man is trapped within his skull, just as he encloses others within prison walls.

In drawing his portrait of oppression, Shelley could depend on the evil reputation of Renaissance Italy that had long been a tradition within the English drama. But his treatment of religion goes beyond convention, for Catholicism comes to exemplify this world's commitment to the self. In the preface to the play, Shelley stresses the Catholicism of his characters:

They are represented as Catholics, and as Catholics deeply tinged with religion. To a Protestant apprehension there will appear something unnatural in the earnest and perpetual sentiment of the relations between God and man which pervade the tragedy of the Cenci. It will especially be startled at the combination of an undoubting persuasion of the truth of the popular religion with a cool and determined perseverance in enormous guilt. . . .Religion. . .is interwoven with the whole fabric of life. It is adoration, faith, submission, penitence, blind admiration; not a rule for moral conduct. It has no necessary connection with any one virtue. The most atrocious villain may be rigidly devout, and without any shock to established faith, confess himself to be so. Religion pervades intensely the whole frame of society, and is according to the temper of the mind which it inhabits, a passion, a persuasion, an excuse, a refuge; never a check. ("Preface," p. 277)

Far from providing a moral code or a framework of providential order, Catholicism can be used by the individual "according to the temper of the mind" to defend any act, no matter how horrible. A mode of rhetoric that enables the self to view its "darkest purposes" as aspects of God's plan, religion is used to transform and thus to disguise the "sad reality" ("Dedication," p. 275) revealed in Beatrice's lament, "what a world we make, / The oppressor and the oppressed" (V, iii, 74–75). Catholicism is treated not only as a mode of "false consciousness," but also as a perverted form of speech, opposed to true imaginative vision.

This religion poses an especial danger for the nominally innocent characters. Lucretia, Cenci's second wife, is a "good" person; but she is also wholly ineffectual, for her belief in a beneficent providence enables her to avoid the realities of a world ruled by the powerful selfhood of her husband. Catholicism becomes for her an "excuse" not to oppose her husband. Cardinal Camillo relies upon religion as a "refuge" from the terrors of his world. When Cenci reveals to him the horrors he has perpetrated, Camillo's simplistic faith protects him from the truth:

> Hell's most abandoned fiend
> Did never, in the drunkenness of guilt,
> Speak to his heart as now you speak to me;
> I thank my God that I believe you not. (I, i, 117–20)

Religion serves an oppressor like Cenci who can bend it to his "passion," for it masks the brutality of his deeds and persuades the oppressed to accept their lot.

Life in this world is a struggle for domination, a struggle in which those who have tapped the power of the unrestrained self have a decided advantage. However corrupt self-anatomy may be, it rewards its practitioner with power over the institutions of oppression that are manifestations of the principle of self. The power structure of the play, which rests upon the paternal triumvirate of God, Pope, and Cenci as father and lord, is an externalization of the struggle between self and other.

Count Francesco Cenci, parent, nobleman, and friend to the Pope, stands at the center of these oppressive institutions. He uses his position as father to torture his children. As a lord, he often seems to stand beyond the law. And when his sordid acts do become known, he merely buys absolution from the Pope.[17] His power arises from his long delving into the depths of the self. He has sought to explore fully man's interior life and has been lured to its forbidden corners:

> All men delight in sensual luxury,
> All men enjoy revenge, and most exult
> Over the tortures they can never feel—
> Flattering their secret peace with others' pain.
> But I delight in nothing else. I love
> The sight of agony, and the sense of joy,
> When this shall be another's, and that mine.
> And I have no remorse and little fear,
> Which are, I think, the checks of other men.
> This mood has grown upon me, until now
> Any design my captious fancy makes
> The picture of its wish, and it forms none
> But such as men like you would start to know,
> Is as my natural food and rest debarred
> Until it be accomplished. (I, i, 77–91)

Shelley sums up here the destructive nature of the inward turn that we have found in Maturin's Bertram, Coleridge's Ordonio, Byron's Lucifer, and Goethe's Mephisto; it can be found in Musset's Lorenzaccio as well. Free from remorse (like Bertram or Manfred) and fully in the grips of his family's "trick," Cenci finds he must act upon any desire his "captious fancy" uncovers. There is a strong intellectual component in his depravity, for "Invention palls" and the anatomizing intellect must discover new acts "Whose horror might make sharp an appetite / Duller than mine" (I, i, 99, 101–2). Cenci's speech evidences his total immersion in the battle of self and other. The very rhythm of a statement like, "I love / The sight of agony, and the sense of joy, / When this shall be another's, and that mine," follows his mind as it divides the world between the joys of his self and the pain it inflicts on others.

While lust, the only form of love open to Cenci, satisfied him as a youth, he has delighted most in dominating others. Just as Bertram moved from love to hate in his pursuit of self-affirmation, so Cenci moves from lust to torture. In torturing another and in finally destroying him, the Count finds the means of proving his self's power. Shelley masterfully points out that the real goal of such a sadist is to ensure himself through the pain of others that he lives fully and contentedly. He is the Marquis de Sade proving himself through Hegel's Master and Slave relationship.[18] Beholding the terror of others, he can convince himself of his own "secret peace." Hearing them cry out in agony, he can exult in his own pleasure. Feeling them die by his own hands, he can be assured that he truly lives.

Cenci, however, has "progressed" beyond even this delight in physical terror. His oppression of the other has become for him a "spiritual" activity. (We might recall here Lucifer's espousal in *Cain* of man's "spiritual nature.") Cenci no longer derives pleasure from lustful acts, nor even from murder. His voracious selfhood demands subtler stimulation, the subjugation of another's soul:

> I rarely kill the body, which preserves,
> Like a strong prison, the soul within my power,
> Wherein I feed it with the breath of fear
> For hourly pain. (I, i, 114-17)

The Count's latest, ultimate desire is to bend another individual completely to his will, to force another into a mold set by his selfhood. Cenci's account of the growth of his sadistic self traces a movement from the youthful joys of animal pleasures through a time when murder haunted him like a passion to an old age in which the sad music of another's pain can convince him that his own spirit pervades all things. It is to gratify this final "fancy" that Cenci undertakes his assault upon Beatrice.

II

II
SHELLEY AND SHAKESPEARE: THE RAVAGES OF SELF-ANATOMY

WE MAY WONDER why—when *The Cenci* subverts the order of traditional tragedy—Shelley chose to echo repeatedly passages from his great precursors, especially Shakespeare. Shelley's use of Shakespearean reminiscences in *The Cenci* has often been criticized; for example, the Count's speeches echo those of King Lear, and the seeming inappropriateness of such a connection has armed those who wish to attack Shelley's drama as a failed imitation of Elizabethan drama.[19] Paul Cantor, however, has argued that it is not enough to cite the parallel passages and then condemn Shelley for borrowing from Shakespeare: "Perhaps a more fruitful approach to *The Cenci* would be to consider the role of Shakespearean echoes in our understanding of the play's significance, rather than in our estimation of its artistic worth."[20] While Cantor uses the echoes to uncover a Shelleyan reinterpretation of Shakespeare, and while I hope to illuminate Shelley's definition of his own characters in relation to Shakespeare's heroes, we both focus on the contrast that Shelley intentionally points out between his play and the plays of his greatest predecessor.

Noting the verbal links between Cenci and Lear that Shelley fashions in the fourth act, Cantor defines the difference between the two characters:

One can learn a great deal about the differences between Shakespeare and Shelley by juxtaposing the ways they choose to portray an authority figure: the kingly Lear, for all his flaws and errors, represents the potential for—and at times the actuality of—a positive force of order in the world, necessary to combat the disordering force of human passion; the degenerate Cenci reflects Shelley's distrust of authority as such, embodying a nightmare vision of the warped principle of order behind both nature and convention in this world.[21]

Cantor identifies the distance between Shakespeare's figure of fallen authority and Shelley's portrait of authority as anarchy. In *Lear*, authority stands against the chaos of passion, against the "dangerous secrets" of the self. Lear may be a vain man who foolishly attempts to bend the world to his will. But the principle of authority he thus betrays is real and valid, and insofar as Lear is true to it he participates in an order greater than himself. In *The Cenci*, power arises from self-anatomy. Institutions merely reflect the self's desire to oppress the other. The echoes that link Cenci to Lear thus highlight the distance between the hero of traditional tragedy, defined in relation to a meaningful order, and the characters of romantic tragic drama who find themselves isolated from true authority in a world ruled by the amoral self. Cenci, in espousing self-anatomy, falls from authority into anarchy.

Shelley is often accused of being unable to create characters like Shakespeare's, but Shelley intends to define his characters through contrasts with Shakespeare's heroes. His use of Shakespearean prototypes to define the loss of traditional heroic stature would have been an entirely practical strategy of characterization in the early nineteenth century. Shelley could rely upon an audience alive to Shakespeare and to the differences between his characters and the Bard's, for the romantic period was the age of Bardolatry in which Shakespeare revivals thronged the stage and in which, as the rather large number of Shakespearean parodies reveals, the audience was prepared to hear the differences between the play before them and a Shakespearean norm.[22] It seems to me that Shelley's adaptations from Shakespeare, far from being the mark of a literary man rejecting the stage, represent a keen sense of the dramatic tradition upon which he could draw to appeal to a contemporary audience. In a sense, Shelley could treat Shakespeare as if his plays were a source of archetypes and myths that could be evoked and adapted. Shelley could look to Shakespeare as the Greek tragedians looked to Homer. Nor is Shelley's play alone in using Shakespeare in this manner. For example, Byron, despite his neoclassical pronouncements, almost always seems to have a Shakespearean prototype in mind when he creates his own dramatic protagonists: behind Manfred stands Hamlet; Marino Faliero recalls Julius Caesar and more importantly Coriolanus; and Sardanapalus appears as an Assyrian Mark Antony. The importance of Shakespeare to the German playwrights of the period is well known. In France, echoes of *Hamlet* and *Julius Caesar* have been found in Musset's *Lorenzaccio*. For many romantic dramatists, Shakespeare's titans are an ideal against which the difficulties of romantic man can be set off.[23]

Shelley uses Shakespeare most pervasively in defining the characters of his play's second generation to demonstrate their involvement in self-anatomy even as they struggle against the oppressive world it has created.[24] The verbal links between Giacomo and Othello in the third act have long bothered critics. Why should Shelley recall Othello, the man the Venetian Senate called "all in all sufficient," in describing the timorous Giacomo? Why echo the speech in which Othello announces the murder of the angelic Desdemona when Giacomo is equivocating about the execution of the demonic Cenci?

We must first remember that Giacomo is not presented in isolation. He appears four times before the final trial scenes (II, ii; III, i; III, ii; V, i), and in each case he has an exchange with Orsino. Orsino seeks to play Iago to Giacomo's Othello, attempting to spur his desire for revenge. Giacomo says as much during their last encounter, in a speech that recalls Othello on Iago:

> 0, had I never
> Found in thy smooth and ready countenance
> The mirror of my darkest thoughts; hadst thou
> Never with hints and questions made me look
> Upon the monster of my thought, until
> It grew familiar to desire. . . . (V, i, 19–24)[25]

While attacking Orsino here, Giacomo also compliments himself. He talks as if he has been able to act upon the "monster of my thought." However, despite the efforts of Iago/Orsino, Giacomo remains an ineffectual Othello. Othello, once he begins to suspect Desdemona, exclaims, "I'll see before I doubt; when I doubt prove; / And on the proof there is no more but this: / Away at once with love or jealousy" (III, iii, 190–93). But Giacomo, having proof of his father's wickedness, is still unable to commit himself to revenge. In fact, he cannot even speak directly of it. When Orsino attempts to elicit from him an admission that he has contemplated the murder of Cenci, Giacomo responds:

> I am as one lost in a midnight wood,
> Who dares not ask some harmless passenger
> The path across the wilderness, lest he,
> As my thoughts are, should be—a murderer. (II, ii, 93–96)

Fantasies of parricide tempt Giacomo, but he is afraid to find any path out of the wilderness of his thoughts. He is paralyzed by his very awareness of his murderous desires. He cannot voice the wordless horrors revealed by introspection, let alone act upon them.

Turning now to the troublesome echoes of Act III, scene ii, we can see how Shelley defines Giacomo through the distance that separates him from Shakespeare's hero. Where the Moor contemplates the murder he is about to commit, Giacomo, musing over an "unreplenished lamp" (III, ii, 9), regrets even his remote participation in the murder that may be taking place at an assassin's hand:

> . . . how very soon,
> Did I not feed thee, wouldst thou fail and be
> As thou hadst never been! So wastes and sinks
> Even now, perhaps, the life that kindled mine:
> But that no power can fill with vital oil
> That broken lamp of flesh. (III, ii, 13–18)

> Put out the light, and then put out the light:
> If I quench thee, thou flaming minister,
> I can thy former light restore,
> Should I repent me; but once put out thy light,

> Thou cunning'st pattern of excelling nature,
> I know not where is that Promethean heat
> That can thy light relume. (*Othello*, V, ii, 7–13)

Othello's speech defines the clarity of his decision to murder Desdemona; Giacomo's speech hovers in uncertainty. Giacomo's repeated echo of Othello's lines on the lamp—"And yet once quenched I cannot thus relume / My father's life" (III, ii, 51–52)—has especially annoyed the critics who ask why Shelley insists upon repeating what they feel to be an inappropriate reference. Yet the double echo is effective, for it indicates the indecisive, circular, and obsessive nature of Giacomo's thoughts. Where Othello can move forward into action, Giacomo is trapped by his inner gaze.

While Giacomo cannot escape the inward turn of his thoughts, his inwardness lacks the richness of the other Shakespearean prototype to whom he is compared—Hamlet. Stuart Curran has identified Giacomo as a "diluted Hamlet, overwhelmed by misgivings and qualms, vainly grasping for the basis of a stable world view."[26] Giacomo wants someone to tell him what to do, as his long obedience to his father and his willingness to follow Orsino demonstrate; but he cannot escape his inner life, though he renders himself impotent in the attempt. Paralyzed by the Cenci "trick," yet wanting to act, Giacomo embodies an extreme version of the introspective passivity that romantic critics like A. W. Schlegel found in Hamlet.[27] Shelley demonstrates not only that the brand of subjectivism embraced by Giacomo leads to inaction, but also that the interior life it creates is shallow, for all of its hypnotic allure. Shelley defines precisely his character through these Shakespearean prototypes. Self-anatomy makes of Giacomo both a failed Othello and a diluted Hamlet.[28]

If the second generation of characters offers a true hope for reform, that hope is Beatrice Cenci, daughter to the depraved Count. Beatrice resembles her father in certain important ways. In fact, her similarity to him paradoxically gives her the potential power to liberate the world that he exploits. Beatrice shares with her father a strength of mind and will that protects them from the more debilitating effects of their family's inward turn. Orsino tells us of Beatrice's command of self-anatomy, but he explains that she does not attempt, as her father does, to bend the will to the desires of the self; rather, she urges a turn against these desires:

> Yet I fear
> Her subtle mind, her awe-inspiring gaze
> Whose beams *anatomize* me nerve by nerve
> And lay me bare and *make me blush* to see
> My hidden thoughts. (I, ii, 83–87; my emphasis)

Shelley dramatizes Beatrice's ability to resist the seductive insights of self-anatomy during her first moments on stage. We see Beatrice struggle against her skeptical intellect that would reduce life to a vicious charade, as she tries to protect her trust and faith in others. For example, she veers towards a condemnation of Orsino, knowing his faults (I, ii, 30–31, 43), but she constantly returns to a charitable view: "Ah no! forgive me. . . . Here I stand bickering with my only friend" (I, ii, 34, 45). She tries to inspire him to deserve her trust, urging him to feel shame for his selfish thoughts. He, however, lacks her ability to combat his inner desires:

> So Cenci fell into the pit [through self-anatomy]; even I,
> Since Beatrice unveiled me to myself,
> *And made me shrink from what I cannot shun,*
> Show a poor figure to my own esteem,
> To which I grow half reconciled. (II, ii, 114–18; my emphasis)

Camillo also pays homage to the power that Beatrice possesses. He describes her as an angelic figure who might even dispel the "fiend" within Cenci's self:

> Where is your gentle daughter?
> Methinks her sweet looks, which make all things else
> Beauteous and glad, might kill the fiend within you. (I, i, 43–45)

Beatrice can beautify and gladden the world, for she does not project upon it the self's dark desires. Rather, she struggles to remain true to what she calls her "innocence." The insistence by Beatrice and by other characters, even after the murder of her father, that she is innocent has bothered many critics, but this is because they construe her innocence in moral terms.[29] Camillo's hope that her innocence will prove equal to Cenci's "fiend" suggests, however, that her innocence is defined in relation to her father's pursuit of self-anatomy. Much as in Blake's poetry where innocence is understood through its relationship to experience, so in *The Cenci* innocence is defined through its opposition to self-anatomy; these are not so much moral categories as modes of consciousness. Beatrice remains innocent as long as she rejects the lure of the self. She alone in her world seems to have the power to confront the inner life and yet to resist it. Shelley says of her in his preface, "Beatrice Cenci appears to have been one of those rare persons in whom energy and gentleness dwell together without destroying one another. . ." ("Preface," p. 278). Where Cenci exalts the self and Lucretia remains powerless in her passive piety, Beatrice seems capable of harnessing the self's energies to reform the world in keeping with a vision of innocence.

Beatrice's role should be that of another Prometheus. However, she discovers that her world lacks a mode of innocent action, a lack signaled by the absence of a love interest in the play. Love has perhaps a larger place in Shelley's vision than in that of any other poet. It is after all in the love of Asia that Prometheus discovers the fulfillment that marks the imaginative transformation of his world. For Beatrice, however, love is not a possibility. She tells Orsino that she might have loved him in the past, but "All the love that once / I felt for you, is turned to bitter pain" (I, ii, 20-21). She still feels charitable towards him "as a sister or a spirit might," but hers is a "cold fidelity" offering no hope of fulfillment (I, ii, 25-26). Love is the first casualty of self-anatomy, for the inward turn alienates the self from the other. While Beatrice resists the most violent aspects of her family's "trick," self-anatomy still isolates her from others, thus undermining the potential she possesses to reform her world. As Shelley says in his preface, she was "a most gentle and amiable being, a creature to adorn and be admired, and thus violently thwarted from her nature by the necessity of circumstance and opinion" (p. 275).

In her inability to act upon her innocence, Beatrice resembles Schiller's Max, the "beautiful soul" who finds that all actions in his world are corrupted; Iphigenia, who is like Beatrice in a number of ways,[30] differs on this point, for Goethe's heroine does discover a mode of action—or at least a mode of speech—that can embody her vision. Shelley's portrait of Beatrice differs from that of both Max and Iphigenia in that he shows his figure of innocence cruelly forced to enter the world of experience, the world of self-anatomy. Beatrice is raped by her father and then discovers that her only possible responses to his assault necessarily involve her in the struggle of self and other. Either she must submit to his violation and be slowly corrupted, or she must strike back. While Shelley clearly regards such revenge as a "pernicious mistake," Beatrice's path is tragic because her world offers her only this course of violent, heroic resistance:

Undoubtedly, no person can be truly dishonoured by the act of another; and the fit return to make to the most enormous injuries is kindness and forebearance, and a resolution to convert the injurer from his dark passions by peace and love. Revenge, retaliation, atonement, are pernicious mistakes. If Beatrice had thought in this manner she would have been wiser and better; but she would never have been a tragic character.... ("Preface," p. 276)

Beatrice's tragedy arises because she cannot remain true to her innocence in acting within her world: innocence will either remain mute potentiality or become tragically corrupted in its attempt to actualize itself.

Shelley once again uses Shakespearean echoes to define Beatrice's dilemma. Many critics are bothered by the fact that Shelley links Beatrice to both Desdemona and Lady Macbeth; Milton Wilson summarizes the conflict:

...and, whereas the darker side of Beatrice resembles Lady Macbeth, the brighter side at moments in the last act reminds us of Desdemona. It is hard to imagine Lady Macbeth and Desdemona in the same heroine, but Shelley's unconscious reminiscences of Shakespeare force us to do so.[31]

In fact, Shelley uses these reminiscences quite consciously to place Beatrice through her relationship with her Shakespearean prototypes. Beatrice is a Desdemona who finds she must become a Lady Macbeth to combat her father. A Desdemona/Lady Macbeth matches perfectly with Shelley's definition of Beatrice as a "gentle and amiable being" "violently thwarted from her nature." Still, she remains committed to the values embodied by her Desdemona aspect even as she acts in her Lady Macbeth aspect. It is this attempt to turn from self-anatomy to embrace innocence that so offends her father and provokes his assaults. And it is her attempt to maintain her allegiance to a vision of innocence even as she is forced to act in contradiction to it that constitutes her heroism.

III
CENCI AND BEATRICE: SHELLEY'S DRAMATURGY OF SELF AND INNOCENCE

THE CENCI CENTERS upon the conflict between Cenci and Beatrice, between the apostle of the isolated self and an innocent with the thwarted potential to liberate man from the "principle of self." Cenci has tried to mold his world to his own nightmarish desires, and Beatrice is the last person to resist him. We have already heard Cenci announce his drive to dominate the other not only physically, but also spiritually: "I rarely kill the body, which preserves, / Like a strong fortress, the soul within my power..." (I, i, 114–15). Just as he locks his family within the fortress of Petralla where his command is unassailable, so does he desire to imprison the soul in an isolated mode of consciousness that he can control. In his incestuous assaults upon Beatrice, Cenci tries to imprison her soul by forcing her into an awareness of the "dangerous secrets" that lie within her. Cenci hints at his designs upon Beatrice throughout the early scenes, but it is in the fourth act that he explains them clearly:

> Might I not drag her by the golden hair?
> Stamp on her? Keep her sleepless till her brain
> Be overworn? Tame her with chains and famine?
> Less would suffice. Yet so to leave undone
> What I most seek! No, 'tis her stubborn will
> Which by its own consent shall stoop as low
> As that which drags it down. (IV, i, 6–12)

Having already raped Beatrice, Cenci realizes that physical subjugation alone will not conquer her soul. He hopes to tame her will in order to make her like himself:

> I will drag her, step by step,
> Through infamies unheard of among men:
> She shall stand shelterless in the broad noon
> Of public scorn, for acts blazoned abroad,
> One among which shall be. . . What? Canst thou guess?
> She shall become (for what she most abhors
> Shall have a fascination to entrap
> Her loathing will) to her own conscious self
> All she appears to others. . . . (IV, i, 80–88)

We hear in this speech the voice of the master of self-anatomy, who knows only too well how that which is abhorrent within the self can entrap one who gazes too long upon it.[32] Cenci feels certain that if he could only tame Beatrice's will, if he could only force her to gaze long and hard at the vicious, perverted desires that exist within all men but which she has always rejected, then she would become "as low / As that which drags it down," become "what she most abhors"; that is, she would become a replica of his own self. Cenci dreams of perpetuating his own demonic selfhood by impressing it completely upon another, as when he hopes that his incestuous union with Beatrice will bring forth a child blending his features with hers (IV, i, 145–49). Such a conquest would be the ultimate triumph in his war against the other.

Cenci's rape of Beatrice provides Shelley with a perfect emblem of the struggle between them, revealing their relationship as a version of the battle between the oppressor and the oppressed. Moreover, rape perverts the bond of love into a paradigm for the hateful domination of the other by the self. The incestuous nature of their union not only intensifies this conflict, but also suggests some deep link between them, a possibility that Cenci could really convert Beatrice into a second version of himself. More clearly than Bertram's insistence that Imogine prove herself in adultery, more clearly than Manfred's destructive desire for his *döppelganger* Astarte, more clearly than the incestuous bond between Cain and Adah—Cenci's rape of Beatrice reveals the secret desire of the romantic villain-hero: to impose his self so totally on another that he or she is willing to turn against everything else to join in a perverse union; and ultimately, to make the world a vast replica of his own selfhood. This desire is the demonic counterpart of the romantic dream of transforming the world through the imagination: where a visionary would remake the world according to a transcendent ideal, a Cenci would render the world a mirror for the basest aspects of his own self.

Many, perhaps most, critics believe that Cenci fulfills his wish. Antonin Artaud in his adaptation of *The Cenci* has Beatrice say, "I fear that death may teach me that I have ended by resembling him."[33] There are moments within Shelley's own play that support such an interpretation. Beatrice does appear to adopt her father's habit of meeting charges with lies and pious exclamations of God's support for her actions. She also has a nightmare vision of a universe dominated by her father, where "all things then should be. . . my father's spirit" (V, iv, 60). Such a vision would seem to signal Cenci's success.

However, Shelley, unlike Artaud, does not have Beatrice go to her death with thoughts of her father. In the final scene she rejects her vision of his domination ("'Tis past / Whatever comes my heart shall sink no more"; V, iv, 77–78), just as throughout the play she turns away from his mode of consciousness. Even Cenci comes to admit that he has failed to achieve the transformation he would force upon her: "I must give up the greater point, which was / To poison and corrupt her soul" (IV, i, 44–45). Shelley denies Beatrice the visionary solution open to Prometheus, but he does allow her to discover a heroic mode of consciousness which enables her to remain free of her father's perverted self-anatomy. To dramatize the differences between these two characters, Shelley grants Beatrice a completely different stage presence from the one he gives to the Count.

It is often assumed that, since Shelley was essentially a lyric poet, there is little point in analyzing his dramatic techniques. When attention is paid to his dramaturgy, it is usually to point out his debts to earlier playwrights or to the conventions of the day. For example, some contend that *The Cenci* is a rather conventional melodrama, pitting absolute good against absolute evil; Cenci is seen as a melodramatic villain or a gothic villain-hero, and Beatrice is viewed as a suffering innocent, like the Bianca of Milman's *Fazio*.[34] Cenci does have many of the stock traits of the stage villains of the day; Camillo's account of Cenci's life could serve as the biography of any one of the innumerable depraved stage noblemen: "I stood beside your dark and fiery youth / . . . . I marked / Your desperate and remorseless manhood; now / Do I behold you in dishonoured age / Charged with a thousand unrepented crimes" (I, i, 49–54). It is also true that Shelley's Beatrice shares qualities with her suffering stage sisters.

However, Shelley is not interested in pitting one more wailing innocent against a conventional villain. Rejecting the trivial moralizing that was the hallmark of such melodramatic encounters, he transforms the struggle between good and evil by viewing it in the light of his analysis of self-consciousness. He demonstrates that Cenci's Gothic traits—his depravity, his inward-turned melancholy, and his outward turns of violence—all manifest his preoccupation with the self and its struggle with the other. Cenci is not a Gothic villain-hero who wins our sympathy by showing remorse for his actions. He is rather a remorseless battler at war with his fellow men, fascinating because he reveals the dark side of the romantic quest into the self. He fully exemplifies the "vicious and insane wish" that Coleridge discovers in *Bertram*: the demand that we love his selfhood but not his qualities and actions, a demand made even of his God. Nor is Beatrice a frail maiden, a moral innocent preyed upon by an evil father. She is a forceful exponent of an innocent mode of consciousness tragically destroyed even as she heroically clings to her own vision. Rather than reducing Shelley's play to melodrama, we need to see how he transformed the conventions of the stage to pursue his tragic study of consciousness.

Shelley uses speech and action—the primary resources of the drama—to differentiate the modes of consciousness his characters adopt. This is perhaps clearest in his handling of soliloquies. E. S. Bates has catalogued twelve soliloquies in *The Cenci*,[35] but no one has noted the importance of their distribution amongst the characters: Count Cenci has six of these speeches, Orsino has four, Giacomo one, and the last, not really a soliloquy but a speech spoken over the sleeping Beatrice, is given to Bernardo. Beatrice never speaks a soliloquy; she is never on stage alone. If we consider the importance of self-anatomy in the play, this distribution has a clear significance. Cenci's inward turn is given dramatic reality as we see him time and again talking to himself and questing deeper into his own darkest thoughts. Orsino, who would like to have the power of a Cenci, is almost as fond of soliloquizing. Giacomo, who is paralyzed by his turn to the self, indulges in an inner monologue only once. Shelley thus manages to link him to the vice of self-anatomy while distinguishing him from Orsino and Cenci, who delight in it. The fact that Beatrice never engages in a soliloquy demonstrates her resistance to her family's inward turn.

As his use of soliloquies suggests, Shelley alters his dramaturgy to present his characters' varying relationships to self-anatomy. Since the play centers upon the conflict between Cenci and Beatrice, the ways in which they are presented differ the most. Count Cenci walks through the play delivering what is essentially a long monologue. For Cenci, "the heart triumphs with itself in words" (I, i, 139). His best moments on stage are found in his soliloquies, and all of his other impressive moments partake of the soliloquy: his opening discussion with Camillo reminds the Cardinal of what a fiend might say to itself; his scene with Lucretia in the fourth act is not really a dialogue, but a tirade; even the scene of the feast in the first act finds Cenci delivering a speech, not engaging in conversation. Cenci emerges from his long dialogue with his own self only to issue commands, lectures, and curses—all modes of speech that assert the power of the will over the world.

Cenci's acts complement his words. He appears as a man of action, the only truly active character in the play except for Beatrice. However, he acts for himself, not for an audience. Shelley could not, of course, stage Cenci's ultimate act—the rape of Beatrice. But he makes a virtue of this necessity by establishing in Cenci a desire for hidden action wholly in accord with his nature. Announcing in the first scene that when he commits crimes in the future it will be with secrecy—"Henceforth no witness—not the lamp —shall see" (I, i, 21)—Cenci is continually beset by the anxiety that others might see him or overhear him (I, i, 137–139; II, i, 174-81). The traditional hero performs his deeds in public view, on the battlefield or in the court, for only then can he acquire the fame that ratifies his heroic stature. Cenci, seeking to "flatter" his "secret peace," acts only for himself and perhaps for the God who is a projection of his own worst nature. If we recall Bertram's vision of being lost at sea with his enemy on a plank, battling with him for life and death, then we have an image of Cenci's preferred mode of action: an isolated struggle between self and other.

Beatrice is dramatized in a wholly different way from Count Cenci, for Shelley wants to depict her as the one person in the play who continually confronts the dangers of the inner life only to overcome them. Where Cenci's best moments on stage are essentially monologic and his acts secret, Beatrice is seen only with others, primarily in moments where she stands forth to present herself clearly and to engage others in debate: in the banquet scene, where she confronts her father; in the fourth act, where she urges the murderers to their deed; in the fifth act, where she faces down her accusers; and to a lesser extent, in her various parrying exchanges with Orsino. All of her acts are public attempts to make contact with another. Where Cenci asserts himself in monologues, curses, and commands, Beatrice seeks to engage others through discussions, pleadings, and exhortations.

The only moments in which Beatrice seems to founder upon the self's "dangerous secrets" occur at the beginnings of the second and third acts when she appears to be going insane. Some critics have found these "mad scenes" overly long and undramatic. Yet Shelley certainly had the right to expect them to work on stage. As the case of Imogine in *Bertram* suggests, such "mad scenes" had become a theatrical convention. Eliza O'Neill had overwhelmed audiences with her portrayal of the mad Bianca in *Fazio*, and it was, of course, O'Neill whom Shelley had in mind for the part of Beatrice. Shelley once again draws upon a conventional piece of stage business, but only to reinterpret it. These intense moments were generally used to reveal the inner workings of the character's mind and to win sympathy for her.[36] Beatrice's madness arises from an unbearably acute sense of the self and of its struggle with the other. When madness strikes, she finds herself cut off from others, wandering in a private inner world in which she is the fallen victim of an omnipresent and terrifying other, her father (see III, i, 13–25). This is surely an intense, emotional moment, but it is not in such moments that Shelley reveals Beatrice. Rather these scenes display the threats to her identity, based as it is in innocence. If Beatrice shared the limitations of her fellow sufferers, of Lucretia or Giacomo, her insanity would comprise her final fate and these "mad scenes" would define her as they do Imogine and Bianca. But Beatrice battles back from madness. She repeatedly resists giving voice to the horrors she has undergone,[37] knowing that if she dwells upon them she might indeed become "what she most abhors." Rather than wallow in a passive, inward-turned response to the rape, she turns outward to discover an act that will obliterate the event from her consciousness—"something which shall make / The thing that I have suffered but a shadow / In the dread lightning which avenges it . . ." (III, i, 87–89). She fights her madness to engage those around her: "You see I am not mad: I speak to you" (II, i, 34). The triumph of dialogue over monologue evidences Beatrice's victory over self-anatomy. She moves beyond her temporary madness to her final confrontation with her father and herself.

Beatrice cannot allow her father's act to define her. She must struggle heroically to preserve her identity of innocence. Her innocence having been attacked in fact, she now asserts it in vision. Such an assertion involves her in an apparent falsehood. What appears to her as an imaginative vision strikes us as a self-justifying piece of fancy. What she calls her "holier plea" (III, i, 212) is made on behalf of innocence, but she uses it to justify murder.

Shelley tells us that Beatrice should not have murdered her father, that she should have endured as Prometheus did. In turning to murder, she involves herself in the struggle of self and other; she destroys the other, her father, to preserve her own selfhood. However, it is clear that *for Beatrice* the murder holds out the hope for a transformation of the world. Believing the murder done, she proclaims, "the world / Is conscious of a change. Darkness and Hell / Have swallowed up the vapour they sent forth / To blacken the sweet light of life" (IV, iii, 40–42). In particular, she feels herself freed:

> The deed is done,
> And what may follow now regards not me.
> I am as universal as the light;
> Free as the earth-surrounding air; as firm
> As the world's centre. (IV, iv, 46–50)

She speaks as if she and her world were experiencing the type of transformation that occurs in *Prometheus Unbound*.[38] For her, the murder not only eradicates the rape; it is also a revolutionary act that liberates her world from the rule of self-anatomy. To understand Beatrice and her heroism, we must accept the sincerity with which she endorses this vision of rebirth through violence.

However, Shelley's play makes clear that she is mistaken. Even as she voices her new feeling of freedom, Savella raises the cry of murder over the discovered corpse and arrests Beatrice and her family. Like so many romantic rebels, like Schiller's Moor and Fiesco or Byron's Marino Faliero, Beatrice finds that violent revolt fulfills rather than breaks the cycle of oppression she opposes. She can attain no visionary solution in her world. Her actions lead to murder, and her innocence thus becomes a dream, not a realized vision. Beatrice continues to believe in her dream, as the only defense she has against the "sad reality" of her world. For some, such a stance makes her a hypocrite, virtually as evil as Cenci.[39] But rather than hearing in the final scenes the voice of Cenci speaking through a perverted Beatrice, we should instead listen to the voice of a thwarted visionary who can only gesture toward a higher truth she herself cannot attain. She is tragic in her inability to discover the ideal solution of a Prometheus. But she is also heroic in her persistent refusal to bow to her father and to his vision.

The Beatrice of the final act possesses the intense ambiguity that always marks the tragic hero. While many critics find Beatrice's continued espousal of her own innocence demonic, Shelley dramatizes the power of that innocence to convince those around her that she is, despite her crimes, in some sense angelic. Her strength arises from the fact that her dream of innocence is preferable to the reality of oppression against which it struggles:

> 0 white innocence,
> That thou shouldst wear the mask of guilt to hide
> Thine awful and serenest countenance
> From those who know thee not! (V, iii, 24–27)

Beatrice is not alone in proclaiming her innocence. Giacomo describes her standing "like God's angel ministered upon by fiends" (V, i, 43-44); at the trial, Camillo finds her to be "as pure as speechless infancy" (V, ii, 69). We see her ability to draw others into her dream most strikingly in the trial scenes of the fifth act, where Beatrice pits her innocence against the oppression of her world. To understand the Beatrice of the last act, we must turn to the final moments of *King Lear* in which the power of Lear's love for Cordelia almost makes us believe she is still alive; again, at the end of Ibsen's *John Gabriel Borkman*, the intensity and—one might almost say—the sheer insanity of Borkman's final speech has the ability to transform his world into a realm of idealized capitalism. Beatrice, too, has the power momentarily to subjugate the world to her heroic identity. So absolute is her sense of her own innocence that she convinces Marzio, the hired assassin, that he should retract his accusations against her:

> Torture me as ye will:
> A keener pang has wrung a higher truth
> From my last breath. She is most innocent!
> Bloodhounds, not men, glut yourselves well with me;
> I will not give you that fine piece of nature
> To rend and ruin. (V, ii, 163–68)

Beatrice's dream of innocence projects a "higher truth" than her world can offer. Her espousal of that truth, her martyrdom for it, evinces her heroic victory over her father's attempt to bend her to an experience of the self's perversity.

Her tragedy, however, lies in her inability to find an act commensurate with her own dream. When she moves against her father to protect her innocence, she compromises that very innocence. Even Beatrice comes to realize that "I am cut off from the only world I know" (V, iv, 85), the world of innocence. Unlike Goethe's Iphigenia who finds a way beyond violence and cunning, Beatrice must act in the world of self-anatomy, the world of the oppressor and the oppressed. More striking, her language is also bound by that world. She does not find, as Iphigenia and Orestes do, an interpretive key to unlock her prison door through imaginative language. She cannot speak the visionary tongue of the last act of *Prometheus Unbound*, where language is a "perpetual Orphic song." It is as if she lived in a world where the only language was that of Prometheus's curse or that of Goethe's "Parzenlied," where language itself is betrayed by the inward turn of the self. She finds herself forced to adopt the rhetoric of Catholicism that Shelley analyzes in his "Preface." She cannot break through beyond the limitations of her world, but rather dreams of a God who protects the innocent. Beatrice pits her beneficent God against Cenci's demonic God, but both must rely upon religious rhetoric, not vision, in their struggle. In this world where there is no true human contact based on self-knowledge and love for the other, Beatrice must fashion an ultimate Other, a God who will support her identity of innocence even as it is under assault. Clearly, for Shelley, Beatrice is in error. Compared with the visionary success of a Prometheus or even the tempered victory of an Iphigenia, Beatrice's life seems one of failure. She has not attained the true "God" of poetic vision. But she has escaped the "Mammon" of the "principle of self." She finally acts to preserve her own self, but only in a heroic attempt to create herself as a sign of innocence within a world where true innocence is not yet a possibility.

Beatrice is tragic because she cannot rise above her historical period. She has a glimpse of the eternal truths of the imagination, but her involvement in the rhetoric of her world distorts them, leading her into the "pernicious mistake" of revenge. Iphigenia's humane myth of *Bildung* can become an actuality within her play, because she lives on the borderline of human history, moving from the world of theocentric myth to that of human art. But Beatrice, a potential visionary, finds herself trapped within history, cut off from both myth and a new Mythus of the imagination: "The crimes and miseries in which she was an actor and a sufferer are as the mask and the mantle in which circumstance clothed her for her impersonation on the scene of the world" ("Preface," p. 278).

Shelley's emphasis upon the historical basis of his drama, and especially upon its Catholic background, now appears as a key to the play. It is the "circumstance and opinion" ("Preface," p. 275) of Beatrice's historical period, its "sad reality," that "violently thwarted her true nature," preventing her from perceiving the "high idealisms" of the imagination.[40] Like one of Schiller's time-trapped protagonists, Beatrice can offer only a partial solution to her difficulties, a solution heroic in its resistance to a debased world but tragic in its failure to complete man's imaginative quest. Even though Shelley's play is primarily concerned with the tragedy of self, it still draws us to the heartland of romantic historical tragedy: the tragedy of thwarted revolt.

At the conclusion of *The Cenci*, Beatrice faces her entrapment within history. Having escaped her father's world of the self only to fail to attain the visionary heights, she seeks to create herself as a historical emblem of the struggle of innocence against oppression. Her final act is to impress her dream of innocence upon her younger brother, Bernardo:

> One thing more, my child:
> For thine own sake be constant to the love
> Thou bearest us; and to the faith that I,
> Though wrapped in a strange cloud of crime and shame,
> Lived ever holy and unstained. And though
> Ill tongues shall wound me, and our common name
> Be as a mark stamped on thine innocent brow
> For men to point at as they pass, do thou
> Forbear, and never think a thought unkind
> Of those, who perhaps love thee in their graves.
> So mayest thou die as I do; fear and pain
> Being subdued. Farewell! Farewell! Farewell! (V, iv, 145–56)

Beatrice tries to write her own history. For all of Shelley's disagreements with Byron over dramaturgy,[41] his heroine ends with a stance similar to that of Sardanapalus or Marino Faliero. Like them, she seeks to create herself as a historical exemplum even as she finds herself trapped by history. Unable to break through to vision, she enters history as a martyr for a dream of innocence.

IV

THE THEATER OF SELF-KNOWLEDGE

I BEGAN THIS discussion by noting that Shelley wrote *The Cenci* with the contemporary theater in mind; but he also wrote it in an attempt to rival the great tragic masterpieces of the past. While he mentioned the play in the same breath as the works of Coleridge, Milman, and Maturin, he also linked it to dramas by Sophocles, Shakespeare, and Calderón.[42] How do we reconcile these two sets of influences? The answer lies in Shelley's ideas on imitation and on tragedy. Shelley opposed any simple imitation of past models for he felt that the drama of each new epoch had to respond to the "spirit of the age"; he tried to demonstrate in *A Defence of Poetry* how inextricably bound up with the social and cultural conditions of its day the drama must be. Mere imitation produces false art, for it imposes outmoded forms on present reality. Shelley even found fault with his greatly admired Calderón for having attempted to return in his religious *autos* to dramatic practices that no longer had any direct relationship to social and cultural institutions.[43]

There is, however, a reciprocal danger. In cultivating the spirit of the age, the dramatist often finds himself erecting as an absolute truth a fleeting opinion. This is what Shelley objected to in the contemporary melodrama: it claims to reveal moral truths while in fact it contains only "specious flatteries of some gross vice or weakness with which the author, in common with his auditors, are infected" (*Defence*, p. 285). In Shelley's view, a poet "would do ill to embody his own conceptions of right and wrong, which are usually those of his place and time . . ." (*Defence*, p. 283).

In a sense, Shelley sees the dramatic poet as facing a situation much like that which Beatrice confronts. Like her, the dramatist must struggle against the "circumstance and opinion" of his place and time in history to discover a mode of language that will communicate with those around him without betraying his imaginative vision. If we recall Shelley's description of Beatrice's crimes as "the mask and mantle in which circumstance clothed her for her impersonation on the scene of the world," we must be struck by the similarity between this portrait of a woman caught within history and Shelley's discussion of the poet's commitment to the false doctrines of his day: "The distorted notions of invisible things which Dante and his rival Milton have idealized are merely the mask and the mantle in which these great poets walk through eternity enveloped and disguised" (*Defence*, p. 289–90). The difference between Beatrice and the poet is that she remains trapped within history, while the poet breaks through to vision to "walk through eternity."

These ideas form the basis of Shelley's critique of contemporary drama. He criticized the neoclassical remnants of his day for aping the forms of the past and attacked the popular melodrama for preaching the false doctrines of the present. He strove in *The Cenci* to create a modern dramatic form that would reveal the enduring lesson of tragedy. By turning to the contemporary stage, he avoided the imitation of tried and thus untrue dramatic forms. Turning to the visions of past tragic masters, he shunned the parochial views of his lesser contemporaries. He hoped thus to create in *The Cenci* a play that would serve the same function for his age that *Oedipus Rex* did for ancient Athens and *King Lear* did for Shakespeare's London.

And what is this function that modern drama should share with the tragedies of the past? In both the preface to *The Cenci* and in his *Defence*, Shelley argues that tragedy teaches the knowledge of the self:

The highest moral purpose aimed at in the highest species of the drama, is the teaching the human heart, through its sympathies and antipathies, the knowledge of itself. . . . ("Preface," p. 276)

In a drama of the highest order there is little food for censure or hatred; it teaches rather self-knowledge and self-respect. (*Defence*, p. 285)

If we recall the quotation in which Shelley opposes poetry and the "principle of self" as the God and Mammon of the world—only one can be served—then it becomes clear that the "self-knowledge and self-respect" taught by poetic tragedy must serve as charms against this "principle of self." Tragedy combats self-anatomy.[44] While self-anatomy involves a turn inward, self-knowledge involves a turn outward. Taught by the drama through the heart's sympathies and antipathies, the audience can come to understand itself and others. Shelley's discussion of Athenian tragedy in the *Defence*, from which the above statement about self-knowledge is quoted, supports such a reading:

The tragedies of the Athenian poets are as mirrors in which the spectator beholds himself, under a thin disguise of circumstance, stript of all but that ideal perfection and energy which every one feels to be the internal type of all that he loves, admires, and would become. . . . Neither the eye nor the mind can see itself unless reflected upon that which it resembles. The drama, so long as it continues to express poetry, is as a prismatic and many-sided mirror which collects the brightest rays of human nature and divides and reproduces them from the simplicity of these elementary forms and touches them with majesty and beauty, and multiplies all that it reflects and endows it with the power of propagating its like wherever it may fall. (*Defence*, p. 285)

In tragedy, the spectator beholds himself, but only insofar as he possesses "the brightest rays of human nature." Tragedy turns the gaze of the spectator outward through imaginative sympathy so that he can identify with the ideal type he should become and not the self he is. Self-anatomy traps the individual within his own subjectivity. Self-knowledge leads one towards a paradoxical "internal type" of the ideal which embraces "all that he loves, admires and would become," that is an internal type of all that one is not. Self-anatomy entices the individual inward and turns him against his fellow man. Self-knowledge fulfills the individual through the other in whom he can discover his ideal "anti-type."[45]

The attainment of self-knowledge through the heart's antipathies and sympathies involves the "restless casuistry" which Shelley sees as typifying our response to Beatrice:

It is in the restless and anatomizing casuistry with which men seek the justification of Beatrice, yet feel that she has done what needs justification; it is in the superstitious horror with which they contemplate alike her wrongs and their revenge, that the dramatic character of what she did and suffered, consists. ("Preface," pp. 276–77)

There have been some ingenious discussions of this "restless casuistry."[46] It is often seen as a negative process, an exercise that Shelley rejects; in that it is "anatomizing," this casuistry might even strike us as resembling self-anatomy. However, it also comprises "the dramatic character" of Beatrice's tragedy and must therefore contribute to the self-knowledge Shelley sees as the goal of drama. It seems to me that Shelley's "restless and anatomizing casuistry" is his version of the tension between sympathy and judgment that we have discovered in other plays of the period and that Coleridge makes the basis for his discussion of Maturin's *Bertram*. Beatrice engages both our sympathy and our judgment. Even though she has committed a murder, we feel that in some fundamental sense she is innocent.

This tension in our response remains "restless" and "anatomizing" as long as we continue to vacillate between moral pronouncements and emotional justifications. However, eventually this tension can lead us to question the two poles that define it. When we begin to doubt conventional moral judgments because they are not in accord with our heart's sympathies and to wonder whether sympathies that do not coincide with judgment can be more than self-indulgence, then we move beyond casuistry towards vision. The play reveals that the morality which would condemn Beatrice is merely an instrument of oppression and that her innocence is in part a dream of the self. Conventional morality collapses with the Catholicism of Count Cenci; pure empathy is challenged by Beatrice's self-preserving, if not self-serving, proclamations of innocence. We learn to understand Beatrice and her fellow characters not through moral categories or in empathetic response, but from the viewpoint of imaginative truth. We fully understand Beatrice only when we both recognize how far she stands from the mode of imaginative consciousness and action possessed by Prometheus and at the same time respect her allegiance to her sense of this ideal. In coming to such an understanding, we acquire the self-knowledge that lies in the recognition of the ideal.

Far from being a closet dramatist, Shelley used the techniques of the contemporary stage to draw his intended audience beyond conventional responses towards his own imaginative ideals. We can perhaps see this more clearly if we redefine the tension between sympathy and judgment as a conflict between the monodrama and the melodrama. *The Cenci* has struck some as a melodramatic struggle between absolute good and absolute evil. It has appeared to others as a monodramatic study, in which the characters appeal to us through histrionic displays of emotion. However, within *The Cenci*, these two forms compromise each other. The moral vision of melodrama is brought into question when evil appears emotionally appealing and good becomes involved in crime; we discover the melodramatic attempt to construct an absolute moral vision to be part of the oppressive world of "anarchy" that the play rejects. Again, the expressive, monodramatic moments of the play come to be understood as symptoms of self-anatomy; we learn to see monologues, "mad scenes," and so on not as opportunities to empathize with the characters, but as revelations of their preoccupations with the self.

Had *The Cenci* been performed in the early nineteenth century, the contemporary viewer could have entered the world of the play feeling he was on conventional ground, but he would have found that ground cut away as Shelley forced him to play off his conventional responses against one another until they canceled one another out. At that moment, the viewer might have glimpsed the vision of the play behind the mask and mantle of convention. And as a key to that vision, Shelley provided those troublesome Shakespearean echoes that resound so strangely throughout the play, suggesting by comparing them with their titanic prototypes that these characters are trapped within the lesser world of self-anatomy and that a greater drama of the imagination remains to be played. Having finished *The Cenci*, Shelley went on to write the final act of that greater drama— *Prometheus Unbound*.

The movement beyond casuistry to self-knowledge through vision enables the audience to attain a deeper insight than that won by the characters in the play. The characters are tragically trapped in their sad historical reality, the world of self and other, but the audience sees beyond this world to the eternal truths of the imagination, the "internal type" of the ideal: watching the performance of the characters' entrapment within the self, we are liberated.

Shelley's theater of self-knowledge has much in common with the dramaturgy of other romantic playwrights. Benjamin Bennett has discovered a similar theory of the drama in the German plays of the period; drawing on Kleist, he defines the drama as "an exercise for the spectator in problematic self-consciousness, an attempt to conduct the spectator's self-consciousness 'through the infinite' in order that the little community in the theater become the model and seed of a revitalized humanity...."[47] Jerome McGann touches upon a related idea in his discussion of Byron's plays. Arguing that the point of Byron's dramas was not to arouse melodramatic suspense but "to make the audience thoughtful and self-conscious," McGann suggests that Byron's designation of his plays as "mental theatre" had a larger significance than "its specialized meaning of simple 'closet drama'": "The general Byronic theme of the need for self-consciousness tends to suggest this. Moreover, the term 'mental theatre' seems to be another of Byron's verbal equivocations intended to mean both 'drama of self-consciousness' and 'closet drama.'"[48] While McGann sees Byron's theater as intensifying the self-consciousness of the audience and Bennett sees the German drama leading its viewers beyond the self, both recognize the dynamics of selfhood as a key to romantic dramaturgy. They agree with Shelley that the self is not only a theme *within* the play, but a problem for the audience attacked *by* the play. Schiller's discussions of the drama, Coleridge's analysis of *Bertram*, and Hazlitt's theory of tragedy all share with Shelley's treatment of the tragic a concern with the drama's impact on the spectator and his relation to his own selfhood or ego.[49] In the hands of the romantics the theater becomes a powerful tool in the investigation of the self and a means of promoting self-knowledge in the audience.

Still, such knowledge is only for the audience, not for the protagonists of romantic tragic drama. They cannot experience on stage the liberating movement out of the self we find in watching them. Schiller's characters can find only a partial humanity that reveals their entrapment in a limited identity. Byron's Cain and Manfred must struggle on in the consciousness of their divided state as "fiery dust." Shelley's Beatrice must struggle to maintain her belief in her identity of innocence even though it is "violently thwarted" by her world. Denied vision, these characters must shoulder the burden of their selfhoods. It is important that their inability to break out of the self into imaginative vision forces them to define themselves in history: Cain journeys away from Paradise to eke out an existence in the realm of historical time Lucifer defines; Beatrice tries to ensure through Bernardo that history will record her as a martyr for a dream of innocence. Still, these characters maintain the link between heroism and the tragic. Insofar as they struggle to preserve their identities even as they humble themselves to the limits of history, they prove their heroism. But insofar as they are trapped within history rather than liberated into vision, they are tragic. They can find a heroic identity, but—tragically—not a fully imaginative humanity.

As we reflect on the gap between Beatrice caught in the world of self-anatomy and the audience that can perceive the ideal type she gestures towards, between Byron's "mobile" spectator and his history-bound characters, or between the plot Schiller creates for his characters and the plots they try to craft for themselves, we begin to sense that the tragedy of these romantic protagonists is defined by the distance between their sense of themselves and the vision of the spectator, by the distance between the stage world and the world of imaginative vision. We can now see what those romantics who worked within contemporary stage conventions gained: the nineteenth-century theater, which at first appears as a debased medium hostile to visionary poetry, is discovered as a means to image the limited world of the present that awaits the liberating power of the imagination.

Goethe tried to close the gap between the spectator's vision and that of his protagonists, granting Egmont a glimpse of the future and allowing Iphigenia to enact a myth of history that binds the vision of the ideal to the progress of history. In *Faust*, he went even further, seeking to bridge the distance between the stage and the poetry of vision. *Faust* is both the period's greatest victory over the limits of its stage and an indication that its theater could not finally contain the entirety of the romantic vision; for *Faust* demonstrates that the full pattern of romantic thought, the full movement from the problems of self and revolt to their resolution, can begin in the stage drama of the first part of the play but ends in the barely dramatized vision of the second part, what I have termed, following Blake, "visionary forms dramatic." These "visionary forms dramatic" do not so much represent an escape from the actual theater to a mental theater as they represent the hope that the imagination can liberate us from the present restricted world bodied forth on the stage, and usher in the real drama of the life of vision.

Nonetheless, most romantic dramas remain within the "sad reality" of the historical world that could be portrayed on the nineteenth-century stage. Shelley, the visionary poet of *Prometheus Unbound*, reflects this turn to the stage world of self-anatomy and historical violence in his attempt to offer his age a tragedy to match the masterpieces of the past. We find a similar turn in the dramas of the French romantics and particularly in Musset's *Lorenzaccio*. Trying to stage both the glory and the frustration of the revolutionary spirit that had so decisively shaped France, Hugo, Dumas, Vigny, and Musset found in a theater of limits a way to present the tragic conflict between individual and community, between revolutionary act and visionary ideal.

CHAPTER SEVEN
NEOCLASSICISM,
MELODRAMA, AND
FRENCH ROMANTIC
DRAMA

Romanticism came early to France, as early as Rousseau; but, despite Constant's *Wallstein* and de Staël's enthusiasms for German drama, despite rumblings in the second decade of the nineteenth century and increasingly vocal proclamations like Stendhal's *Racine et Shakespeare* in the third, romanticism did not become a major force in Paris theaters until the late 1820s. This long delay is surely linked in part to the fact that the French people had to live through the revolutionary events which spurred much of romanticism elsewhere, but it is also a function of the French romantics' need to displace the traditional literary drama to make way for a new form.

The German romantics had to create a national dramatic tradition. In England, playwrights hoped to revive a once-great tradition. In France, the romantics found themselves struggling against the tradition of neoclassicism that in the 1820s was still firmly entrenched at the Comédie Française and was still seen by many critics and key portions of the theater audience as the only "legitimate" drama. Thus, in France, the popular drama, particularly the melodrama, was not so much a threat to the romantics as an arsenal of weapons to be drawn upon in the struggle against the neoclassical establishment. The history of French drama between the Revolution of 1789 and 1830, the year of the "battle" of *Hernani* and another Revolution, has been seen as a struggle between neoclassicism and the melodrama, with the latter proving victorious.[1] While the theatrical situation was much more complex—we should not forget the presence of the *vaudeville* or the rise of the "well-made" play—such an account does delineate the boundaries within which romantic drama developed in France.

We must not, however, confuse French romantic drama with the melodrama. The romantics borrowed from this popular form, but it was neoclassical tragedy they sought to replace; that is, they hoped to use melodramatic devices to create a modern rival to traditional tragedy. Thus, in one sense, French romantic drama is an attempt to combine the practices of the melodrama with those of neoclassicism. The romantics' tendency to call their plays *drames* and to turn to prose while still reaching for tragic effects suggests this hybridization. Yet, finally, these romantic plays set themselves in opposition to both rival forms, seeing them as embodiments of partial visions. French romantic drama finds the tragic in the moment when man, revolting against the closed world embraced by neoclassical tragedy, finds he cannot break free into a renewed world but is instead trapped within the melodramatic pattern of violence issuing in a resurgent old regime.

This fall from established order into a violence that finally results in a renewed but diminished order also outlines a vision of revolt and of the Revolution itself. Hugo declared, "The physiognomy of this epoch will be determined only when the French Revolution, which personified itself in society in the form of Bonaparte, personifies itself in art."[2] This call is not so much a demand for art committed to a particular ideology; after all, Napoleon's own ideological relationship to the Revolution is ambiguous. What Hugo seems to want is a work of art that embraces all of the contradictions and tensions of the Revolution, much as Napoleon might be said to have done.

Still, Hugo's search for an art work equal to the task of embodying the Revolution does raise the issue of the relationship between the dramas written during the romantic period and politics. In France, the drama could not remain aloof from the political realm. After all, the Revolution had demanded propaganda plays; Napoleon had banned them. Under the restored monarchy, censorship was in force, prohibiting, for example, the production of Hugo's *Marion Delorme*. Under the July Monarchy, Hugo was again censored when *Le Roi s'amuse* was removed from the stage after its opening night. Political events could grant plays an ideological twist they might not otherwise have possessed. Arnault's conventional *Germanicus* (Comédie Française, 1817) was banned after a riot, the difficulty arising not in response to the play's vision but because its author was an exiled ally of Napoleon.[3] Even foreign plays could be caught up in political battles. Revolutionary Paris welcomed *The Robbers* as a call to liberty, equality, and fraternity. When an English acting troop appeared at the Porte-Saint-Martin in 1822, crowds still incensed by memories of French defeats pelted actors with eggs and potatoes.

Some plays gained political significance through circumstance; some clearly had a political content. But we must be careful not to identify any particular dramatic form with a particular political view. For example, neoclassicism might at first seem to be the style for political reaction, given its links with the golden years of the *ancien regime*. However, in the hands of artists like David and dramatists like Chénier, neoclassicism also became the style of the Revolution. Then it was appropriated by Napoleon. Again, the melodrama, as a popular form, might be thought to express the people's discontent and their aspirations, but its escapism marks it more as a palliative than as propaganda.

What of romantic drama? Despite Hugo's assertion of the link between romanticism's stylistic revolt and the Revolution (as when, for example, he called 1830, the year of *Hernani,* a "literary '93"), the political positions of French romantics ranged from the conservatism of Chateaubriand to Hugo's growing liberalism; it is difficult to accept Hugo's definition of romanticism as "*liberalism* in literature."[4] Still, there is a sense in which French romantic drama—in fact all romantic drama—is deeply political. We can get at this aspect of romantic drama by borrowing Irving Howe's definition of the political novel that he sees as coming into being in the years following Napoleon:

It is at this point, roughly speaking, that the kind of book I have called the political novel comes to be written—the kind in which the *idea* of society, as distinct from the mere unquestioned workings of society, has penetrated the consciousness of the characters in all of its profoundly problematic aspects, so that there is to be observed in their behavior, and they are themselves often aware of, some coherent political loyalty or ideological identification. They now think in terms of supporting or opposing society as such; they rally to one or another embattled segment of society; and they do so in the name of, and under prompting from, an ideology.[5]

Romantic drama, from *Götz* with its study of the shift from the medieval to the modern world, to *Lorenzaccio* with its portrayal of a failed revolt, is political in this sense: not that it embraces a particular ideological position but that it presents a society open to or threatened by profound change and characters who seek to further or hinder that change. *Hernani* may seem a call for revolt; *Lorenzaccio* may seem to outline the futility of rebellion. Goethe may have penned both *Egmont* with its operatic vision of liberty and *The Natural Daughter* with its bleak view of the Revolution. But all of these plays, as their involvement with a dynamic sense of history dictates, create worlds in which man must confront radical shifts in the political, social, and cultural orders. In the sense that romantic tragic drama typically sets forth the defeat of revolutionary hopes, with all political movements compromised, these plays may be deeply antipolitical: their true hope may lie with vision rather than with political action. But they are not apolitical.[6]

However, neoclassical tragedy and melodrama, rivals of French romantic drama during the 1820s, were not political in Howe's sense. Neoclassicism offered a society above and beyond fundamental change. Even when it took subjects from history, the very style of neoclassicism seemed to assert continuity and convention; even when liberal sentiments were voiced (as in Casimir Delavigne's plays), the focus is not upon the possibility of a significant shift in society but upon the intrigues between private individuals. In the melodrama, an eternal moral order is discovered beneath any shifts within society. Melodrama seeks the revelation of virtue, not the exploration of ideology. Neoclassicism and the melodrama could become ideologically charged forms within particular situations: there is a sense, for example, in which the theaters under Napoleon sought to bolster the Empire, offering neoclassicism, on the one hand, as an image for the upper classes of an eternal world immune to historical change, and melodrama, on the other, as a morality lesson for the masses, a lesson that teaches that violence leads only to a return to virtue. Still, neither form explored politics as a problem.

The "personification" of the age of revolution that Hugo sought was not to be found in any of the alternative forms that arose in the French theaters of the early nineteenth century, but only in romantic drama itself. While the most famous play on the Revolution—Büchner's *Danton's Death*—was not written in French, *Lorenzaccio* comes closest to this ideal embodiment of the rhythms of revolt; and we can read much of French drama after 1789 as pursuing this personification, with certain key works adumbrating the romantics' plays and others turning to neoclassical or melodramatic models.

I
CHÉNIER'S *CHARLES IX*: TRAGEDY AND HISTORY

ON THE EVE of the Revolution, the neoclassicists still controlled the French stage. The Comédie Française exercised a monopoly over the legitimate drama more powerful than that of the comparable patent theaters in London. There had certainly been challenges to the national theater and its repertoire. New theaters and theatrical forms had sprung up, and even the Comédie's offerings betrayed a movement away from its strict espousal of a neoclassical ideal. Still, when Marie-Joseph Chénier, friend of Danton and brother of the poet killed by the Revolution, offered his *Charles IX* to the Comédie in 1788, he submitted a play that adhered to neoclassical rules. While his tragedy's inflammatory ideas first prevented its production, Chénier had written in alexandrines, observed the unities, used a small cast, made no gesture towards the mixture of genres, and retained such devices as the Voltairean narrator. It seemed as if even the most revolutionary spirit had to bow to the strictures of neoclassical form.[7]

Not that neoclassicism lacked revolutionary credentials. David had created for painting a republican neoclassicism opposed to the aristocratic rococo, and Chénier hoped to do the same for the drama. Jean Starobinski has written of David's turn to traditional neoclassical forms in his depictions of revolutionary oaths and the parallel turn in Chénier's plays:

> To express the hero's fidelity to this oath, the painter finds he has to manifest his own fidelity to aesthetic standards. This was the intention of poets like Marie-Joseph Chénier, who tried to give the Revolution its own drama. In it, the rigor of Racinian tragedy was strictly imitated with great care taken over versification. Only the subject was topical, as in *Charles IX,* which at the end of 1789, for the first time in the French theater, showed a king of France as a criminal. It was a strange survival, which made use of rationalist arguments: Its proponents refused to see that such tragedy was doomed to mere repetition.[8]

In stressing the allegiance of revolutionary classicism to past forms, Starobinski correctly suggests that a play like *Charles IX,* despite its republican content, could never envision a world remade but must instead repeat the patterns of traditional tragedy; this is one reason why revolutionary classicism could not provide romanticism with a dramatic form. Chénier, however, seems aware of the limits his form places upon him and uses them to define Charles's tragedy as an entrapment within the patterns of the past.

Chénier's play centers around the St. Bartholomew's Day Massacre. It depicts a vacillating Charles IX urged to the suppression of the Protestants by the Queen Mother, members of the nobility, and the Church. Those who counsel against the massacre, clearly the author's spokesmen, argue that the king should rule in accordance with the laws and in harmony with the people. Possessing what Chénier calls an "irresolute, timid, and cruel character,"[9] Charles agrees with first one side and then the other, until he is finally persuaded to order the assault. In the final scene, however, he comes to realize that he has made a horrible mistake. He has turned against his own people and authored a national tragedy.

We can glimpse the tension between Chénier's formal decorum and his bloody content if we examine his use of a formal feature borrowed from earlier neoclassical dramas, the appearance of a narrator who comes on stage to report a catastrophe. The Chançelier de l'Hospital acts as a messenger but does not, as do so many of his predecessors, enter to announce the death of a son, the murder of a favorite, or the hidden truth of some family relationship. The tragic action no longer centers upon an individual who is caught in a neoclassical intrigue of love and honor affecting only the few people at the summit of society who form the court. *Charles IX* presents a tragedy of an entire nation, and thus the Chançelier arrives to paint a tableau of public destruction:

> Within our walls the blood flows in rivers.
> All those who live, except for the hangmen,
> All quake; heaven itself has veiled its light,
> And Paris now is only a vast lair
> Where the dead. . . . (V, ii)[10]

Here, the King of Navarre interrupts, unable to bear the horror of this report of the St. Bartholomew's Day Massacre. The tragedy occurs when the wrangling at court comes to an end and an action against the Protestants is ordered, when we move from the hermetically sealed world of the neoclassic court into the arena of historical events.

However, the play itself never discards the formal limits of the neoclassical palace tragedy. The events that make up the content of the play may take place in the streets of Paris, but Charles never leaves the court; and herein lies his tragedy. Charles is presented with two possible courses of action. The first, set forth by his mother and her associates and finally accepted by Charles, brings violent destruction down upon the nation and also entraps Charles within the court. The second would free Charles from the court to have him remake the nation in the image of an ideal. Eleanor Jourdain has argued that all of Chénier's historical dramas present a vision of an "ideal national life":

In fact justice is hardly done Chénier, if the success of his tragedies is put down to their significance in the political order. His vision of France, which dominates his whole *théâtre,* expresses an ideal beyond that of the majority of writers of his day. . . . In his pamphlet, *De La Liberté du Théâtre en France,* Chénier showed that he considered the function of the stage to be the representation of the ideal national life, while by a counter current the representation of the stage should affect that life. The function of tragedy, he considered, was to draw the whole attention of a people to historical facts that threatened this life.[11]

In *Charles IX,* Coligny and the Chançelier de l'Hospital promote this vision. They call for a France defined by freedom and enlightenment.[12] The Chançelier envisions a Golden Age at the end of history and its chronicle of oppression. He would liberate Charles from the confines of the court to .

unite him with his people in a perfect social order. Coligny also urges Charles to break with the past and the court to lead the French against their Spanish enemies. Both want to escape the pattern of French history, for it has been a sequence of tragedies preventing France from becoming the Eden it could be.

For Chénier, Charles is tragic because he sides with the past, not the future. Charles, torn between the rival factions of his court, cannot establish a firm identity for himself. He stands in striking contrast to the conventional figures of French neoclassical tragedy who were, like the protagonists of English heroic drama, monolithically conceived. Constant, writing in 1809 during Napoleon's continuing effort to preserve the neoclassical tradition, spoke of the solidity of these heroes: "We have a need for unity which makes us reject everything in the character of our tragic figures which hinders the unique effect we wish to produce."[13] Charles longs to become such a forceful character, a hero free from the inner divisions that beset him. Unfortunately, he can take on the trappings of the neoclassical hero only by following the court's advice to pursue violence. If he is to be such a hero, he must define himself within the world of the neoclassical court, and that means he must commit himself to repeat past mistakes and thus to will a tragedy.

Charles's career must be a tragedy of repetition, since for Chénier only the past is tragic. The play's subtitle, "A School for Kings," indicates Chénier's hope that he can educate the people and their rulers to avoid the violence that erupts in the Massacre and thus to shape their history into a grand march towards the ideal French nation. The goal of Chénier's theater is to lead the nation on a progressive, enlightened course that would enable man to transcend tragedy.

In locating tragedy in the moment when the protagonist is caught between a vision of the future and the history of violence that still shapes the present, Chénier's play looks forward to romantic tragic drama. But since tragedy is for him a feature of the *ancien regime* and not of the republican future, traditional forms must be used even as they restrict the playwright's ability to dramatize the historical crisis at the center of his play. Chénier's play offers a paradoxical relationship between form and content: Charles's entrapment within a world of courtly intrigue makes him tragic from a revolutionary perspective; but to present that entrapment, Chénier had to adopt a traditional form. While Chénier's selection of an act of historical violence for his climax is an innovation, that violence is firmly identified with the past and encapsulated within a traditional form that keeps the Massacre offstage.

We see here one attempted resolution of the tension between conventional literary structures and the new content that found its way into the drama during the revolutionary era, a tension that can also be defined as that between neoclassical tragedy and the melodrama. Further experiments were undertaken in the Parisian theaters, particularly during the revolutionary years and again during the 1820s, times when the theaters were under less rigid governmental control. Interestingly, such plays were usually further from the vision of romantic drama than was *Charles IX*.

II
THE SEARCH FOR A FORM AND THE
AVOIDANCE OF TRAGEDY

DURING THE REVOLUTION, a number of playwrights joined Chénier in adapting neoclassical tragedy; as Chénier did in his *Caius Gracchus* and *Tibère,* they often adopted a classical subject as well. However, they went further than he did in remaking the tradition in the light of revolutionary doctrines. For example, Charles-Phillippe Ronsin, at one time a general for the Republic and later executed as a supporter of Hébert, wrote a number of plays that preserved some traditional features (the alexandrine, for example) and rejected others (he abandoned the five-act structure). The distinguishing mark of his plays, however, is that their polemic message takes precedence over any evocation of the tragic. In his *Arétaphile ou La Révolution de Cyrène* (Louvois, 1792), the Plutarchan heroine dies after trapping Cyrene's tyrannic usurper, thus clearing the way for the joyous revival of the republic under her husband. Again, Ronsin's *La Ligue des fanatiques et des tyrans* (Théâtre de Molière, 1791) is tragic in that it concludes with the death of the hero, Sélimars; but Sélimars forbids mourning since a republican army has at the same time defeated the counterrevolutionary alliance. In such plays, the tragedy of the individual is a small discordant note in a hymn to republican victory. These plays are in fact closer to romance than to tragedy. The same can be said of another group of plays that might have discovered a type of revolutionary martyr tragedy; these plays dealt with the deaths of such figures as Marat and Barra, but generally placed more emphasis upon anticipated republican victory than upon grief over the martyr's death.[14]

Maréchal's *Judgment Day for Kings,* mentioned in chapter 2 as an exemplary revolutionary propaganda play, goes even further to make a complete break with conventional tragedy. Written in prose and set on an island far from the neoclassical court, this is a drama of universal liberation in which all of the crowned heads of Europe perish in a volcanic eruption, as even nature joins the revolutionary cause. Men and women of high estate die in this play, but their deaths are merely a comic interlude in a romance of republican victory. The play celebrates the demise of the aristocratic, providential world and thus the destruction of traditional tragedy. In *Charles IX,* the ideal national life lay in the future, so man could still find life tragic in embracing the past. In Maréchal's play, where every republican desire achieves instant gratification, revolution appears as the virtual end of history: there is no time for tragedy. Tragedy can arise within history only when history is freed from apocalyptic patterns to appear as a series of time-bound struggles.[15] Revolutionary plays like Maréchal's offer secular Last Judgments, putting the past to the torch as time begins anew, much as the revolutionary calendar attempted to open up the future free from the intrusions of traditional temporal rhythms.

The logic of Maréchal's play is close to that of Saint-Just's revolutionary pronouncements: "Republican government has as its principle virtue; if not terror"; "The human heart advances from nature to violence, from violence to morality."[16] The pattern of history enunciated by Saint-Just and staged by the revolutionary drama might appear to follow the three phase movement we find in romantic poetry. The journey out of nature through violence to morality sounds deceptively similar to the movement from innocence through experience to a higher innocence. Romantic tragic dramas, like *Wallenstein* and Byron's *Marino Faliero,* reveal the distortion in equating these two patterns; for they insist upon the destruction that results when man must use violence to win his way free from the past. Maréchal and Saint-Just, however, hail violence as the harbinger of an apocalyptic moment of revolt that brings history to a joyful conclusion. Terror breeds virtue; the dawn of the new age must be blood red.

The rhythm of these revolutionary dramas may distance them from romantic drama, but it reveals how close they are to the pattern of the melodrama, which developed in the theaters of revolutionary Paris and drew in part upon such republican plays as *Judgment Day for Kings* and *Les Victimes Cloitrées.* The melodrama retained the revolutionary pattern of terror issuing in virtue; some melodramas gestured towards revolutionary themes in focusing upon struggles between rich and poor, the powerful and the disadvantaged. We might recall Nodier's contention that melodrama was "the only popular tragedy appropriate to our age" in that its frenzied action mirrored the chaotic events through which the French nation had passed.[17]

However, as we saw in chapter 2, the melodrama did not follow the revolutionary drama in prophesying a world remade through revolt. It envisioned instead the resurgence of the traditional moral order. Melodramatic terror is not a unique phase in man's progress towards a virtuous polity. Violence is a recurring episode in the continuing revelation of an eternal, but hidden, moral order. If the melodrama displaces the emotions and deeds of the revolutionary era onto the stage, it is to assert that the Revolution was not a cataclysmic step forward to a new human order but part of a periodic testing of Providence.

While *Charles IX* gestured towards historical tragedy, most of the neoclassical plays that followed, even the most innovative, froze historical acts into heroic gestures. The melodrama, while born of the Revolution and offering a "revolutionary" theatrical technique, offered lessons in morality, not essays into history. We can sense how far the early nineteenth-century French theater was from offering a tragic account of historical man when we note that Lebrun's *Marie Stuart,* an adaptation of Schiller's play, struck audiences at the Comédie Française as an innovation in 1820, twenty years after the first German performance of *Maria Stuart*.[18]

A number of playwrights sought a form for history plays outside of the opposing camps of neoclassicism and the melodrama. The circle of writers around Stendhal, that included Mérimée and Vitet, wrote plays that came to be known as "scènes historiques." They were episodic works in prose that sought to offer an objective portrait of an age. They were loosely organized, for comic and tragic plots were seen as distorting the historical truth. These writers oppose history to the drama. Vitet, for example, described his efforts as "historical facts presented in dramatic form, but without any pretension of composing a drama." Interestingly, these plays dealt largely with moments of turmoil and revolt, with Mérimée writing *La Jacquerie,* Rémusat *L'Insurrection de Saint-Domingue,* and Vitet *La Ligue.* These "scènes historiques" had some impact on French romantic drama, especially upon *Lorenzaccio,* but they could not by definition spark a revival of the drama or a renewal of the tragic vision.[19] The "well-made" play offered another mold within which to pour historical events, though these plays treat history as comedy with chance seen as ruling change and trivial acts revealed as the true cause of great events, as can be seen in Lemercier's *Pinto* (1799), a precursor to the "well-made" treatment of history, or in Scribe's *A Glass of Water (Un Verre d'eau;* 1840), the "masterwork" of the genre.

Another group of plays sought a compromise between neoclassical tragedy and melodramatic innovations. Often seen as precursors of the romantic drama,[20] these plays are really attempts to shore up the declining appeal and prestige of neoclassical drama. Still, the theater of the 1820s was groping for new forms, and thus playwrights introduced innovations even when tackling classical subjects. Etienne de Jouy's *Sylla* treated audiences to crowd scenes, and Michel Pichat's *Léonidas* was given a spectacular, even melodramatic production.[21] French history continued to inspire a number of plays, including François Ancelot's *Louis IX* (Comédie

Française, 1819). The Bible lay behind Guiraud's *Maccabees* (Odéon, 1822) and Alexandre Soumet's *Saul* (Odéon, 1822). Schiller was adapted by Lebrun, and Shakespeare loomed behind Lemercier's *Jane Shore* (Comédie Française, 1824). The neoclassical camp was opening its gates to change, but the changes were small and the plays rather timid. It is thus not surprising to find Lemercier and Jouy joining such classicists as Arnault in objecting to the staging of Dumas's *Henri III et sa cour* in 1829.[22]

The most interesting of these intermediate playwrights is Casimir Delavigne who had a string of successes beginning with his *Sicilian Vespers* (*Les Vêpres siciliennes;* Odéon, 1819). Maurice Descotes explains that Delavigne's compromise between neoclassicism and proto-romantic innovations offered an increasingly bourgeois audience their own brand of neoclassicism in which the rules, which had come to represent high culture, nobility, and even morality, were preserved while historical subjects and some liberal themes were introduced.[23]

Sicilian Vespers, treating the Sicilian revolt against French occupation, does broach the key romantic themes of selfhood and revolt. Lorédan, son of the rebel leader Procida but also friend of the French governor Monfort, murders his friend for his father's cause only to feel remorse for what he comes to see as an assassination. He kills himself as his punishment. We would seem to have here a presentation of the rebel's double bind, desiring liberation but being forced to become a terrorist. However, Lorédan joins the revolt not out of conviction but because he is jealous of Monfort's attentions to Amelie, who seems to prefer the governor to her fellow Sicilian. The revolutionary theme is obscured by a conventional love intrigue. Again, Monfort and Procida at first seem to have some complexity, some internal division. Monfort is described as having the heroic charisma of a Gothic villain-hero:

> Superb, impetuous, sure of success,
> He dazzles the court with his magnificence,
> He compels loyalty even by his rashness.
> He might sacrifice, without any check to his desires,
> His life to his duty, his duty to his pleasure. (I, i)[24]

Procida, the victorious patriot, appears bloodthirsty and almost inhuman in the pursuit of his goal; he might remind one of Octavio Piccolomini. However, both characters finally fall into conventional heroic molds, with Monfort dying for love and country and Procida mourning the son who has been sacrificed to liberate Sicily. Delavigne has a sense of those romantic features that might please his audience, but he makes sure that these features are securely tucked away within a conventional framework.

His *Marino Faliero* (Comédie Française, 1829) shows promise but again disappoints. The play has been seen as offering all of romanticism's stage innovations.[25] But, whatever its formal experiments—involving scene changes, fights on stage, and spectacular sets—it backs off from the romantic vision. As in Byron's play on the subject, we witness the movement of Faliero from nominal ruler of Venice to leader of a rebel force. An insult to his wife by a young nobleman who is barely punished by the aristocratic council of the Forty again prompts the doge's revolt. At times, Delavigne seems to echo Byron's play, but he treats the story in a completely different way from that of the English poet. In the preface to his play, Byron explains his approach: ". . . before I had sufficiently examined the records, I was rather disposed to have made it turn on jealousy in Faliero. But, perceiving no foundation for this in historical truth, and aware that jealousy is an exhausted passion in the drama, I have given it a more historical form."[26] Byron rejects a love theme for his play to concentrate upon history; he defines the doge not through jealousy but through the absolutism that marks his self-conception.

Delavigne's play, however, returns to the "exhausted passion." Steno may only have been voicing unfulfilled desires when he insulted the doge's wife, but she is, in fact, in love with the doge's nephew, Fernando, whom Faliero treats like a son. The opening scenes are devoted to the lovers, and the play centers less upon the political implications of Faliero's deeds than upon the private ties among the characters, as Fernando and Elena struggle between love and guilt and Faliero feels the pangs of jealousy. The play closes not with the doge's vision of Venice's destruction (Delavigne does include it, adopting a key feature of Byron's play only to displace it from the center of his drama) but upon the reconciliation between Faliero and his wife.

The characters change with this shift in focus. Faliero is not the proud, impetuous hero of Byron's play; he is a good old man, who places his faith in his young wife and nephew and is more concerned with them than with the glory of his name or of Venice. To give an example of the weakening his character undergoes: Byron's Faliero makes the decision to massacre all his fellow aristocrats, a decision which brings to a head the contradiction the revolt poses to the noble rebel; in Delavigne's play, the doge confronts the same question, but as he hesitates to answer, a warning cry goes up that scatters the rebels without a decision being made—his goodness is not compromised by a fateful command. The character of Israel Bertuccio also reveals the distance between the two plays. Byron's dedicated revolutionary who urges fanatic devotion to the rebel cause is transformed by Delavigne into a man who feels more attached to his role as Faliero's old comrade–in–arms than he does to the revolt. Bertuccio's key scenes (I, viii; V, i) focus on his commitment to his former commander.

The only character who is more intriguing in Delavigne's version than in Byron's is Steno who appears masked at the party staged in the second act to observe Elena for whom he has conceived a passion. Celebrating "This night of drunkenness...what tumult! Ah! disorder is sweet" (II, xiii), Steno captures the mood of *Lorenzaccio* and has some of the aristocratic fascination that marks Gothic figures as well as Egmont and Schiller's Fiesco. He has the energy and the self-awareness that are missing from the other characters, as he explains his philosophy to his host, Lioni:

> But excess revives us; it grants charm to everything.
> One love is enough for you; mine wanders
> From the slave of Smyrna to the noble Roman,
> And from the courtesan it reascends to the beauties
> That your ball promises for my enchanted eyes.
> The play at the casino piques my interest;
> But I must squander money there or I die from boredom. (II, iv)[27]

As such a speech indicates, Delavigne has a feel for the emotions, the settings, and the subjects that were vital to romantic drama; but he does little with them. They are finally window dressing for a neoclassical display of the struggle between duty and love; his formal innovations find no counterpart in his vision.

Romantic playwrights could and did learn from their early nineteenth-century precursors, from melodramatists and neoclassicists, writers of "scènes historiques" and forgers of compromise between tradition and innovation. However, the vision of romantic tragic drama finally sets it apart from these rival forms. As we have seen, the key alternatives of neoclassicism and melodrama are included within romantic tragic drama to embody thematic points. Thus, neoclassical tragedy could be evoked to define a lost heroic society. Musset's Lorenzo dreams of being a Brutus; the audience might well imagine his longing to become a character from Corneille or Voltaire. Hernani, as an outlaw, has been cast out from the neoclassical world of heroic codes and social titles to which his rival, Don Ruy de Gomez, still belongs. Just as Euripides' figures stand behind the characters in Goethe's *Iphigenia* or as Shakespeare's creations shadow the protagonists of English romantic drama, so do the monumental figures of neoclassical tragedy loom in the background of French romantic plays.

The melodrama offered a "revolutionary" theatrical style that the French romantics imitated; but they used it to define a trap into which the protagonist falls. Melodramatic patterns enter the romantic drama as a nightmare of failure in which the rebel finds that he has embraced violence against the powers that be, only to contribute to the restoration of their power. Lorenzo's revolt ends by strengthening tyranny in Florence.

Antony's last act of violence is made in homage to conventional morality.

Neoclassical tragedy and the melodrama simply lacked the means to stage central romantic concerns. Neither offered ways to stage the exploration of the self. As Constant noted, neoclassical tragedy required a fixed, absolute character; the melodrama offered moral types, not inward-turning voyagers into the interior. Again, neoclassical tragedy tried to maintain the brand of providential drama the romantics knew was no longer possible. The melodrama, ahistorical in its portrayal of virtue's perpetual victory and antitragic in its insistence that violence finally contributes to that triumph, opposes romantic drama's vision of history and revolt.

As dramatic forms, neoclassicism, melodrama, and their progeny may have been opposed, but as visions they were secret sharers in a belief in providential order; official and popular culture alike offered images of security—of fixed identities and inevitable outcomes—in troubled times. Only romantic drama confronted the possibility that the modern revolutionary age had put an end to such certainty, and thus only romantic drama could stage the tensions and anxieties of revolt.

III

THE THEATER OF REVOLT

VIRTUALLY EVERY MAJOR French romantic author contributed to the struggle to replace neoclassical tragedy with romantic tragic drama. Vigny wrote some celebrated plays and provided a romantic version of Shakespeare. Dumas won for the romantics their greatest theatrical successes. Lamartine, Nerval, Gautier, and Balzac all played lesser roles in the romantic battle for the stage.[28] But it was Victor Hugo who stood at the head of the romantic forces. While he wrote neither the most memorable play of the period nor the most popular, he demonstrated more forcefully than any other French writer that the romantic poets could offer the stage a literary drama worthy of supplanting official neoclassicism and capable of presenting the tragedy of revolt.

In recognition of Hugo's importance, most accounts of French dramatic history locate the romantic theatrical achievement between the years 1830, when Hugo scored his first stage success with *Hernani,* and 1843, when *Les Burgraves* failed and Hugo retired from the stage. While this conventional set of dates distorts history somewhat (Dumas's historical drama *Henri III et sa cour* was staged in 1829, Vigny's seminal translation of *Othello* was performed the same year, Hugo's own *Cromwell* had been written in 1827, and a definably romantic presence was noted on the Parisian stage until 1850), the choice of 1830 as the *terminus a quo* for French romantic drama is suggestive. A revolutionary year, 1830 reinforced the importance of revolt and its frustrations. Plays as different as Dumas's *Antony,* the popular *Robert Macaire* of Frédérick Lemaître, and Musset's *Lorenzaccio* reflect the hopes raised by the July Revolution and the disappointments that attended the July Monarchy.[29] This new revolt did not usher in the grand, terrible days of the Revolution and Napoleon, but the petty and money-mad era savaged in Balzac's novels. The pattern of French romantic drama, of a heroic revolt degenerating into an affirmation of a petty order, of a tragic descent from grand action to a melodramatic triumph of order through violence, seemed to be enacted on the historical stage.

Hugo's first important play, written before the July Revolution drove home the distance between the present age and past glories, already rests upon the awareness that traditional systems of order have lost their power, an awareness we have found in *Götz* and *Wallenstein, Cain* and *The Cenci.* In *Cromwell* (1827), Hugo presents his protagonist as a rebel who creates a world devoid of an established order. Calling Cromwell the "gigantic prototype of the religious reformation, of the political revolution of England," ("colossal prototype de la réforme religieuse, de la révolution politique d'Angleterre"; 1: 444),[30] Hugo sees him as a rebel who destroys the orders of the past by uprooting the official church and murdering the king, acts strikingly similar to those of the Paris revolutionaries of '89 and '93.

Hugo offers a Cromwell who is unhappy with the world he has brought about. Whereas the traditional Church articulated a shared vision of the divine plan, Cromwell's Puritans engage in endless arguments over Scripture; human interpretation replaces divine truth. Cromwell, however, turns to an astrologer for a direct revelation of the supernatural. Again, the king stood at the summit of his society, holding a position given meaning within a hierarchical order. Even though he has all the power of a king and perhaps more, the Lord Protector is seen by Hugo as desiring a kingly title, the sanctified role. Cromwell longs for the providential certainty possessed by the men who lived within the order he has destroyed.

Cromwell is the prototype for all those Hugolian figures who, like Ruy Blas, desire recognition within a meaningful social structure and who, like Hernani, insist upon discovering within their lives a mysterious fateful pattern, the mark of a postprovidential destiny. Significantly, in the preface to *Ruy Blas,* Hugo links that play to *Hernani,* arguing that both works depict a society without a strong central government (1: 1495). In *Hernani,* he tells us, he sought to portray the life of the Spanish nobility before the establishment of a sovereign monarch. In *Ruy Blas,* he depicted the collapse of the monarchy. In both plays, as in *Cromwell* and the later *Burgraves,* Hugo chooses moments in history when man must confront the collapse of order or create a new order. Hugo's defense of these plays on historical grounds is often and for the most part justly criticized; he is rarely concerned with accurately portraying an age. But if *Ruy Blas* and *Hernani* do not tell us much about Spanish history, they do confront the central fact of post-Revolutionary history—the absence of absolute cultural and social structures. These plays engage history in a significant way, not by sticking to the facts nor by providing bits of local color, but by depicting men who must shape history by offering order to a world that is without God or King. Hugo's plays, like those of Schiller, are historical in that they show men working to make their own history; they are also thus political in Howe's sense.

In the plays of the other French romantics, we find a comparable sense of the loss of traditional order. In *Chatterton,* Vigny's poet/protagonist isolates himself from the bourgeois society of his own time to live in the imagination as a monk of the tenth century where he can discover the beauty and truth ignored by his age. In Dumas's *Antony,* the author's spokesman argues that the French Revolution destroyed the code of manners within which man had defined himself; this playwright-within-the-play explains that modern dramatists must turn to the past to discover a milieu in which the social order endowed individual identity with a meaningful shape. Musset's *Lorenzaccio* emphasizes the distance between an oppressive present and Florence's golden past.[31] In such plays, society either lacks order or enforces a limiting order. To move beyond such an order, the romantic protagonist must revolt.

Rebels fill the French stage under the romantics. Cromwell and Lorenzo are revolutionaries seeking a total change in the political structure of their societies. Hernani and Ruy Blas may have less coherent political programs, but they, too, protest against oppressive societies. Others struggle for personal or spiritual values rather than explicitly political goals. Vigny's Chatterton cries out against a world that, by chaining man in the market place, places material gain above spiritual development. Like one of Schiller's frustrated idealists, he demands the right to discover his full humanity free from the roles society would force upon him: "I have made up my mind not to disguise myself and to be myself to the very end, always to listen to my heart, whether it speaks in compassion or in indignation, and to resign myself to fulfilling the law of my being" (I, v).[32] In Dumas's *Antony* and *Kean,* the man of passion and genius finds that bourgeois society cannot accept him. It insists that he conform to codes of behavior and deference that would limit and belittle the power of his character. Society demands that Antony sacrifice his passion to a hypocritical moral code and that Kean bow to those who possess a superior social position even though his genius sets him above them.[33] Antony and Kean join with their fellow romantic protagonists in revolt; for only through revolt can they free themselves from the moral, social, and political restrictions that seek to shape them to the limits of their unheroic and empty world.

Revolt is the dialectic counterpart of the inward turn that seeks to discover an ideal within the self, for revolt is the outward action taken in hope of creating a world that will support that ideal self-definition. Still, with the exception of *Lorenzaccio,* we do not find in French romantic drama the same subtle analysis of the dangers of "self-anatomy" that we discover in the plays of Shelley or Goethe. While it is clear that Chatterton pits an inner vision against his materialistic world and that Dumas's Kean finds his identity in the disorder of his genius and not in the order of his world, these characters do not possess the complex inner life of a Faust or a Beatrice Cenci.

Of course, French romanticism was more fully involved in the "social question" than either German or English romanticism. Hugo could proclaim that in France, home of the Revolution, the nineteenth century had two names: romanticism and socialism. Social thinkers like Ballanche, Michelet, Lamennais, Fourier, and above all Saint-Simon had a greater impact on the French romantics than, for example, Godwin had on the English poets. The idea of Society often takes the central place in French romanticism that theories of the individual Imagination held in English romanticism and a concern with Culture held in German romanticism. The Saint-Simonians called to the French romantics to reform society through art. Writers like Hugo and Vigny took up the challenge and, perhaps as a result, tended to emphasize their protagonists' outward, social revolt, not their inner struggles.[34]

The protagonists of French romantic drama can, as a result, seem hollow figures. In some of these plays, the central figure appears to be the least defined of the characters, a weakly portrayed thematic mouthpiece. In *Chatterton,* for example, Vigny's poet/protagonist lacks the solid stage presence of the capitalist John Bell with whom he lives. Even figures like Lord Talbot and the Lord Mayor who appear only briefly in the final act seem more fully defined than Chatterton.[35] This apparent weakness in the handling of the central character is certainly intentional. John Bell and the others have accepted a role within society and can thus be defined on stage through that role: Bell as a capitalist, Talbot as a member of the nobility, and so on. The man who is willing to accept the limits of the social world can be presented on stage through society's code of manners, dress, and behavior. But a protagonist like Chatterton, who rejects society, requires a different stage presence. He cannot be defined through the rules and acts that make up the social world presented on stage.

The presentation of such an ideal character obviously poses a problem for the dramatist. As Théophile Gautier put it in an essay on Hugo's *Angelo,* dramatic "characters are made visible by shadows,—and there is nothing less dramatic than virtuous people."[36] Hugo's mode of characterization, his mixture of the sublime and the grotesque, is an attempt to solve this difficulty. In order to avoid the undramatic stance of the ideal character, Hugo conjoins the sublime identity towards which his protagonists gesture with a grotesque but powerful stage presence. Lucrèce Borgia would bore us as a doting mother, but she commands our attention as a scheming poisoner. Triboulet's demand to be seen as an ideal father interests us only because he appears as a caustic and even vicious grotesque.

Of course, this method of characterization has come under heavy attack. For these figures do not so much explore their selves as invoke them through the heroic gestures of revolt; moreover, the sublime/grotesque opposition seems to some to be perilously close to the antitheses between good and evil invoked in the melodrama.[37] It is true that the French romantics and Hugo in particular develop their plays around pairs of terms: genius and disorder, heaven and hell, angel and devil. It is also true that such oppositions mark the plays of Pixérécourt and his fellow melodramatists.

However, Hugo uses these antithetical pairs to place his figures beyond the terms of the antithesis and thus beyond melodramatic moralism. When in *Marion Delorme,* Didier says of the heroine, "Oh God, the angel was a demon!" ("O Dieu! l'ange était un démon!"; 1: III, vii), this pronouncement does not signal Hugo's acquiescence to a melodramatic moral vision; rather, it places Marion beyond conventional moral definition. Her human complexity cannot be reduced to either category, "angel" or "demon." Again in Hugo's *Marie Tudor,* the Queen says to her lover, "Either your eyes are those of an angel, or those of a devil." He responds, "Neither devil nor angel, but a man who loves you" (2: II, i).[38] The point being made may not be subtle, but it is clear: the absolute moral categories that were invoked on the melodramatic stage must be discarded if we are to penetrate to the truth of man's humanity. Hugo's characters demand to be taken in their entirety, not in some delimited form demanded by society's moral vision. Similarly, Dumas's Kean demands that society take his disorder along with his genius; Antony, his passion along with his talents; Chatterton—in a speech quoted above—his indignation along with his compassion. Where the melodramatist offers characters conceived as simple wholes or absolutes, the romantic playwrights mix antithetical traits in the same character to assert that man's character can never be captured by a list of qualities. This admixture of the sublime with the grotesque resembles the tension between sympathy and judgment central to the English drama. The grotesque features of a figure invite us to join his world in judging him, but we must sympathize with his sublime qualities. The French romantics thus attempt to rescue their characters from the world of the melodrama by re-introducing the internal division often seen as a key to tragic characterization.[39]

This use of apparently melodramatic devices to move beyond the melodrama has led some to call French romantic drama "merely theatrical."[40] It is true that, where the English created a theater of the self, the French offered a theater of revolt that delights in the postures and trappings of heroic action. However, this intense theatricality is necessary to plays in which the protagonist does not so much possess a selfhood as seek to discover one through a revolt that would catapult him beyond the limited world depicted on stage. An extreme theatricality is used to summon up a world beyond the stage. This is also the function of granting the protagonist a more "poetic" style of speech than that given to the other characters. This use of heightened language can be found even in the prose plays of the period. In Hugo's prose dramas the reach towards a poetical prose can seem strained, but in *Lorenzaccio* and *Chatterton* Musset and Vigny are able to suggest the superior sensitivity and imagination of their protagonists by granting them a lyrical mode of speech.

The impact of this lyricism is clearest in a verse play like *Hernani.* In his intensely lyric duets with Dona Sol, Hernani offers us a glimpse of his personality free from the limits of his world. When he speaks the language of society, Hernani must give up his lyric identity. As he claims for himself a place within Spanish society, he allows himself to be defined by a role dictated by his family and political relations:

> God, who grants the scepter and gave it to you,
> Made me Duke of Sergorbe and Duke of Cardona,
> Marquis of Monroy, Count Albater, Viscount
> Of Gor, master over regions that I cannot number.
> I am John of Aragon, Grand Master of Avis, born
> In exile, the proscribed son of a father assassinated
> By the order of your father, King Carlos of Castille! (1: IV, iv)[41]

How much more powerful, how much more suggestive is the identity he creates for himself in his lyric tirades:

> You believe that I am perhaps
> A man like all other men, a being
> With sense, who runs straight to the goal of his dreams.

Disillusion yourself. I am a force that drives on!
A blind and deaf agent of funereal mysteries!
A soul of misfortune made of shadows!
Where am I going? I do not know. But I feel myself driven
By a violent wind, by a mad destiny.
I descend, I descend, and cannot stop. (1: III, iv)[42]

In such passages, Hernani gestures wildly towards the identity he would create beyond the confines of his society. If the language that he uses often seems to lack clear referents, it is because his poetic self-conception points beyond present referents to a fuller, more spacious world. If these passages appear excessive, it is because only in excess can he summon the energy to shatter the limits of his world and thus catch a glimpse of the new one he would create.

Significantly, Hernani's lyric flights of self-definition occur in his scenes with Dona Sol; for to a greater extent than in the English or German drama the French protagonists explore the possibility that love can resolve their struggle to create themselves as heroes in a fully human world. We think of Wallenstein, Beatrice Cenci, Marino Faliero, Manfred, and even Faust as isolated figures no matter what their ties to others. But we cannot imagine Hernani without Dona Sol, or Ruy Blas without his Queen. Chatterton's poetic vision is intimately linked to his love for Kitty Bell. Antony's sense of society's injustice arises from his frustrated love for Adèle. The bond between the lovers becomes a sign of a fully human society. Shunned by others, the protagonist finds support and the opportunity to expand lyrically towards his full identity in the society of two created in love. In a sense, these French dramas offer a pair of protagonists; the double death or suicide that closes so many French romantic plays becomes the appropriate ending.

Together, lovers like Hernani and Dona Sol evoke a lyric world that exists beyond the stage world, but it is in the stage world that they must act. A world of light, love, and transfiguration beckons; but man finds he must adopt the tools of darkness, violence, and disguise to reach it. The use of disguise is another feature of French romantic drama that the critics label as a weak, conventional device. But disguise is wholly appropriate to the situation of the romantic protagonist. Disguise is the point of contact between the protagonist's vision of an ideal society and the means he must adopt to pursue that ideal.

The romantic protagonist cannot commit himself to the limits of a social persona without betraying his true identity. However, he can enter into society by donning a mask, playing at a role. Clearly, such a figure can be accused of being a mere theatrical construct, for he plays at having a character rather than possessing one. Yet it is his self-conscious theatricality that frees his identity from any limited definition set by convention. Insofar as the part he plays remains a disguise, he is freed from the prying eyes of society and is able to preserve his selfhood intact. However, as he comes to identify himself with his role, he becomes part of the limited world and his independent selfhood is compromised.

The romantic protagonist dreams of living in a world without the need for disguise. Chatterton, rejecting his society, eschews disguise in a speech quoted above ("I have made up my mind not to disguise myself"). Again, Ruy Blas imagines the rescue of Spain as a removal of disguises: "Let us save the people! Let us dare to be great and strike! / Let us strip the shadows from intrigue and the masks from the knaves!" (1: III, v).[43] But, ironically, it was only through donning a mask that Ruy Blas, the lackey, achieved the power and position needed to change the course of his country's history. Moreover, the role is a part in a drama engineered by Don Salluste, the master of violent revenge. Ruy Blas took up his mask to free his nation; he finds that his role-playing has compromised him and involved him in a petty plot against the queen. Hernani has similar difficulties in keeping clear the distinctions between his various roles and his true identity: is he Jean d'Aragon or Hernani, his social role or his disguise or something else altogether? The fullest treatment of man's struggle with disguise is found in Musset's Lorenzaccio, the man who becomes his mask.

Disguise both indicates the presence of a true but hidden identity and presents visually the rebellious idealist's compromise with the violent means of his world, his entrapment in the present even as he seeks the future. In the preface to *Cromwell,* Hugo says of his protagonist's attempt to fulfill his dreams that the commitment to acting upon the ideal in the present brings the "moment when his chimera escapes him, when the present kills the future" ("le moment où sa chimère lui échappe, où le présent lui tue l'avenir"; 1: 446). This last phrase encapsulates the tragedy of revolt. Man is trapped in historical time. He must use the means of the present to make the future. Acting in the present, he must betray his future dreams, bringing them forth in a masked and compromised way. One indication of this dilemma is that the use of disguise seems always to open the way to violence: for example, Lucrèce Borgia and her son destroy each other because she has hidden her identity from him; the complex masking of the *Burgraves* almost leads Otbert to kill his father, Job/Fosco.

French romantic drama stages this destruction of the dream by having the protagonist's ideal romance of love and reform replaced by a violent melodrama of order regained, as can be seen in the works of Dumas. The plays of Dumas are often very close to the melodrama, though he usually works to shift the melodramatic towards the tragic, much as "Monk"

Lewis sought to transform the English Gothic drama. In Dumas's immensely popular *La Tour de Nesle* (Porte-Saint-Martin, 1832), melodramatic patterns overwhelm any interest in the supposedly historical subject. However, while the play does end with a return to order and a defeat of the villains, order is won only through the destruction of both the innocent and the evil. And Buridan, the most interesting figure in the play and another of Dumas's images of genius in revolt against power, is a morally mixed character whose destruction is deserved yet lamented; for the energy he embodies is desperately needed by the society he seeks to rule. There are horror and loss in this play, if not tragic terror and pity.

Dumas's *Antony* works a different variation upon the melodrama in pursuit of the tragic. Through his love for Adèle, Antony defines himself in opposition to his society. While he is a bastard shut out from society and she is a married woman with an established position, he convinces her that their love stands beyond social convention. He dreams of escaping society to live in freedom and love. However, when her husband returns to discover their affair, Antony murders Adèle. Such a gesture might be seen as an affirmation of their love beyond life in the bourgeois world, as a violent love/death compact. However, Antony survives Adèle to proclaim, falsely, "She resisted me, I killed her" ("Elle me résistait, je l'ai assassinée!"; V, iv). He does not use violence to place their love beyond social judgment. Rather he uses it to preserve Adèle's reputation within society, to restore her place within the limits of social convention. Of course, he also thus insures that he will be condemned by society. He sacrifices his freedom and reduces himself to a villainous role in a melodramatic plot of virtue's resistance to vice. Yet Dumas's play moves beyond mere melodrama by suggesting that there is a tragic distance between Antony's vision of love and the melodramatic social order of the present that he must rejoin in order to serve his mistress.

Hernani, often seen as the quintessential French romantic play, offers an opportunity to bring together the various points I have been making, and it clearly reveals French romantic drama's revisionist use of neoclassical tragedy and the melodrama. The world of *Hernani* lacks the order that marked traditional tragedy, as can be seen if we compare it with a neoclassical model, Corneille's *Cid,* which shares a number of features with *Hernani* and is mentioned by Hugo in his preface. Like Hernani, Rodrigue loves a woman, Chimène, only to find their union blocked by a representative of the older generation and traditional ways, in this case, Chimène's father, Don Gomès. Where Hernani violates Silva's honor and betrays his hospitality, thus provoking him to revenge, Rodrigue kills Don Gomès, forcing Chimène to seek retribution. Just as Charles V intervenes to pardon the plotters and to marry Hernani to Dona Sol, so does the King of Castille restore order at the end of Corneille's play, granting Chimène to Rodrigue. Interestingly, Rodrigue earns a new name through his exploits, that of the Cid; the complexities surrounding the naming of Hernani have already been mentioned.

Of course, this last point of comparison reveals the great differences between the two plays. As Hernani, Jean d'Aragon dons an antisocial disguise, but Rodrigue earns a social title, a badge of fame. Rodrigue can win an objective social status because the *Cid* takes place within a world with a well-defined social order, a clear political hierarchy, and a respected if not all-powerful ruler. The clarity of this order and its code of conduct define the conflict: Rodrigue loves Chimène but must fight her father to protect his father's honor; Chimène loves Rodrigue but must seek revenge for her father's death. Such well-defined problems are open to resolution, a resolution that replaces revenge with love and displaces violence from the squabbles within the court to the war against the Moors.

In *Hernani,* however, there is no accepted order. As the preface to *Ruy Blas* makes clear, Hugo conceived *Hernani* as treating a transitional period in which the fiercely independent aristocrats found their power taken from them as an absolute monarchy was established; we may be reminded of *Götz* when we think of Hugo's play as a portrait of the decline of proud noblemen. Initially, at least, this society lacks the firm order that hierarchy and an aristocratic code grant the world of the *Cid.* Neither personal nor political relations are clear. Thus, in the first act, we meet a king hiding in a cupboard to mask his sexual misadventures, a young nobleman forced into revolt against the crown, and an aging aristocrat trying to live in the past.

Each of the central male characters responds differently to this collapse of order. The subtitle of the play, "Tres para una," suggests that we have three men in pursuit of one woman; more than that, however, as is clearer with the three main characters in *Ruy Blas* (see "Preface," 1: 1494), the three men embrace different dramatic visions, different plots for their world. Silva seeks to preserve the traditional way of life. As his famous appeal to his ancestors' portraits in the third act reveals, his identity is tied to the past. His socio-political goal is to maintain the aristocratic code against both the insurrection of common robbers and the intrusion of the king. His personal goal is to marry Dona Sol, thus binding the new to the old. Silva would like to see life as comedy, in which his long life devoted to honor is consummated in marriage and revived through love. But comedy is for younger men. His plans failing, life for him takes on the plot of a neoclassical tragedy where oaths are binding and love must pay a debt to wronged honor.

Don Carlos initially sees life as a farcical pursuit of pleasure. He seems to value nothing, as he seeks to abduct Dona Sol and later violates the honor of Silva. On the one hand, he helps reveal the pretense of Silva's vision of himself as comic hero, for Don Carlos turns Silva into a *senex* guarding a young girl. On the other hand, Carlos becomes a villain in Silva's tragedy of revenge. However, Carlos is transformed after he communes with the spirit of Charlemagne. He renounces personal goals for public power and stability. In a sense, Carlos tries to form the kind of order that the King of Castille can create at the end of Corneille's play. More precisely, however, the half-comic, half-serious Don Carlos, who acts the villain in his pursuit of Dona Sol before being "converted" into the Emperor Charles V, tries to grant his world a melodramatic shape; Georges Lote has seen the close of the fourth act as Carlos's attempt to stage a melodramatic victory.[44] In that he fails, at least as far as Hernani and Silva are concerned, we see the gap that opens between order and the violence used to secure it, between virtue and terror. And in that the play moves beyond this melodramatic denouement, we are also given a dramatic image of the insufficiency of melodramatic patterns from the romantic perspective: melodrama is something to be contained within a larger dramatic rhythm.

Hernani's plot is made up of Silva's and Carlos's plottings: Silva's plan to marry Dona Sol and Carlos's planned abduction of her; Carlos's schemes to become Emperor and Silva's plot against the King; Carlos's acts as Charles V and Silva's return for revenge. For a play sometimes thought of as lyric and undramatic, all of these schemes make for considerable plot conflict. Still, the center of the play does lie outside these plots, for Hernani eschews such scheming. His deeds do not shape the action of the play. Tellingly, he wins Dona Sol through an act of the King; he meets his death through an act of Don Ruy de Gomez.

Hernani, much like a romantic dramatist, finds himself caught between the plots of neoclassical tragedy and the melodrama. However, Hernani's characteristic mode of action is not a plot—a scheme to get something—but escape. As is the case with other romantic protagonists, Hernani's response to the collapse of traditional order is a desire for a new world. As a bandit, he seems to be modeled on Karl Moor, Schiller's archetypal rebel, but he is less interested in reform of society than retreat from it. He flings his protest against society as such, as he dreams of creating a community of two with Dona Sol, telling her, "I need you to help me forget the others!" ("J'ai tant besoin de vous pour oublier les autres!"; 1: I, ii). The new world he seeks is beyond the confines of everyday life; he wants to expand lyrically towards some other reality.

Charles Affron has said of Hugo's play that "the movement of the play is away from plot, temporal contingency, and conventional portraiture, towards a purely lyric sphere."[45] It would be more accurate to say that Hernani dreams of escaping the world of his rivals' plots to win a purely lyric sphere. Becoming Hernani, he has escaped the political realm that would trap him within the role of Jean d'Aragon. He would escape all limitations by leaping into eternity with Dona Sol. The series of disguises he adopts—as Hernani, as a member of Carlos's entourage, and as a pilgrim—suggests that his identity lies outside any role. He acts within the world, but only to suggest that his "true" self lies elsewhere. His speech also gestures beyond the world of conventional language to a visionary realm. In a sense, Hernani tries to escape plot in poetry, to escape the metonymic order of contiguity and continuity in the metaphoric order of congruence and communion. He always seeks the unplottable—freedom, a visionary love, death. His struggle is against those who would emplot life, who would tie his identity to a particular time, a particular place, a particular sequence of events, a particular name. As long as Hernani remains aloof from the plots of others, he sustains his lyric independence. But once he joins the plot against Don Carlos and, more important, once he accepts the plot for life outlined by Carlos as Emperor, Hernani finds himself trapped within the world he would flee. Poetry gives way to plot, vision to drama.

We can better understand the dilemma facing Hernani if we examine the opposition between love and hate which is as central to his play as it is to *Bertram* and in a different way to *The Cenci* or *Don Carlos*. Within Hugo's play, love offers liberation, whether it be the libertinism of Don Carlos, the long-deserved rest sought by Don Ruy de Gomez, or the visionary freedom celebrated by Hernani. Hate, however, threatens to bind each of these men to a limited project and a restricted role. Carlos pursues the bandit Hernani and thus becomes a conventional figure of authority. Don Ruy de Gomez is consumed with jealousy of his younger rivals and thus appears as an old man trying to keep a young girl from her rightful mate.

Hernani struggles between his love for Dona Sol and his hatred for the King, as his soliloquy at the end of the first act indicates:

> For an instant
> I stood wavering between love and hate;
> My heart is not large enough for both you and her.
> In loving her, I forgot the burden of your hate;
> But, since you wish it, since it is you who come
> To remind me, very good, I remember!
> My love weighs down the uncertain balance
> And falls completely on the side of my hate. (1: I, iv)[46]

Hate usually wins in these internal battles. If Hernani could escape with Dona Sol, he could live a life of love, but his world continually summons him back to violence. After Carlos abducts Dona Sol, Hernani finds it easy to commit himself wholly to revenge, hatred, and death; he becomes one of the plotters, defined by his role in their scheme.

Yet violence and hatred seem to be set aside at the close of the fourth act. Becoming Emperor Charles V, Carlos renounces both love and hate, Dona Sol and revenge on the plotters. Hernani gives up his vendetta and rejoins society to enjoy his love. Here the play would end if it were either the *Cid* or a melodrama.

But, of course, the play moves on to the deaths of Hernani, Dona Sol, and Silva. Carlos's order does not resolve the problems of his world. To begin with, it has no place for Silva; it does not balance the equation of love and hate. On the night of Hernani's marriage, a marriage that might image the rebirth of Spanish society, Silva returns as the voice of the past; his world has been destroyed to make way for Carlos's new order. Silva recalls Hernani to the identity he has sought to discard, to the past he has sought to escape. This final confrontation is not merely an abstract balancing of emotional counters. Hugo is not only depicting the private conflicts of the characters in his play, but also charting the convulsive historical movement from the age of the free aristocracy to one in which a central monarch will rule. While the melodramatist can move blithely through violence to order, the historical dramatist must ascertain the loss wrought by historical change. Silva—the representative of the free nobility now in decline—returns to claim from Hernani a debt of violence and hatred. Don Ruy demands that Hernani kill himself as a sacrifice to redeem the violence that has been wrought against his world.

Hernani himself has also lost something in changing his name and ways to become a member of the new society of Charles V. He has chosen the literal order of Carlos over the imaginative freedom he has always sought. He has thus betrayed himself to the world of social roles and political plots he has always rejected, and he is now subject to its rules. Silva's demand that Hernani commit suicide to fulfill his oath, often criticized as a forced means to a catastrophic end, in fact reveals by being mechanical that what we witness here is a victory of the binding role over the freely evoked identity, of the closed world of an actual social order over the open vision of an ideal society, of metonymic patterns of plot over metaphoric gestures of the imagination.

Of course, dying together, Hernani and his beloved Dona Sol sever all ties with this world of violence and move in their final lyric duet towards a vision in which they evoke the full identities they would discover in their love. Hernani remains true to his identity beyond the stage even in his highly dramatic death. In a sense, we get here a double ending similar to that at the end of *Egmont* in which there is an opposition between vision and the denouement of the plot. However, while Goethe's *Egmont* moves to free its protagonist from the limits of the stage, *Hernani* offers an image of an almost impossible gap between the stage world of hate and death and the visionary world of love and life. The rebel cannot bridge that gap, for his revolt forces him to adopt the violent means against which his revolt is directed. Vision does not become enacted as it does at the end of *Faust;* it is perhaps finally freed but only in the moment of death.

Hernani marked an important moment in the development of French romantic drama not only because it became a rallying point for the shock troops of young romantics or because it was a well-publicized victory for the leader of the romantic school; it was central because it marked the moment when the pattern of French romantic drama became clear. This pattern invoked neoclassical tragedy and the melodrama but only to use them to discover a new brand of tragedy. In a sense, French romantic drama reveals the tragedy of a society that sees its choices—at least as they are dramatized—limited either to a return of a discredited old regime or to the violent victory of an order that has all of the limitations of the past with none of its glory. This tragedy of man caught between neoclassical nostalgia and melodramatic nightmares found its greatest embodiment in Musset's *Lorenzaccio.*

CHAPTER EIGHT
MUSSET'S *LORENZACCIO:*
INNOCENCE, EXPERIENCE,
AND THE TRAGEDY OF
REVOLT

The first scene of Alfred de Musset's *Lorenzaccio* plunges us immediately into the debauchery that has come to dominate Florence under Alexandre de Medicis. The Duke impatiently awaits a fifteen-year-old girl he hopes to corrupt. His cousin Lorenzo—known to most of Florence by the deprecatory nickname "Lorenzaccio"—has acted as his panderer. Assuring the Duke that the girl will come, Lorenzaccio titillates his cohort with a loving catalogue of the joys of seducing a young innocent. We first discover Lorenzo as a man who delights in betraying "middle class mediocrity personified" ("la médiocrité bourgeoise en personne"; I, i, 38; p. 5)[1] into the hands of the jaded Duke.

What sort of hero does Musset offer? This play, often seen as French romanticism's best candidate for the honorific of "tragedy," challenges in its very first scene our preconceptions of the heroic and the tragic. Certainly, few figures we would call tragic heroes impress us less at the outset than does Lorenzo. Tragedies typically move quickly to establish the greatness of their heroes. We see Oedipus as king and victor over the Sphinx before we discover him as the tragically deluded slayer of his father and the husband of his mother. Macbeth returns as a valiant defender of Scotland and only then begins to plot against Duncan. Even Richard III, who wastes no time in informing us he will "prove a villain," does so in an impressive manner that points to his strength and energy.

But the only "greatness" Lorenzo demonstrates initially is a certain skill as a procurer. A roué who serves a bastard "butcher boy" imposed on Florence by the Pope and the Emperor, Lorenzo hardly appears heroic. Lorenzo does not even initially adopt a stance typical of other romantic protagonists. He might have been portrayed as another Beatrice Cenci, an innocent struggling against a depraved world; or as a Chatterton, a recluse seeking to withdraw from an oppressive milieu; or as a Hernani, a noble outlaw in revolt against society. Although such characters may not sit at the summit of their worlds, they impress us by rejecting their petty and oppressive societies. Lorenzo, however, seems at first to delight in his vice-ridden city. He appears as a knowing reveller, not a strayed innocent; a figure at the center of Florentine life, not a recluse; a spy amongst the republicans, not a rebel. We do, of course, learn later in the play that Lorenzo is closer to a Beatrice or a Hernani than we might think. Indeed, Lorenzo will tell us that he became "Lorenzaccio" only to mask his plans to liberate Florence. But if Lorenzo is to be revealed as a heroic idealist, if we are to find that Lorenzaccio is merely a role, then why does Musset go to such lengths to demean his protagonist? Musset devotes almost the entire first act to depicting the base Lorenzaccio. We see him as a panderer (I, i), a drunk (I, ii), a spy (I, iv; I, vi), and a coward (I, iv). We hear only his mother's vague allusions to a possible nobility within him (I, vi). What has happened to the traditional strategy of establishing the stature of one's protagonist? Why so much Lorenzaccio before we are introduced to the virtuous Lorenzo?

Much has been made of *Lorenzaccio's* dependence upon *Hamlet*;[2] perhaps an answer to the question of Lorenzo's presentation lies in this similarity. Musset may simply adopt a Shakespearean model to free himself from the limitations of neoclassical and melodramatic modes of characterization, the one statuesque and the other moralizing. Hamlet, particularly as the nineteenth century understood him, would appear the perfect prototype for Musset to follow in his depiction of a young idealist adopting a persona to act within a corrupt world. The parallel would seem promising, for Hamlet, too, wears a mask, playing the madman as much as Lorenzo plays the debauchee. Hamlet, like Lorenzo, feels himself ordained to murder a member of his own family and acts out a role to accomplish this execution. Hamlet, who has within him something inexpressible which "passes show," might even presage the romantic protagonist who finds he cannot discover his full identity within the limits of his world. Musset's striking portrait of his protagonist might then appear mere imitation, another instance of romantic Elizabethanizing.

Our examination of Shelley's use of Shakespearean echoes has taught us to suspect such arguments. There is little simple imitation in the plays of the major romantic writers. When they draw upon Shakespeare—or upon the Greeks, as Goethe does in *Iphigenia in Tauris*—they do so with a thematic purpose, often to illuminate the differences, not the similarities, between their protagonists and the heroes of traditional tragedy. Such a purpose defines the relationship between *Lorenzaccio* and *Hamlet*; for the parallels between the two plays and their central figures are inexact.

We meet Hamlet before he assumes his madman's role. We know him to be a heroic figure; we are told that he is a brilliant student, an excellent swordsman, the envy of the court, and a potentially great ruler—he is the "observ'd of all observers," as Ophelia tells us. His claim upon our attention has been established in the past, prior to the play. We immediately grant him our sympathy, even our admiration. When we see him play the madman, we understand and support his reasons for doing so. Shakespeare makes sure we will empathize with Hamlet as a hero, even though we may later come to judge him as he pursues his "mad" acts. Lorenzo's case is vastly different. *Lorenzaccio* begins, as it were, with the second act of *Hamlet*. Musset's protagonist has already donned his mask when we meet him. We do not share in his deception; we are deceived.

If Hamlet is a hero who dons a debilitating mask, Lorenzo is a flawed character who dons a mask in the hope of creating himself as a hero. There is no way for Lorenzo to establish a heroic identity within his decadent society. He has perhaps been noble in the past. He certainly dreams of being great in the future. But in the present, he is neither. Beneath Hamlet's disguise there is something the audience believes to be heroic. Beneath Lorenzo's mask, there are only the confusion and alienation of the isolated self as it struggles to discover a coherent identity. For the moment, his mask is his only way of becoming a unified character. Musset must present Lorenzaccio and not a noble Lorenzo because at the moment the play begins Lorenzo is only a dream.

Musset's departure from the model of *Hamlet* points to the crucial difference between the traditional figure like Hamlet who *is* a hero and the romantic protagonist who wants *to become* a hero. Through his analysis of Lorenzo's masking, Musset explores the double tragedy that faces romantic man. From one perspective, Lorenzo's reliance on his role points to the tragedy of his selfhood: he cannot create the integrated identity sought by romantic man but must bear behind his mask the divisions of his self-consciousness. From another perspective, Lorenzo's mask is a sign of his revolt, an instrument in his violent effort to realize his ideal—literally, a means of getting close to Alexandre. Lorenzo is thus clearly linked both to figures like Beatrice Cenci who seek a full identity behind the "mask and mantle" of their social role and to figures like Hernani who take on a new identity as a sign of their revolt against society. Lorenzo is central to a discussion of romantic tragic drama, because he appears to be the least heroic of figures—he is as distant from the firm, self-possessed figures of French neoclassical drama as he could be—and yet he is still heroic insofar as he seeks an ideal: a reformed Florence and a renewed self. Romantic tragic drama sought to discover tragedy in an increasingly unheroic age; *Lorenzaccio* tests the limits of this project.

I
LORENZO AND FLORENCE: INNOCENCE AND EXPERIENCE

LORENZACCIO IS IN part a story of lost innocence, both the innocence of a man and that of a city. Musset's play takes place in Florence after the collapse of the Florentine Republic and the return to power of the Medicis, a return abetted by the Emperor and the Pope.[3] We have already seen that Musset moves swiftly to reveal this Florence as a place of violence and decadence. Alexandre rules as a brutal and debauched autocrat. His court lives in idle pleasure, but the nobility has been stripped of any real power and the people lead miserable lives in the shadow of court fêtes. Alexandre maintains his rule through a network of spies and with the aid of German mercenaries. He is accompanied by an assassin; exiles choke the roads from Florence.

If the first scene of the play establishes a brutal present, in the second we hear longings for an ideal Florentine past:

Florence was once (it was not so long ago) a good house well built. All the great palaces, which are the homes of our leading families, were its columns. There was not one, of all these columns, that was greater than the next. Together they supported a venerable and strongly reinforced arch, and we could walk beneath it without fear that a stone might fall upon our heads. (I, ii, 245–52)[4]

The Florence of the Republic is seen here as a cohesive and well-organized society. Each of the noble families had a place within the city's political structure and the people could live safely within that structure. However, as the same citizen tells us, the city changed when "two bad architects"— the Emperor and the Pope—"decided to take one of those columns, that of the Medicis, and make it a tower" (I, ii, 252, 256–58; p. 9).[5] Replacing the checks and balances of the Florentine Republic, a single tyrant now rules over everyone:

It does no good for the Florentine families to cry out, or for the people and the merchants to protest: the Medicis govern by means of their garrison. . . . a bastard, half a Medici, a boor that heaven created for a butcher boy or a farm hand, corrupts our daughters, drinks our wine, smashes our windows. (I, ii, 268–70, 273–76; pp. 9–10)[6]

Musset suggests that Florentine history has followed the pattern that we have found in other romantic plays of a fall from cohesive order into oppressive anarchy. Musset's Italy is not unlike Shelley's and quite like Byron's. An autocrat, who is, in Shelley's terminology, an "anarch" in that he uses his power to destroy rather than to support human life, rules through robbery and rape. As in Byron's *Marino Faliero*, the disruption of the social order has left both the aristocrats and the people without a meaningful place in the political system. Many romantic plays trace the fall of a traditional hierarchical society; Musset's play like Byron's history plays or Shelley's *Hellas* makes a similar point by lamenting the collapse of a republic.

Florence longs for a redeemer. Several candidates offer themselves for the part, the Strozzi and La Marquise Cibo among them. The most important of these potential redeemers is, however, Lorenzo himself who plans to end tyranny by murdering Alexandre. His attempt to redeem his city is the most interesting, for it involves him in a revolt that brings about his own fall.

While we first meet Lorenzo as Lorenzaccio, the figure of experience standing in the midst of Florentine corruption, we learn that his "youth was as pure as gold" ("Ma jeunesse a été pure comme l'or"; III, iii, 558; p. 56). Significantly, he spent it away from Florence at the pastoral retreat of Cafaggiuolo. Cafaggiuolo—which Lorenzo remembers as a place of peace, study, and communion with nature—remains for him an emblem of innocence, an innocence he also discovers in a series of pure young girls: his aunt Catherine, Pierre Strozzi's daughter Louise, and Jeannette, a girl from his youth. His thoughts of these girls mingle with recollections of his childhood to evoke a world of innocence quite different from Florence:

Poor Philippe! a daughter as beautiful as the day! Once upon a time, I sat near her under the chestnut-tree; her little white hands, how she was working! How many days I have spent, sitting under the trees! Ah, what peace! What a horizon at Cafaggiuolo! How pretty Jeannette was, the young daughter of the concierge, as she was drying her clothes! How she chased the goats that came walking over her linen stretched upon the grass! The white goat with the long slender feet would always come back. (IV, ix, 747–56)[7]

Beautiful women, nature, the white of innocence—these form a litany of memories, reminding him that somewhere a life exists that stands apart from Florentine decadence.

Such a life is for him, however, only a memory. Lorenzo's mother, who also pays homage to the innocent childhood of her Renzo or Lorenzino, provides us with a striking image of his fall from innocence:

Ah, Catinna, if we want to sleep peacefully, we must never have certain dreams. It is too cruel to have lived in a fairy palace where angels sang and to have been rocked to sleep by your son, and then to have awakened to a blood-filled hovel, filled with the debris of orgies and human remains, and held in the arms of a hideous spectre who destroys you while still calling you mother. (I, vi, 1078–85; p. 24)[8]

This passage is doubly important, for it repeats the image of Florence as a mighty piece of architecture that has fallen into decay and links that image to Lorenzo's transformation from an innocent youth into a hideous debauchee. This link is reinforced by the fact that Lorenzo was by birth entitled to a throne. But his mother now finds that Florence has become a slaughter house and her son the monstrous henchman of the butcher boy.

Lorenzo's fall from innocence has left him alienated and inwardly divided, suffering all of the torments of the self explored in *The Cenci*. We must understand that Lorenzo is not defined simply as a virtuous man who wears a mask of depravity. If he were to remove his garb as Lorenzaccio, we would not discover the innocent Renzo cowering underneath. Lorenzo is portrayed not as possessing layers of differing personality traits, but rather as having passed through several different identities over time. As in *The Cenci*, the depiction of the "fall" of man and of his society engages not moral categories but modes of human consciousness and action. As in the plays of Hugo, we are asked to understand the central character as he escapes from the absolute moral distinctions that marked the contemporary melodrama. In general, we can assert that while the melodrama attempts to divide mankind into those who are good and those who are evil, the romantic drama seeks to trace man's development from innocence into experience and perhaps beyond.

Lorenzo's identity thus lies strewn over time. In the past there may have been an innocent Lorenzo who decided to play a role, but he has now only an inner chaos of memories and hopes from which the mask represents his only escape. Lorenzo finds one of the greatest agonies of his fallen state in his alienation from his own past. The innocent Renzo can appear to his present self only as a "ghost."[9] When Lorenzo looks within, he discovers what Georges Poulet has called the "interior distance": "The contemplation of the past is thus the contemplation of the interior abyss into the depths of which, step by step, one has fallen down all the way to the present. How did one pass from such a height to such a depth, from such a plenitude to such a misery?"[10] This "interior distance" measures Lorenzo's fall from the "plenitude" of innocence to the "misery" of experience.

Divided within, Lorenzo reveals in his external role as Lorenzaccio further features of his fallen mode of consciousness. Lorenzaccio seems to possess two salient characteristics: a penetrating intellect and a delight in low pleasures. He resembles Shelley's Count Cenci whose turn to an analytic and isolated intellect is linked to a craving for increasingly extreme sensual stimulation.[11] Lorenzaccio's intelligence and wit are among the first things we notice about him. There is in him something of the Byronic irony that Musset admired so much,[12] but it has become decidedly corrosive. His mother complains that Lorenzo is marked by "an ignoble irony and a contempt for everything" ("une ironie ignoble et le mépris de tout"; I, vi, 1068–69). His ability to penetrate the hypocrisy of his society has led him to doubt and to belittle everything and everyone around him. When he first ventured forth into Florentine life, he rapidly became convinced that corruption ruled man:

I was just entering into life, and I saw, on my approach, that everyone was doing what I was doing. All the masks fell before me. Humanity lifted its dress and showed itself to me in all its monstrous nudity as if I were a skilled pupil worthy of her. (III, iii, 735–40; p. 59)[13]

Once he became conscious of the depravities of the world of experience, Lorenzo's piercing intellect could not turn from them: "The hand which has once raised the veil of truth can never let it fall again" (III, iii, 782–83; p. 60).[14] The analytic intellect does not, however, remain an objective observer as it peers into the depths of vice. Like Shelley's Count, Lorenzo finds that the anatomizing mind teaches the will "dangerous secrets" and lures him "into the depth of darkest purposes." He finds that the isolated intellect, seeing through man's often hypocritical virtues, leaves man's most vicious desires free to seek fulfillment:

By Heaven! What kind of man of wax am I? Has vice, like the robe of Dejanira, become so much a part of my body that I can't speak with my own tongue? The very air between my lips is vile despite myself. I was going to corrupt Catherine. I think I would corrupt my mother if it occurred to my brain to do so. (IV, v, 428–34; p. 73)[15]

Lorenzo, who understands man's vices, ends up as Lorenzaccio, who delights in them: "Vice used to be a garment for me, but now it is glued to my skin" (III, iii, 792–94).[16]

Lorenzo's innocence was, like that of Blake's Thel, partially mere ignorance. His fall into the divisive and depraved world of experience is in part a movement from pastoral retreat to urban chaos. But Lorenzo need not have come to Florence. As he himself tells us, no one compelled him to leave Cafaggiuolo (IV, iii, 165–66). Why then did he journey into the fallen world of Florence?

At the center of the play (III, iii), Musset presents the central encounter between Philippe Strozzi and Lorenzo, where Lorenzo attempts to tell the story of his life. Philippe, his sons imprisoned by Alexandre, feels that the time for revolt has finally come. He appeals repeatedly to Lorenzo, whom he has befriended despite his reputation, demanding that Lorenzo cease playing his role as Alexandre's panderer and join the republican ranks. Lorenzo parries these demands that he reveal a virtuous man beneath the mask of debauchery; he knows that no such man exists in the present. Instead, he tells Philippe of his virtuous past: "No matter how I seem to you now, Philippe, I once was virtuous. I believed in virtue, in human greatness, as a martyr believes in his God" (III, iii, 551–53; p. 56).[17] Knowing this virtue to be lost to him, Lorenzo explains, in the central speech of the play, what propelled him out of his innocence:

My youth was as pure as gold. But in twenty years of silence, a thunderbolt was forming in my breast. Truly, I must have been the spark for that thunderbolt, for suddenly, one night, seated in the ruins of the Colosseum, I rose, stretched my young arms toward heaven, and swore that I would kill one of my country's tyrants. At that time I was a quiet student, occupied only with art and science. How can I explain the strange vow I made? Perhaps it is what a man feels when he falls in love.

. . . .

I was happy then. My heart and hands were at peace. I was entitled to the throne, and I had but to let the sun rise and set, to see all human hopes flower around me. Men had influenced me neither toward good nor evil, but I was good, and, to my everlasting sorrow, I wanted to be great. But I must confess that if Providence led me to the decision to kill a tyrant, whoever he might be, pride led me to it also. What more can I say to you? All the Caesars of the world spoke to me of Brutus. (III, iii, 558–69, 574–83; pp. 56–57)[18]

This night at the Colosseum brought a moment of discontinuity, a sudden transition from one mode of existence to another. Had Lorenzo remained as he had been, the honest and virtuous figure of innocence, he tells us he would have grown to possess a life marked by "all human hopes." The organic imagery surrounding this path not taken (the cycle of the sun, the blossoming of the good life) contrasts with the imagery of catastrophe—the thunderbolt—that marks his break with his earlier life.

Lorenzo has had a secure niche within society, within the natural order of things. But he revolts. He breaks with his pastoral youth and hurls himself into urban experience; for he "wanted to be great," wanted to be a "modern Brutus" ("Brutus moderne"; III, iii, 729; p. 59). We might complain that Musset has Lorenzo mouth cliches about a vague destiny that dooms him as if he were a figure out of a Gothic melodrama. However, the vagueness of any providential element in Lorenzo's call to action is intentional. The Greek Orestes may be commanded by Apollo. Hamlet may be told by a ghost to seek revenge. But the romantic protagonist can no longer look to the gods or the fates to single him out for a heroic destiny. A Hernani seeks revenge because revenge enables him to cast himself in a heroic role. Shelley's Beatrice and Goethe's Iphigenia stand against their worlds because they hear a voice within themselves, not because they are called by the gods. Similarly, Lorenzo cannot be certain whether it is Providence or pride—God or the self—that urges him to action. An important element of his peculiarly romantic heroism is that he is willing to act without that certainty.

There are hints in the play of an alternative, non-tragic path for Lorenzo, but they prove misleading. Lorenzo sets forth from Cafaggiuolo still possessing the ideals of innocence. He enters the world of Florentine experience to shape its future according to these ideals. In romantic lyric, this descent into experience is often seen as a fortunate fall that enables man to create a "higher" or "organized" innocence. Within Musset's play, Philippe Strozzi voices a belief in the reality of this pattern. Philippe leads the republican nobles, but he has never engaged in any action to realize his ideals. Still a voice of innocence, he represents what Lorenzo might have become had he continued on his path of study and solitude. As Lorenzo puts it, Philippe has "lived alone. . . . Like a bright beacon you have remained motionless beside the ocean of men, and you have seen in the waters the reflection of your own light" (III, iii, 657–60; p. 58).[19] When we first meet Philippe at the beginning of the second act, he seems to question his stance as an isolated philosopher; he fears that his ideals may be only dreams and corruption and evil the realities of man's experience (see II, i, 5–32). Yet even in questioning his beliefs, Philippe moves to reassert them: "'Republic'—we must keep that word. It is only a word, but it means much to the people, and they will rise when they hear it" (II, i, 32–35; p. 26).[20]

Philippe resembles a Schillerian "beautiful soul" who is in touch with an ideal vision of life and who has had no experiences that have forced him to compromise his vision. Philippe stands apart from the corruption of Florence, still believing in "Virtue, Modesty, and Liberty" ("à la vertu, à la pudeur et à la liberté"; III, iii, 701; p. 59), and thus he can still envision an ideal end to its history. He argues that Lorenzo himself, despite all he has done as Lorenzaccio, can be redeemed if he saves his nation:

> But, if you were virtuous, when you have delivered your country you will become so again. To think that you are virtuous, Lorenzo, this is what makes my old heart rejoice. Then you will be able to throw away your hideous disguise, and you will once again become as pure a metal as the bronze statues of Harmodius and Aristogiton. (III, iii, 774–80; p. 61)[21]

Here, in his central statement of faith, Philippe argues that the fall of Florence and Lorenzo's loss of innocence can both be transcended, that his society can once again become an Edenic republic and that Lorenzo can prove himself as pure as the tyrannicides, Harmodius and Aristogiton. Moreover, this man of peace and scholarship believes that such redemption can be won through violence: the murder of Alexandre. Philippe sees no contradiction between his ideal vision and the violence he advocates. He does not believe that experience can contaminate the ideals of innocence. For him, Lorenzo's fall is a fortunate one, since it enables Lorenzo to commit the liberating murder that the innocent idealist could never accomplish; and afterwards Lorenzo can shed his experience of vice and violence as if it were a "hideous disguise."

Philippe might seem to endorse a version of the romantic triumph of innocence and vision, but his advocacy of violence must for us strike a discordant note. Philippe does not envision a transformation of man and his world through imagination and love. Rather, he believes that freedom and dignity can be won through murder. In the world of *Lorenzaccio*, the lure of violent action corrupts even the idealist, even the "beautiful soul." We can better define Philippe's stance if we turn once more to Saint-Just's maxim on virtue and terror. Saint-Just and the drama of the Revolution accepted the necessity of terror for the promulgation of revolutionary virtue. Philippe, too, endorses murder, but he wants to pass quickly over this descent into violence; characteristically, in the passage quoted above, he leaps from Lorenzo's past virtue to his future purity without mentioning the murder that must be committed to get from one point to the other. He tries to mask his acceptance of revolutionary terror by adopting the rhetoric of the romantic belief in man's progress through experience to a visionary innocence. Like other French romantic plays, *Lorenzaccio* demonstrates the tragic difference between these two positions and suggests that the attempt to cover up the realities of revolutionary violence with idealistic rhetoric plays into the hands of the established order: the belief of Philippe and his kind in an apocalyptic moment of violence capable of remaking the world prevents them from organizing a more practical revolt.[22]

Lorenzo himself has no illusions about the ability of revolt to triumph innocently. He knows the world of Florence too well to believe that action within that world can escape the taint of vice and violence. Nor can he believe with Philippe that the murder of Alexandre will, in fact, liberate their country. Not only does he warn Philippe away from compromising his beliefs through action (see III, iii, 488–519), but he also foresees the failure of his own attempt to change the course of Florentine history:

I'll make a wager with you. I am going to kill Alexandre. Once my deed is accomplished, if the republicans act as they should, it will be easy for them to establish a republic, the finest that ever flourished on this earth. Let's say they may even have the people with them. I wager that neither they nor the people will do anything. (III, iii, 815–20; p. 61)[23]

Lorenzo dreams of a golden age, but he is certain that it will not come about. He is even more certain that his actions will not return him to innocence. The burden of his discussion with Philippe in their central scene is that to act in the world of experience necessarily corrupts man. Like Shelley's Beatrice, Lorenzo lives in a world stripped of the romantic hope of regeneration. But where Beatrice struggles to keep her sense of her own innocence apart from the deed she must perform—she denies that she has committed a murder—Lorenzo is fully aware that he must adopt fallen means in the pursuit of his ideal end. Again, his relation to his mask as Lorenzaccio defines him. When he first adopted his disguise, he believed that it would preserve the innocence it hid: "When I began to play my role of the modern Brutus, I marched in my new habit of the vast brotherhood of vice, as a child of ten marches in the armor of a fairy-tale giant" (III, iii, 728–32; p. 59).[24] However, as we have seen, Lorenzo discovers that he cannot play a part in the world of experience without becoming part of it. The man no longer uses the mask; the mask begins to define the man just as the "robe of Dejanira" glues itself to the skin.

The striking aspect of Lorenzo's heroic project is that he understands how it has led to his degradation, yet he continues to pursue it. No other figure in romantic drama shares Lorenzo's awareness of the degree to which the world of fallen consciousness and action shapes even the noblest man, though there is a suggestion of this awareness in Byron's figures. Most romantic protagonists continue to assert their ideal identities apart from their worlds: Beatrice still insists upon her innocence; Faust continues to assert his titanic sense of himself; Hernani dies invoking a world transformed. Lorenzo realizes that he has created a demonic parody of his ideal self. He recognizes that as Lorenzaccio he has adopted a role that reduces him to a negative element within the various orders of his world; that is, he has allowed himself to be defined morally as an evil man and ideologically as a tool of the oppressors. He has sacrificed himself to his world. One key to his heroism and his tragedy is his willingness to lay upon the altar of experience the innocence that so many other romantic figures seek to preserve. Lorenzo has completely compromised his sense of self in striving for the ideal in a debased world. And in the end he has come to realize that his ideal itself will not be achieved through his struggle. How then, as Philippe asks, can Lorenzo act? How can he murder Alexandre, if he does not believe this assassination will redeem either Florence or himself? To answer that question, we need a better sense of what it means to Lorenzo to be a hero.

II
LORENZO: THE MODERN BRUTUS

LIKE GOETHE'S GÖTZ and Egmont, Schiller's Moor, Byron's Marino Faliero, and so many other romantic protagonists, Lorenzo finds himself trying to be a hero in a world that no longer supports heroism. We should here recall Hegel's argument in *The Philosophy of Fine Art*[25] that heroes can arise only within those cultures which allow the individual to determine the limits of heroic activity, where social bonds and roles do not compromise heroism. In such a society, the individual is free to be heroic; his world ratifies his heroism by placing him at its summit, a position that reveals his freedom from external constraints. If we compare the world of the epic with that of the novel, we find that while the epic world consists of a loose confederation of independent individuals whose free heroic acts are recognized as such by their society, the novelistic world consists of a more highly organized society in which the individual must recognize many claims and restrictions upon his actions that prevent him from performing any heroic deed. The traditional hero need not bow to the limits of his society, for his society will adjust in accordance with his heroic acts. Modern society, however, attempts to shape the individual, to prevent any potential hero from changing the order of things. We have on the one hand a figure like Achilles, who can withdraw himself freely from the Greek cause to prove to the Greeks that he is their greatest hero; and on the other hand, we have Balzac's Rastignac who must at the end of *Père Goriot* turn back to Paris even though he knows he can define himself there only within a limited set of rules and roles. The traditional hero is, paradoxically, both free and part of his society. The modern protagonist is both restricted and alienated from his world.

Lorenzo and Rastignac were both created in 1834 and both live in a society that offers the individual only limited and corrupted means of action. When Lorenzo departs from his home in Cafaggiuolo for Florence, he resembles Rastignac leaving the provinces for Paris: they are both young innocents trying to prove themselves in the big city. But there is a difference between them. Rastignac learns to accept the limits of his world, to define himself through them. Lorenzo may know thoroughly the limitations of Florentine society. He may have penetrated his fallen society to its deepest recesses. Nonetheless, he still wants to prove himself a hero in opposition to this fallen and unheroic world. In this he is not so close to Rastignac as he is to Rastignac's would-be mentor, Vautrin—another man who adopts a mask to pursue what he sees as a heroic revolt against a corrupt society. Lorenzo wants to prove himself an epic hero even though he is living in the world of the bourgeois novel; to restate this within the context of the romantic battle for the stage, he wants to possess the stature of the Greek and Roman heroes of neoclassical tragedy, but his world—like that of the melodrama or bourgeois drama—is one that diminishes man.

Like all the protagonists of romantic tragic drama, Lorenzo wants to fashion himself in the image of the heroes of the past. More specifically, like Schiller's Karl Moor, Lorenzo is a great admirer of the heroes in Plutarch.[26] All of the Caesars of his world call out to him to become a Brutus, to revolt in the name of an ideal republic. Yet within his world there is no role comparable to that of the republican assassin of Julius Caesar. The means for the virtuous rebel to act so directly and in concert with others do not exist. If he could have emulated this Brutus, Lorenzo would never have had to become Lorenzaccio. He finds the more accurate model for his role to be the earlier Brutus, the destroyer of the Tarquins, who had to assume the part of a madman in his effort to oust the tyrants. Tarquin's Brutus and Caesar's Brutus are both mentioned within the play; some critics have felt that either Lorenzo or Musset confuses them.[27] Actually, Lorenzo's tragic situation is in part defined by the fact that he must, like the earlier Brutus, take on a role rather than act directly like the Brutus who joined the pact against Caesar. Lorenzo wants to emulate the second Brutus, but he finds he must act like the first, compromising his heroic self-image by taking on an all-consuming disguise: "Brutus pretended to be mad in order to kill Tarquin, and what astonishes me about him is that he did not really lose his mind" (III, iii, 796–98; p. 61)[28]

Lorenzo strikes us as heroic because he decides to pursue his goal even though he realizes how his world has warped him. Throughout the third and fourth acts he tries to explain his reasons for his continued struggle. At times, feeling the futility of his deeds, he is ready to commit the murder merely for its sensational effect on others. Forced to play a role, he seems concerned only with staging the final *coup de théâtre:*

Whether men understand me or not, whether they act or not, I'll have said all I have to say. Let them call me what they will, Brutus or Herostratus, I don't want them to forget me. My entire life is at the end of my dagger, and whether Providence favors me or not, in two days man will appear before the tribunal of my will. (III, iii, 889–901; p. 62)[29]

Lorenzo, trapped within a disfiguring disguise, seems to accept here his situation within an unheroic world. If he cannot be a hero, he will still perform an extraordinary act—even though it will be open to an unheroic interpretation. Lorenzo no longer cares whether he is known as a modern Brutus or as a Herostratus, who burned down the temple of Artemis so that others would remember him. Lorenzo realizes that in his world that reduces the hero to an overnight sensation, no apparent difference exists between these two figures. He will play out his role and let others judge him as they will.

But this explanation of his actions does not fully satisfy Lorenzo. Even as he submits to the judgment of his unheroic society, he still claims for himself a heroic perspective from which he can judge—"before the tribunal of my will"—those who will judge him. At other moments, he attempts to break through the limits of his role as Lorenzaccio to attain the vision granted other romantic protagonists like Chatterton or Hernani. In the fourth act, Lorenzo speaks a number of impassioned soliloquies. Finding that he cannot be a hero for society, he wonders whether he is a hero in the eyes of some divine spectator. If his fellow men see him as a Herostratus, perhaps God still sees him as a Brutus. He asks, "Am I the hand of God? Is there a halo above my head? When I enter this room and want to draw my sword, I am in fear of drawing the flaming sword of the Archangel, and falling in ashes on my prey" (IV, iii, 179–83; pp. 74–75.)[30] Yet even as he tries to cast himself in the role of a divine avenger, he seems to realize that there are no such providential figures in his world. He contrasts himself to Orestes who was called to revenge by the spirit of his father (IV, iii, 168–69); he could equally have chosen Hamlet. While such figures of providential tragedy are visited by ministers of another realm who direct their actions for good or evil, Lorenzo must make his own choices. No *deus ex machina* will descend to proclaim him a hero before those who see him as a villain.

In these speeches, Lorenzo once again oscillates between his desire to be a hero and his entrapment within his world, between his vision of himself as the modern Brutus and his role as Lorenzaccio. Having lost his innocence, he refuses to accept his part in the whirl of experience but cannot break through beyond it. Thus, in his discussion with Philippe in the third act and again in his soliloquies in the fourth act, Lorenzo returns time and again to his earlier innocence. If he cannot create the future, he can remember and cherish the past. At the close of his scene with Philippe he offers this explanation for his decision to follow through on the murder:

You ask me why I am going to kill Alexandre? Do you want me to poison myself or jump into the Arno? Do you want me to become a spectre and that in striking this skeleton (*He strikes his breast*), no sound should arise? If I am a shadow of myself, do you want me to break the only thread which today joins my heart to a few fibers of the heart that I had in the past? Do you realize that this murder is all that is left to me of my virtue? (III, iii, 855–64)[31]

Lorenzo has lost himself in his role. There is little left within him of the virtuous youth except the desire to be a hero. He has but one strong bond with his virtues and ideals: the murder he decided to commit in their name. Hoping to achieve virtue through terror, Lorenzo has adopted the violent and vile means of his world only to find that they have come to dominate him. *Lorenzaccio* carries Saint-Just's maxim on virtue and terror one step further to reveal its tragic implications: if the present world is not virtuous, then terror must be adopted to alter it; but when the use of terror corrupts the virtuous terrorist, he finally finds that his virtue has been reduced to terror. Lorenzo finds that the only sign of his former innocence is a murder.

In the monologues of the fourth act, Lorenzo begins to see the murder not only as a sign of his former innocence, but also as an act of homage to innocence itself. As the moment of the murder approaches, memories of his childhood and images of the innocent women in his life fill his thoughts. He begins to cast himself in the role of the protector of the innocent. Finding himself on the verge of corrupting Catherine, he insists that in fact he is her defender and that the murder of Alexandre will save her: "Poor Catherine! you would die nevertheless, like Louise, or allow yourself to fall into the eternal abyss like so many others, if I were not here" (IV, v, 451–53).[32] Just as in the third act he tried to persuade Philippe to remain apart from the world of violence and to allow him to be the instrument of revolt, so now he sees himself as the protector of the innocents of his world, shielding them from the fall he has experienced. He has sacrificed his own innocence in the hopes of remaking the world in the light of a great ideal only to find that the world of experience is stronger than those who would change it. He now prays that his sacrifice will at least protect the innocence of others.

By the time Lorenzo commits the murder, we sense that he is seeking the revenge of the world of innocence upon that of experience. Alexandre, the brutish and tyrannical lout who seems to have no thought other than for his own pleasure and no energy other than that which can be wasted in a night of debauchery, stands as an emblem of the world of experience. Lorenzo now demands that a sacrifice be made to the innocence he has lost. Lorenzo speaks several times of the murder as if it were a wedding night (III, i; IV, ix; IV, xi). Alexandre believes that Lorenzaccio has arranged for him to seduce Catherine. But this is one seduction that will not succeed, one "wedding" that will not be consummated. The "maiden" will not lose her innocence and pass into the world of experience, as have so many women seduced by the Duke. Rather Lorenzo, who casts himself as the bride, will strike dead the man of experience. It is as if Lorenzo wanted to halt the passage of innocence to experience, the passage he has made to his regret. If he cannot create a future of "organized innocence," then he will protect the simpler innocence that was his in the past. Lorenzo realizes his tragic fate in the murder of Alexandre: he proves his heroism by acting upon his ideal of innocence, yet the murder as he now conceives it is an admission of defeat.

But for the moment, Lorenzo experiences victory. Since he commits the murder in the name of innocence, it is appropriate that for a moment after he has killed Alexandre, Lorenzo seems to recapture the rapport with innocent nature that was his in Cafaggiuolo:

What a beautiful night! How pure the air is! Breathe, breathe, O heart filled with joy!. . .How soft and fragrant are the evening winds! How wonderfully the flowers of the fields are budding! 0 magnificent nature! O eternal tranquility! (IV, xi, 912–13, 918–20; p. 82)[33]

But as the final act of the play demonstrates forcefully, Lorenzo lives not in innocent nature but in fallen Florence; he finds himself not in a tranquil, timeless moment, but in the onward rush of history.

III
THE TRAGEDY OF REVOLT

WHILE LORENZO MAY find in his murder of Alexandre a private significance linking him to the innocence of the past, within his society his act is political and has the potential to shape the future. When Lorenzo meets Philippe Strozzi in Venice after the murder, Philippe welcomes him as a true "modern Brutus" and the creator of a new age:

Oh, our new Brutus! I believe you, and I embrace you. Then liberty is saved!. . . The Duke is dead! There is no hate in my joy. There is only the purest, most holy love for my country. As God is my witness! (V, ii, 260–65; p. 87).[34]

Despite all that has happened to him during the play—the degradation of his country, the imprisonment of his sons, the murder of his daughter, his own exile—Philippe still believes in the purity of revolt. He sees Lorenzo redeemed, recreated as the Brutus of his dreams; and Philippe goes on in this same scene to see Lorenzo's act as the spark of a general revolt, for "the flash of a single sword may light up an entire century" ("l'éclair d'une seule épée peut illuminer tout un siécle"; V, ii, 339–40; p. 88). Philippe is certain that the republican millennium is at hand.

However, the entire fifth act proves him wrong. In the very first scene, we find that political maneuvering in Florence has brought about not a republic but the ascension of a new Medici. Côme de Medicis is to be installed as the new figurehead Duke through whom the Pope and Emperor will rule Florence. Throughout the act, we see the destruction and dispersal of revolutionary hopes and forces. We witness the cowardice of the aristocratic republicans (scene i); the compromise between a revolutionary leader and the king of France, another autocrat with designs on Florence (scene iv); the defeat of the students (scene vi);[35] and the luring of the people from thoughts of revolt to bread and circuses, mysticism, and an acceptance of the powers that be (scenes i, v, and viii). The act closes with the pageant of the crowning of the new Duke and with his speech, in which it becomes clear that the tyranny imposed upon Florence by the Pope and the Emperor will wear a more politic face than it did under the debauched Alexandre, but that its force will continue undiminished.

To judge the conclusion of the play and of Lorenzo's life, we must examine the fates of the other important characters in the play; for they represent—as do the secondary characters in *The Cenci* or perhaps more relevantly Hamlet—the alternative paths the protagonist does not take.

The Strozzi family represents one set of alternatives. Philippe, as we have seen, is a dreamer who has planned a republic but never tried to build it and has thus managed to maintain his passive innocence. His son, Pierre, however, is a man of action, playing Laertes to Lorenzo's Hamlet. Pierre is involved in much of the action of the play, for he strikes again and again in the hopes of stirring up revolt. In the end, his turn to action compromises him. Attempting to depose Alexandre, a puppet of the Emperor and the Pope, Pierre becomes a pawn of the king of France, a lackey to another autocrat. While Philippe at least preserves his ideals, action leads Pierre to self-betrayal.

The Strozzi subplot involves the world of public action. The Cibo subplot, on the other hand, while it has socio-political import, involves an attempt to change the order of things through personal and private action. One might ask why Lorenzo did not use his status as Alexandre's favorite to influence him for the better. La Cibo provides the answer, for her plan of becoming Alexandre's mistress to convert him to the republican cause fails miserably. In Lorenzaccio's Florence, even the hope of redeeming the world through love is tainted; La Cibo's love merely serves Alexandre's lusts. She attempts to serve her ideals by adopting the ways of the world. She succeeds only in demeaning herself.

Each of these characters attempts to write a plot for the history of his city, casting himself in the leading role. La Cibo wants to believe that her world can be reformed through love; she would like to be an Asia finding in Alexandre a fallen Prometheus. She finds, however, that she must play out a bedroom intrigue in which she becomes a mistress striving to control events by slipping in bits of advice between kisses. With history reduced to petty scenes played behind closed doors, she becomes part of a bourgeois drama. Pierre would write for himself a neoclassical play, full of noble words and stirring actions. Philippe, the optimist who believes that virtue can win out even through violence, thinks like a melodramatist; he would reduce history to a battle between the good republicans and the evil Alexandre. As we have seen, their self-aggrandizing visions merely serve the powers against which they struggle. Each of these characters offers a plot for history that reduces its complexities. Each is defeated by the limitations of his or her vision.

Since the fifth act presents the defeat of these visions and the reassertion of Medici power, some commentators on the play have seen the conclusion of *Lorenzaccio* as returning to its opening situation; a few have even found in the play a vision of cyclical history or of the meaninglessness of history.[36] It is true that no revolution has taken place, that power remains in virtually the same hands. Still, there has been a meaningful change in Florence: the impetus for revolt has been blunted. At the beginning of the play, everyone was crying out for change—Philippe and the republicans, La Cibo, Lorenzo, and the people themselves. At the end of the play, the ranks of the opposition have been thinned: the Strozzi are in exile, the Marquise Cibo is compromised, the students have been subdued, and the people are ready to accept their new Duke. It is as if Florence demanded only the token death of Alexandre, as if it wanted to play out for itself a ritual sacrifice of a king without the cathartic change, the rebirth such a sacrifice might bring. Now that they have had the spectacle of the slain leader, the citizens seem prepared to accept their new ruler and to return to a life of tyranny and foreign oppression.

There is another important change in Florence at the conclusion of the play, for there is a new power behind the throne—Cardinal Cibo. The Cardinal is the one character who successfully plots his way through the twistings of Florentine history. While Lorenzo has fought against Alexandre, the Cardinal is Lorenzo's true enemy; in fact, his opposite. While Lorenzo struggles to preserve his ideals in a hostile world, the Cardinal embraces the ways and means of that fallen world. Where Lorenzo finds himself disoriented and debased by his role as Lorenzaccio, Cibo remains untroubled by the fact that he dons the garb and dignity of the priesthood to pursue personal power. The Cardinal has no sense of himself apart from the power he wants to exercise and thus feels no tension in adopting roles that grant him power, as the role of priest grants him power over the Marquise, for example; he can *be* the role he plays, having neither Lorenzo's interior distance nor Hamlet's something within which passes show. Lorenzo assumes his troubling role to usher in an ideal republic, to remake his world according to his vision of human greatness. Cardinal Cibo plays his role with relish to reaffirm the reality of brute power and Machiavellian stratagem. Lorenzo, at his moment of triumph, bursts into a lyric evocation of innocent, timeless beauty. The Cardinal celebrates his moment of victory in silence, allowing Côme de Medicis to deliver a politic speech that masks the brutality of his rule. Interestingly, Musset uses the actual speech Cosimo de Medici gave upon his ascension to power. Within Musset's text, the lyric moment at the end of the fourth act gives way to fact in the final scene, just as man's dreams of the future have given way to the onrush of history. Lorenzo would have moved his world towards vision. Cibo stages a victory of the literal.

But what of Lorenzo in the final act? Does he succeed in casting himself in the role of the modern Brutus? Philippe greets him in Venice as a hero, but Lorenzo does not share in his enthusiasm:

I wear the same clothes, I always walk upon my legs, and I yawn with my mouth; there is nothing changed in me but a misery; that is, that I am more hollow and more empty than a tin statue. (V, vi, 628–31)[37]

In seeing himself as a tin statue, Lorenzo draws upon an important imagery pattern in the play, one that defines his career. When in the third act he tells Philippe of his decision to murder a tyrant, he describes himself as a statue stalking the streets (III, iii, 592–96), an image that suggests both the heroic power he felt within and his sense of alienation from all around him. However, as he goes on to tell the story of his descent into the world of experience, of his life as Lorenzaccio, he no longer speaks of himself as a heroic statue, but instead says he has been reduced to a plaster mask (III, iii, 634). Philippe—in a passage already quoted—asserts his faith in Lorenzo's redemption, by imagining Lorenzo arising after the murder to become "as pure a metal as the bronze statues of Harmodius and Aristogiton." When we remember that Lorenzo proclaimed, "My youth was as pure as gold," we have charted his development through this chain of images from noble youth to hounded terrorist.

The final image of the tin statue fits Lorenzo's status as a man striving to become a hero in an unheroic world. Lorenzo wants to discard his role as Lorenzaccio and mold the chaos of his inner life into the fixed and powerful identity of a hero. As we have already seen, his world works in two ways to defeat that desire: it impinges upon the individual, forcing a role upon him, and it refuses to recognize in him the heroism he has imaged for himself. Lorenzo discovers that his potentially heroic deed has won him only condemnation:

When I was going to kill Clement VII, a price was put on my head in Rome. Now that I've killed Alexandre, naturally there's a price on my head all over Italy. If I were to leave Italy, I'd be hunted all over Europe; and at my death the Good God wouldn't fail to post my eternal condemnation at every crossroads of the universe. (V, vi, 617–23; p. 91)[38]

Lorenzo has discovered a fame of sorts. He may not be a Brutus, but he has certainly become a Herostratus. (Pierre sees the murder as a mere publicity stunt—"A curse on that Lorenzaccio, who thinks he's somebody"; "Maudit soit ce Lorenzaccio, qui s'avise de devenir quelque chose!"; V, iv, 433–34.) Lorenzo has made Florence pay attention to him. He has let them know that he is not merely a Lorenzaccio. But his identity is not ratified by fame. It is denied and denigrated in infamy. His image of the tin statue is exact: it may shine and attract attention, but within, all is hollow.

Revolt seems to promise a total change that will engender a world in which terror is banished and virtue is universal; society will be remade and the revolutionary will be reborn. The tragedy is that the change may never be forthcoming, that the rebel may find himself justifying ever increasing violence in the name of ever distant ideals. The revolutionary gesture is an attempt to leap out of the self and the present into a heroic future, but Musset insists upon the historical nature of the act of revolt. For him revolt is not a timeless act of heroic virtue, but a concrete act of historical violence. The final twist in Lorenzo's tragedy is that man must live in history. Lorenzo revolts to escape his fallen selfhood and liberate his oppressed country, to create himself as a hero and Florence as a perfect republic. However, the society Lorenzo works to create would have to exist before he acted if he were to be truly heroic, for only then would he *be* a hero ratified by fame. As it is, he plays at being Lorenzaccio, hoping to become a hero within a society that holds him in contempt. Thus, rather than catapult himself into an ideal future, he gives himself over to history. The history all men—the Cardinal as well as the Marquise, Alexandre as well as Philippe—make together, and not some ideal future Lorenzo would envision, will judge him. Lorenzo stakes his sense of himself and his vision of the future of his society on an act of revolutionary terror that he still hopes will render him and society virtuous. But in adopting the violent means of his world, he betrays the virtuous end for which he fights. His revolt merely reaffirms the oppressive powers that be and reduces him to a footnote to history.

We can get a better sense of Lorenzo's stance at the end of the play if we compare him with the central character of the nineteenth-century's most famous play on revolt and one that tackles the Revolution itself: Büchner's *Danton's Death*. The plays share a great deal: they both treat key moments of revolt; they both evoke an atmosphere of debauchery amidst political activity; Musset and Büchner both turn to an open structure; Musset's Plutarchan allusions are met by the revolutionaries' Roman rhetoric in Büchner's play; and so on. Yet, finally, the plays come at the revolutionary situation from different angles. While *Lorenzaccio* traces Lorenzo's steps up to his act of terror and then moves swiftly to his death, Büchner's play, as its title suggests, recounts Danton's movement towards death after his acts of terror—most important, the September Massacre—are behind him, after he renounces the Terror and becomes its victim.

Danton stands at the beginning of his play where Lorenzo stands at the end of his. At the beginning of the second act, Danton gives a speech that is reminiscent of Lorenzo in Venice after the murder; he responds to Camille Desmoulins's complaint that "we have no time to lose!": "And yet, time loses us!—How tedious it is always to have to put one's shirt on first and then pull up one's trousers; to spend the night in bed and then in the morning have to crawl out again and always place one foot in front of the other—and no one even imagines it could be otherwise" (II, i).[39] Danton shares with Lorenzo a disillusionment with revolutionary acts that do not radically transform man. It is not merely a question of changing rulers or even the rules of society; it is a question of changing man himself, of unlocking the mind-forged manacles and cleansing the doors of perception. Unless man is remade, revolution becomes merely a means of substituting one executioner for another. However, the revolutionary who acts in history cannot achieve such an apocalyptic transformation. He cannot make time begin again. The future he seeks to create arises from the debased present.

Danton shares with Lorenzo—and with their shared prototype, Hamlet—a propensity to doubt. All three find that this questioning makes it increasingly difficult to act. All three finally find themselves most comfortable in a situation where they can allow themselves to be killed; in a sense, they commit suicide. Danton knows there is something rotten in the state of France. At times he feels he was born to set it right. But he can no longer bring himself to act. He enters the political realm again only when it is clear that he will become a martyr. While he has sought to flee politics—in sensation, in sex, even oblivion—he now finds he can be a political actor without having to act: he can become a victim, not the executioner. In Danton, we would seem to have reached the point where the romantic rebel finally rejects the contradiction between ideal and action, becoming a martyr rather than descending into the Terror that action would demand. And, thus, in a sense, Büchner writes the martyr tragedy sought by those revolutionary playwrights who staged the death of key figures like Marat.

Danton is not, however, a martyr for the Revolution as understood by those who control it. He rejects the two clearest visions of the French Revolution set forth in his play, that of Robespierre and that of the Dantonistes, Camille, Philippeau, and Hérault-Séchelles. Robespierre believes that the Revolution will end not only the domination of the aristocratic class but also an entire way of life that he deems sinful. When he accuses the followers of Hébert or of Danton of being allies with the aristocrats, his concern is not just that they may be literally plotting with France's enemies; he senses a more insidious alliance, a brotherhood of vice in which the revolutionaries give themselves over to aristocratic ways. This is the burden of his speech in I, iii ("Vice is the aristocracy's mark of Cain"); and he warns Danton that "there are certain times when vice becomes high treason" (I, vi).[40] Robespierre's goal is to construct a virtuous Republic, which he believes in turn will produce virtuous men. Man lost his goodness when he fell from nature into society. He must now fight his way back to virtue and freedom. This struggle is known as the Terror, the destruction of the old vice-ridden ways and of anyone who clings to them. His view is close to that of Philippe Strozzi, another idealist willing to stoop to violence.

While Robespierre awaits the creation of Virtue through the Terror, Camille and those like him believe the Revolution has gone on too long; as Hérault-Séchelles puts it, "The Revolution must end and the Republic begin" (I, i).[41] The Dantonistes want order—not the chaos of the Terror—but they want a minimal government that would allow each individual to pursue his desires. If Robespierre would make man virtuous through the law, Camille would have the law bow to man's drives, even his vices:

The Constitution must be a transparent veil that clings close to the body of the people. Through it we must see the pulsing of each vein, the flexing of every muscle, the quiver of every sinew. Her body can be beautiful or ugly, because it has the right to be exactly what it is; and we have no right to dress her as we see fit. (I, i).[42]

Camille imagines not a virtuous Republic but a sensualist's Utopia in which every desire will be fulfilled.

Neither position can satisfy Danton. Robespierre's view collapses into the gap between his rhetoric and reality, between his professed idealism and his tactics as a terrorist. In Danton's eyes, Robespierre's virtue appears a timid rejection of life. His Terror is another word for self-serving executive murder. His control of the Revolution seems that of a man carried along by a wave of violence, who finds formulas to justify mass executions. As Danton says, "Isn't there something inside you that whispers sometimes, quietly, secretly, that you lie, Robespierre, you lie?" (I, vi).[43] Robespierre's position collapses because he has an abstract view of the individual and of human character. Camille's falls because it is blind to the social realities that surround him. For Camille, the self-satisfied leader of the Revolution, revolt may be over. But for the people, the Revolution will not be over until they are fed and housed, capable of living a decent life. To them, the freedom that Camille talks of is as abstract as Robespierre's virtue. What good is the freedom to pursue happiness if you are not guaranteed the necessities of life? Danton's acceptance of Camille's position would be akin to Lorenzo's accepting the world vision of Lorenzaccio: man is marked by vice, and thus one should learn to enjoy the fallen world.

Danton turns from Robespierre and Camille, just as Lorenzo rejects the positions of Philippe and of his own Lorenzaccio mask. But I do not believe that this rejection leads Danton to the nihilism that some find in him. In the first scene of the play, he suggests that "our statue of Liberty has not yet been cast" ("die Statue der Freiheit ist noch nicht gegossen"; I, i). Here and elsewhere, he suggests that the Revolution is just beginning. He realizes the Revolution is not over, but he cannot believe its proper course lies with Virtue and Terror, some abstract plan. For him the Revolution is chaos, "the world-god yet to be born" (IV, v).[44] As chaos, the Revolution is the process of putting things in question—not just the state or God or morality but everything within man that seems fixed and static. His pursuit of sex is not a self-satisfied wallowing in pleasure. It is a way of putting his identity in question, of putting himself at risk in trying to know what it is to be another person ("Know one another? We'd have to crack open our skulls and drag each other's thoughts out by the tails"; I, i).[45] His involvement in the Revolution is also a questioning, a testing, for he does not believe anyone controls the Revolution: "We didn't make the Revolution, the Revolution made us" (II, i).[46] Danton, like so many of his romantic precursors, strives to imagine a selfhood freed from the restraints of the present, and he hopes to find in history a force to replace the fate and providence in which he can no longer believe.

Danton would clear away the debris of the present; he would embrace history as the birth pangs of chaos, of a world we cannot yet conceptualize. While his position is, thus, for the most part defined in opposition to what is, rather than as a clear affirmation of what will be, he finally turns to the same values, the same forces as do other romantic protagonists: imagination and love. He may not be a visionary poet; he may in fact doubt the ability of rhetoric to capture reality. But the vitality of his speeches and his intense concern with language demonstrate his involvement with the power of words. He may not be an idealized lover, as he wanders from brothel to tavern, but he surely seeks some bond with another person, whether that bond be one of sympathy or of sensuality. As they are led to the scaffold, Danton and Hérault-Séchelles try to embrace, only to be separated by the executioner. Danton asks, "Are you trying to be crueler than death? Do you think you can prevent our heads from kissing down there in the basket?" (IV, vii).[47] These are not grand nor visionary words; they are almost grotesque. Yet they reveal the strength of Danton's language—his ability to break out of the tired rhetoric of his world—and they embrace love in the midst of death, community in the midst of official barbarity, friendship in the midst of betrayal. Danton dies a martyr for the Revolution—not Robespierre's or Camille's—but a revolt that would overturn the past in pursuit of a world remade by love, and love in all of its forms, from the sensual delights of Marion to the friendship of his comrades and the deep bond between Danton and Julie. In his own strange way, Danton—like Faust—finds at death that human love is all that can redeem us.

Thus, Danton, for all of the savage irony of his play, for all of its bleak assessment of the Revolution, is given more than Lorenzo. He can still affirm something that escapes the violence and debased rhetoric of his world; he can, in some sense, escape his historical moment. Lorenzo is more fully enmeshed in his fallen, historical world. Yet Lorenzo dies a hero, or at least a potential hero. The difficulties involved in creating oneself as a hero within historical time can be seen if we return to the contrast between the traditional hero and the romantic protagonist with which I began this discussion of *Lorenzaccio*. Since the hero of traditional tragedy lives within a static, hierarchical world, his career, his tragedy, follows essentially an upward and downward course: the rise and fall of a great man; the tragedy of the wheel of fortune that raises men up only to destroy them in the turnings of its immutable cycle. It is not that time is unimportant in these plays; after all, Hamlet hesitates and Macbeth desires an act that will in some sense bring an end to time. But, as the pattern of rise and fall suggests, time is organized according to providential and hierarchical structures.[48] The characterization of the traditional hero also takes a hierarchical cast. Marked by his place in society, he is further defined as possessing a higher and a lower nature, his heroism usually arising from his higher qualities and his destruction from his lower ones. This hierarchical characterization is perhaps clearest in a simplified model of neoclassical tragedy where the conflict is defined as the split between head and heart, between noble ideals and base passions. A character establishes himself as a hero through a commitment to these ideals and finds his tragedy in the power of his passions.

Shakespeare's mode of characterization, while different, is also hierarchical. To simplify greatly, his tragic figures are poised between an ideal type and a reductive stereotype. Hamlet's vision of man as noble in reason, the paragon of animals, and yet the quintessence of dust is central to this mode of characterization. Man strives to become an ideal type: the perfect king, scholar, son, warrior, or lover. But he is always threatened with the possibility of becoming a tyrant, a pedant, a momma's boy, a *miles gloriosus*, or a fop. Within Macbeth lies the henpecked husband; within Coriolanus, the "boy of tears"; within Lear, the senile parent; within Othello, the old cuckold. One way in which Shakespeare creates such a sense of depth in his characters is by suspending them between the ideal realization of their potentials and the grotesque reduction of them.[49] These figures become tragic by willing both sides of their character, by asserting the full register of their identities and thus committing themselves not only to what is ideal but also to what is base. If they had turned to only the ideal, they would have become figures of romance; if they had been only a reductive stereotype, they would have become comic. The hierarchical mode of characterization enables Shakespeare to portray them as tragically embracing both alternatives simultaneously.

The romantic protagonist is not defined in this hierarchical fashion. He is defined within historical time. His relation to time differs from that of the traditional character, for events no longer follow providential and hierarchical patterns; they are part of the history that men make for themselves. For the romantic protagonist, ideal and base characteristics are arrayed not in a static hierarchy, but within different moments in time. The rhythms of thought behind romantic drama are temporal: the passage from innocence into experience and perhaps to a higher innocence; if not virtue, *then* terror.

For the romantic protagonist, the ideal type he wishes to become exists only in the future, only at the end of a historical process in which he must participate. The traditional hero may have been suspended between an ideal and a grotesque version of himself; but the romantic protagonist finds that his ideal lies in a perhaps unachievable future, while the present offers far too many opportunities for becoming a mere grotesque. Lorenzo wants to be an ideal hero in a virtuous republic, but he lives in the corrupt present and thus has only the grotesque role of Lorenzaccio to play. The traditional hero found his heroism in the ideal and his tragedy in the coexistence of the all-too-human grotesque that he must assert as part of his total identity. The romantic protagonist finds his tragedy in his inability to reach the ideal and his potential heroism in avoiding becoming a grotesque.

Lorenzo may not create himself as a modern Brutus, but he convinces us of his heroic potential by avoiding the reductive identities adopted by the other characters. In the final act, La Cibo has become a compromised woman, Pierre has turned into a lackey for the king of France, and Philippe remains an exiled Quixote. Lorenzo rejects the reductive roles offered by his society and finally wearies of even his Lorenzaccio mask. He cannot within the play be the hero he desires to be, but he refuses to be anything else. He proves himself potentially heroic by virtue of *not* being something within his world. His character thus becomes void of content; he becomes the hollow statue. Still, his refusal to sustain a grotesque role points, although in a wholly negative way, towards the full humanity that is the goal of the romantic protagonist. Denied the humanistic breakthrough of an Iphigenia, the lyric vision of a Hernani, or even the final glimpse of love given Danton, Lorenzo still makes himself a sign of man's greatness by absenting himself from a society that denies all greatness. His last act of homage to his own humanity is a final negation. He commits suicide, walking out into the street to be struck down by an assassin and hurled into Venice's lagoon by a raging mob. In his last moments, Lorenzo seems not unlike Karl Moor, ready to be seized by some family man who could use the reward placed on his head; but Lorenzo has none of Moor's stagey heroism, no desire to make a final impression on people. He thus protects his mute but potential heroism. He dies tragically frustrated, yet his death has the force of a sacrificial indictment of an unheroic world.

If the conclusion of *Lorenzaccio* seems darker than that of the plays of Goethe, Schiller, Shelley, or even Büchner, it is because Musset excludes from his drama any hint of an imaginative resolution to the tragic situation. Goethe tries to place individual tragedies within the pattern of a larger imaginative romance. Schiller sends Wallenstein to a fate not unlike Lorenzo's, but he also creates Max, the "beautiful soul" who embodies an ideal free from the divisions of modern life. In *The Cenci*, Beatrice finds she must act in violation of her sense of herself, but she can still bear witness to her vision of innocence. In *Danton's Death*, Danton at least has his lovers and his language freed from rhetoric. In all of these plays, we are able to glimpse the man or woman behind the mask, the vision beyond the theater. Lorenzo, however, can make no positive gesture to an imaginative vision beyond his world. He can look back to his innocent childhood. He can try to preserve his heroic potentiality for some ideal future. But he can never embrace in the present a vision of a world remade.

Of course, several powerful readings of *Lorenzaccio* do find Musset pitting a vision against the sordid realities of Florence; and they find, interestingly enough, that it is the vision of an artist.[50] Some critics have found Lorenzo himself to be an artist of sorts, a Michelangelo of murder as it were. Others have found in the figure of Tebaldeo Freccia, the young artist whom Lorenzo meets and hires in the second act, a foil to Lorenzo who offers a resolution to the difficulties of self-consciousness and revolt; art, not revolt, is seen as a means of escaping the self and remaking the world. While there is some evidence that Musset at one time thought of devoting more attention to the idea of art in *Lorenzaccio*, David Sices has persuasively argued that Musset moved to limit the appeal of art and to stage instead what Sices calls the "triumph of reality."[51] We can go further. In *Lorenzaccio*, the artist remains not an attenuated emblem of a solution, but one more indication of the problems besetting his world. Whatever trappings of the artist may surround Lorenzo, he still performs an act of destructive violence, not of imaginative creation. While Tebaldeo insists that his life as an artist involves him in a "realization of dreams," he also reveals the rather limited nature of his dreams. Content to prettify the slaughter-house that is Florence, Tebaldeo envisions no transformed world. He adopts the doctrine that the people's suffering is justified if it creates a situation in which artists can work.[52] Tebaldeo Freccia is no image of the romantic artist struggling to reform the world through the imagination and love. He is no Prometheus, no Los, no Faust. He is willing to leave the world alone if the world will allow him to pursue his art for its own sake and to enjoy his private love for his mother and his mistress. Far from offering a solution to Lorenzo's problems, he is one more symptom of the division in his world between art and act, vision and reality.

Musset's *Lorenzaccio* answers Hugo's call for an art work capable of "personifying" revolution. While the neoclassicists, revolutionary dramatists, melodramatists, and writers of "well-made" plays all failed to capture both the glory and the terror of their revolutionary age, Musset—a disciple of Schiller, the creator of modern historical drama—does capture the rhythm of the rise and fall of revolutionary ideals, a rhythm that seemed to be that not only of the July Revolution but of its greater prototype as well.[53] Musset also establishes the deep links between the difficulties of self-consciousness and the turn to revolt. Lorenzo tries to find in revolt the means to bridge the distance between self and role, the individual and the community; but he then flounders in the gap that arises between his concrete act and the ideal future he would create. In his world, the self is reduced to a role; revolt becomes a game that finally serves the masters. There is no vision in this world, only playacting. While in *The Cenci* the "mask and mantle" that envelopes Beatrice is an emblem of art that cannot break through to the imagination but must instead adopt the limited forms of the day, and while *Iphigenia in Tauris* stages an unmasking that is the prelude to the creation of a humane world, Musset's *Lorenzaccio* sees in disguise man's necessary entrapment in the self and his inability to find actions that match his vision. Lorenzo is trapped in the world of Mephistophelean theatrics. Musset denies more absolutely than any other romantic dramatist the possibility of a visionary solution to the dilemmas faced in romantic tragic drama. In Kleist's *Prince Friedrich of Homburg*, we have another, though less somber, meditation on vision and the stage; but Kleist's play does not so much portray man denied vision and trapped in playacting as raise the question of whether we can ever know the difference between imaginative creation and theatrical posturing.

CHAPTER NINE
KLEIST'S *PRINCE FRIEDRICH OF HOMBURG:* THE TRAGEDY OF NON-TRAGIC MAN

With regard to chronology, Kleist seems an odd choice for the final chapter of this study. He died in 1811, a suicide; his dramatic career was over before that of Byron, Shelley, Hugo, or Musset had begun. Goethe's *Götz* had been published years before Kleist's birth, yet Goethe outlived Kleist by more than two decades. I turn to Kleist now because his dramas, while written during the earlier decades of the romantic movement, already point the path the drama would take after romanticism. Modern drama is closer in spirit to Kleist than to Schiller or Goethe, Shelley or Hugo. In moving from the plays of Schiller and Goethe to those of Shelley and Musset, I have traced a darkening of the vision of romantic tragic drama; but all of these playwrights share the project of discovering a romantic tragedy, a modern heroism. Kleist's dramatic corpus recapitulates the rhythms and themes of romantic drama, but the variations he works on these patterns begin to undermine key elements of the romantic tragic vision and to move towards the tragicomic sense of life found in more recent plays.

Kleist's dramatic work was remarkably varied. Besides his tragic dramas, he wrote two comedies, *The Broken Jug* (*Der Zerbrochene Krug*) and *Amphitryon*, and a tale of patriotic gore, *The Battle of Arminius* (*Die Hermansschlacht*). His tragic dramas turn to a great many models. His early *Feud of the Schroffensteins* (*Die Familie Schroffenstein*) draws upon both the popular *Ritterdrama* and Shakespeare. His *Katherine of Heilbraun* (*Kätchen von Heilbronn*) reveals the influence of the romantic circles.

Penthesilea reworks Greek myth. *Robert Guiscard*, which Kleist destroyed in a melancholy fit, was modeled on *Oedipus Rex*. His masterwork, *Prince Friedrich of Homburg*, draws upon a number of earlier works, Shakespeare's *Measure for Measure* and Goethe's *Egmont* and *Tasso* among them. Important as these influences were, it was Schiller who had the most profound impact on Kleist.[1] In a sense, Kleist's dramatic corpus reiterates that of Schiller, but in a more somber key. Like Schiller, Kleist tried to rival *Oedipus Rex*, like him tried to capture the spirit of Shakespeare and to evoke the atmosphere of the dramas produced by the romantic circles. Most important, in *Prince Friedrich*, Kleist attempted the key Schillerian form—the history play—and remade it in keeping with his own vision. If this study, which first turned to Schiller, ends with Kleist, it is in part because Schiller's younger contemporary already redefined in a distinctively modern way the mode of historical drama that Schiller had created.

I
PRINCE FRIEDRICH AND HISTORICAL DRAMA: THE CHAOS OF CHANCE

THE INFLUENCE OF a number of Schiller's plays has been traced in *Prince Friedrich*, *The Robbers* and *Don Carlos* among them; and standing behind the entire play is the magnificent precedent of the *Wallenstein* trilogy. *Wallenstein* was Kleist's favorite amongst Schiller's plays, amongst all drama, one could almost say.[2] It is thus not surprising that *Prince Friedrich* bristles with reminiscences from the trilogy, especially from *The Piccolomini*. Verbal echoes abound.[3] The situations in the two plays are similar; both treat military and diplomatic relations between Germans and Swedes during the seventeenth century. Many striking moments in Kleist's play recall episodes in Schiller's. For example, the tale of Froben's death is modeled on the report of Max Piccolomini's death. The central characters in *Prince Friedrich* parallel figures in *Wallenstein*; the relations among the Prince, Natalie, and the Elector recapitulate those among Max, Thelka, and Wallenstein.

None of these local reminiscences, however, shapes Kleist's play as thoroughly as does his confrontation of the central problem posed in Schiller's trilogy. We have seen that *Wallenstein* is a drama of plots and plotting, a play about man's attempt to shape his life and history. In Schiller's play, most men fail miserably in this attempt; Wallenstein fails grandly; and Max, the "beautiful soul," places himself beyond the entanglement of human plots, beyond the lures of self and revolt. Kleist's *Prince Friedrich* also treats man's attempt to shape history and to control life; it also portrays characters trapped in the self and caught up in revolt. Kleist, however, re-works Schiller's version of historical drama, questioning even the partial successes Schiller grants to Wallenstein and Max. Most strikingly, Kleist's historical drama challenges the very status of history as a ground for heroic and tragic action. In *Wallenstein*, history may escape man's control, but by the end of the trilogy Wallenstein has managed to stake out a heroic, tragic destiny in historical time. While in most romantic plays, history replaces fate, in *Prince Friedrich* chance rules the field of historical action. One can find no fixed destiny in Kleist's historical world, only reversals and accidents.

The very first scene of *Prince Friedrich* establishes this pattern of reversal. As the play opens, we discover the Prince, lost in dreams, sitting in a garden making a wreath for himself. He is absorbed in a vision of the triumph he hopes to win on the battlefield. The Elector and his entourage emerge from the palace to view the Prince's strange distraction. Intrigued by the young man's somnambulistic state, the Elector decides to play a "jest" on him (see V, vi, 1708).[4] The Elector believes he understands the Prince's dream and seeks to control his sleep-walking vision of glory by introducing into it an emblem of triumph, the chain and wreath he has the Princess Natalie hold out to the Prince. The Elector treats the Prince as if he were a comic puppet, feeling certain he knows just which strings to pull to get an amusing reaction from the young man.

But the jest does not work out as planned. The Prince's heartfelt response, his apparent love for Natalie, shames the witnesses. This jest takes a sudden serious turn, the mood of the scene shifts abruptly, and we find ourselves strangely drawn to this young man who only a minute before struck us as the rather ridiculous butt of the Elector's joke. The Elector, who appeared in control of the situation, is forced to flee back into his palace. He has not been able to shape the Prince's dream. Even his attempt to give the dream a conclusion fails. The company retreats into the palace, but the Prince retains one of Natalie's gloves. For the Prince, the dream will linger on into waking reality.

This brief scene provides an emblem of Kleistian man's inability to control his life, to shape his future. This play does not present a hero struggling against an inexorable chain of historical causes and effects. Instead, life appears dominated by personal quirks and freak accidents. We might consider the Elector's "jest" as a playlet. He believes he knows what will happen when he toys with the Prince, and thus he writes a script for the Prince's dream, the performance of which he wants to direct. But the Prince, and life, are not so easily controlled. Perhaps man's plans for the future are merely artful illusions, mere playacting.

This possibility challenges both the Prince and the Elector. Most readings of Kleist's play focus upon the differences between these two characters, between the mature, realistic Elector and the adolescent, idealistic Prince, between the rational planner and the emotional dreamer.[5] However, we should not let their clear differences blind us to their common task. They struggle, albeit in different ways, to create an order for life that would allow man to explore freely his full humanity. The Prince will be more concerned with establishing his own heroic humanity and the Elector will work for an abstract social order, but they share a common enemy—the chaos of chance and inner division that lies threateningly beneath the surface of the initial scene of the play.

Kleist's world hovers dangerously close to this chaos. Like the Prince a believer in his destiny and like the Elector the creator of a *Lebensplan*, the young Kleist became convinced, in what is called his "Kant Crisis," that man could not know or shape his world; his dread of the chaos he saw facing him led to the first of many breakdowns.[6] His plays return time and again to this tension between the desire to know and to control life and the realization that life escapes human knowledge and will. For example, Kleist's first play, *The Feud of the Schroffensteins*, a *Ritterdrama* that owes much to *Romeo and Juliet*, portrays two families that act upon what they perceive and reason to be true only to find that appearances have deceived them and led them to destruction. Kleist seems to argue that neither sensual perception nor reason can help man chart his course through the chaotic twistings of life. Nor is there any help in turning from the external world to one's inner feelings, for the play also systematically demonstrates the error of intuitive judgments. In the later *Penthesilea*, Kleist further suggests that an abstract and artificial law provides little protection from the deceptions of the external world and the confusions of the inner one. The importance to Kleist of these ideas is indicated by their presence even in his two comic works, *Amphitryon* and *The Broken Jug*.

In *Prince Friedrich*, by the close of the first act, we have seen the two central characters express their faith in their ability to control the future. As we will see, the Prince believes that an inner vision has revealed to him the shape of things to come, while the Elector is certain he can order events by making man obey the law. The second act, however, reverses their convictions, casting them adrift in a world of deception.

There are three major movements to the second act—the battle, the false report of the Elector's death, and the arrest of the Prince. Each hinges upon a failure to know or to control reality. First, we see the failure of the Elector's battle plan, for the Prince refuses to follow orders and attacks at the wrong moment. Significantly, while the Prince disregards the Elector's rational plan to follow the dictates of the heart, emotions prove no better guide than the intellect; if the Elector failed to plan for every contingency, the Prince's emotionalism only compromises the German victory.

The second movement of the act centers upon the mistaken belief that the Elector is dead. Everyone thinks he has seen him struck down while riding his white horse into battle to rescue the Prince. However, a messenger soon arrives to announce that everyone has been deceived: the Elector's groom, Froben, exchanged horses with his sovereign when he realized that the white horse was a conspicuous target; it was he who was killed—interestingly, not in heroic battle, but in the attempt to lead the horse to safety. Then, in the final segment of the act, we discover the Elector seeking assurances that Homburg had not, in fact, led the cavalry attack, for he has called for the arrest of whoever was responsible for this violation of his plan. His officers inform him that the Prince was injured before the battle and thus could not have been in command.[7] At this moment the Prince enters with the Swedish standards he has captured. He explains that he did lead his troops, and the Elector orders Homburg's arrest.

This act drives home again and again the fallibility of man's perceptions and his inability to control events. By the end of the act, the Elector's victory has been compromised and the order he wished to establish challenged. More drastically, the destiny of the Prince has undergone a total reversal. He believed himself to be guaranteed fame. He finds himself in prison, awaiting sentencing. In a sense, the first act presents two hypotheses about how to master life, the Prince's dream vision and the Elector's law; the second act tests these hypotheses and finds them both wanting. Throughout the rest of the play, the Prince and the Elector scramble to reassert their control over events. Still, nothing that happens later can eradicate the impression left by the second act: life is chaotic, beyond man's control. Moreover, in that it centers on the battle, this act more clearly than the others depicts the historical realm. In plays from *The Robbers* to *Lorenzaccio*, historical action presents the romantic protagonist with an impasse, but also with an opportunity to prove himself heroic; history replaces fate in the tragic hero's life. In Kleist's play, history, lacking the power of fate and moved by chance, presents a less dignified arena in which to pursue one's goals. The Prince and the Elector still seek to create a heroic and fully human sense of life despite the uncertainties of their world. In portraying their struggles, Kleist questions two key romantic stances—that of the "beautiful soul" like Max and that of the cultural artificer like Wallenstein or, more powerfully, Iphigenia.

PRINCE FRIEDRICH: BEAUTIFUL SOUL OR CASE STUDY?

WHEN WE FIRST meet the Prince in the opening scene, we learn of his tendency to escape present realities in dreams. We find that he believes he can glimpse the future through such visions. When Hohenzollern displays the Prince to the Elector, he tells of his friend's dream:

> Somnambulating!
> On that bench! You would never have believed it!
> Enticed here by the moon, asleep but busy,
> He dreams with the eye of his own posterity,
> Weaving his own splendid wreath of fame. (I, i, 24–28)[8]

Impatient with the present, with the pace of historical time, the Prince wants to seize the future now, and thus he wreathes for himself the laurel he hopes posterity will award him. His impetuosity has robbed the Elector of two victories prior to the opening of the play; incapable of awaiting the right moment, the rash Prince has struck too early, leaping to the attack. The Prince, like his fellow romantic protagonists, lives in historical time— in fact, in the same period as Wallenstein and Max Piccolomini—but the Prince is constitutionally incapable of accepting the limits of history. In romantic drama, man can possess only a potential heroism when he is caught in history. The Prince wants to be a hero, not merely to possess the potential to become one. As we have seen in plays from *Egmont* to *Lorenzaccio,* one way the romantic dramatists defined the difficulties their protagonists faced was to situate these would-be heroes in an unheroic world that denies them the recognition, the fame, necessary to the hero. As Hohenzollern makes clear, the purpose of the Prince's dream is to establish in vision a fame that has been denied him in reality. The Prince himself says as much when he later speaks of the vision:

> And he, the Elector, with a brow like Zeus,
> Held a wreath of laurel in his hand:
> He steps up close before my very eyes;
> As if to inflame my whole soul, he winds
> The chain from his own neck about the wreath
> And hands it, to be pressed upon my locks...
> . . . .
> High above me, like the muse of glory,
> She lifts the garland with its swinging chain
> As if about to crown a hero's head. (I, iv, 158–63, 172–74)[9]

As the transformation of the Elector and the as-yet-unknown girl into gods suggests, the Prince believes that this dream has granted him a contact with a higher, ideal realm. Although on earth, in human history, his actions may not be recognized as heroic, may in fact strike us as comic, he finds in his dream the hope that the "gods" will see in him the hero he feels himself to be. The dream provides a way to transcend, at least for the moment, the travails of historical man, but only because the Prince is certain that his vision is a revelation and not a delusion, that his inner gaze focuses not upon the isolated self but on an ideal world.

Of course, in that he retains Natalie's glove from the dream, the Prince awakes like Keats's Adam to find that his dream is real, at least in part. Armed with this token of fulfillment, he attends the officers' meeting at the close of the first act to receive the Elector's orders for the next day's battle. As he slowly realizes that Natalie, the Elector's adopted daughter, is the girl from the dream, he becomes completely oblivious of the military discussion. What need has he of tactics when he has a vision of future glory and, in the glove, its proof? Why need he worry over historical events on the battlefield when he already knows the future? The act ends with his triumphant vision in which threatening chance is transformed into the bountiful goddess of Fortune:

> Already, Fortune, you have touched my brow
> And tossed a pledge to me as you rolled by,
> Shook from your horn of plenty with a smile:
> But today, elusive offspring of the gods,
> I shall capture you upon the battlefield
> And spill out all your blessings at my feet,
> Even if, with iron sevenfold,
> You're shackled to the Swedes' triumphal car! (I, vi, 358–65)[10]

The second act, as was noted earlier, undermines his dream-induced solutions to romantic man's predicament. Chance, not Fortune, rules. His inner vision proves an unreliable guide. Hoping for fame, he finds himself in prison, sentenced to death. Yet, when at the beginning of the third act we visit with Hohenzollern the Prince in his prison, we find Homburg still trusting in Fortune, still believing in his destiny. His dream still counts for more with him than do the ominous actions taken by the Elector. With his dream in direct conflict with his actual situation, the Prince begins to see present reality as a charade, a view he has already expressed upon his arrest, where he accuses the Elector of yearning "to play the Brutus" ("Mein Vetter Friedrich will den Brutus spielen"; II, x, 777). In prison, he tells Hohenzollern that he finds his trial to be another bit of playacting on the Elector's part. He believes his sovereign is merely going through the motions

THE HERO AND THE EDUCATOR: CULTURE, MORTALITY, AND ILLUSION

WHILE BOTH THE Elector and the Prince have had their approaches to life challenged, neither ceases his attempt to impose his will on the world: the Prince continues to seek heroic stature and the Elector moves to protect his beloved law. The doubts the play has raised about their projects, however, make it impossible for either character to pursue his goal blindly. The Prince can no longer be certain he has a direct and immediate contact with a higher realm of value. The Elector cannot see the law as objective and universal. Both must affirm their visions self-consciously, willing them despite the objections that have been raised.

The final action of the play is set in motion when the Elector writes to the imprisoned Homburg to grant him a choice: affirm the law by accepting his sentence or free himself by rejecting the rules of war as unjust (IV, iv, 1307–13). The Elector, recognizing now that the law is not an absolute value, no longer demands obedience to it, but instead establishes it as an agreement into which the Prince may enter. Attempting to reaffirm the law, the Elector must admit its precarious, contractual nature.

Of course, the Prince does come to accept his sentence, but not exactly for the reasons the Elector might wish. By taking responsibility for his actions, the Prince appears to turn from his dreams of heroism to confront present realities. By willing his own death to uphold the law, he would seem to reject the self's delusions in favor of an external ideal. However, while there is something grand and centrally human in the Prince's descent into the historical present and thus into death, we must remember that he still quests for fame and glory. He now seeks to prove himself a hero and to reap a hero's reward in death. He sees in the law a new escape route, another way to convert his isolated self into a heroic identity. Throughout the scene in which he wonders how he should answer the Elector, the Prince repeatedly notes that his sovereign has acted nobly and that he should respond in a like manner. He seems to be trying on a role:

> He faces me with so much dignity,
> I won't confront him totally unworthy!
> Guilt, important guilt, weighs on my breast.
> If I must argue with him for my pardon,
> I'd just as soon know nothing of his mercy! (IV, iv, 1380–85)[30]

The Prince, realizing that events have finally offered him a heroic part, leaps at the chance to die nobly. The note he sends off to the Elector ac-

demanded by duty before descending like a *deus ex machina* to give his "play" a happy ending:

> How could he summon me before this bench
> Of heartless judges, sitting there like owls,
> Hooting a dirge of firing squads at me,
> Unless he meant, serenely, with his veto,
> To step into the circle like a god?
> No, friend, he conjures up this night of clouds
> Around my head, in order, like the sunrise,
> To break all radiant through their murky sphere:
> And this caprice I surely can permit him. (III, i, 852–60)[11]

Believing his arrest, trial, and sentencing mere caprices of the Elector, the Prince is willing to indulge his sovereign in what the Prince sees as a comedy. To protect his dream vision from the contradictions of reality, the Prince reduces life to theater.

When Hohenzollern questions the Prince's certainty that the Elector will save him, Homburg once again claims an inner revelation, though now he grounds his confidence not in a dream vision but in his intuition about the Elector ('Auf mein Gefühl von ihm!''; III, i, 867). The Prince's espousal here of intuition or feeling has often and correctly been noted as a key to his personality.[12] Since reality is a game for the Prince, he can turn confidently from this charade to what he incorrectly believes to be the truth within himself. Like so many other romantic protagonists, he finds his world lacking in comparison to the riches of his inner vision. More exactly, he sees himself as a "beautiful soul," like Schiller's Max who can follow inclination without being led astray through the incredibly complex tangle of plots that make up *Wallenstein*.

The Prince is modeled on Max, in the sense that Max is a beautiful soul, while the Prince aspires to be one. Homburg certainly adopts the appropriate rhetoric. Amid the battle, when the Swedes begin to retreat, the Prince demands that the cavalry attack immediately. Reminded by Kottwitz that they are to await further orders, the Prince cries, "Await commands! O Kottwitz, do you ride so slowly?/ Have you not felt the orders in your heart?" (II, ii, 474–75).[13] The Prince believes that if he follows his feelings, he will, like Max, inevitably act right. But Homburg lives in a world far different from Max's. Max's intuitions truly intimate an ideal moral order that, in the present, conflicts with reality. Similarly, Shelley's Beatrice finds an internal vision of innocence which she can oppose to her fallen world. But the Prince lives in a world denied even an ideal. In his world, feelings are hardly a certain criterion for action. Intuitions arise from the dreams of the self rather than descend from an ideal order. Thus, the Prince's intuitions are time and again incorrect. The "orders" he hears in his heart urge him to attack at the wrong moment, almost leading to the Elector's death and certainly compromising the German victory; his sense of the Elector's attitude towards the trial is also wrong. While in Schiller the beautiful soul holds out the hope that feeling can provide a link with a transcendent order, in Kleist the beautiful soul is an *ignis fatuus* by which the Prince hopes to light his way through the labyrinth of his world.

The inner life of the Prince is finally as chaotic as the outer world opposed to it. This inner confusion accounts for the sense many readers have of "deeper" motives existing for the Prince's actions. The Prince's inner life consists not only of intuitions of a higher order but also of a morass of feelings often tied to semiconscious desires. For example, when the Prince discusses his dream with Hohenzollern in the first act, it is clear that Homburg seeks more than glory. The mysterious girl in the dream moves him strangely. Her image touches upon some desire he has apparently not yet admitted fully to himself. When he mentions her to Hohenzollern, a puzzling debate ensues over the identity of the girl. Hohenzollern puts forth several candidates, none of whom we meet. He keeps emphasizing this dream girl and jokes with the Prince about his amorous intentions towards various women in the court. Hohenzollern wants to dismiss the dream as an instance of erotic wish fulfillment. If he can convince the Prince that his dream was of Countess Platen or Madam Bork, then the Elector's jest is safe. The Prince, however, sees his dream as a sign from a higher realm, from the "gods." Where his friend would reduce it to a manifestation of the subconsciousness, the Prince would elevate it into a revelation granted by a higher consciousness. I do not believe Kleist intends us to accept either interpretation; rather, he shows us the confusion that reigns within the self. For the Prince, no clear distinction exists between feeling and desire, and therefore, he cannot tell whether his intuitions are ideal visions or the self's dreams of desire.

Kleist cannot accept the notion that simple introspection and a refined sensibility will lead one to virtuous and effective action. His characters are far too confused and tortured for such easy certainty. For example, the title character of *Katherine of Heilbraun,* who is often seen as a beautiful soul, follows an inner vision that proves correct; but her feelings lead her to adopt such a bizarrely masochistic role that we wonder whether she is a model to be emulated or a psychological case to be studied. In *Penthesilia,* the Amazon queen cannot distinguish among her commitment to her people's law of love conquest, her lust for Achilles, and her hatred of the Greeks; her internal confusion lures her to murder her beloved in one of the most barbaric "love-deaths" of romantic literature. Again, Kleist's point is not that the sexual data of the subconscious is the final or true cause of his characters' actions. Rather his point is the confusion of realms, his protagonists' inability to separate higher from lower aspects of the self. Hohenzollern typifies a man all too ready to see life ruled by the mechanism of desire, a clearly limited view.[14] Kleist shares neither Homburg's idealizing view nor Hohenzollern's reductive one. Those who follow Hohenzollern in offering a psychological reading of *Prince Friedrich,* by giving priority to desire over vision, miss the complexity of the play. Kleist's treatment of Homburg is not so close to modern depth psychology as it is to Manfred's tortured realization that there is no truth in the traditional hierarchy of reason, will, and desire, that man is "Half dust, half deity, alike unfit / To sink or soar . . . / Contending with our low wants and lofty will" (I, ii, 40–41, 44).

The Prince's feelings for the Elector are clouded by such confusion, despite his claim that he can intuit his sovereign's intentions. The Prince talks often of the Elector as a father. One of the reasons he feels certain the Elector will not execute him is that he is convinced he has been as "Dear as a son" to the Elector ("Wert wie ein Sohn"; III, i, 830). Such father-son references have led some critics to discover an Oedipal antagonism between the Elector and the Prince.[15] Once again, my point is not that such a psychological reading is correct, but that this search for a "deeper" motive for the characters' actions is made possible by the nature of feeling in the play. When the Prince sees himself as a beloved son to a fatherly Elector, he strives to see their relationship, as he sees everything pertaining to himself, in ideal terms. However, the evocation of an ideal father-son tie simultaneously calls up the sometimes violent tensions of actual filial bonds.

The Prince's self-confidence falters when he begins to lose his ideal perspective on his relationship with the Elector and to view it as beset with hidden tensions. Already, at the close of the second act, he suggests that the Elector's treatment might turn violent. He sees the Elector as Brutus ready to sacrifice his son and proclaims, "By God, in me he will not find a son / To do him homage at the headman's block!" (II, x, 782–83).[16] Under Hohenzollern's proddings during the prison scene, he questions his bond further. Hohenzollern, trying to understand why the Elector is intent upon sentencing the Prince, mentions that the Elector has considered using the marriage of his adopted daughter Natalie to seal a peace treaty with the Swedes, only to discover that she has already committed her heart to another. Hohenzollern hints that the Elector's displeasure over the Prince's suit to Natalie has really led to his trial and death sentence. Hearing this report, the Prince, who only a moment before protested his innocence, despairs:

> . . . now all is clear to me;
> My courtship of her plunges me to ruin:

> Know that I'm to blame for her refusal,
> Because the Princess is bethrothed to me. (III, i, 925–28)[17]

There is more in this outburst than a realization that he has obstructed the Elector's diplomatic plans. The situation of the Prince, Natalie, and the Elector, of course, echoes that among Max, Thelka, and Wallenstein, one also marked by a conflict between love and diplomacy; but Homburg transforms a dynastic and political problem into a psychological one. He allows himself to be convinced that he has unconsciously hurt the Elector's pride (III, i, 914–16). He begins to believe that sexual jealousy has poisoned his relationship with his "father," the Elector, and the Elector's "daughter," Natalie. In accepting such an interpretation of his sovereign's actions, the Prince undermines his faith in his own intuitions. He sees himself no longer as a beautiful soul experiencing lofty emotions, but as a man caught in a net of all-too-human desires. His belief in his destiny crumbles as he replaces his own idealizing vision with Hohenzollern's reductive approach.

By paralleling Homburg to Schiller's Max, Kleist undermines the idea of the beautiful soul or innocent who, in Schiller and elsewhere, offers one possible solution to the difficulties facing romantic man. Schiller offers Max as an almost prelapsarian figure, one who has not fallen into self-consciousness and thus has avoided what Kleist, in his essay "On the Puppet Theater," recognized as the "disorders that consciousness could produce in the natural grace of humankind."[18] As his essay makes clear, Kleist believes that the innocence Schiller grants Max is, after the "fall," found only in animals with their unconscious instincts or in mechanical constructs like puppets from which man's divisive consciousness has been removed.[19] Kleist thus rejects a mode of characterization important in romantic drama, one that enables not only Max but also figures like Beatrice Cenci and Chatterton to appear heroic by clinging to an innocence opposed to the fallen world of consciousness and "self-anatomy." We cannot understand Kleist's Prince if we turn him into a beautiful soul. Homburg clearly desires innocence, but he cannot attain it.

We again misconceive Homburg's character when, in correctly identifying him as a self-conscious inhabitant of the fallen world, we see him as wholly defined by that world. We may well find the psychological complexity of the self-involved Prince so interesting that we forget that this complexity is a problem he struggles to overcome. In a sense, prelapsarian figures of innocence like Max have no individual psychology. Their inner feelings echo an ideal order rather than a unique psyche. Insofar as the Prince possesses psychological complexity, he has fallen from an ideal innocence into a chaos of thoughts, emotions, and desires. When we identify the Prince with this chaos rather than with the desire to transcend it, we reduce him to a psychological case study. He is, instead, a heroic figure who fights to find a wholeness of character on the far side of his psychological perplexities.

Kleist, like his fellow romantics, sought not only to delineate the state of self-consciousness, but also to explore ways to "redeem" the "fall" into selfhood. In his puppet essay, Kleist sees man cut off from prelapsarian innocence, but seeking to transcend self-consciousness: "But Paradise is locked and bolted and the Cherub is behind us. We must make a journey around the world, to see if the back door has perhaps been left open"; "we would have to eat of the tree of knowledge a second time to fall back into the state of innocence." Man can fulfill and thus transcend his selfhood if he will expand his consciousness to include all of creation, if he will travel around the entire world to discover a backdoor to Eden. Man will then attain the "infinite" consciousness—and with it, the grace or wholeness—of a god: "grace" appears "most purely in that bodily form that either has no consciousness at all or an infinite one, which is to say, either in the puppet or a god."[20] Man's goal in this schema is to transcend the psychology of human consciousness to become like a god who holds all creation in his awareness. Blake's prophetic epics that seek a cosmology in an expanded and unified human psychology and Shelley's *Prometheus Unbound* that unveils a world shaped by the human imagination are visionary works in which man attains the infinite consciousness of a god by breaking the isolation of self-consciousness and uniting with the cosmos. Goethe's *Iphigenia in Tauris,* while not written in a visionary mode, is an example of a romantic drama that rediscovers a connection between the inner world of man's emotions and an ideal external order; and again, man achieves the status of a god, as Iphigenia replaces Diana as man's redeemer. While romantic drama rarely breaks through to this imaginative union between man and world, we misread romantic plays any time that we forget this visionary goal and reduce the characters who struggle towards it to the psychological difficulties they would overcome.

In Kleist's play, the Prince refuses to remain in the confusion that follows upon the fall into self-consciousness, but he does not pursue the path towards infinite consciousness recommended by the essay on the marionettes. Instead, he seeks to flee from self-consciousness back into the innocent oblivion of nature. Troubled by events and by Hohenzollern's proddings, the Prince is forced to become self-aware. Most important, his confidence in the future shaken, he must face the probability of his death. When he goes to plead for his life with the Elector's wife, Homburg's heightened consciousness of self has narrowed to a pitiful concern for his own survival:

And the man who upon Life's pinnacle today
Still views the future like a fairyland
Shall tomorrow rot between two narrow boards,
A tombstone there to testify: he was! (III, v, 989–92)[21]

The Prince has sought a personal paradise on earth, a "fairyland" of the future. When he realizes that not heaven on earth but a grave within it lies in wait for him, he breaks down completely. He renounces his dreams: "I give up every claim to happiness. / As for Natalie, don't forget to tell him / I desire her no longer" (III, v, 1022–24).[22] He has lost all confidence in his destiny. He now desires only life. Most important, the Prince still wishes to escape the exigencies of historical time; he still struggles against the complexities of the self. However, he seeks neither the ideal innocence grasped by the beautiful soul nor the infinite consciousness achieved by the fully imaginative man. Instead, he seeks to sink himself in inhuman nature, avoiding in its cycles of survival and its instinctual patterns both history and the self:

I go to my estates along the Rhine,
There to build and to destroy again,
To sow and reap until I drip with sweat,
Consume alone, as if for wife and child;
And when I've harvested, to sow again;
And thus within a circle chase this life,
Till sinking down at evening, it expires. (III, v, 1030–36)[23]

In this speech, the Prince might seem to embrace the earthly life as Goethe's Orestes does when he dedicates himself to the pursuits of the earthly plain. Homburg, however, actually renounces a distinctly human life, for he here abandons his project of giving meaning to life. He will follow nature rather than try to bend the world to his vision. Having fallen into the hell of self-consciousness, he is willing to isolate himself from his fellow men and to renounce his own humanity if only he can escape the turmoil he feels. The Prince cannot confront the mediate, self-conscious life that is the lot of the romantic protagonist. Homburg's desperate pursuit of an unconscious state suggests that the would-be innocent, perhaps even the beautiful soul, turns away from a fully human life. In any event, the Prince's attempt to live life as a beautiful soul has failed. It is now the turn of the Elector, who seeks the ideal not in an inner vision but in the idea of the law.

III

THE ELECTOR: MASTER BUILDER OR TYRANT?

THE ELECTOR IS clearly distinguished from the dreamy, inward-turned Prince. He repeatedly warns the Prince about his fantasizing, and he arrests the Prince for following the orders "in his heart" rather than those set down in the battle plan. Still, the Elector shares with Homburg a desire to control life and to shape the twists and turns of history. His opening "jest" on the Prince is only one of many instances where he tries to write a script for the future. He acts throughout the play like a stage manager, directing a trial here, a triumph there, and orchestrating the climactic scene of the play. His plan of battle is his most ambitious script, offering parts to thousands of soldiers. In each case, his planning seeks to force events into the pattern set by his vision of human life, a vision for him embodied in the law.

The Elector first voices his deep concern for the law at the end of the second act where he explains why he must punish the man who has brought him victory in the battle just concluded:

> Our success today was brilliant.
> Tomorrow I'll give thanks before God's altar.
> Yet were it ten times greater, that would not
> Excuse him, through whom fortune granted it:
> I must fight still other battles after this one,
> And I demand adherence to the law. (II, ix, 729–34)[24]

While we might see the Elector's demand for obedience as a bit obsessive, his reasons for it are clear. He fears the rule of chance in life and history; and as we have seen, in Kleist's world he has good reasons for such fears. For the Elector, the only way man can ensure that his life will have order and that the future will not bring some horrible reversal is to pit a set of human laws against inhuman chance. The Elector sets forth this position in the great debate of the fifth act, when he counters Kottwitz's argument that the Prince, in disobeying the law, has shown the Germans how to win future victories:

> I want no illegitimate victory,
> Fortune's bastard child; I want the law,
> The upright mother of my crown, secure
> To bear me an entire race of victories. (V, v, 1566–69)[25]

For the Elector, fortune, the Prince's bountiful goddess, is only inhuman chance and as such the enemy he hopes to defeat through the rigors of the law. In the Elector and the Prince, Kleist presents the two sides of the romantic protagonist's attempt to rescue his world from the chaos threatening it: the Prince—striving to be like Max Piccolomini, Beatrice Cenci, or Chatterton—turns against the confusion of the present to find an ideal in the visions of the self; the Elector—closer to Iphigenia, Sardanapalus, or Ruy Blas—seeks a cultural ideal and a political program that at least appear objective.

Kleist's play challenges the Elector's belief in the law just as it threatens the Prince's faith in his dreams. When Natalie brings the Prince's suit to the Elector in the fourth act, she presents a contrasting vision to the Elector's belief in the law as the cornerstone of human order. She comes to plead for the Prince's life, but more important she wants to protect his freedom:

> I do not want to have him for myself . . .
> Let him wed whatever wife he will,
> I only want to see him live, dear uncle,
> Apart, free, independent, self-sufficient,
> Like the single flower that gives me pleasure. (IV, i, 1085–89)[26]

Natalie argues that to destroy the Prince for following his inner independence would be "inhuman" ("unmenschlich"; IV, i, 1110) in her eyes. She does not deny that society needs the law, but she contends that order must not be won at the expense of the individual:

> In fact, what you, who have been raised in camp,
> Would call a loss of order, willfully
> To suspend the judges' sentence in this case,
> To me inaugurates the fairest order:
> The battle code shall govern, that I know,
> But so shall tenderhearted feelings.
> The Fatherland that you established for us
> Stands, a solid fortress, noble uncle:
> It shall weather much more dangerous storms
> Than this unanointed victory.
> The future shall enlarge it wonderously,
> A grandchild's care will make it grow more lovely,
> With towers numerous, like a fairyland,
> A joy to friends, a terror to all foes! (IV, i, 1125–38)[27]

The Elector cannot remain unmoved by Natalie's pleadings. Her vision of an ideal freedom argues for the same values as does his vision of man's life under the law. Seeing himself as the creator of a humane society, he must smart under her epithet "inhuman." However, the terms Natalie uses to depict her vision must bother him. Like her beloved Prince of Homburg, she would overlook the significance of present actions to embrace a vision of the future. Just as he has viewed the "future like a fairyland" ("die Zukunft. . . wie ein Feenreich"), so is her vision marked by "towers numerous, like a fairyland" ("Mit Zinnen, üppig, feenhaft"). She would create between the Prince's present transgressions and this dream of a Utopian state a space in which Homburg's free spirit might blossom.

The Elector cannot accept this displacement of freedom and order into the future. He wishes to establish in the present an order that will guarantee a future shaped by the human will. Nor does freedom mean the same thing to him as it does to Natalie. She defines it as the ability to transgress the law in pursuit of one's individuality. The Elector sees freedom, as a Kantian might, in man's curtailment of his will in obedience to the law. She would free the Prince through an arbitrary exercise of the Elector's will over the law. He believes he can make all men free by refusing to put his will above others, by insisting they all obey the law.

Much critical debate has been waged over the nature of the law espoused by the Elector. Some see it as the means by which a godlike Elector creates order for his world; others see it as an oppressive Prussian institution, rightly opposed by those like Natalie who endorse the spirit of mercy.[28] His law is finally neither of these things though partaking of both. Such readings err for they argue that Kleist intends us to accept the law as absolutely correct or to reject it as ruinously limited. Kleist, however, is not so much interested in endorsing a particular program for order or freedom as he is in detailing the difficulties man has in discovering the boundaries of freedom and authority in a postprovidential world. In Kleist's world, no institution possesses absolute validity, for each is a human construct. If the law appears at times to present a providential plan, if the Elector appears godlike, it is because Providence has absconded from this world, leaving a vacuum that the Elector tries to fill. However, the law, unlike a divine decree, has no absolute claim upon man: it is a contract to which men must consent.

The crucial point about the law, then, is that it is a human institution. The Elector himself comes to realize that, unlike the rulers of the past, he does not speak with the authority of the divinely anointed. Constantly contrasting himself with omnipotent tyrants,[29] the Elector defines his position as a constitutional monarch, ruling by man-made law, not through divine fiat. Like Wallenstein, upon whom he is modeled, the Elector attempts to discover a plan that will bring a human shape to a life no longer charted by the gods; but where Wallenstein ceaselessly searches the stars for providential reassurance, the Elector recognizes he has only human law with which to work.

We see in Kleist's play, as we have seen in Goethe's *Iphigenia* or Byron's *Cain,* the abyss of relativism that opens when the society of men displaces providential order, human interpretation replaces divine truth, and imagination supplants revelation. Since the Elector seeks in a human institution a way beyond this anxious relativism, he may remind us particularly of Iphigenia. Just as Iphigenia is the creator of a new social order, so is the Elector, as Natalie has told us, the founder of the Fatherland. Their respective communities differ, however. The institution that Iphigenia creates—that of the guest-right—is seen to arise from the common spirit of man; the spiritual education that Goethe's characters undergo uncovers an order for life grounded in the depths of the human heart. The Elector's order originates in no such inner truth. If—as is often claimed—his order is objective or rational, it is because it is the abstract creation of the human intellect and will. As Natalie makes clear, this order stands opposed to "tenderhearted feelings," demanding that they be subordinated to the law. Insofar as the law embodies not some inner spiritual truth but an abstract system which—if anything—denies the feelings of the individuals under its sway, it can appear arbitrary and even oppressive in its demand for obedience.

Where Iphigenia ushers in a human triumph over the inhumanity of life lived under cruel gods, the Elector's support of the law appears as an all-too-human attempt to shore up the ruins left after the collapse of providential order. The Elector comes to recognize the precariousness of his own ideal at the close of his interview with Natalie. He asks her what the Prince feels about his sentence, confident that the Prince shares his vision of the law. He is startled when Natalie tells him of the Prince's collapse. Kleist tells us the Elector is "utterly amazed" ("im aussersten Erstaunen") upon learning of the Prince's abject visit to beg his life from the Electress (stage direction, IV, i, 1156). The Elector has believed that the law brings man freedom and dignity, but it has brought the Prince to his knees. The elder man must now face the destructiveness of this institution through which he had hoped to elevate man. Just as Kleist has questioned the Prince's turn to the self to discover a vision of innocence, so he challenges the Elector's belief that the institution of the law will create an ideal human order. In Kleist's hands the innocence of the beautiful soul becomes a lost illusion, and the espousal of cultural ideals a failed search for an external absolute.

cepting his fate—the contents of which are never exactly revealed to us—is not solely a heroic gesture; it is also a script for a tragic conclusion to his life. The Prince still wants to see himself as a Max Piccolomini dying in pursuit of an ideal or a Karl Moor sacrificing himself to the moral order of his world. There *is* something heroic in his action, but there is also something stagey. He may be a tragic hero within the play he would write for himself, but not yet within Kleist's drama.

When the Prince comes before the assembled officers in the fifth act to defend the Elector, he certainly tries to pass himself off as a tragic hero. In his central speech, he explains why he is now willing to die:

> It is my absolute desire
> To glorify the sacred code of battle,
> Broken by me before the entire army,
> With voluntary death. What do I care
> For one more victory, brothers, over Wrangel,
> In my much more glorious triumph over pride,
> That devastating enemy within us? (V, vii, 1749–58)[31]

If this speech does not sound strange to our ears, then we have missed Kleist's point. The Prince has never voiced any belief in the "sacred code of battle," not even in accepting the death penalty. His desire has always been to win individual glory, and even his decision to die rested upon his wish to appear noble before his sovereign. And who has ever accused the Prince of pride? He has been a rash fool, a dreamer, but not a proud overreacher. He now ascribes to himself the pride of a tragic figure, calling his fault "Ubermut"—the fault of Goethe's titanic Tantalids. Homburg rewrites his adolescent impetuosity as *hubris* to translate his bungled life into the realm of high tragedy.

We cannot doubt the power of the role he adopts. Like Shelley's Beatrice who in the final act of *The Cenci* possesses the power to persuade those around her of her innocence, Homburg convinces the audience of his heroism, and he certainly convinces his fellow soldiers. Kottwitz and the others cannot express their admiration. The Prince finally wins the renown he has sought. He now claims the other prizes he has imagined for himself; Natalie, whom he could not win in life, becomes his in death:

> She is Prince Homburg's bride...
> Condemned victorious, after Fehrbellin,
> His ghost still marches with the battle flags,
> And he who wants her must contend with him! (V, vii, 1790–93)[32]

The Prince, who has always had qualified success on the battlefield, is now pictured by the Elector as an avenging war god, winning victory in ghostly form. Fame, Natalie, and victory—the Prince wins all he has ever dreamed of. In his own eyes and in those of his fellow officers, he has become a hero.

Finished with life, the Prince wants the death that will ensure his heroic stature. Having made his reckoning with the world (V, viii, 1807), Homburg delivers a soliloquy that is his equivalent of the summary vision of the traditional tragic hero:

> Now, O Immortality, you're mine!
> Your light, intenser than a thousand suns,
> Pierces the bindings of these earthly eyes.
> Mighty pinions grow on both my shoulders,
> My spirit soars into the silent aether;
> And like the ship, abducted by the wind,
> That sees the lively harbor shrink and vanish,
> So below me life grows dark and fades away:
> Colors I can still perceive, and forms;
> Then all lies beneath me in a mist. (V, x, 1830–39)[33]

This speech recalls in several respects the soliloquy the Prince delivers at the close of the first act. Both speeches are addressed to a personified abstraction—Fortune in the earlier speech, Immortality here. Both evidence the Prince's belief that he has obtained all the goddess can offer. Similar images occur in both passages, of sailing and of riches strewn beneath one's feet (compare I, vi, 356 and V, x, 1835; I, vi, 362–65 and V, x, 1836–38). The latter monologue resolves the longing set forth in the earlier speech. There is, of course, an important difference between them: his earlier vision foresaw future victory granted by Fortune; now he sees himself winning immortal fame through death. Still, as the Prince attempts to give a final shape to his life, it is clearly his personal destiny that concerns him and not any external, cultural ideal like the law. The Prince is ready to die because he believes he has created himself as a tragic hero.

The Elector, however, has other plans for him. Having had his "jest" fail, his battle plan compromised, and his vision of the law challenged, the Elector now attempts to reassert his control by placing his own interpretation upon the Prince's acceptance of the sentence. He argues that the chaotic action of the play should be understood as a school run by himself through which the Prince has passed to learn the lessons of the law (V, ix, 1818–23). The Elector suggests that he has created a *Bildungsprozess* to usher the boyish Prince into maturity. The Prince sees himself as a great tragic hero. The Elector sees him as a raw youth who has finally made good.

To enforce his interpretation of events, the Elector restages the dream vision he presented to the Prince in the first act, only this time the wreath and Natalie are given to him. The original dream is now apparently fulfilled in reality. The Prince faints at what might appear to be his moment of triumph and when awakened by cannon fire, exclaims, "No, tell me! Is it a dream?" ("Nein, sagt! Ist es ein Traum?"; V, xi, 1856). Kottwitz replies that of course it is a dream, and the play closes with the other officers raising the Brandenburg battle cry. The Elector would seem to have successfully staged an appropriate graduation ceremony for the pupil he claims to have guided through the school of the law.

What is the dream in this final scene and what the reality? The Prince has played his part as a tragic hero so well that he is willing to die to complete it. The Elector has staged a magnificent spectacle to demonstrate the power of his beloved law. We are swept up by both their attempts to give the events we have seen a final shape. Yet we witness their final triumphs knowing that the Prince's and the Elector's visions do not have the power or authority the two men once sought. The Prince wanted to be the hero of an interior ideal, but his heroism is grounded not in an inner vision but in the perception of others: he has not so much become a hero as he has successfully played at being one. As for the Elector, he sought an absolute in the law only to find it to be a precarious, uncertain human construct. His order is finally as rhetorical and theatrical as the Prince's heroism. In Kleist's world, man can create only an artificial order that is the product of his will and not a fact of the universe.

Still, the Prince's heroism is no longer that of an isolated dreamer. If he plays a role, it is a role applauded by others. And the Elector has demonstrated that the law is not the willful oppression of a solitary sovereign, but a contract for which the Prince is willing to sacrifice himself. The two may discover artifices rather than absolutes, but they convince their fellow Brandenburgians that together they have unveiled a meaningful order within which man can achieve heroic and even tragic stature; that is, the Elector and the Prince convince their society that they have restored what was lost in the fall from providential order.

While we may see the Prince and the Elector merely as coauthors of a "play" to which they attach a triumphant ending, Kleist seems to grant that "play" considerable importance. There is a strong suggestion that this vision of order and heroism, though illusionary in some sense, is nonetheless necessary. Life without heroism is petty and not fully human. Life without order condemns man to the chaos of chance. This is the lesson of *Michael Kohlhass,* Kleist's great novella. Kohlhass, finding his world oppressive, revolts against it only to bring chaos to Germany. The order against which he rebelled is itself objectionable, but finally any order is preferable to the inhuman confusion that arises with its collapse. After his claims have been recognized by the law, Kohlhass willingly sacrifices himself to it. He can acknowledge the necessity of even a flawed order, for he has lived outside it. While the Prince in accepting death does not attain Kohlhass's social awareness, he, too, chooses to sacrifice himself to the institution of the law while realizing the extent to which social order is an illusion. When external reality becomes chaotic and thus, from man's standpoint, virtually meaningless, then illusion and the dream become the only possible human reality. Within a world where any vision is preferable to what lies outside it, man needs his cultural illusions, and the posturing of a Homburg is the only brand of heroism left.

If we read *Prince Friedrich of Homburg* as moving beyond a chaotic reality to celebrate the triumph of an artificial, but meaningful, cultural order, then we link the play to works like Goethe's *Iphigenia in Tauris;* both plays can be seen to endorse artifice as the means by which man liberates himself from inhuman nature to create a humane culture. We may even find in the final theatrical order evoked by the Prince and the Elector a movement towards Schiller's idea of the "aesthetic state":

If in the *dynamic* state of rights man encounters man as force and restricts his activity, if in the *ethical* state of duties he opposes him with the majesty of law and fetters his will, in the sphere of cultivated society, in the *aesthetic* state, he need appear to him only as shape, confront him only as an object of free play. *To grant freedom by means of freedom* is the fundamental law of this kingdom.[34]

We might see Kleist's play charting a similar pattern: from the Prince's "dynamic" view in which man would earn glory through individual force and prowess; through the Elector's espousal of the "ethical state" with its emphasis on the law; to an "aesthetic state" where order is the product of playacting. Reading the play in this way, we bring it closer to the vision of Goethe and Schiller; we connect it to the central romantic quest for an imaginative order for human life, the search for a reality that is a work of art.

Yet *Prince Friedrich* raises new challenges to such a movement from history to vision, from the self to imagination, from tragedy to romance. Opposing the dream of cultural triumph staged at the close of the play is the reality of death. During the last two acts, as the Prince and Elector sketch out a script for their society to follow, the Prince also comes to a new understanding of death and thus to a new relationship with life. As Natalie rushes to the Prince's cell to bring him the Elector's pardon, we see Homburg alone, musing:

Life's a journey, says the holy man.

Admittedly, a short one. From six feet
Above the ground to six feet under it.
I wish that I could rest me halfway there! (IV, iii, 1286–89)[35]

This is one of three soliloquies given the Prince. While the other two—at the ends of the first and last acts—set forth his longing for fame and public recognition, this speech reveals Homburg's private thoughts on life and death. Having overcome his panic upon learning of the death sentence, the Prince reevaluates his life. He has always looked forward and upward for glory, but now he desires to "rest" "halfway there"; facing the loss of earthly life, he begins to value it.

This change in the Prince is most fully revealed in the penultimate scene of the play. Having just heard the Elector claim that he has run a "school" for the Prince and having overheard Homburg contend that he possesses immortality, we seem ready for the triumphal climax. But then comes one of the shifts in tone of which Kleist is a master. The Prince, imagining himself in his final soliloquy drifting higher and higher above a receding and misty earth, suddenly breathes the exquisite odor of some flowers at his feet. As many have noticed, this brief moment in which the Prince inquires of his guard about the flower recalls a discussion in the first act concerning the unusual presence in Brandenburg of the laurel the Prince uses to weave his wreath. In the first act, the laurel was central to the Prince's dream as an emblem of future victory. Now, ready for death, Homburg can appreciate the humbler flower that lies at his feet, not as a sign of fame but as part of the richness of the earthly life. The movement of the Prince's feelings resembles the development in Keats's "Ode to a Nightingale." Having ascended on the "viewless wings of Poesy" to an imaginative height, Keats can turn to celebrate the flowers that lie at his feet, unseen but filling the air with their sweet odors; significantly, the poet earns the right to delight in a completely meaningful earthly life because he is "half in love with easeful Death." Similarly, the Prince feels himself soaring to the heights only to turn to the earth he can now appreciate because he is about to die. In a sense, this is the first moment the Prince has ever lived fully in the present, in touch with earthly things. The Prince reveals an aspect of simple humanity we have not seen in him—or in any other character in the play. He takes a flower from his guard, saying, "I'll take it home with me to put in water" ("Ich will zu Hause sie in Wasser setzen"; V, x, 1845). The Prince, who still believes he is to be executed and thus knows he will never again return home, touches us in a new way here. This small incident reveals that the Prince has come to an experience of life that strikes us as more fully human than either his prior somnambulistic existence or the Elector's dedication to an abstract ideal.

This moment in the garden with the Prince prevents us from accepting completely the closing triumph of the play. The Prince does not strike us as merely a young man who has finally made good by accepting the law; nor are we satisfied with his own theatrical self-image as the proud, tragic figure. For us, the play has become a tragic drama in which a conflict exists between the full humanity the Prince has achieved in confronting death and the cultural triumph staged for Brandenburg society.

Both the Elector and the Prince have tried to provide their world with a script. Finally, neither succeeds in enclosing life within the outlines of his plot. In fact, their competing visions compromise each other. The Elector's perception of the immaturity of the Prince and his understanding of the need for order in his world undermine the Prince's grandiose self-conception. The Prince's very real suffering and his new-found appreciation of life give the lie to the Elector's cultural dream. The final scene presents a tense opposition. The Elector asserts an order for his world in the final triumph, and our judgment tells us he is correct in doing so. The Prince, however, has found in life a richness which lies outside the Elector's abstract cultural vision and with which we must empathize.[36] When the dream is restaged, we see it both as a triumph—the immature Prince has become Brandenburg's hero, and thus his dream has become reality—and as a moment of horror—the Prince has come to grips with the reality of mortal human life only to be told that his experience has been a dream. The dream-become-real provides a comic ending for Brandenburgian society, but it can be only a moment of terrible anguish for the Prince as it turns his entire life into an illusion.

We can better understand the impact of the conclusion if we compare it to a work that may have been on Kleist's mind as he wrote *Prince Friedrich:* Calderón's *Life is a Dream.* The contrast between these two plays can provide us with further insight into the differences between traditional drama and romantic drama. Calderón's play, like *Prince Friedrich,* is concerned with the education of a prince and with the relationship between dream and reality. Basil, the king of Poland, has imprisoned his son, fearing death at his hands. Segismund, raised in a dungeon, is finally released, but only in what appears to him as a dream staged by Basil. In this "dream," he appears to win glory and love. But Segismund does not act in this little experiment as the king wishes, and thus he is again banished to his prison. Having experienced this "dream," Segismund adopts the philosophy that life is a dream and that one should live it to the fullest until he "wake into the dream that's death." Events work out so that Segismund is again freed, but now believing all is a dream, he behaves in a noble and wise manner, winning victory and fame for himself. In the final scene, he restores order to his world, divided by strife and confusion. As everyone wonders at his wisdom, he sets forth his philosophy:

> Why do you marvel, since
> It was a dream that taught me and I still
> Fear to wake up once more in my close dungeon?
> Though that may never happen, it's enough
> To dream it might, for thus I come to learn
> That all our human happiness must pass
> Away like any dream, and I would
> Here enjoy it fully ere it glide away. (III, 745–52)[37]

As a providential play, *Life is a Dream* rests upon the idea that this earthly life is a mere dream from which we awake into the true life after death. In Kleist's play, there is no such promise of a final reality. There is only the order that man creates for himself. Segismund can create a social order that reflects an ultimate order. His tragic perception of the transitoriness of life and his conviction that as a result "ripeness is all" essentially accord with the structure of his world. Segismund has learned through his experience of the dream how he should live, and thus his statement that life is a dream can be a cry of victory.

For Kleist's Prince, the confusion of life and dream that greets him in the final scene of the play can cause only anguish. Taught not by his own misleading dreams but by the reality of death, the Prince believes he has won through illusion to an appreciation of the beauty and truth of life. This celebration of life from the vantage point of death cannot, however, provide the Prince with an idea of order. It is the Elector who must create order for Brandenburgian society; but this order does not recognize the reality the Prince believes he has discovered—in fact it robs him of that reality and thrusts him back into a world which no longer concerns him. Where *Life is a Dream* closes with an alignment of human society and an absolute order, Kleist's drama drives a wedge between the artificial order man must create and the realities of the mortal world.

In a sense, Kleist's play denies the possibility of tragedy, or at least anything resembling traditional tragedy. The Prince in seeking heroic stature and the Elector in pursuing an absolute order together have attempted to construct a tragic world in which a titanic individual comes into conflict with an immutable order—the prideful hero against the ideal but exacting law. But life in Kleist's play eludes man's grasp, undermining his noble poses and revealing the precariousness of any order he may affirm. In such a world, man cannot attain the heights scaled by the tragic hero because there are no heights and no clear idea of the heroic. In Calderón's play, Segismund can be a hero of tragic dimensions because his world has a providential, divinely comic order that defines the tragic value of man's earthly life. In Kleist's play, man cannot be tragic because his world lacks any final order that would guarantee the significance of tragic heroism. This world is not providential but ironic, a world in which each new vision, each new heroic stance, shatters against the teeming chaos of life.[38] Man may delight in the play of cultural forms, but each form captures only a piece of life; thus man laments his inability to live in the simpler, more vivid world that the Prince discovered in the garden.

In his play Kleist goes further than do the other romantic dramatists I have discussed in denying man a breakthrough into a visionary existence, and thus he raises doubts about romantic tragic drama's redefinition of tragedy in relation to the pursuit of vision. In Goethe's *Iphigenia* and *Faust,* man can discover an imaginative order for life beyond the snares of self and history. In Shelley's *The Cenci* and even in Büchner's *Danton's Death,* individuals can at least glimpse the ideal world they would create. Kleist, however, begins to subvert the movement from innocence through experience to vision that provides romantic tragic drama with its underlying ideal. In *Prince Friedrich,* Kleist wonders whether innocence is not self-delusion, the experience of history a plunge into chaos, and vision mere playacting. Where romantic tragic drama holds out the hope of an imaginative breakthrough and discovers tragedy in man's inability to achieve such a vision while he is trapped in the self and violence, Kleist's play concludes with what appears to be such a triumph only to suggest it is merely a dream, not a vision. Romantic tragic drama presents a world of role-playing men trying to break out of theatrics into vision; Kleist stages a vision only to ask whether it is not just another piece of theater. Kleist reminds us that if man must create order, life itself is without an absolute order. If man discovers freedom in his attempt to shape his own destiny, that freedom rests upon a relativism that threatens to rob life of any final truth. The tragic ceases to describe the fate of the individual hero; it becomes the central fact of human existence. The world, tragically, lacks a final, meaningful order; and the order that modern culture must create to shape this chaos has no room for tragedy, no room for heroes. Kleist's tragic vision arises from his sense that life is neither a dream from which we awake to discover the divine, nor a stage with heroic actors struggling to break through into vision; life is chaos, and the dream and the theater are man's only defenses against it. We no longer need tragic heroes. The world as chaos is tragic enough—or worse, perhaps merely absurd—and what we need are fine actors who can enchant us into a dream of order that might keep at bay the horrors that surround us.

V

ROMANTIC TRAGIC DRAMA AND MODERN TRAGICOMEDY

WHEN MAN CAN no longer attain tragic heroism and instead life itself appears tragic, we begin to move out of the realm of romantic tragic drama and into that of tragicomedy. By "tragicomedy," I do not mean the type of play written by Renaissance or Baroque playwrights like Beaumont and Fletcher, but rather the distinctively modern dramatic type that has also been called bourgeois drama, "metatheatre," and theater of the absurd.[39] While many critics see tragicomedy as the modern version of tragedy, we do encounter here many plays that are in fact "anti-tragic"; for they reject the idea of the hero as an idealization and the vision of a final order as an illusion. Man is no longer a grand and noble creature capable of the magnificent gestures of past heroes, let alone their tragic sacrifices. Life is no longer seen as highly ordered and richly meaningful; it appears chaotic and absurd or mechanical and meaningless. If heroism remains, it has been reduced to the drive to survive possessed by Mother Courage or to the despairing antics of Beckett's clowns. Plays like Sartre's *Flies* evoke the mythic order of traditional tragedies only for the purposes of irony. The rituals pursued by Beckett's and Pinter's characters neither possess a divine sanction nor provide an opportunity—like that given to Iphigenia—for humanistic interpretation; these rituals are mere routines pursued to make bearable the confusions of modern life.

Plays devoted to the tragicomic vision cannot attain the heights of tragedy, for tragicomedy sees tragic glory as a falsification of life; but neither can they be pure comedies, for they testify to what is lost with the passing of tragic heroism. Eric Bentley has suggested that for Brecht life is a comedy, and the tragedy is that man will not realize it.[40] Such a statement is central to modern tragicomedy; for this form rests upon the idea that life is not commensurate to man's idealizations. This in turn suggests that life lacks significance and that ideals are false. Where the romantic dramatist finds tragedy in man's failure to remake his world, the tragicomedist finds absurd a world that dooms man's attempts to make life more significant than it is.

Romantic tragic drama lies between traditional tragedy and twentieth-century tragicomedy. The romantic dramatists struggled to affirm man's heroic stature and to discover an order for their world, but they were already writing plays that confronted the problems that have produced modern tragicomedy. Romantic tragic drama is a great protest against an oncoming reduction of man and devaluation of life. The romantic dramatists realized that they no longer had heroes supported by a hierarchical order or plots derived from divine myth or a vision of a providential order. But they struggled to recreate tragedy by depicting extraordinary men fighting to create themselves as heroes and to discover a plot for history that would move life towards an ideal human order. Romantic tragic drama sought to find the hero in the man who discovers his full individuality, a modern equivalent to myth in the processes of history, and a replacement for providential order in a vision of a humanized world.

But as Kleist's play suggests, the vision of romantic tragic drama rested on very precarious ground. Inner tensions that suggest man can never fully control his selfhood already beset the individual. History begins to appear as a series of violent chance occurrences. The idealized vision of romantic humanism sounds too much like mere rhetoric. Kleist still seeks to assert an order and a brand of heroism. But neither the self nor the ideal provides a solution to man's dilemmas in this play. Kleist's doubts are prophetic. The vision of romantic tragic drama soon began to waver in the face of the three great reductions of modern culture: the reduction of the self to its lower drives, of history to socioeconomic forces beyond man's control, and of man's imaginative ideals to the rhetoric of language games.

Of course, the history of modern drama has not been a simple story of a tragicomic assault upon romantic idealizations. Many modern dramatists have sought to reground the romantic tragic vision, relocating its rhythms in everyday life—as in Ibsen's plays—or in a new sense of myth—as in Wagner's operas. An interesting and extreme attempt to rework the vision of romantic drama—and one that suggests the complex relationship between romantic and modern attitudes towards the tragic—is found in Nietzsche's *The Birth of Tragedy*. While Nietzsche discusses Greek tragedy, his analysis tells us a great deal about nineteenth-century conceptions of the tragic, as his use of Schopenhauer and his turn to Wagnerian music drama might suggest.

Nietzsche discovers in tragedy a combination of Apollonian and Dionysian art. The Apollonian artist experiences a dream vision of beauty and order. The Dionysian artist shares in the intoxicating experience of undifferentiated being.[41] Tragedy traces a movement out of Dionysian intoxication to an Apollonian dream vision of order and finally to a shattering of that vision as the drama returns to Dionysus's chaos. More specifically, the hero—who is, for Nietzsche, always Dionysus adopting a mask and the Apollonian language of epic—defines himself against the Dionysian chorus' communal experience of chaos by following Apollo, the "apotheosis of the *principium individuationis*."[42] The hero, the follower of a god who demands self-control and self-knowledge, seeks within himself a structure to project upon his chaotic world.[43] However, he cannot find a final order. He can only create a *dream* of order—that is, an Apollonian work of art. His belief that he has found within himself a pattern for his world indicates that his pursuit of individuation has in fact led him to "excess and *hubris*," "the hostile spirits of the non-Apollonian sphere."[44] His illusion of order is shattered, as he surrenders himself once more to the experience of the underlying Dionysian chaos.

However accurate as a portrait of Greek tragedy, Nietzsche's tragic pattern does resemble that of romantic drama. In the dialectic struggle between Apollo and Dionysus, we hear echoes of the tension between the romantic protagonist seeking to be a hero of an ideal order and the anarchic oppression of his world. However, Nietzsche breaks with the romantics in his sense of the final vision taught by tragedy. For the romantics, man discovers the tragic by failing to break through into true vision. For Nietzsche, tragic chaos is the truth of life and any vision of order is an illusion. Nietzschean tragedy teaches man that there is no final structure to life, that any pattern he creates is a mere human construct forged in violence against the chaos that is reality. If man accepts this truth, he can then turn to the self-conscious creation of illusion—to art—as the means to redeem life. For Nietzsche, tragedy envisions man arising time and again from the chaos of life to create an artful order, a work of art that for the moment solaces him but in the destruction of which he should finally delight. For that destruction prepares the way for new creation and thus ensures the freedom and creative joy of the future. Nietzsche continues the romantic project of redefining the tragic, but he approaches modern tragicomedy in his rejection of imaginative apocalypse and in his commitment to self-consuming works of art that leave the chaos of reality unchanged. In Nietzsche, we sense the movement away from romantic tragic drama—where art, particularly the art of the stage, is merely a prelude to vision—towards modern tragicomedy—where we are constantly reminded that art is, after all, art and that man's lot is to act in a play doomed to have a short run.

We may feel that Nietzsche's turn from the imagination's apocalypse to the solaces of self-conscious art was inevitable. We may continue to insist that the romantic attempt to recreate tragedy was a mistake, that the romantics should have accepted the harsher vision of the modern world, that they should have written forward-looking tragicomedies and not backward-looking tragedies. But even if romantic tragic drama was a mistake and a failure, it was also a glorious gamble risked in the hope of creating a vision of man and his world that would preserve the nobility and richness of life at the very moment when the providential guarantees of such qualities were collapsing.

It was also a gamble that had an important, though often subterranean, influence on the best dramas to come. Tragicomedy may be the central modern equivalent to traditional tragedy, but in the quest for a modern style of heroism and a vision of human order for modern times, playwrights have returned repeatedly to the romantic dramatists for inspiration. We need to be reminded of the impact romantic drama had upon virtually every important modern playwright—on Ibsen who read Byron, Goethe, and Hugo and produced a play by Musset; on Strindberg who immersed himself in Goethe and Schiller and wanted to translate Byron; on Artaud who rewrote *The Cenci;* and on Sartre who reworked Dumas's *Kean.* The dream of writing historical tragedy did not end with the romantics. Ibsen wrote his massive *Emperor and Galilean* and Strindberg created a Vasa Trilogy; Shaw, Brecht, Eliot, Camus, and Weiss have all attempted to adapt historical tragedy to their own ends. The search for a modern hero did not end with Beatrice Cenci or Wallenstein. Their descendants include Ibsen's Solness and Borkman, Pirandello's Henry IV, Shaw's Joan, and even Miller's Proctor. And surely the great humanist vision of these plays has continued to exert an appeal, even on those like Brecht who have set out to debunk it.[45] Modern times may suggest that romantic tragic drama was a doomed attempt to preserve a vision that life no longer supports, but in the theater the heroic and tragic protest of romanticism continues.

PREFACE

1. Théophile Gautier, *A History of Romanticism,* vol. 8 of *The Complete Works of Théophile Gautier*, trans. and ed. F. C. DeSumichrast (London: Postlethwaite, Taylor and Knowles, 1909), 105.
2. George Steiner, *The Death of Tragedy* (London: Faber & Faber, 1961), pp. 106–283. For similar views, see Geoffrey Brereton, *Principles of Tragedy* (Coral Gables, FL: University of Miami Press, 1968); Joseph Wood Krutch, "The Tragic Fallacy," in *A Krutch Omnibus* (New York: Morrow Quill Paperbacks, 1980), pp. 14–27.
3. Morris Weitz, *Hamlet and the Philosophy of Literary Criticism* (Chicago: University of Chicago Press, 1964), p. 307.
4. Susan Sontag, *Against Interpretation and Other Essays* (New York: Farrar, Strauss & Giroux, 1961), pp. 132, 133.

CHAPTER 1: ROMANTICISM AND TRAGEDY

1. See, for example, R. B. Sewall, *The Vision of Tragedy* (New Haven: Yale University Press, 1959), p. 84; George Steiner, *The Death of Tragedy* (London: Faber & Faber, 1961), *passim;* and Geoffrey Brereton, *Principles of Tragedy* (Coral Gables, FL: University of Miami Press, 1968), pp. 183–88. However, Tom F. Driver, *Romantic Quest and Modern Query* (New York: Delacorte Press, 1970), is closer to my view that we find a tragedy of the open world in nineteenth- and twentieth-century drama.
2. R. R. Palmer, *The Age of Democratic Revolution: 1760–1800: A Political History of Europe and America* (Princeton: Princeton University Press, 1959 & 1964), 2 vols.
3. Friedrich Hebbel, "Preface to *Maria Magdalena*," in *Masterpieces of the Modern German Theatre*, ed. Robert W. Corrigan (New York: Macmillan, 1967), p. 75.
4. Steiner, *Death of Tragedy,* p. 193.
5. Ibid., pp. 193–98.
6. Ibid., p. 135.
7. Ibid., p. 8.
8. Ibid., p. 31.
9. Peter Brooks, *The Melodramatic Imagination* (New Haven: Yale University Press, 1976), p. 107.
10. Having accepted the boundaries for traditional tragedy set by Steiner and others (See *Death of Tragedy*, pp. 113–14, 193) and thus having placed the break in the tragic tradition between Racine and Rousseau, I clearly must slight the important place of eighteenth-century drama. For a different view, in which an English dramatic tradition from Beaumont and Fletcher to the romantics is perceived, see Joseph Donohue, *Dramatic Character in the English Romantic Age* (Princeton: Princeton University Press, 1970).
11. All quotations from Shakespeare's plays are taken from *The Riverside Shake-*

speare, ed. G. Blakemore Evans et al. (Boston: Houghton Mifflin, 1974). Act, scene, and line numbers will be given in the text.

12. For example, John Jones, in *On Aristotle and Greek Tragedy* (London: Chatto & Windus, 1962), argues that we have "imported" the hero into Greek tragedy, which imitates an action not human beings (see esp. pp. 12–46). Walter Benjamin finds the hero in Greek tragedy but not in the modern drama that arises with the Baroque; see *The Origin of German Tragic Drama*, trans. John Osborne (London: NLB, 1977), pp. 57–158.

13. Hegel, *Hegel on Tragedy*, ed. Anne and Henry Paolucci (1962; rpt., New York: Harper & Row, 1975), p. 102.

14. *The Complete Works of Christopher Marlowe*, ed. Fredson Bowers (Cambridge: Cambridge University Press, 1973), 2.

15. Northrop Frye, *Anatomy of Criticism* (Princeton: Princeton University Press, 1957), pp. 33–34, 37, 209–10. Frye's view of tragedy has clearly influenced my own.

16. Heinrich Wilhelm Gerstenberg's comment is from his *Briefe über Merkwürdigkeiten der Litteratur* (1766) and is quoted in René Wellek, *A History of Modern Criticism 1750–1950*, 1 (New Haven: Yale University Press, 1955), 177. Mill's genre theory, set forth in his essays "What is Poetry?" and "The Two Kinds of Poetry" (1833), is discussed by M. H. Abrams, *The Mirror and the Lamp* (1953; rpt., New York: Norton, 1958), esp. pp. 23-24, 148. Mill owed much to Wordsworth, on whom see Abrams, "Wordsworth and Coleridge on Diction and Figures," *English Institute Essays: 1952* (New York: Columbia University Press, 1954), pp. 171–201. For Schlegel, see his *Course of Lectures on Dramatic Art and Literature*, trans. John Black, rev. ed. (1846; rpt., London: H. G. Bohn, 1861), pp. 45–46. Hegel finds a division between form and vision in modern art since it possesses "a significance which goes beyond the classical form of art" and thus "destroys the completed union of the Idea and its reality"; Hegel, *On Art, Religion, Philosophy: Introductory Lectures to the Realm of Absolute Spirit*, ed. J. Glenn Gray (New York: Harper & Row, 1970), p. 114. See also Hugo's preface to *Cromwell* (1827), where Hugo discusses dramatic form in relation to its attempt to embody both the sublime and the grotesque, and Shelley's *A Defence of Poetry* (1821, 1840), where Shelley suggests that the poet's imagination escapes the limits of any form, perhaps poetry itself. Murray Krieger discusses the rise of the division between the form of tragedy and the tragic vision in *The Tragic Vision: The Confrontation of Extremity* (1960; rpt., Baltimore: Johns Hopkins Press, 1973), pp. 1–21.

17. Raymond Williams, *Modern Tragedy* (Stanford: Stanford University Press, 1966), p. 32. Hegel argued against the "false notion of *guilt* or *innocence*" in tragedy; *On Tragedy*, pp. 70–71. Schopenhauer attacked the notion of poetic justice, finding the "true sense of tragedy" in man's atonement for "the crime of existence itself"; *The World as Will and Idea*, trans. R. B. Haldane and J. Kemp (New York: Doubleday, 1961), p. 265. Hugo's merger of the sublime and the grotesque renders drama morally as well as aesthetically mixed;

and Shelley in the preface to *The Cenci* (1819) contended that tragedy had to eschew "what is vulgarly termed a moral purpose," in *Poetical Works*, ed. Thomas Hutchinson and rev. G. M. Matthews (Oxford: Oxford University Press, 1970), p. 276.

18. Robert Langbaum, *The Poetry of Experience* (1957; rpt., New York: Norton, 1971), p. 12.

19. Shelley, "Dedication" to *The Cenci*, in *Poetical Works,* pp. 274–75.

20. As Hegel notes; *On Tragedy*, pp. 110–12.

21. Hugo, *Cromwell*, in Pléiade edition of *Théâtre Complet*, ed. J. J. Thierry and Joseph Mélèze (Paris: Gallimard, 1963), 1.

22. I realize that the model of romanticism that I draw upon here, grounded in the work of Frye, *A Study of English Romanticism* (New York: Random House, 1968); Bloom, *The Visionary Company*, rev. ed. (1961; rpt., Ithaca: Cornell University Press, 1971); and Abrams, *Natural Supernaturalism* (New York: Norton, 1971), has come under increasing attack, most strongly from the deconstructionists. See, in particular, Paul De Man's essays, "The Rhetoric of Temporality," in *Interpretation: Theory and Practice*, ed. Charles S. Singleton (Baltimore: Johns Hopkins Press, 1969), pp. 173–209, and "The Intentional Structure of the Romantic Nature Image," in *Romanticism and Consciousness*, ed. Harold Bloom (New York: Norton, 1970), pp. 65–77. I am also aware of the attempts of critics like Anne Mellor, *English Romantic Irony* (Cambridge: Harvard University Press, 1980) and Tilottama Rajan, *Dark Interpreter: The Discourse of Romanticism* (Ithaca: Cornell University Press, 1980) to find a position between those who idealize the romantic imagination and those who deconstruct it. For my purposes, the idealizers provide a useful model of the fulfillment of romanticism's cultural dreams; whether that ideal remains unquestioned in romantic lyrics and romances or whether romantic texts consciously or unconsciously undermine their own ideals, romantic tragic drama is best defined in contrast to the visionary pattern in which self-consciousness is transformed into imagination and violence into love. In a sense, then, my study of romantic drama joins those studies that seek a romantic mode that is neither naively idealizing nor ironically deconstructive, that mode in my view being tragic drama.

23. Schiller, *On The Aesthetic Education of Man in A Series of Letters*, trans. Reginald Snell (1954; rpt., New York: Frederick Ungar, 1965), p. 36. Michelet, *History of the French Revolution*, trans. Charles Cocks and ed. Gordon Wright (Chicago: University of Chicago Press, 1967), esp. pp. 10–11.

24. Geoffrey Hartman, "Romanticism and 'Anti-Self-Consciousness,' " in *Beyond Formalism* (New Haven: Yale University Press, 1970), pp. 298–310.

25. On Blake's myth, see Frye's *Fearful Symmetry* (Princeton: Princeton University Press, 1947), and Bloom's *Visionary Company* (pp. 5–123, esp. 33–49); Kleist's essay "On the Puppet Theater" is translated in *An Abyss Deep Enough: Letters of Heinrich von Kleist with a Selection of Essays and Anecdotes,* trans. and ed. Phillip Miller (New York: E. P. Dutton, 1982), pp. 211–16.

26. From a letter to Byron, 8 September 1816, in *Letters of Percy Bysshe Shelley*, ed. Frederick Jones (Oxford: Clarendon Press, 1964), 1:504.

27. Abrams, "English Romanticism: The Spirit of the Age," in *Romanticism and Consciousness*, pp. 91–119.

28. Shelley's comment is from his letter of 13 October 1817, *Letters*, 1:564. See Michelet, *History of the French Revolution*, pp. 10–11. On Goethe's "Neptunism" and "Vulcanism," see Werner Kohlschmidt's *A History of German Literature 1760–1805*, trans. Ian Hilton (New York: Holmes & Meier, 1975), pp. 337–62; the terms refer to rival geological theories discussed in *Wilhelm Meisters Wanderjahre* (bk. 2, chap. 9) and the "Classical Walpurgisnacht" of *Faust 2*, Act II.

29. Nineteenth-century Shakespeare criticism does devote much time to character. See Arthur Eastman, *A Short History of Shakespearean Criticism* (New York: Random House, 1968), pp. 35ff.; Augustus Ralli, *A History of Shakespearean Criticism* (London: Oxford University Press, 1932), 1:108–58; Langbaum, *Poetry of Experience*, pp. 160–81; and Donohue, *Dramatic Character in the English Romantic Age*, pp. 189–343. Hegel argues that romantic tragedy "accepts in its own province from the first the principle of subjectivity" (*On Tragedy*, p. 79); Goethe and Schiller maintain that tragedy "represents man as an internal agent," while epic depicts his external, objective deeds, in "On Epic and Dramatic Poetry," in *Goethe's Literary Essays*, ed. J. E. Spingarn (1921; rpt., New York: Index Reprint Series, 1967), pp. 100–103. Terry Otten, *The Deserted Stage: The Search for Dramatic Form in Nineteenth-Century England* (Athens, OH: Ohio University Press, 1972), argues that in nineteenth-century drama character replaces plot as the "soul of the action."

30. Hegel, *On Tragedy*, p. 61.

31. Ibid., p. 86. Hegel makes this comment about the characters of Shakespeare, who was for Hegel and for many romantic critics a romantic dramatist.

32. I see the adoption of a "sentimental" ideal opposed to the world as representing an intermediary stance between a "naive" unity with the world and an imaginative transformation of it. See Schiller's *Naive and Sentimental Poetry/On the Sublime*, trans. Julius Elias (New York: Frederick Ungar, 1966).

33. Goethe, *Wilhelm Meister's Apprenticeship*, bk. 4, chap. 13, trans. Thomas Carlyle, *The Works of Thomas Carlyle in Thirty Volumes,* Centenary Edition (1899; rpt., New York: AMS Press, 1969), 23:282.

34. On this point, see Ilse Graham, *Schiller: A Master of the Tragic Form* (Pittsburgh: Duquesne University Press, 1974) and *Schiller's Drama: Talent and Integrity* (New York: Barnes & Noble, 1974).

35. Albert Camus, *The Rebel*, trans. Anthony Bower (1954; rpt., New York: Random House, 1956), pp. 20–21. On revolt and nineteenth-century literature, see Morse Peckham, *Beyond the Tragic Vision* (New York: George Braziller, 1962); Robert Brustein, *The Theatre of Revolt* (Boston: Little, Brown, and Company, 1962); and John P. Farrell, *Revolution as Tragedy: The Dilemma*

of the Moderate from Scott to Arnold (Ithaca: Cornell University Press, 1980).

36. Camus, *Rebel*, p. 21.

37. Ibid., p. 10.

38. Hugo, *Ninety-Three*, trans. Helen Dole (New York: T. Y. Crowell, 1888), p. 359.

39. See, for example, Steiner's comments on the meliorist strain in Ibsen's plays; *Death of Tragedy*, p. 291.

40. Mircea Eliade, *The Myth of the Eternal Return, or Cosmos and History*, trans. Willard Trask (Princeton: Princeton University Press, 1971), esp. pp. 141–62.

CHAPTER 2: THE FORM OF ROMANTIC TRAGIC DRAMA

1. On this split between stage and page, see, for example, Allardyce Nicoll, *Early Nineteenth Century Drama 1800–1850*, vol. 4 of *A History of English Drama 1660–1900* (Cambridge: Cambridge University Press, 1960). Michael Booth says that "there undoubtedly was a separation between literature and drama, or to be more precise a separation between men of letters and the occupation of the dramatist"; *The Revels: History of Drama in English*, vol. 6, *1750–1880* (London: Methuen, 1975), 45.

2. Michael Booth, *Prefaces to English Nineteenth-Century Theatre* (Manchester: Manchester University Press, 1980), p. x.

3. Josephine Miles, *Eras and Modes in English Poetry*, 2nd ed. (1957; rpt., Berkeley: University of California Press, 1964), p. 123.

4. Ronald Paulson, *Representations of Revolution (1789–1820)* (New Haven: Yale University Press, 1983), p. 4.

5. Geoffrey Hartman, "Reflections on Romanticism in France," in *Romanticism: Vistas, Instances, Continuities*, ed. David Thornburn and Geoffrey Hartman (Ithaca: Cornell University Press, 1973), p. 54.

6. Paulson, *Representations*, pp. 1–36, esp. 24–25, 34.

7. Shelley attacks both the remnants of neoclassical tragedy and the popular melodrama in *A Defence of Poetry*, in *Shelley's Prose*, ed. David L. Clark, rev. ed. (1954; rpt., Albuquerque: University of New Mexico Press, 1966), p. 285. Stendhal contrasts romanticism as the art which pleases his contemporaries with neoclassicism which offers works which pleased their great-grandfathers; *Racine et Shakespeare* (1823), in *Revolution in the Theatre: Romantic Theories of Drama*, ed. Barry V. Daniels, Contributions in Drama and Theatre Studies, no. 7 (Westport, CT: Greenwood Press, 1983), p. 126. A. W. Schlegel complains about the sterility of German drama under the influence of French neoclassicism in *Course of Lectures on Dramatic Art and Literature*, trans. John Black, rev. ed. (1846; rpt., London: H. G. Bohn, 1861), pp. 508–10.

8. See J. J. Jusserand, *Shakespeare en France* (Paris: Colin, 1898); E. L. Stahl,

Shakespeare und das deutsche Theater (Stuttgart: W. Kohlhammer, 1947); N. W. Bawcutt, "The revival of Elizabethan drama and the crisis of Romantic drama," in *Literature of the Romantic Period 1750–1850,* ed. R. T. Davies and B. G. Beatty (Liverpool: Liverpool University Press, 1976), pp. 96–113; A. D. Harvey, *English Poetry in a Changing Society, 1780–1825* (London: Allison & Busby, 1980), pp. 142–47.

9. See Nicoll, *Early Nineteenth Century Drama,* p. 89: "It is not too much to say that Shakespeare cast a blight upon the would-be higher drama of the time."

10. Robert Rosenblum, *Transformations in Late Eighteenth-Century Art* (Princeton: Princeton University Press, 1967), p. 53. On the theme of the "Exemplum Virtutis," see pp. 50–106.

11. On Nash, see Nikolaus Pevsner, *An Outline of European Architecture* (1942; rpt., Baltimore: Penguin, 1966), p. 378; Terence Davis, *The Architecture of John Nash* (London: Studio, 1960).

12. Rosenblum, *Transformations,* pp. 24–27.

13. In *Transformations,* Rosenblum has discussed the variety of "classicisms" found in the visual arts, pp. 3–49.

14. See Robert L. Herbert's *David, Voltaire, "Brutus" and the French Revolution: An Essay in Art and Politics* (New York: Viking, 1972).

15. Alfieri, "Dedication" to *The First Brutus* in *The Tragedies of Vittorio Alfieri,* ed. Edgar Alfred Bowring (1876; rpt., Westport, CT: Greenwood Press, 1970), 2:264. On Ronsin and Legouvé, see H. Carrington Lancaster, *French Tragedy in the Reign of Louis XVI and the Early Years of the French Revolution, 1774–92* (Baltimore: Johns Hopkins Press, 1953), pp. 119–24, 153–55. On Chénier, see chapter 7 below.

16. See Nikolaus Pevsner and S. Lang, "Apollo or Baboon," *Architecture Review* 104 (1948): 279n; M. L. Clarke, *Greek Studies in England 1700–1830* (Cambridge: Cambridge University Press, 1945).

17. See Shelley's "Preface" to *Prometheus Unbound* in *Poetical Works,* ed. Thomas Hutchinson and rev. G. M. Matthews (Oxford: Oxford University Press, 1970), pp. 204–7, esp. 205; and his "Preface" to *Hellas,* pp. 446–48, esp. 447.

18. Frederick Antal, *Classicism and Romanticism with Other Studies in Art History* (New York: Basic Books, 1966), p. 2.

19. On the London theaters, see Joseph Donohue, *Theatre in the Age of Kean* (Totowa, NJ: Rowman & Littlefield, 1975), pp. 31–56; Greater London Council, *Survey of London,* vol. 35: *The Theatre Royal Drury Lane and the Royal Opera House Covent Garden* (London: Athlone Press, 1970); R. Leacroft, *The Development of the English Playhouse* (Ithaca: Cornell University Press, 1973); and *The Georgian Playhouse: Actors, Artists, and Architecture 1730–1830,* An Exhibition designed by Iain Mackintosh (London: Arts Council of Great Britain, 1975). On French staging, see M. J. Moynet, *L'Envers du théâtre* (Paris: Hachette, 1873). See also Marvin Carlson, *The German Stage in the Nineteenth Century* (Metuchen: Scarecrow Press, 1972); and *The French Stage in the Nineteenth Century* (Metuchen: Scarecrow Press, 1972).

20. Renato Poggioli, *Theory of the Avant-Garde,* trans. Gerald Fitzgerald (Cambridge: Belknap Press, 1968), esp. pp. 43–59.

21. See Helen Damico, "The Stage History of *Werner,*" *Nineteenth-Century Theatre Research* 3 (1975): 63–81.

22. On non-verbal dramatic techniques, see Marian Hannah Winter, *The Theatre of Marvels,* trans. Charles Meldon (New York: Benjamin Blom, 1964). On the dramatization of revolutionary events, see Marie-Hélène Huet, *Rehearsing the Revolution: The Staging of Marat's Death, 1793–1797,* trans. Robert Hurley (Berkeley: University of California Press, 1982). On the drama of the Revolution in general, see Marvin Carlson, *The Theatre of the French Revolution* (Ithaca: Cornell University Press, 1966). On Sylvain Maréchal, see Maurice Dommanget, *Sylvain Maréchal, L'égalitaire, "L'homme Sans Dieu": Sa vie, son oeuvre 1750–1803* (Paris: Lefeuvre, 1950), pp. 258–73. On *Pizarro,* see John Loftis, *Sheridan and the Drama of Georgian England* (Oxford: Basil Blackwell, 1976), pp. 124–41; and Joseph Donohue, *Dramatic Character in the English Romantic Age* (Princeton: Princeton University Press, 1970), pp. 125–56. On the harlequinade, see Booth, *Prefaces,* pp. 150–57.

23. Holcroft, *A Tale of Mystery* (London: R. Philips, 1802).

24. Ralph Cohen, "On the Interrelations of Eighteenth-Century Literary Forms," in *New Approaches to Eighteenth-Century Literature, Selected Papers from the English Institute,* ed. Phillip Harth (New York: Columbia University Press, 1974), p. 49.

25. Hegel, *On Tragedy,* ed. Anne and Henry Paolucci (1962; rpt., New York: Harper & Row, 1975), p. 58.

26. See Hegel, *On Tragedy,* pp. 1–30. Schelling also argued that the drama witnessed the union of the lyric and the epic; see René Wellek on Schelling in *A History of Modern Criticism 1750–1950,* 2 (New Haven: Yale University Press, 1955), 80–81. In the preface to *Cromwell* (1827), Hugo envisioned literature as moving from lyric to epic to drama.

27. The text for *Pygmalion, scène lyrique,* written in 1762, was set to music in 1770; the piece was first performed in Paris in 1772. For the text, see the Pléiade edition of Rousseau's *Oeuvres Complètes,* ed. Bernard Gagnebin and Marcel Raymond (Paris: Gallimard, 1961), 2:1224–31. Rousseau called the piece a "mélo-drame" in his "Observations sur l'*Alceste* Italien de M. le Chevalier Gluck" (1774 or 1775). On *Pygmalion,* see Paul De Man, *Allegories of Reading* (New Haven: Yale University Press, 1979), pp. 160–87. On *Pygmalion*'s progeny, see Jan van der Veen, *Le Mélodrame musical, de Rousseau au romantisme* (The Hague: M. Nijhoff, 1955).

28. Tennyson's comment, reported by W. J. Rolfe, is quoted in A. Dwight Culler, "Monodrama and the Dramatic Monologue," *PMLA* 90 (1975): 369.

29. Goethe's monodrama, *Proserpina,* begun in 1776 at Gluck's request, received an independent performance only in 1814; the germanophile William Taylor translated the play in *Historic Survey of German Poetry* (London: Treuttel and Würtz, 1830), 3:312–16. Other German monodramas include the *Ariadne auf Naxos* (1774) of Georg Benda and Jean Christian Brandes,

and Benda's later *Medea* (1782). Lewis's *The Captive, A Monodrama or Tragic-Scene* was performed once at Covent Garden on 22 March 1803. Other English experimenters with the monodrama include Taylor's friend Frank Sayers (see his *Dramatic Sketches* of 1792) and Southey who placed five monodramas in *The Poetical Works of Robert Southey Collected by Himself in Ten Volumes* (London: Longman, Orme, Brown, Green and Longmans, 1837), 2:101–16.

30. An account of the performance, with Lewis's letters about it to his mother, is included in Mrs. Cornwell Baron-Wilson, *The Life and Correspondence of M. G. Lewis* (London: Henry Colburn, 1839), 1:231–35; the text is also given, 1:236–41. The play is discussed by Culler, by Louis Peck, *A Life of Matthew G. Lewis* (Cambridge: Harvard University Press, 1961), pp. 90–91, and by Joseph Irwin, *M. G. "Monk" Lewis* (Boston: Twayne, 1976), pp. 77–79.

31. Culler, "Monodrama," p. 368.

32. Baillie, "Introductory Discourse" to *A Series of Plays* (1798–1812; rpt., New York: Garland Press, 1977), 1:38.

33. Ibid., p. 59.

34. Culler, "Monodrama," p. 372.

35. On these developments, see Robert Langbaum, *The Poetry of Experience* (1957; rpt., New York: Norton, 1971); and Terry Otten, *The Deserted Stage: The Search for Dramatic Form in Nineteenth-Century England* (Athens, OH: Ohio University Press, 1972).

36. The French critic Geoffroy saw melodrama as a descendent of the eighteenth-century tragedies of Voltaire and Crébillon; see Charles-Marc Des Granges, *Geoffroy et la critique dramatique sous le Consulat et l'Empire 1800-1814* (Paris: Hachette, 1895), pp. 401–13. Arnold Hauser, in *The Social History of Art,* trans. Stanley Godman (New York: Random House, 1951), 3:689–95, also sees the melodrama as a popularized form of tragedy, though recognizing the influence of such forms as pantomime. Félix Gaiffe, in *Le Drame en France au XVIIIᵉ siècle* (1910; rpt., Paris: A. Colin, 1971), argues that the "drame bourgeois" of Diderot lay behind the melodrama. Alexis Pitou correctly asserts against these views the popular origins of the melodrama in "Les Origines du mélodrame français à la fin du XVIIIᵉ siècle," *Revue d'histoire littéraire de la France* 18 (1911): 256–96.

37. For the statistics on performances of Kotzebue's plays, see Carlson, *German Stage,* pp. 37–40; and W. H. Bruford, *Theatre, Drama and Audience in Goethe's Germany* (London: Routledge & Kegan Paul, 1950), pp. 261–64. On Kotzebue's influence, see L. F. Thompson, *Kotzebue: A Survey of his Progress in France and England* (Paris: Champion, 1928); and Andrée Denis, *La Fortune littéraire et théâtrale de Kotzebue en France pendant la Révolution, le Consulat et l'Empire* (Paris: Champion, 1976), 3 vols.

38. On Pixérécourt, see W. G. Hartog, *Guilbert de Pixérécourt* (Paris: Champion, 1913). Armand Charlemagne's statement is from his *Le Mélodrame aux boulevards, facétie littéraire, historique et dramatique par Placide le Vieux* (Paris: Impr. de la Rue Beaurepaire, 1809). Pixérécourt included a

"Tableau Chronologique" listing performances in his *Théâtre Choisi* (Paris: Tresse, 1841), 1:lxiv.

39. Nicoll, *Early Nineteenth Century Drama*, p. 82.
40. For example, Holcroft translated *Coelina* as *A Tale of Mystery;* Pixérécourt borrowed frequently from Kotzebue, as Frank Rahill has shown in *World of Melodrama* (University Park, PA: Pennsylvania State University Press, 1967); Coleridge talks of the debts German dramatists such as Kotzebue owe to the English tradition in his review of *Bertram*, in *Biographia Literaria: Edited with his Aesthetical Essays,* ed. J. Shawcross (Oxford: Oxford University Press, 1907), 2: 184.
41. Peter Brooks, *The Melodramatic Imagination* (New Haven: Yale University Press, 1976), p. 15.
42. Nodier, "Introduction" to Pixérécourt, *Théâtre Choisi,* 1:vii–viii.
43. Ibid., p. viii.
44. On the development of spectacle, see Michael Booth, *Victorian Spectacular Theatre 1850–1910* (Boston: Routledge & Kegan Paul, 1981).
45. Hegel, *On Tragedy,* p. 92.
46. Ibid.
47. Nodier called romantic drama melodrama "dressed up in the artificial pomp of lyricism"; "Introduction," p. vii.
48. Both comments come from Pixérécourt's *Dernières réflexions sur le mélodrame (1843),* included in *Théâtre Choisi,* 4:493, 498.
49. Nodier, "Introduction," p. viii.
50. Robertson Davies, in *The Revels,* 6:224.

CHAPTER 3: SCHILLER AND THE IMPORTANCE OF GERMAN ROMANTIC DRAMA

1. The introduction of German materials into England can be traced in *The Reception of Classical German Literature in England 1760–1860: A Documentary History from Contemporary Periodicals,* ed. John Boening (New York: Garland, 1977), 10 vols. See, also, V. Stockley, *German Literature as Known in England 1750–1830* (London: Routledge, 1929); Frederic Ewen, *The Prestige of Schiller in England 1788–1859* (New York: Columbia University Press, 1932); Fritz Strich, *Goethe and World Literature,* trans. C. A. M. Sym (1949; rpt., London: Kennikat Press, 1972); and F. W. Stokoe, *German Influence in the English Romantic Period 1788–1818* (New York: Russell & Russell, 1963).
2. See, for example, Coleridge, *Biographia Literaria: Edited with his Aesthetic Essays,* ed. J. Shawcross (Oxford: Oxford University Press, 1907), 2:182–84; the tag "German School," while reflecting German influence, also owes something to the distinction drawn by the Schlegels and de Staël between Mediterranean classicism and northern romanticism.

On the assimilation of German literature by French writers, see Fernand Baldensperger, *Goethe en France* (Paris: Hachette, 1904); Jean Giraud, "Alfred de Musset et trois romantiques allemands," *Revue d'histoire littéraire de la France* 18 (1911): 297–334, 19 (1912): 341–75; Edmond Eggli, *Schiller et le romantisme français* (Paris: J. Gamber, 1927), 2 vols.; Charles Dédéyan, *Victor Hugo et l'Allemagne* (Paris: M. J. Minard, 1964); Lillian Furst, *Counterparts* (Detroit: Wayne State University Press, 1977); and Furst, *The Contours of European Romanticism* (Lincoln: University of Nebraska Press, 1979). Any account of German influence must include the popular Kotzebue; see L. F. Thompson, *Kotzebue: A Survey of his Progress in France and England* (Paris: Champion, 1928); and Andrée Denis, *La Fortune littéraire et théâtrale de Kotzebue en France* (Paris: Champion, 1976), 3 vols.

3. On German Baroque drama, see Walter Benjamin, *The Origin of German Tragic Drama,* trans. John Osborne (London: NLB, 1977); and Judith Popovitch Aikin, *German Baroque Drama* (Boston: Twayne, 1982). On the importance of the Baroque to the theater in Goethe's and Schiller's day, see W. H. Bruford, *Theatre, Drama, and Audience in Goethe's Germany* (London: Routledge & Kegan Paul, 1950), pp. 1–39. On Gottsched, see R. R. Heitner, *German Tragedy in the Age of Enlightenment* (Berkeley: University of California Press, 1963). On Lessing, see H. B. Garland, *Lessing, The Founder of Modern German Drama,* 2nd. ed. (1949; rpt., London: Macmillan, 1962); and F. J. Lamport, *Lessing and the Drama* (Oxford: Clarendon, 1981). See, also, Benno von Wiese, *Die deutsch Tragödie von Lessing bis Hebbel* (Homburg: Hoffman und Campe, 1948).

4. See, for example, Walter Silz, *Early German Romanticism* (Cambridge: Harvard University Press, 1929), pp. 54–82; and Benjamin Bennett, *Modern Drama and German Classicism: Renaissance from Lessing to Brecht* (Ithaca: Cornell University Press, 1979). See, also, Fritz Strich's demonstration that Goethe and other German writers were received abroad as romantics in his *Goethe and World Literature,* cited above; and Korff's discussion of the period as a "Goethezeit" in *Geist der Goethezeit* (Leipzig: Koehler & Amelang, 1923–1954), 5 vols.

5. Schlegel's comment appeared in the first issue of his periodical *Europa* (1803); it is cited in Hans Eichner, *Friedrich Schlegel,* (New York: Twayne, 1970), p. 93. For an account of the productions of *Ion* and *Alarcos,* see Marvin Carlson, *Goethe and the Weimar Theater* (Ithaca: Cornell University Press, 1978), pp. 165–66, 176–78.

6. From Schlegel's famous definition of romantic poetry as "progressive universal poetry," printed as an Aphorism in the *Athenaeum* (1798); it appears as "Aphorism 116" in Schlegel, *Dialogue on Poetry and Literary Aphorisms,* trans. Ernst Behler and Roman Struc (University Park, PA: Pennsylvania State University Press, 1968), pp. 140–41.

7. On Grillparzer's *Ahnfrau,* see V. Wiese, *Deutsch Tragödie,* pp. 382–88; Bruce Thompson, *Franz Grillparzer* (Boston: Twayne, 1981), pp. 27–32; and W. E. Yates, *Grillparzer: A Critical Introduction* (Cambridge: Cambridge University Press, 1972), pp. 47–58. See Carlyle's essay, "Life and Writings of Werner," included in *The Works of Thomas Carlyle in Thirty Volumes,* Centenary Edition (1899; rpt., New York: AMS Press, 1969), 26.

8. Bruford, *Theatre,* p. 1.

9. See Goethe's remark to Riemer, 26 December 1813, where he attacks popular art as such: "What does not please is the right thing; the new art corrupts because it wants to please"; in *Goethes Gespräche,* ed. F. von Biedermann (Leipzig: F. W. von Biedermann, 1909), 2:221; quoted in René Wellek, *A History of Modern Criticism,* 1 (New Haven: Yale University Press, 1955), 216.

10. Quoted in Bruford, *Theatre,* p. 358.

11. Friedrich Schlegel, *Lectures on the History of Literature,* trans. Henry Bohn (London: Bohn, 1859), p. 382.

12. See his letter to Goethe, 20 March 1802, in *Correspondence between Goethe and Schiller from 1794 to 1805,* trans. L. Dora Schmitz (London: G. Bell, 1898), 2: 412, where he sees *Don Carlos* as "cut out much too broadly"; in another letter to Goethe, 2 October 1797 (1: 410), he speaks of his "former rhetorical style." References to the Schiller-Goethe correspondence will be to this translated edition.

13. See, for example, his letters to Goethe of 13 November 1796 (1:254–55), 18 November 1796 (1:258–60), and 4 April 1797 (1:303–4).

14. Letter to Goethe, 2 October 1797 (1:410).

15. "Mir ekelt vor diesem tintenklecksenden Säkulum, wenn ich in meinem Plutarch lese von grossen Menschen" (I, ii). All quotations from *The Robbers* or the *Wallenstein* trilogy are from *The Robbers and Wallenstein,* trans. F. J. Lamport (New York: Penguin, 1979). Act and scene numbers will be given in the text. Except for brief passages, the original will be given in the notes. The text used is Schiller, *Sämtliche Werke,* ed. Gerhard Fricke, Herbert G. Göpfert, and Herbert Stubenrauch (Munich: Carl Hanser, 1965); *Die Räuber* is in Band 1; *Wallenstein,* in Band 2.

16. "Da verrammeln sie sich die gesunde Natur mit abgeschmackten Konventionen . . . "; "Das Gesetz hat zum Schneckengang verdorben, was Adlerflug geworden wäre. Das Gesetz hat noch keinen grossen Mann gebildet, aber die Freiheit brütet Kolosse und Extremitäten aus" (I, ii).

17. See E. L. Stahl, *Friedrich Schiller's Drama: Theory and Practice* (Oxford: Clarendon Press, 1954), pp. 9–10.

18. See, for example, Margaret Scholl, *The Bildungsdrama of the Age of Goethe* (Frankfurt: Peter Lang, 1976), which treats *Don Carlos, Tasso,* and *Prince Friedrich of Homburg.*

19. On the relationship between politics and personality in Schiller's figures, see Stahl, *Schiller's Drama,* pp. 9–44; Oskar Seidlin, "Schiller: Poet of Politics," in *A Schiller Symposium,* ed. A. Leslie Wilson (Austin, TX: Department of Germanic Languages, University of Texas, 1960), pp. 31–48; and Frederick Garber, "Self, Society, Value and the Romantic Hero," in *The Hero in Literature,* ed. Victor Brombert (Greenwich, CT: Fawcett, 1969), p. 220. On *Tell,* see William Mainland's preface to his translation of the play (Chicago: University of Chicago Press, 1972), pp. xi–xxxi.

20. "Pfui! Pfui über das schlappe Kastraten jahrhundert, zu nichts nütze, als die Taten der Vorzeit wiederzukäuen und die Helden des Altertums mit Kommentationen zu schinden und zu verhunzen mit Trauerspielen" (I, ii).

21. "Ein merkwürdiger, wichtiger Mensch, ausgestattet mit aller Kraft, nach der Richtung, die diese bekömmt, notwendig entweder ein Brutus oder ein Cati-

lina zu werden" ("Vorrede," p. 486). Lamport does not include the preface from which this statement is taken. It can be found in Schiller, *Works: Early Drama and Romances,* trans. Henry Bohn (London: H.G. Bohn, 1853), p. xiv.

22. See Schiller's "Über die tragische Kunst," in *Sämtliche Werke,* 5: esp. 379; excerpted in *Dramatic Theory and Criticism: Greeks to Grotowski,* ed. Bernard Dukore (New York: Holt, Rinehart and Winston, 1974), esp. p. 452, where he criticizes the villains in *Othello* and *The Robbers.* See, also, Stahl's discussion of this point in *Schiller's Drama,* pp. 81–83.

23. "Stelle mich vor ein Heer Kerls wie ich, und aus Deutschland soll eine Republik werden, gegen die Rom und Sparta Nonnenklöster sein sollen" (I, ii).

24. Critics disagree about Schiller's idealism. Drawing upon his philosophical essays, some see it as a brand of Kantianism that renounces instinct in favor of the moral life; others have argued that his idealism is essentially an aesthetic concept, a means of seeing the world as a work of art. For a summary of the dispute, see Ilse Graham, *Schiller's Drama: Talent and Integrity* (New York: Barnes & Noble, 1974), pp. 1–6.

25. See Schiller's comments on Posa in his "Briefe über *Don Carlos,"* in *Sämtliche Werke,* 2:225–67, where he speaks of the Marquis as so certain of success that he tries to use the king to free Flanders (pp. 244–45).

26. Letter to Goethe, 4 April 1797 (1:303).

27. Letter to Goethe, 2 October 1797 (1:410).

28. Note that Shelley, in the preface to *The Cenci,* argued that his material was suitable for tragedy because it was known by all and felt to be significant in a way similar to the Oedipus myth and the legend of King Lear; *Poetical Works,* ed. Thomas Hutchinson and rev. G. M. Matthews (Oxford: Oxford University Press, 1970), p. 276.

29. Letter to Goethe, 2 October 1797 (1:410).

30. See Ilse Graham, *Schiller's Drama,* pp. 9–44, where she uses *Fiesco* to demonstrate how Schiller's characters, in striving for the full, free personality that he defined as the goal of an aesthetic education, come to see themselves as static art objects and thus betray the fluid potential of character developing in time. Musset's *Lorenzaccio* follows *Fiesco* in this analysis of art and identity.

31. "Preface," to *Robbers,* p. xiv. "Wer es einmal so weit gebracht hat (ein Ruhm, den wir ihm nich beneiden), seinen Verstand auf Unkosten seines Herzens zu verfeinern, dem ist das Heiligste nicht heilig mehr—dem ist die Menschheit, die Gottheit nichts—Beide Welten sind nichts in seinen Augen" ("Vorrede," 485).

32. See Schiller, "Briefe über *Don Carlos,"* *Werke,* 2:245, 259, where he describes Posa as a "Schwärmer" whose pursuit of the ideal brings him to treat his fellow men as means rather than ends.

33. Hegel, *On Tragedy,* ed. Anne and Henry Paolucci (1962; rpt., New York: Harper & Row, 1975), p. 86.

34. *"zwei Menschen wie ich den ganzen Bau der sittlichen Welt zugrund richten würden"* (V, ii).

35. "Lasst ihn hinfahren! Es ist die Grossmannsucht. Er will sein Leben an eitle Bewunderung setzen"; "Mankönnte mich darum bewundern" (V, ii).
36. See, for example, *Wallenstein's Camp,* sc. 11:

> When the word is spoken, who has not seen
> How we all move in harmony, like a machine?
> Who is it has forged us so tightly together
> That none can distinguish the one from the other?
> Why, no man other than Wallenstein!

> Greifen wir nicht wie ein Mühlwerk flink
> Ineinander, auf Wort und Wink?
> Wer hat uns so zusammengeschmiedet,
> Dass ihr uns nimmer unterschiedet?
> Kein andrer sonst als der Wallenstein!

See, also, scs. 2 and 6.
37. See, for example, his claim in *Wallenstein's Death,* III, xv, that "This War will swallow us all. / Austria wants no peace, and for that reason, / Because *I* work for peace, so I must fall"; "Dieser Krieg verschlingt uns alle. / Östreich will keinen Frieden, darum eben, / Weil *ich* den Frieden suche, muss ich fallen."
38. Coleridge may have been the first to attack Schiller's use of astrology, when he complained, "Astrology is made prophetic and yet treated ludicrously. The author as philosopher is in complete discord with himself as Historian"; in *Complete Poetical Works of Samuel Taylor Coleridge,* ed. E. H. Coleridge (1912; rpt., Oxford: Oxford University Press, 1957), 2:298n. Stahl agrees with Coleridge, *Schiller's Drama,* pp. 102–3.

CHAPTER 4: GOETHE AND ROMANTIC DRAMA: VARIATIONS ON A THEME

1. Erich Heller, "Goethe and the Avoidance of Tragedy," in *The Disinherited Mind* (1952; rpt., New York: Farrar, Straus and Cudahy, 1959), pp. 37–63; George Steiner, *The Death of Tragedy* (London: Faber & Faber, 1961), pp. 185, 166–72.
2. Schlegel, from *Athenaeum* (1798), "Aphorism 116," in *Dialogue on Poetry and Literary Aphorisms,* trans. Ernst Behler and Roman Struc (University Park, PA: Pennsylvania State University Press, 1968), pp. 140–41; see also his "Essay about the Different Styles in Goethe's Early and Late Works" (1799–1800), pp. 106–13.
3. On the resolution offered in Musset's comedies, see David Sices, *Theatre of Solitude: The Drama of Alfred de Musset* (Hanover, NH: University Press of New England, 1974), pp. 65–89. On the link between Schiller's aesthetics and his tragic dramas, see Ilse Graham, *Schiller: A Master of Tragic Form: His Theory in his Practice* (Pittsburgh: Duquesne University Press, 1974); and *Schiller's Drama: Talent and Integrity* (New York: Barnes & Noble, 1974). On Shelley, see chapter 6, below.

4. Hegel, *Hegel on Tragedy,* ed. Anne and Henry Paolucci (1962; rpt., New York: Harper & Row, 1975), pp. 110–11.

5. The translation of *Egmont,* by Willard Trask (Woodbury, NY: Barron's Educational Series, 1960), will be given in the text with act and scene numbers. Except for brief passages, the original will be given in the notes. It is taken from the "Hamburg" edition of *Goethes Werke,* Band 4, *Dramatische Dichtungen,* Band 2, ed. Wolfgang Kayser (Hamburg: Christian Wegner, 1968); the German text identifies scenes by setting.

6. Hegel, *On Tragedy,* p. 99.

7. Schiller first pointed out this gap in his review, "Über *Egmont,* Trauerspiel von Goethe," in *Sämtliche Werke,* ed. Gerhard Fricke and Herbert Göpfert (Munich: Carl Hanser, 1967), 5:934–36.

8. "Soll ich den gegenwärtigen Augenblick nicht geniessen, damit ich des folgenden gewiss sie?" (II, "Egmonts Wohnung").

9. Benjamin Bennett, in *Modern Drama and German Classicism: A Renaissance from Lessing to Brecht* (Ithaca: Cornell University Press, 1979), pp. 121–50, traces Egmont's descent into the self.

10. "Er scheint mir in allem nach seinem Gewissen zu handeln" (I, "Palast der Regentin"). In Act II, ii, Orange states, "Egmont, for many years all our circumstances have been of the greatest concern to me; it is as if I stood over a game of chess, and I consider no move of our opponent without significance"; "Egmont, ich trage viele Jahre her all unsre Verhältnisse am Herzen, ich stehe immer wie über einem Schachspiele und halte keinen Zug des Gegners für unbedeutend" (II, "Egmonts Wohnung"). Machiavelli tells us in I, ii what Margaret has said of him: " 'You see too far, Machiavelli. You should be a historian; those who act can be concerned only with the next step' "; " 'Du siehst zu weit, Machiavell! Du solltest Geschichtschreiber sein: wer handelt, muss fürs Nächste sorgen' " (I, "Palast der Regentin").

11. "Dass ich fröhlich bin, die Sachen leicht nehme, rasch lebe, das ist mein Glück; und ich vertausch es nicht gegen die Sicherheit eines Totengewölbes. Ich habe nun zu der spanischen Lebensart nicht einen Blutstropfen in meinen Adern, nicht Lust, meine Schritte nach der neuen bedächtigen Hofkadenz zu mustern" (II, "Egmonts Wohnung").

12. "Dass andrer Menschen Gedanken solchen Einfluss auf uns haben! Mir wär es nie eingekommen; und dieser Mann trägt seine Sorglichkeit in mich herüber.—Weg!—das ist ein fremder Tropfen in meinem Blute. Gute Natur, wirf ihn wieder heraus! Und von meiner Stirne die sinnenden Runzeln wegzubaden, gibt es ja wohl noch ein freundlich Mittel" (II, "Egmonts Wohnung").

13. "Ich freue mich nur über das Geschehene; und auch über das nicht leicht: denn es bleibt stets noch übrig, was uns zu denken und zu sorgen gibt" (IV, "Wohnung des Herzogs von Alba").

14. "Längst hatt ich alles reiflich abgewogen und mir auch diesen Fall gedacht, mir festgesetzt, was auch in diesem Falle zu tun sei; und jetzt, da es zu tun

ist, wehr ich mir kaum, dass nicht das Für und Wider mir aufs neue durch die Seele schwankt" (IV, "Wohnung des Herzogs von Alba").

15. "Noch steh ich aufrecht, und ein innrer Schauer durchfährt mich" (V, "Gefängnis").

16. "0 Sorge! Sorge! die du vor der Zeit den Mord beginnst, lass ab!—Seit wann ist Egmont denn allein, so ganz allein in dieser Welt? Dich macht der Zweifel hülflos, nicht das Glück" (V, "Gefängnis").

17. "Junger Freund, den ich durch ein sonderbares Schicksal zugleich gewinne und verliere, der für mich die Todesschmerzen empfindet, für mich leidet, sieh mich in diesen Augenblicken an; du verlierst mich nicht. War dir mein Leben ein Spiegel, in welchem du dich gerne betrachtetest, so sei es auch mein Tod. . . . Ich lebe dir, und habe mir genug gelebt" (V, "Gefängnis").

18. "Durch ihn bin ich der Sorgen los und der Schmerzen, der Furcht und jedes ängstlichen Gefühls" (V, "Gefängnis").

19. Schiller was the first to note this "operatic quality"; "Über *Egmont," Werke,* 5:942.

20. *The Autobiography of Johann Wolfgang von Goethe,* trans. John Oxenford (1848; rpt., Chicago: University of Chicago Press, 1972), 2:424–25. Ronald Peacock, in *Goethe's Major Plays* (New York: Hill and Wang, 1959), p. 42, has suggested we forget the remarks on the daimonic. Bennett's *Modern Drama and German Classicism* offers a good discussion of the controversy surrounding these remarks (p. 324, n. 4) and puts them to good use (pp. 127–39).

21. Goethe, *Autobiography,* 2:424.

22. In several *Conversations of Goethe with Eckermann and Soret,* trans. John Oxenford (London: George Bell & Sons, 1874), Goethe stressed the "productive" power of the daimonic individual, his ability to influence and change others (11 March 1828, pp. 304–12; 28 February 1831, 2 March 1831, pp. 523–26; 8 March 1831, pp. 527–28; 18 March 1831, pp 535–36). Goethe finishes his portrait of Egmont as a daimonic individual by revealing his lasting influence through the operatic finale.

23. Schiller, letter to Körner, 21 January 1802, in *Schillers Briefe,* ed. Fritz Janas (Stuttgart: Deutsche-Verlag Anstalt, 1892–1896), 6:335. Goethe apparently agreed; he told Eckerman that Schiller "proved to me that I myself, against my will, was romantic, and that my *Iphigenia,* through the predominance of sentiment, was by no means classical and so much in the antique spirit as some people supposed"; *Conversations with Eckermann,* 21 March 1830, p. 467.

24. Goethe, letter to Schiller, 19 January 1802, in *Correspondence Between Schiller and Goethe,* trans. L. Dora Schmitz (London: G. Bell, 1898), 2:393. Schmitz gives "human" for the German *human;* the phrase is "ganz *verteufelt human,"* meaning "quite devilishly [or damnably] humane."

Henry Hatfield, in *Goethe: A Critical Introduction* (Cambridge: Harvard University Press, 1963), p. 57, finds in the comment the mature Goethe's skepticism towards an earlier work. Oskar Seidlin, in "Goethe's *Iphigenia* and the Humane Ideal," in *Goethe: A Collection of Critical Essays,* ed. Victor Lange (Englewood Cliffs: Prentice-Hall, 1968), p. 51, finds it a "Mephistophelean" warning against seeing Iphigenia as an ideal.

25. Letter to Goethe, 20 January 1802 (2:394).

26. On the romantics' use of classical forms, see chapter 2. On romantic inversion of traditional myth, see Northrop Frye, *A Study of English Romanticism* (New York: Random House, 1968), pp. 3–49. On Goethe and Greece, see E. M. Butler, *The Tyranny of Greece over Germany* (1935; rpt., Boston: Beacon Press, 1958); Henry Hatfield, *Aesthetic Paganism in German Literature from Winckelmann to the Death of Goethe* (Cambridge: Harvard University Press, 1964); Humphrey Trevelyan, *Goethe and the Greeks,* (1941; rpt., New York: Octagon Books, 1972).

27. All quotations from *Iphigenia* are from the translation by Charles E. Passage (New York: Frederick Ungar, 1963). Passage uses only act and line numbers; scene numbers are given for cross-reference to the German text, in *Goethes Werke,* Band 5, *Dramatische Dichtungen,* Band 3, ed. Josef Kunz (Hamburg: Christian Wegner, 1952). Except for brief passages, the original will be given in the notes:

> ... aber Götter sollten nicht
> Mit Menschen wie mit ihresgleichen wandeln:
> Das sterbliche Geschlecht ist viel zu schwach,
> In ungewohnter Höhe nicht zu schwindeln.
> Unedel war er nicht und kein Verräter,
> Allein zum Knecht zu gross, und zum Gesellen
> Des grossen Donnrers nur ein Mensch. So war
> Auch sein Vergehen menschlich; ihr Gericht
> War streng.... (I, iii, 315–23)

28. From Hölderlin's commentary on his translation of *Oedipus Rex,* quoted in Michael Hamburger's edition of Hölderlin, *Poems and Fragments* (1966; rpt., Cambridge: Cambridge University Press, 1980), p. 7.

29. Goethe, *Autobiography,* 2:278–79.

30. Goethe discusses Satan in the same section of his *Autobiography,* 2:278; he begins his comments with Prometheus on p. 277.

31. From Goethe's "Prometheus," in *Goethe, The Lyricist: 100 Poems in New Translations,* trans. E. H. Zeydel, University of North Carolina Studies in the Germanic Languages and Literatures, no. 16 (Chapel Hill: University of North Carolina Press, 1955), pp. 35, 37.

32. Graham points out that Tantalid violence involves deception and mistaken identity; Hippodamia, for example, is wrongly accused of murdering Pelops's first born, and Thyestes eats his children unaware. See Graham, *Goethe: Portrait of an Artist* (New York: Walter de Gruyter, 1977), pp. 65–70.

33. The older view of Iphigenia is represented by Butler, *Tyranny of Greece over Germany,* pp. 93–105, and by Peacock, *Goethe's Major Plays,* who sees Iphigenia as "innocent, saintly, and remote" (p. 65). Graham, in *Goethe,* p. 63,

argues that the "plaster cast which has enveloped the figure of Iphigenia for so long, has audibly begun to crack." We need to hear the Tantalid in Iphigenia. Far from being the pious woman she is often made out to be, she announces from the first that she serves her goddess reluctantly (I, i, 36). Every gesture of submission to the gods is qualified with a protest (see I, i, 7–9, 23–29).

34. "Ein lügenhaft Gewebe knüpf' ein Fremder / Dem Fremden, sinnreich und der List gewohnt, / Zur Falle vor die Füsse; zwischen uns / Sei Wahrheit!" (III, i, 1078–81).

35. "Es ist der Weg des Todes, den wir treten" (II, i, 561).

36. "Was ist es? Leidet der Göttergleiche? / Weh mir! es haben die Übermächt'gen / Der Heldenbrust grausame Qualen / Mit ehrnen Ketten fest aufgeschmiedet" (III, ii, 1306–9).

37. "Und das Geschlecht des alten Tantalus / Hat seine Freuden jenseits der Nacht" (III, ii, 1298–99).

38. "Von dir berührt, / War ich geheilt; in deinen Armen fasste / Das Übel mich mit allen seinen Klauen / Zum letzten Mal" (V, vi, 2119–22).

39. Es löset sich der Fluch, mir sagt's das Herz.
    Die Eumeniden ziehn, ich höre sie,
    Zum Tartarus und schlagen hinter sich
    Die ehrnen Tore fernabdonnernd zu.
    Die Erde dampft erquickenden Geruch
    Und ladet mich auf ihren Flächen ein,
    Nach Lebensfreud' und grosser Tat zu jagen. (III, iii, 1358–64)

40. In "Shakespeare Ad Infinitum," Goethe argued that Greek tragedy centers upon fate, while modern tragedy stresses individual free will; in *Goethe's Literary Essays,* ed. J. E. Spingarn (1921; rpt., New York: Index Reprint Series, 1967), pp. 178–80. *Iphigenia* charts such a movement from a classical to a modern tragic idea.

41. ". . . ich sinn' und horche, / Ob nich zu irgendeiner frohen Flucht / Die Götter Rat und Wege zubereiten" (II, i, 601–3).

42. "Mit seltner Kunst flichtst du der Götter Rat / Und deine Wünsche klug in eins zusammen" (II, i, 740–41).

43. While Thoas and his Tauridians are often seen as barbarians, Graham in *Goethe,* pp. 65–70 and Bennett in *Modern Drama and German Classicism,* pp. 108–10 point out that the Greeks are as barbaric. Thoas has the virtues and limitations of a good burgher. As he sums up his vision, "The most fortunate of men, / Be he king or commoner, is he / Whose welfare is assured in his home"; "Der ist am glücklichsten, er sei / Ein König oder ein Geringer, dem / In seinem Hause Wohl bereitet ist"; I, iii, 228–30. For many, the law requiring death to strangers brands the Tauridians as barbaric, but this barbarism is rather pious, performed in submission to divine will. Iphigenia's interruption of the sacrifice is seen as an usurpation of the gods' rights by Thoas (I, iii, 528–31) and Arkas (I, ii, 63–73, 92, 117).

44. "Ruf' ich die Göttin um ein Wunder an? / Ist keine Kraft in meiner Seele Tiefen?" (V, iii, 1881–85).

45. "Jetzt kennen wir den Irrtum, den ein Gott / Wei einen Schleier um das

Haupt uns legte, / Da er den Weg hierher uns wandern hiess" (V, vi, 2108–10).

46. "Gewalt und List, der Männer höchster Ruhm, / Wird durch die Wahrheit dieser hohen Seele / Beschämt" (V, vi, 2142–44).

47.   Verbann' uns nicht! Ein freundlich Gastrecht walte
      Von dir zu uns: so sind wir nicht auf ewig
      Getrennt und abgeschieden. Wert und teuer,
      Wie mir mein Vater war, so bist du's mir,
      Und dieser Eindruck bleibt in meiner Seele.
      Bringt der Geringste deines Volkes je
      Den Ton der Stimme mir ins Ohr zurück,
      Den ich an euch gewohnt zu hören bin,
      Und seh' ich an dem Ärmsten eure Tracht:
      Empfangen will ich ihn wie einen Gott,
      Ich will ihm selbst ein Lager zubereiten,
      Auf einen Stuhl ihn an das Feuer laden
      Und nur nach dir und deinem Schicksal fragen. (V, vi, 2153–65)

48. I will argue that *Iphigenia* balances tragedy with triumph, but an alternative approach would be to confront the issue of the "happily concluded" tragedy. See, for example, Walter Kaufmann, in *Tragedy and Philosophy* (1968; rpt., New York: Doubleday, 1969), pp. 80–86, where he notes Greek plays that end with reconciliation and Aristotle's preference for such conclusions.

49. Bennett argues powerfully along these lines in *Modern Drama and German Classicism,* pp. 97–120. See also, Sigurd Burkhardt, *The Drama of Language: Essays on Goethe and Kleist* (Baltimore: Johns Hopkins Press, 1970), pp. 33–56.

50. All quotations from *Faust* are from the translation by Walter Arndt in the Norton Critical Edition of the play, ed. Cyrus Hamlin (New York: Norton, 1976). Since the two parts of *Faust* are divided differently, I will identify the part and line number for the first part of the play, the part, act, and line number for the second part. Except for brief passages, the original will be given in the notes; the text used is the "Hamburg" edition of *Goethes Werke,* Band 3, *Dramatische Dichtungen,* Band 1, ed. Erich Trunz (Hamburg: Christian Wegner, 1949).

51. "Weh! steck' ich in dem Kerker noch?"; "Beschränkt von diesem Bücherhauf"; Und fragst du noch, warum dein Herz / Sich bang in deinem Busen klemmt? / Warum ein unerklärter Schmerz / Dir alle Lebensregung hemmt? / Statt der lebendigen Natur..." (1: 398, 402, 410–14).

52.   Drum hab' ich mich der Magie ergeben,
      Ob mir durch Geistes Kraft und Mund
      Nicht manch Geheimnis würde kund;
      Dass ich nicht mehr mit sauerm Schweiss
      Zu sagen brauche, was ich nicht weiss;
      Dass ich erkenne, was die Welt
      Im Innersten zusammenhält,
      Schau' alle Wirkenskraft un Samen,
      Und tu' nicht mehr in Worten kramen. (1: 377–85)

53. Shelley, *Prometheus Unbound*, IV, 412–17, in *Poetical Works*, ed. Thomas Hutchinson and rev. G. M. Matthews (Oxford: Oxford University Press, 1970). Coleridge, *Biographia Literaria: Edited with his Aesthetical Essays*, ed. J. Shawcross (Oxford: Oxford University Press, 1907), 1:202.

54. "War es ein Gott, der diese Zeichen schrieb, / Die mir das innre Toben stillen, / . . . Die Krafte der Natur rings um mich her enthüllen?" (1: 434–5, 438).

55. See Heinrich Rickert, *Goethes Faust* (Tubingen: Mohr, 1932), pp. 113–21; Eudo C. Mason, *Goethe's Faust: Its Genesis and Purport* (Berkeley: University of California Press, 1967), pp. 130–47.

56. "Ich fühle Mut, mich in die Welt zu wagen, / Der Erde Weh, der Erde Glück zu tragen" (1: 464–65).

57. "In Lebensfluten, im Tatensturm / . . . Ein wechselnd Weben, / Ein glühend Leben. . ." (1: 501, 506–7).

58. Keats, *Hyperion*, bk. 3, 112–20, 130, in *The Poems of John Keats*, ed. Miriam Allott (London: Longman, 1970).

59. Kleist, "On the Puppet Theater," in *An Abyss Deep Enough: Letters of Heinrich von Kleist with a Selection of Essays and Anecdotes*, ed. Philip B. Miller (New York: E. P. Dutton, 1982), pp. 211–16.

60. "Ich bin der Geist, der stets verneint! / Und das mit Recht; denn alles, was entsteht, Ist wert, dass es zugrunde geht. . ." (1: 1338–40).

61. "Ein Teil von jener Kraft, / Die stets das Böse will und stets das Gute schafft" (1: 1335–36).

62. "Du hast sie zerstört, / Die schöne Welt, / . . . Baue sie wieder, / In deinem Busen baue sie auf!" (1: 1608–9, 1620–21).

63. "Ihm hat das Schicksal einen Geist gegeben, / Der ungebändigt immer vorwärts dringt. . ." (1: 1856–57).

64. "Denn schlepp' ich durch das wilde Leben, / Durch flache Unbedeutenheit, / . . . Und seiner Unersättlichkeit / Soll Speis' und Trank vor gier'gen Lippen-schweben; / Er wird Erquickung sich umsonst erflehn. . ." (1: 1860–61, 1863–65).

65. Vorbei und reines Nicht, vollkommnes Einerlei!
Was soll uns denn das ew'ge Schaffen!
Geschaffenes zu nichts hinwegzuraffen!
'Da ist's vorbei!' Was ist daran zu lesen?
Es ist so gut, als wär' es nicht gewesen,
Und treibt sich doch im Kreis, als wenn es wäre.
Ich liebte mir dafür das Ewig-Leere. (2: V, 11597–603)

66. Und was der ganzen Menschheit zugeteilt ist,
Will ich in meinem innern Selbst geniessen,
Mit meinem Geist das Höchst' und Tiefste greifen,
Ihr Wohl und Weh auf meinen Busen häufen,
Und so mein eigen Selbst zu ihrem Selbst erweitern,
Und, wie sie selbst, am End' auch ich zerscheitern. (1: 1770–75)

67. "Und diese Glut, vonder ich brenne, / Unendlich, ewig, ewig nenne. . ." (1: 3064–65).

68. "Sich hinzugeben ganz und eine Wonne / Zu fühlen, die ewig sein muss!" (1: 3191–92).

69. "Welch ein himmlisch Bild / Zeigt sich in diesem Zauberspiegel!"; "Ist's möglich, ist das Weib so schön?" (1: 2429–30, 2437).

70. Erhabner Geist, du gabst mir, gabst mir alles,
    Warum ich bat. Du hast mire nicht umsonst
    Dein Angesicht im Feuer zugewendet.
    Gabst mir die herrliche Natur zum Königreich,
    Kraft, sie zu fühlen, zu geniessen. Nicht
    Kalt staunenden Besuch erlaubst du nur,
    Vergönnest mir, in ihre tiefe Brust,
    Wie in den Busen eines Freunds, zu schauen.
    Du führst die Reilhe der Lebendigen
    Vor mir vorbei, und lehrst mich meine Brüder
    Im stillen Busch, in Luft und Wasser kennen.

    . . . .

    Dann führst du mich zur sichern Höhle, zeigst
    Mich dann mir selbst, und meiner eignen Brust
    Geheime tiefe Wunder öffnen sich. (1: 3217–27, 3232–34)

71. 0 dass dem Menschen nichts Vollkommnes wird,
    Empfind' ich nun. Du gabst zu dieser Wonne,
    Die mich den Göttern nah und näher bringt,
    Mir den Gefährten, den ich schon nicht mehr
    Entbehren kann, wenn er gleich, kalt und frech,
    Mich vor mir selbst erniedrigt, und zu Nichts,
    Mit einem Worthauch, deine Gaben wandelt.
    Er facht in meiner Brust ein wildes Feuer
    Nach jenem schönen Bild geschäftig an.
    So tauml' ich von Begierde zu Genuss,
    Und im Genuss verschmacht' ich nach Begierde. (1: 3240–50)

72. "Bin ich der Flüchtling nicht? der Unbehauste? / Der Unmensch ohne Zweck und Ruh' " (1: 3348–49).

73. "Was ist die Himmelsfreud' in ihren Armen?"; " . . . sie, mit kindlich dumpfen Sinnen, / Im Hüttchen auf dem kleinen Alpenfeld, / Und all ihr häusliches Beginnen / Umfangen in der kleinen Welt" (1: 3345, 3352–55).

74. Goethe was aware of the execution for infanticide of Susanna Margarethe Brant in 1772; Mason discusses the possible influence of this event in *Goethe's Faust*, pp. 68–72. Seduction had provided a subject for domestic tragedies since Lessing's *Miss Sara Sampson*. The Storm and Stress writer Heinrich Leopold Wagner wrote a play on infanticide, *Die Kindermörderin* (1776). Goethe accused Wagner of stealing the idea; *Autobiography*, 2:235, and see Mason, pp. 192–95.

75. Schelling's remarks come in his lecture course on the philosophy of art, excerpted in the Norton edition of *Faust*, cited above, pp. 437–39.

76. On this point, see Georg Lukács, *Goethe and His Age*, trans. Robert Anchor (1968; rpt., New York: Grosset & Dunlop, 1969), pp. 160–67, 174.

77. We hear that in the Imperial world "The floodtide of rebellion rolls"

("Schwalle / Des Aufruhrs"; 2: I, 4772–811). Mephisto tells us that during Faust's journey things have progressed to the point where "the realm broke up in anarchy" ("Indes zerfiel das Reich in Anarchie"; 2: IV, 10242–51, 10260–71). The Emperor voices his desire to become a heroic leader through the violence of the civil war in IV, 10407–22, where he claims, "A rival Emperor profits me—I feel / My sovereignty's never been more real" ("Ein Gegenkaiser kommt mir zum Gewinn: / Nun fühl' ich erst, dass ich der Kaiser bin"). The irony is obvious.

78. See the final scene of the fourth act, "The Rival Emperor's Tent," in which the Emperor learns how constrained his actions now will be and exclaims, "Why not sign over all the realm while we're at it!" ("So könnt' ich wohl zunächst das ganze Reich verschreiben"; (2: IV, 11042).

79. Goethe told Eckermann that "the character of the chorus is quite destroyed by the mourning song: until this time it has remained thoroughly antique, or has never belied its girlish nature; but here of a sudden it becomes nobly reflecting, and says things such as it has never thought or could think"; *Conversations*, 5 July 1827, p. 265.

80. Noch hab' ich mich ins Freie nicht gekämpft.
    Könnt' ich Magie von meinem Pfad entfernen,
    Die Zaubersprüche ganz und gar verlernen,
    Stünd' ich, Natur, vor dir ein Mann allein,
    Da wär's der Mühe wert, ein Mensch zu sein. (2: V, 11403–7)

81. "Eröffn' ich Räume vielen Millionen, / Nich sicher zwar, doch tätig-frei zu wohnen. / . . . Im Innern hier ein paradiesisch Land, / Da rase draussen Flut bis auf zum Rand. . ." (2: V, 11563–64, 11569–70).

82. Shelley, *Prometheus Unbound*, III, iv, 201.

83. Mann, "Goethe's *Faust*," in *Essays of Three Decades*, trans. H. T. Lowe-Porter (New York: Alfred A. Knopf, 1947), p. 5.

84. Alles Vergängliche
    Ist nur ein Gleichnis;
    Das Unzulängliche,
    Hier wird's Ereignis;
    Das Unbeschreibliche,
    Hier ist's getan;
    Das Ewig-Weibliche
    Zieht uns hinan. (2: V, 12104–11)

85. Harold Bloom, "The Internalization of Quest-Romance," in *Romanticism and Consciousness*, ed. Bloom (New York: Norton, 1970), p. 8.

CHAPTER 5: *BERTRAM*, BYRON, AND ENGLISH ROMANTIC DRAMA

1. S. T. Coleridge, *Biographia Literaria: Edited with his Aesthetical Essays*, ed. J. Shawcross (Oxford: Oxford University Press, 1907), 2:181.

2. See *Byron's Letters and Journals*, ed. Leslie Marchand, vol. 9 (Cambridge: Belknap Press, 1979), 35; Boleslaw Taborski, *Byron and the Theatre* (Salz-

burg: Institute für Englische Sprach und Literatur, 1972), pp. 60–63; Hazlitt, *"Bertram,"* from *A View of the English Stage,* in *Complete Works,* Centenary Edition, ed. P. P. Howe (London: J. M. Dent and Sons, 1930), 5:304–8; Dale Kramer, *Charles Robert Maturin* (New York: Twayne, 1973), pp. 59–71; Robert Lougy, *Charles Robert Maturin* (London: Associated University Presses, 1975), pp. 41–51. On Coleridge's reaction to the staging of *Bertram,* see Alethea Hayter, "Coleridge, Maturin's *Bertram,* and Drury Lane," in *New Approaches to Coleridge: Biographical and Critical Essays,* ed. Donald Sultana (London: Vision Press, 1981), pp. 17–37.

3. John Genest, *Some Account of the English Stage* (1832; rpt., New York: Burt Franklin, 1965), 7:579.

4. *Report from the Select Committee Appointed to Inquire into the Laws Affecting Dramatic Literature* (1832), reprinted in *Irish University Press Series of British Parliamentary Papers: Stage and Theatre,* 1 (Shannon: Irish University Press, 1968), 3.

5. Gilbert B. Cross, *Next Week—"East Lynne": Domestic Drama in Performance 1820–1874* (Lewisburg: Bucknell University Press, 1977), p. 17.

6. See Bertrand Evans, *Gothic Drama from Walpole to Shelley* (Berkeley: University of California Press, 1947), pp. 16–30, 239–45, 90–131, 133–43.

7. Genest, *English Stage,* 7:88, 210, 421.

8. Coleman, testimony before *Select Committee,* p. 66; letter to Sir William Knighton, 29 February 1824, in Richard Brinsley Peake, *Memoirs of the Coleman Family* (1841; rpt., New York: Benjamin Blom, 1971), 2:400.

9. Lewis, *The Castle Spectre* (London: J. Bell, 1798); act and scene numbers will be given in the text. On Lewis, see Mrs. Cornwell Baron-Wilson, *The Life and Correspondence of M. G. Lewis* (London: Henry Colburn, 1839), 2 vols.; Louis Peck, *A Life of Matthew G. Lewis* (Cambridge: Harvard University Press, 1961); and Joseph Irwin, *M. G. "Monk" Lewis* (Boston: Twayne, 1976).

10. Coleridge, *Biographia,* 2:192–93.

11. On melodrama and working class theaters, see Michael Booth, "East and West End: Class and Audience in Victorian London," *Theatre Research International* 2 (1977): 98–103. Ronald Paulson discusses images of revolt as generational, Oedipal conflicts in *Representations of Revolution (1789–1820)* (New Haven: Yale University Press, 1983). For a reading of English romantic drama as a ritual murder of a father figure by the son, see Erika Gottlieb, *Lost Angels of a Ruined Paradise: Themes of Cosmic Strife in Romantic Tragedy* (Victoria, Canada: Sono Nis Press, 1981).

12. See Cross, *"East Lynne,"* pp. 106–67.

13. Miles Peter Andrews and Frederick Reynolds, *Mysteries of the Castle* (London: T. N. Longman, 1795); James Boaden, *Fountainville Forest* (London: Hookham & Carpenter, 1794).

14. Starobinski, *1789: The Emblems of Reason,* trans. Barbara Bray (Charlottesville: University of Virginia Press, 1982), pp. 35–40. On Lovelace as a precursor of such figures, see Anthony Winner, "Richardson's Lovelace: Character and Prediction," *Texas Studies in Language and Literature* 14 (1972): 45–60.

15. J. G. Holman, "Preface," *Red Cross Knights* (London: Cawthorn), pp. i–ii.
16. See Clara F. McIntyre, "The Later Career of the Elizabethan Villain-Hero," *PMLA* 40 (1925): 874–80, and "Were the 'Gothic Novels' Really Gothic?" *PMLA* 36 (1921): 644–67; for a different view, see Frederick Garber, "Self, Society, Value, and the Romantic Hero," in *The Hero in Literature,* ed. Victor Brombert (Greenwich, CT: Fawcett, 1969), pp. 216–17.
17. Lewis, *Alfonso, King of Castille,* 2nd ed. (London: J. Bell, 1802).
18. Baillie, *Orra* in *A Series of Plays: In Which it is Attempted to Delineate the Stronger Passions of the Mind: Each Passion Being the Subject of a Tragedy and a Comedy* (1798–1812; rpt., New York: Garland Press, 1977), 3.
19. Baillie, "Introductory Discourse," in *Series of Plays,* 1:38–43.
20. Ibid., p. 65.
21. In Act V, scene iv, Baillie, *De Monfort,* in *Series of Plays,* 1, De Monfort exits, proclaiming:

> Here, officers of law, bind on those shackles;
> And, if they are too light, bring heavier chains.
> Add iron to iron; load, crush me to the ground:
> Nay, heap ten thousand weight upon my breast,
> For that were best of all.

22. The note is not in the Garland reprint; it can be found in *The Dramatic and Poetical Works of Joanna Baillie* (London: Longman, Brown, Green, and Longmans, 1851), p. 104.
23. Coleridge, *Biographia,* 2:188.
24. Langbaum, *Poetry of Experience* (1957; rpt., New York: Norton, 1971), p. 83.
25. Coleridge, *Biographia,* 2:191–92.
26. Maturin and his defenders protested that the work was moral. Later editions of the play contained a preface that praised its moral posture. Others agreed with Coleridge, including Genest who felt "there is something unpleasant in the characters of Bertram and Imogine"; *English Stage,* 8:533.
27. Coleridge, *Biographia,* 2:192–93.
28. Hazlitt argues that tragedy does not purge us of terror and pity, but rather replaces egotism with sympathy or fear and pity for others; see his discussion of *Othello,* in *Characters of Shakespeare's Plays,* in *Complete Works,* 4:200, where he talks of how tragedy "substitutes imaginary sympathy for mere selfishness." On Hazlitt's theory of tragedy, see W. P. Albrecht, *Hazlitt and the Creative Imagination* (Lawrence, KA: University Press of Kansas, 1965), pp. 92–105; and Elizabeth Schneider, *The Aesthetics of William Hazlitt* (Philadelphia: University of Pennsylvania Press, 1933), pp. 137–39. Shelley is discussed in the next chapter. We find investigations of the isolated self throughout English romantic drama, in, for example, Lamb's *John Woodvil* (1801), whose protagonist claims, "I to myself am chief" (II, i); or in Wordsworth's *Borderers* (1795–6, 1842), where Oswald pursues the power and freedom to be gained in freeing the intellect from all ties, urging Marmaduke to become a fellow-laborer "to enlarge / Man's intellectual empire" (IV, 1854–55).

29. Coleridge, *Biographia,* 2:193–94. Interestingly, Gottlieb finds a similar ambiguity in the natural setting—the "darkness of the cavern"—in Coleridge's *Remorse;* see *Lost Angels,* p. 71.

30. Maturin, *Bertram, or The Castle of St. Aldobrand* (London: J. Murray, 1816); act and scene numbers will be given in the text.

31. Maturin has Bertram assert his isolation and uniqueness. Bertram insists, "The wretched have no country" (II, iii). Other men inspire him with horror ("Off—ye are men—there's poison in your touch"; I, iii). He sees himself both as inhuman ("I was a man, I know not what I am"; II, i), and as something more than human, possessing a "fiend-like" glory (IV, i).

32. Coleridge, *Remorse,* in *Complete Poetical Works,* ed. E. H. Coleridge (1912; rpt., Oxford: Oxford University Press, 1957), 2; act, scene, and line numbers are given in the text.

33. Coleridge makes a similar objection to Kotzebue, whose melodramas force "one part of our moral nature to counteract with another—as our pity for misfortune and admiration of generosity and courage to combat our condemnation of guilt"; *Coleridge's Shakespeare Criticism,* ed. T. M. Raysor (Cambridge: Harvard University Press, 1930), 1: 60. See Joseph Donohue, in *Dramatic Character in The English Romantic Age* (Princeton: Princeton University Press, 1970), p. 294. Gottlieb, in *Lost Angels,* pp. 45–71, finds moral ambiguity in *Remorse* itself, despite Coleridge's attempts to close the play upon moral absolutes. Terry Otten locates a similar ambiguity, arising from a confrontation with evil, in *Christabel,* which he compares to *The Cenci; After Innocence: Visions of the Fall in Modern Literature* (Pittsburgh: University of Pittsburgh Press, 1982), pp. 31–42.

34. On Byron's desire for success in the theater, despite various disclaimers, see David V. Erdman, "Byron's Stage Fright: The History of His Ambition and Fear of Writing for the Stage," *ELH* 6 (1939): 219–43. On Byron's involvement with the theater and the performances of his plays, see Taborski, *Byron and the Theatre,* pp. 19–75, 152–380.

35. All quotations from Byron's plays are from *Poetical Works,* ed. Frederick Page and rev. John Jump (Oxford: Oxford University Press, 1970); act, scene, and line numbers will be given in the text. On *Werner,* see Terry Otten, *The Deserted Stage: The Search for Dramatic Form in Nineteenth-Century England* (Athens, OH: Ohio University Press, 1972), pp. 67–72; Thomas J. Carr, "Byron's *Werner:* The Burden of Knowledge," *Studies in Romanticism* 24 (1985): 375–98.

36. See George Ridenour, *The Style of Don Juan* (New Haven: Yale University Press, 1960), pp. 19–88; E. D. Hirsch, "Byron and the Terrestrial Paradise," in *From Sensibility to Romanticism,* ed. Fredrick W. Hilles and Harold Bloom (Oxford: Oxford University Press, 1965), pp. 467–86; Robert F. Gleckner, *Byron and the Ruins of Paradise* (Baltimore: Johns Hopkins Press, 1967); Jerome McGann, *Fiery Dust* (Chicago: University of Chicago Press, 1968), esp. pp. 266–73; Otten, *After Innocence,* pp. 19–31; and Paul Cantor, *Creature and Creator: Myth-making and English Romanticism* (Cambridge: Cambridge University Press, 1984), pp. 135–55.

37. For contemporary critical reactions to the play, see *Byron: The Critical Heritage,* ed. Andrew Rutherford (New York: Barnes & Noble, 1970), pp. 214–27. William Battine wrote in 1822 *Another Cain, A Mystery,* about which he said, Byron's "*Cain* has the merit of poetical talent; my *Cain* the merit of truth." For a discussion of the reactions to the play, see Truman Guy Steffan's edition, *Lord Byron's Cain: Twelve Essays and a Text with Variants and Annotations* (Austin: University of Texas Press, 1968), pp. 309–426.

38. On this point, see McGann, *Fiery Dust,* esp. pp. 205–73; Harold Bloom, *Visionary Company,* rev. ed. (1961; rpt., Ithaca: Cornell University Press, 1971), pp. 248–52.

39. While Adah is Cain's sister and wife, their love is treated differently from that of Manfred for Astarte since there are no other eligible mates. However, Lucifer tells them that in the years to come such an incestuous relationship will be branded as sinful (I, i, 360–77).

40. In a letter to Murray, 3 November 1821, *Letters and Journals,* 9:53: Byron wrote of Lucifer's strategy in his dealings with Cain:

> Cain is a proud man—if Lucifer promised him kingdoms etc.—it would *elate* him—the object of the demon is to *depress* him still further in his own estimation than he was before—by showing him infinite things—& his own abasement—

41. See McGann, *Fiery Dust,* pp. 266–69.

42. One might think of Arnold's stance in *Culture and Anarchy,* where he criticizes the various classes as "barbarians," "philistines," and the "populace." The attempt seems to be to distance oneself from any specific class or interest group in order to envision a general culture that will replace the present corrupt society. See Robert Langbaum, "The Victorian Idea of Culture," in *The Modern Spirit* (New York: Oxford University Press, 1970), pp. 37–50; John P. Farrell, *Revolution as Tragedy: The Dilemma of the Moderate from Scott to Arnold* (Ithaca: Cornell University Press, 1980); Daniel Watkins, "Violence, Class Consciousness, and Ideology in Byron's History Plays," *ELH* 48 (1981): 799–816.

43. Bloom, *Visionary Company,* p. 271; see also Ridenour, *Style of Don Juan,* pp. 162–66.

CHAPTER 6: SHELLEY'S *THE CENCI:* THE TRAGEDY OF "SELF-ANATOMY"

1. *The Cenci,* printed first in September, 1819, in an edition of 250 copies at Leghorn, was reprinted in England in 1820.

   Hunt wrote of Shelley that "had he lived, he would have been the greatest dramatist since the days of Elizabeth, if indeed he has not abundantly proved himself such in his tragedy of the Cenci"; *Imagination and Fancy,* 3rd ed. (London: Smith, Elder, and Co., 1846), pp. 295–96. Henry Crabb Robinson reports that Wordsworth called *The Cenci* "the greatest tragedy of the age"; *Henry Crabb Robinson on Books and Their Writers,* ed. Edith Morly (Lon-

don: J. M. Dent, 1938), 1:409. Beddoes, who felt the play dwarfed his efforts, proclaimed it "will be remembered centuries hence" as "a tragedy
inferior to none in our literature or any other"; from a review of *Monte-
zuma*, in *The Works of Thomas Lovell Beddoes*, ed. H. W. Donner (Oxford:
Oxford University Press, 1935), p. 542. Stuart Curran discusses the reaction
of literary men to Shelley's play in *Shelley's 'Cenci': Scorpions Ringed with
Fire* (Princeton: Princeton University Press, 1970), pp. 13–20. For contemporary reviews, mainly negative, see *Shelley: The Critical Heritage*, ed.
James E. Barcus (London: Routledge & Kegan Paul, 1975), pp. 163–224.

2. See Kenneth N. Cameron and Horst Frenz, "The Stage History of Shelley's
The Cenci," *PMLA* 60 (1945): 1080–1105; Bert States, Jr., "Addendum: The
Stage History of Shelley's *The Cenci*," *PMLA* 72 (1957): 633–44; Curran,
'Cenci', pp. 183–256.

   Key readings of *The Cenci* can be found in Curran, *'Cenci'*; Curran, *Shelley's Annus Mirabilis* (San Marino: Henry E. Huntington Library, 1975); Joseph Donohue, *Dramatic Character in the English Romantic Age*
(Princeton: Princeton University Press, 1970); Earl Wasserman, *Shelley: A
Critical Reading* (Baltimore: Johns Hopkins Press, 1971).

3. Allardyce Nicoll, *Early Nineteenth Century Drama*, vol. 4 of *A History of
English Drama 1660-1900* (Cambridge: Cambridge University Press, 1960),
pp. 196–97. Donohue, in *Dramatic Character*, pp. 157–86, corrects the tendency to read the play in isolation from other dramatic works.

4. Mary Shelley tells us in her note to *The Cenci* that Shelley "was not a play-
goer"; in Shelley, *Poetical Works*, ed. Thomas Hutchinson and rev. G. M.
Matthews (Oxford: Oxford University Press, 1970), p. 336. Shelley wrote to
Peacock (20 July 1819) that seeing *The Cenci* "wd. tear my nerves to pieces";
Letters of Percy Bysshe Shelley, ed. Frederick L. Jones (Oxford: Clarendon
Press, 1964), 2:102. Still, Shelley saw quite a few plays, as Curran notes,
'Cenci', p. 158n.

5. See Shelley's *A Defence of Poetry*, in *Shelley's Prose or The Trumpet of a
Prophecy*, ed. David Lee Clark (1954; rpt., Albuquerque: University of New
Mexico Press, 1966), p. 285.

6. Letters to Peacock, 20 April 1818 (2:8); 20 July 1819 (2:102).

7. According to Mary's diary, Shelley saw Kean in *Hamlet* (13 October 1814),
The Merchant of Venice (11 February 1817), and *The Bride of Abydos* (23
February 1818). He saw *Fazio* with Eliza O'Neill as Bianca on 16 February
1817. See *Mary Shelley's Journal*, ed. Frederick Jones (Norman, OK: Okla-
homa University Press, 1947), pp. 20, 77, 92. Mary remarks in her note on
The Cenci that Shelley was "deeply moved" by Miss O'Neill and that she
"was often in his thoughts as he wrote"; Shelley, *Works*, p. 336. Peacock
claimed that she "was always in his thoughts when he drew the character of
Beatrice"; *Memoirs of Shelley*, in *Works of Thomas Love Peacock*, ed. H. F.
B. Brett-Smith and C. E. Jones (New York: AMS Press, 1967), 8:82. Shelley
wrote to Peacock (c. 20 July 1819; 2:102–3) to ask him to arrange a production of the play, stating that "Beatrice is precisely fitted for Miss O'Neill, and

it might even seem to have been written for her"; "The chief male character I confess I should be very unwilling that any one but Kean sh. play."

8. Letter to Charles Ollier, 13 March 1820 (2:178).

9. Shelley heard of the "Peterloo" massacre of 16 August 1819 on September 5 in a letter from Peacock. He immediately wrote *The Mask,* sending it to Hunt for *The Examiner* of September 23; it was not published until 1832. Shelley was working on a copy of *The Cenci* for the press around 11 August 1819; it was published at Leghorn by September 21.

10. Quotations from Shelley will be from his *Poetical Works,* cited above. Quotations from *The Cenci* will be followed by act, scene, and line numbers; the dedication and preface are cited by page number.

11. On this point, see James Rieger, *The Mutiny Within: The Heresies of Percy Bysshe Shelley* (New York: George Braziller, 1967), pp. 113–21.

12. Shelley, *Defence,* in *Prose,* p. 293.

13. On Pound's "usura," see M. L. Rosenthal's "Ezra Pound: The Poet as Hero," in *Modern American Poetry: Essays in Criticism,* ed. Jerome Mazzaro (New York: David McKay, 1970), p. 176. For Shelley's views on self and commerce, see the fifth section of *Queen Mab.*

14. As has long been recognized, *The Cenci* offers a tragic resolution of a situation similar to that in *Prometheus Unbound,* three acts of which were complete when Shelley wrote *The Cenci.* Shelley's plays also differ in their handling of the dynamics of self and vision. See Jean Hall, "The Socialized Imagination: *The Cenci* and *Prometheus Unbound," Studies in Romanticism* 23 (1984): 339–50. On *Prometheus,* see Harold Bloom, *Shelley's Mythmaking* (1959; rpt., Ithaca: Cornell University Press, 1969), pp. 91–147, and *Visionary Company* rev. ed. (1961; rpt., Ithaca: Cornell University Press, 1971), pp. 306–23.

15. Carlos Baker, *Shelley's Major Poetry* (Princeton: Princeton University Press, 1948), p. 143.

16. See Musset's *Lorenzaccio,* IV, v; Goethe's *Faust,* pt. 1, 3249-50.

17. Shelley's link between money and "the principle of self" is dramatized in Count Cenci's concern that he must give up a "third of my possessions" (I, i, 15) to pay for absolution; "I must use / Close husbandry, or gold, the old man's sword, / Falls from my withered hand" (I, i, 126–28). Money as such becomes a key concern in nineteenth-century drama, as the melodrama's rapacious landlords, evictions, forced marriages, and persecutions of the poor suggest; as do Sheridan's *Pizarro,* which pits virtuous Indians against Spaniards fighting for "filthy lucre," and Milman's *Fazio,* where a plot centering on a wife's revenge for her husband's infidelity is set in motion by his avarice. Shelley clarifies the issue by revealing the link between the isolated individual and the power of money in a society where the traditional marks of position—land, family, honor—are under assault.

18. Cenci resembles Sade's spokesmen in seeing God's order as a reflection of the natural evil of man. As the master in a master-slave relationship, Cenci experiences a breakdown in the recognition process, through which one in-

dividual comes to know himself through another, and instead attempts to prove himself through dominating the other. Interestingly, this process ultimately leaves the master with an empty sense of self, but lifts the slave to a higher mode of self-consciousness, a suggestive development for Cenci and Beatrice.

19. See, for example, Nicoll, *Early Nineteeth Century Drama,* p. 197; or Steiner, *Death of Tragedy* (London: Faber & Faber, 1961), pp. 147–48.

20. Paul Cantor, " 'A Distorting Mirror': Shelley's *The Cenci* and Shakespearean Tragedy," in *Shakespeare: Aspects of Influence,* ed. G. B. Evans (Cambridge: Harvard University Press, 1976), p. 92.

21. Ibid., p. 103.

22. See Stanley Wells, "Introduction," *Nineteenth-Century Shakespeare Burlesques,* 1 (London: Diploma Press, 1977), ix–xxvi.

23. Cantor asks "whether Shelley 'believed' in Shakespeare the way Milton believed in the Bible" (p. 96n). In a sense, the romantics did look to earlier creative geniuses as the "Bible" of the imagination; in any event, they could "believe" in Shakespeare in much the same way as Greek tragedians "believed" in Homer. Despite such studies as G. Wilson Knight, *Byron and Shakespeare* (New York: Barnes & Noble, 1966) or A. Sessely, *L'Influence de Shakespeare sur A. de Vigny* (Berne: Chandelier, 1928), we still lack an overall view of the romantics' relation to Shakespeare. Earl Wasserman, "Shakespeare and the English Romantic Movement," in *The Persistence of Shakespeare Idolatry,* ed. Herbert Schueller (Detroit: Wayne State University Press, 1964), pp. 77–103, suggests an approach in viewing Shakespeare as a source of archetypes for the romantics.

24. This generational struggle has been read by some as a commentary on the French Revolution; see, for example, Wasserman, *Shelley,* pp. 94–97.

25. See *Othello,* in *Riverside Shakespeare,* ed. G. Blakemore Evans et al. (Boston: Houghton Mifflin, 1974), III, iii, 106–16.

26. Curran, *'Cenci',* pp. 66–67.

27. A. W. Schlegel, *Lectures on Dramatic Art and Literature,* trans. John Black, rev. ed. (1846; rpt., London: H. G. Bohn, 1861), p. 104.

28. If Giacomo does not become either a Hamlet or an Othello, Orsino proves to be neither a true Horatio nor a successful Iago. Playing a Horatio-like confidant, he repeatedly betrays Giacomo's trust. Seeing himself as an Iagoesque "Joker in the Pack," he proves unable to prompt Giacomo to action; he has tried to write a comic plot for his world, but he has been defeated (V, i, 77–83). (On Orsino and comedy, see Wasserman, *Shelley,* pp. 90, 115–17.) Orsino finally flees in disguise, revealing himself as a victim of self-anatomy, for he cannot "Find the disguise to hide me from myself" (V, i, 103).

29. See Baker, *Shelley's Major Poetry,* pp. 149–50: Beatrice "explicitly rejects the moral position to which she has hitherto been devoted"; Richard Holmes, *Shelley: The Pursuit* (London: Weidenfeld and Nicholson, 1974), p. 524: Beatrice reveals "a cold cruelty of purpose . . . as vicious as her father's"; and John Murphy, *Dark Angel: Gothic Elements in Shelley's Works* (London: Associated University Presses, 1975), p. 181: the "Count has won"

in destroying Beatrice's innocence. For an interesting account of Beatrice's innocence, see Terry Otten, *After Innocence: Visions of the Fall in Modern Literature* (Pittsburgh: University of Pittsburgh Press, 1982), pp. 34–42.

30. See William D. Sims-Gunzenhauser, "Conflict of the Inner Life in Goethe's *Iphigenia* and Shelley's *Cenci*," *Neophilogus* 63 (1979): 95–107.

31. Milton Wilson, *Shelley's Later Poetry* (New York: Columbia University Press, 1959), p. 88.

32. See Prometheus's similar insight, "Whilst I behold such execrable shapes, / Methinks I grow like what I contemplate / And laugh and stare in loathsome sympathy" (I, i, 449–51).

33. Antonin Artaud, *The Cenci,* trans. Simon Watson Taylor (New York: Grove Press, 1970), p. 52.

34. Peter Brooks, *The Melodramatic Imagination* (New Haven: Yale University Press, 1976), pp. 107–8, calls Shelley the "most melodramatic of English romantic poets."

35. E. S. Bates, *A Study of Shelley's Drama 'The Cenci'* (New York: Columbia University Press, 1908), p. 63.

36. Donohue, in *Dramatic Character,* defines such moments as "moments of response" (pp. 47–69); he finds such moments in *The Cenci* (pp. 162–72).

37. See III, i, 85–86, 107–9, 154–55. Wasserman discusses her refusal to dwell upon the rape, in *Shelley,* pp. 112–14.

38. See, for example, the speech of the Spirit of the Hour in *Prometheus Unbound:* "There was a change: the impalpable thin air / And the all-circling sunlight were transformed, / As if the sense of love dissolved in them / Had folded itself round the sphered world" (III, iv, 99–102).

39. See, for example, Wilson, *Shelley's Later Poetry,* p. 85; Cantor, *"The Cenci* and Shakespearean Tragedy," p. 97.

40. Stuart Curran makes a similar point in *Annus Mirabilis,* p. 134.

41. On their disagreements, see Charles E. Robinson, *Shelley and Byron: The Snake and Eagle Wreathed in Fight* (Baltimore: Johns Hopkins Press, 1976), esp. pp. 144–60.

42. While he talks of *Remorse, Fazio,* and *Bertram* in his letters (see above nn. 6 and 7), it is to *Oedipus, Lear,* and *El Purgatorio de San Patricio* that he refers in the preface to the play (pp. 276, 277).

43. *Defence,* in *Prose,* p. 284. Subsequent references to the *Defence* will be given in the text.

44. Wasserman makes a similar argument in his *Shelley,* pp. 84–130, esp. 101–15.

45. See Shelley's essay, "On Love," in *Prose,* pp. 169–71 and *Epipsychidion.*

46. See, for example, Donohue, *Dramatic Character,* pp. 172–83; Wasserman, *Shelley,* pp. 117–21; and Paul Smith, "Restless Casuistry: Shelley's Composition of *The Cenci,*" *Keats–Shelley Journal* 13 (1964): 77–85.

47. Benjamin Bennett, *Modern Drama and German Classicism: Renaissance from Lessing to Brecht* (Ithaca: Cornell University Press, 1979), pp. 54–55.

48. Jerome McGann, *Fiery Dust: Byron's Poetic Development* (Chicago: Chicago University Press, 1968), p. 227 & n.

49. See Schiller, *Sämtliche Werke,* ed. Gerhard Fricke and Herbert Göpfert (Mu-

nich: Carl Hanser, 1967), 5, which contains his theoretical essays on tragedy and his pieces on the theater; there is a selection of this material in *Dramatic Theory and Criticism: Greeks to Grotowski,* ed. Bernard Dukore (New York: Holt, Rinehart and Winston, 1974), pp. 437–75. On Coleridge and Hazlitt, see chap. 5.

CHAPTER 7: NEOCLASSICISM, MELODRAMA, AND FRENCH ROMANTIC DRAMA

1. Marvin Carlson, *The French Stage in the Nineteenth Century* (Metuchen, NJ: Scarecrow Press, 1972), pp. 12–13. On the theatrical situation of the day, see also his *The Theatre of the French Revolution* (Ithaca: Cornell University Press, 1966) and Maurice Descotes's *Le Public de théâtre et son histoire* (Paris: Presses Universitaires de France, 1964).
2. Hugo, "Ymbert Galloix" (1833), in *Philosophie* 1 of *Oeuvres Complètes,* ed. Paul Meurice et al. (Paris: Albin Michel, 1904–52), 184.
3. Carlson, *French Stage,* p. 29.
4. Hugo, *William Shakespeare* (1864), in *Philosophie* 2 of *Oeuvres Complètes,* 208; "Preface," to *Hernani,* in Pléiade edition of Hugo, *Théâtre Complet,* ed. J.-J. Thierry and Josette Mélèze (Paris: Gallimard, 1963), 1:1147. On the romantic dramatists and politics, see Jean Gaudon, *Victor Hugo dramaturge* (Paris: L'Arche, 1955); Henri Lefebvre, *Alfred de Musset dramaturge* (Paris: L'Arche, 1955); Ellie Nower Schamber, *The Artist as Politician: The Relationship between the Art and the Politics of the French Romantics* (New York: University Press of America, 1984); and the essays collected in *Romantisme et Politique 1815–1851: Colloque d'histoire littéraire* (Paris: A. Colin, 1969).
5. Irving Howe, *Politics and the Novel* (New York: Horizon Press, 1957), p. 19.
6. See M. H. Abrams, "English Romanticism: The Spirit of the Age," in *Romanticism and Consciousness,* ed. Harold Bloom (New York: Norton, 1970), pp. 91–119, for an argument that the romantics turned from political revolution to spiritual reformation.
7. As a radical thinker who adopts a traditional form, Chénier is the French counterpart of those eighteenth-century English authors whom Carl Woodring, following the precedent set by the conservative satirists of the *Anti-Jacobin,* calls "Jacobin" writers; *Politics in English Romantic Poetry* (Cambridge: Harvard University Press, 1970). See also, Ronald Paulson, *Representation and Revolution (1789–1820)* (New Haven: Yale University Press, 1983), pp. 1–36.
8. Jean Starobinski, *1789: The Emblems of Reason,* trans. Barbara Bray (Charlottesville: University of Virginia Press, 1982), p. 122.
9. "le caractère irrésolu, timide et cruel": Chénier, "De La Liberté du Théâtre en France" (1789), in *Théâtre de la Révolution,* ed. M. Louis Moland (1877; rpt., Geneva: Slatkine Reprints, 1971), p. 108. *Charles IX* is also in this volume; I give translations in the text, the French in the notes.

10.   Dans nos murs le sang coule en ruisseaux.
       Tout ce qui vit encore, excepté le bourreaux,
       Tout frémit: le ciel même a voilé sa lumière;
       Et Paris maintenant n'est qu'un vaste repaire
       Où la mort . . . .(V, ii)

11. Eleanor Jourdain, *Dramatic Theory and Practice in France 1690–1808*
     (London: Longmans, Green, and Co , 1921), pp. 146–47.

12. See II, iii, where Coligny imagines an ideal kingdom, with a king worthy of
     his title and a people dedicated to commerce and the arts; he dreams of
     "One day when our French, great in courage / Exempt from fanaticism and
     dissension, / Will be able to stand as an example to all the nations" ("Quel-
     que jour nos Français, si grands par le courage, / Exempts du fanatisme et des
     dissensions, / Pourront servir en tout d'example aux nations."

13. Constant, *A Literary and Political Miscellany,* in *Revolution in the Theatre,*
     ed. Barry V. Daniels, *Contributions in Drama and Theatre Studies,* no. 7
     (Westport, CT: Greenwood Press, 1983), p. 82.

14. See in particular Marie-Hélène Huet, *Rehearsing the Revolution: The Stag-
     ing of Marat's Death 1793–1797,* trans. Robert Hurley (Berkeley: University
     of California Press, 1982). On martyr plays, see Walter Benjamin, *The Origin
     of German Tragic Drama,* trans. John Osborne (London: NLB, 1977), esp.
     pp. 69–76; Herbert Lindenberger, *Historical Drama: The Relation of Liter-
     ature and Reality* (Chicago: University of Chicago Press, 1975), pp. 38–53.

15. On apocalypse, history, and tragedy, see Frank Kermode, *The Sense of an
     Ending* (Oxford: Oxford University Press, 1967), esp. pp. 67–89.

16. The first statement is from the "Fragments d'institutions républicaines," in
     Oeuvres Complètes de Saint-Just, ed. Michèle Duval (Paris: G. Lebovici,
     1984), p. 978; the second is quoted by Camus, *The Rebel,* trans. Anthony
     Bower (1954; rpt., New York: Random House, 1956), p. 122, without a
     source being identified.

17. Nodier, "Introduction," to Pixérécourt, *Théâtre Choisi* (Paris: Tresse, 1841),
     1:vii.

18. For example, *Le Journal des Débats* of 13 March 1820 saw *Marie Stuart* as a
     romantic victory, "une victoire des lumières sur les préjugés"; quoted in,
     "Introduction," *Marie Stuart,* ed. Robert Dumeil (Rouen: Publications de
     l'Université de Rouen, 1972), pp. 9–10.

19. For the quotation from Vitet, see *La Ligue, scènes historiques,* Tome 1: *Les
     Barricades* (Paris: Charles Gosselin, 1844), 2. On the "scènes historiques,"
     see J. Marsan, "Le Théâtre historique et le romantisme," *Revue d'histoire lit-
     téraire de la France* 17 (1910): 1–33; M. Trotain, *Les Scènes historiques:
     étude du théâtre livresque à la veille du drame romantique* (Paris: Cham-
     pion, 1923); W. D. Howarth, *Sublime and Grotesque: A Study of French Ro-
     mantic Drama* (London: Harrap, 1975), pp. 110–18. George Sand's "scène
     historique," *Un Conspiration en 1537,* inspired her lover's *Lorenzaccio.*
     The text of Sand's drama is included in Paul Dimoff's *La Genèse de 'Loren-
     zaccio'* (Paris: Droz, 1936), pp. 83–146. Haasan El Nouty draws some con-
     nections between Musset's play and the "scène historique" in general in
     "Théâtre et anti-théâtre au XIX^c siècle," *PMLA* 79 (1964): 604-12.

20. We find, for example, *Le Globe* of 9 November 1824 saying of Ancelot's classicizing adaptation of Schiller, *Fiesque* (Odéon, 1824), that it offered an "alliance between the classicists and romanticists."

21. Carlson calls *Sylla* "probably the best tragedy of the period, and certainly the most popular"; *French Stage,* p. 29. On *Léonidas,* see Léon Séché, "Les Debuts du Romantisme au Théâtre-Français: Le Baron Taylor et le *Léonidas* de Michel Pichat," *Les Annales romantiques* 5 (1909): 241–72.

22. Carlson, *French Stage,* p. 62.

23. Descotes, *Le Public de théâtre,* pp. 245–304.

24.   Superbe, impétueux, toujours sûr du succès,
    Il éblouit la cour par sa magnificence,
    Pousse la loyauté jusqu'à l'imprudence.
    Il pourrait immoler, sans frein dans ses désirs,
    Sa vie à son devoir, son devoir aux plaisirs. (I, i)

Translations of Delavigne will be given in the text with act and scene numbers; the French will be given in the notes. The edition used is *Oeuvres Complètes de Casimir Delavigne* (Paris: Garnier Frères, 1895), 1.

25. P. J. Yarrow, "Three Plays of 1829, or Doubts About 1830," *Symposium* 23 (1969): 373–83.

26. Byron, *Poetical Works,* ed. Frederick Page, rev. John Jump (Oxford: Oxford University Press, 1970), p. 408.

27.   Nuit d'ivresse!... un tumulte! Ah! le désordre est doux....(II, xiii)

    Mais l'excès nous réveille, il donne un charme à tout.
    Un amour vous suffit; moi, le mien se promène
    De l'esclave de Smyrne à la noble Romaine,
    Et de la courtisane il remonte aux beautés
    Que votre bal promet à mes yeux enchantés.
    Le jeu de casino me pique et m'intéresse;
    Mais j'y prodigue l'or, ou j'y meurs de tristesse. (II, iv)

28. Vigny and Dumas are discussed below. Lamartine's *Toussaint Louverture* (Porte-Saint-Martin, 1850) is included in the Pléiade edition of his *Oeuvres Poetiques Complètes,* ed. Marius-François Guyard (Paris: Gallimard, 1963). Nerval's *Leo Burckhart* (Porte-Saint-Martin, 1839) is the most interesting of his several plays. See Jean Richer, "Nerval et ses deux *Leo Burckhart,*" *Mercure de France* 307 (1949): 645–78; and his edition of the play in *Le Drame romantique* (Paris: Club des Libraires de France, 1957). On Gautier's work in the theater, see Claude Book-Senninger, *Théophile Gautier, Auteur dramatique* (Paris: A.-G. Nizet, 1972); Richard Grant, *Théophile Gautier* (Boston: Twayne, 1975), pp. 51–57, 91–106. Balzac's plays have been edited by R. Guisé, *Théâtre,* 3 vols. (Paris: Les Bibliophiles de l'Originale, 1969–1971); they are discussed in Howarth, *Sublime and Grotesque,* pp. 277–84, and in D. Z. Milatchitch, *Le Théâtre de Honoré de Balzac* (Paris: Hatchette, 1930).

29. Dumas's play railed against bourgeois morality. Henri Lefebvre has argued for the relationship between *Lorenzaccio* and the July Revolution in *Alfred de Musset dramaturge. Robert Macaire,* which Gautier called a "great tri-

umph of the revolutionary art which followed on the July Revolution," and which Flaubert claimed as "the greatest symbol of the age" was in part, according to Robert Baldick, a response to the government repressions of 1834 that climaxed in the massacre in the Rue Transnonain that inspired Daumier's print; the message of the play won it both popular success and a censor's ban. See Baldick, *The Life and Times of Frédérick Lemaître* (London: H. Hamilton, 1959), pp. 136–44; the play can be found in an edition by C. Coeuré (Grenoble: Roissard, 1966).

30. All quotations from Hugo's plays and prefaces will be from *Théâtre Complet,* cited above. I give my translations in the text with volume, act, and scene numbers for plays, volume and page numbers for prefaces; the French, except for brief passages, will be given in the notes.

31. See Vigny, *Chatterton,* in *Oeuvres Complètes,* ed. F. Baldensperger (Paris: Gallimard, 1950), 1: esp. I, v; III, i. Dumas, *Antony,* in *Nineteenth-Century French Plays,* ed. Joseph Borgerhoff (New York: D. Appleton-Century Company, 1931), IV, vi. On *Lorenzaccio,* see chapter 8.

32. Vigny, *Chatterton,* I, v: "j'ai résolu de ne me point masquer et d'être moi-même jusqu'à la fin, d'écouter, en tout, mon coeur dans ses épanchements comme dans ses indignations, et de ma résigner à bien accomplir ma loi."

33. See Annie Ubersfeld, "Désordre et génie," *Europe* 490–91 (1970): 107–18.

34. On "social romanticism" in France, see Herbert Hunt, *Le Socialisme et le romantisme en France* (Oxford: Clarendon Press, 1935); David Owen Evans, *Social Romanticism in France* (Oxford: Clarendon Press, 1951); Christophe Campos, "Social Romanticism," in *French Literature and Its Background,* vol. 4: *The Early Nineteenth Century,* ed. John Cruickshank (Oxford: Oxford University Press, 1969), pp. 55–76; Geoffrey Hartman, "Reflections on Romanticism in France," in *Romanticism: Vistas, Instances, Continuities,* ed. David Thorburn and Geoffrey Hartman (Ithaca: Cornell University Press, 1973), pp. 38–61.

35. Howarth makes such an argument about the insufficiency of Vigny's characterization in *Sublime and Grotesque,* pp. 263–77, esp. 269.

36. Gautier, "Victor Hugo," from *Art and Criticism,* vol. 12 of *The Complete Works of Théophile Gautier,* ed. F. C. DeSumichrast (London: Postlethwaite, Taylor & Knowles, 1909), 136.

37. Peter Brooks makes an argument along these lines in *The Melodramatic Imagination* (New Haven: Yale University Press, 1976), pp. 93–109.

38. La Reine: "Ou tes yeux sont les yeux d'un ange, ou ils sont ceux d'un démon." Fabiani: "Ni démon ni ange. Un homme qui vous aime" (2: II, i).

39. See Robert Heilman, *Tragedy and Melodrama: Versions of Experience* (Seattle: University of Washington Press, 1968), pp. 7–18.

40. See, for example, Steiner's comment in *The Death of Tragedy* (London: Faber & Faber, 1961), p. 161: "In regard to French romantic drama, one's sense of artistic failure is drastic. . . . Surely, the reason is that in them the theatre triumphs so relentlessly over the drama."

41. Dieu qui donne le sceptre et qui te le donna
M'a fait duc de Segorbe et duc de Cardona,

Marquis de Monroy, comte Albatera, vicomte
De Gor seigneur de lieux dont j'ignore le compte.
Je suis Jean d'Aragon, grand-maître d'Avis, né
Dans l'exil, fils proscrit d'un père assassiné
Par sentence du tien, roi Carlos de Castille! (1: IV, iv)

42.   Tu me crois peut-être
Un homme comme sont tous les autres, un être
Intelligent, qui court droit au but qu'il rêva.
Détrompe-toi. Je suis une force qui va!
Agent aveugle et sourd de mystères funèbres!
Une âme de malheur faite avec des ténèbres!
Où vais-je? je ne sais. Mais je me sens poussé
D'un souffle impétueux, d'un destin insensé.
Je descends, je descends, et jamais ne m'arrête. (1: III, iv)

43. "Sauvons ce peuple! Osons être grands, et frappons! / Ôtons l'ombre à l'intrigue et le masque aux fripons!" (1: III, v).

44. Georges Lote, *En Preface à Hernani* (Paris: J. Gamber, 1930), pp. 150–68,
esp. 168.

45. Charles Affron, *A Stage for Poets: Studies in the Theatre of Hugo and Musset* (Princeton: Princeton University Press, 1971), p. 42.

46.   Un instant,
Entre aimer et haïr je suis resté flottant,
Mon coeur pour elle et toi n'était point assez large,
J'oubliais en l'aimant ta haine qui me charge;
Mais puisque tu le veux, puisque c'est toi qui viens
Me faire souvenir, c'est bon, je me souviens!
Mon amour fait pencher la balance incertaine,
Et tombe tout entier du côté de ma haine. (1: I, iv)

CHAPTER 8: MUSSET'S *LORENZACCIO:* INNOCENCE, EXPERIENCE, AND THE TRADEDY OF REVOLT

1. Renaud C. Bruce's lively translation of *Lorenzaccio* in the sixth volume of
The Modern Theater, ed. Eric Bentley (New York: Doubleday, 1960) provides
only a partial version of the play. Where possible, I have used Bruce's translation, elsewhere providing my own. I have also used the French form of the
characters' names throughout and not the Italian form adopted by Bruce;
when an Italian name appears, I refer to the historical person, not Musset's
character. The act, scene, and line numbers given with the passages corres-
pond to those assigned in Paul Dimoff's critical edition of the French text,
La Genèse de 'Lorenzaccio' (Paris: Droz, 1936); when Bruce's translations
are used, page numbers for his text are also given. Except for brief passages, I
will give the original French in the notes. Besides Dimoff's invaluable edition, I have found the following critical studies of particular use in tackling
Lorenzaccio: Charles Affron, *A Stage for Poets: Studies in the Theatre of*

Hugo and Musset (Princeton: Princeton University Press, 1971), pp. 199–225; Auguste Brun, *Deux Prose du Théâtre* (Aix-en-Provence: GAP, 1954); Herbert Gochberg, *Stage of Dreams: The Dramatic Art of Alfred de Musset* (Geneva: Droz, 1967), pp. 109–99; Henri Lefebvre, *Alfred de Musset dramaturge* (Paris: L'Arche, 1955); Bernard Masson, *Musset et le théâtre interieur* (Paris: Armand Colin, 1974).

2. See, for example, Pierre Nordon, "Alfred de Musset et Angleterre," *Les Lettres Romanes* 21 (1967): 245–50; Helen Phelps Bailey, *Hamlet in France from Voltaire to LaForge* (Geneva: Droz, 1964), pp. 54–58.

3. For historical details, Musset drew not only upon Sand's "scène historique," *Un Conspiration en 1537,* but also upon Benedetto Varchi's *Storia fiorentina,* the relevant portions of which are excerpted in Dimoff, *Genèse,* pp. 3–80.

4. "Florence était encore (il n'y a pas longtemps de cela) une bonne maison bien bâtie; tous ces grands palais, qui sont les logements de nos grandes familles, en étaient les colonnes. Il n'y en avait pas une, de toutes ces colonnes, qui dépassât les autres d'un pouce; elles soutenaient à elles toutes une vieille voûte bien cimentée, et nous nous promenions là-dessous sans crainte d'une pierre sur la tête" (I, ii, 245–52).

5. "deux architectes malavisé"; "ils ont jugé à propos de prendre une des colonnes dont je vous parle, à savoir celle de la famille des Médicis, et d'en faire un clocher..." (I, ii, 252, 256–58).

6. "Les familles florentines ont beau crier, le peuple et les marchands ont beau dire, les Médicis gouvernent au moyen de leur garnison....un bâtard, une moitié de Médicis, un butor que le ciel avait fait pour être garçon boucher ou valet de charrue, couche dans le lit de nos filles, boit nos bouteilles, casse nos vitres..." (I, ii, 268–70, 273–76).

7. "Pauvre Philippe! une fille belle comme le jour. Une seule fois je me suis assis près d'elle sous le marronnier; ces petites mains blanches, comme cela travaillait! Que de journées j'ai passées, moi, assis sous les arbres! Ah! quelle tranquillité! quel horizon à Cafaggiuolo! Jeannette était jolie, la petite fille du concierge, en faisant sécher sa lessive. Comme elle chassait les chèvres qui venaient marcher sur son linge étendu sur le gazon! la chèvre blanche revenait toujours, avec ses grandes pattes menues" (IV, ix, 746–56).

8. "Ah! Catinna, pour dormir tranquille, il faut n'avoir jamais fait certains rêves. Cela est trop cruel d'avoir vécu dans un palais de fées, où murmuraient les cantiques des anges, de s'y être endormie, bercée par son fils, et de se réveiller dans une masure ensanglantée, pleine de débris d'orgie et de restes humains, dans les bras d'un spectre hideux qui vous tue en vous appelant encore du nom de mère" (I, vi, 1078–85).

9. In II, iv, Maria Soderini, Lorenzo's mother, speaks of seeing the ghost of his former youthful self. In III, iii, Lorenzo talks of walking through Florence with his phantom at his side.

10. Georges Poulet, *The Interior Distance,* trans. Elliott Coleman (Baltimore: Johns Hopkins Press, 1959), p. 190.

11. This same dialectic is pursued in Musset's *Confession of a Child of the Cen-*

tury, where the intellectual skepticism of the eighteenth century leads to the sensationalism of the nineteenth; volume 8 of *The Complete Writings of Alfred de Musset,* trans. Kendall Warren (1892; rev., New York: Edwin C. Hill, 1907), esp. chap. 2, 2–24.

12. On Musset and Byron, see Edmund Estève, *Byron et le romantisme français,* 2nd ed. (Paris: Furne, 1929), pp. 406–48; Pierre Moureau, "L'Ironie de Musset," *Revue des Sciences Humaines* 108 (1962): 501–14.

13. "...j'entrai alors dans la vie, et je vis qu'à mon approche tout le monde en faisait autant que moi; tous les masques tombaient devant mon regard; l'Humanité souleva sa robe, et me montra, comme à un adepte digne d'elle, sa monstrueuse nudité" (III, iii, 735–40).

14. "La main qui a soulevé une fois la voile de la vérité ne peut plus le laisser retomber..." (III, iii, 782–84).

15. "Par le ciel! quel homme de cire suis-je donc! Le Vice, comme la robe de Déjanire, s'est-il si profondément incorporé à mes fibres, que je ne puisse plus répondre de ma langue, et que l'air qui sort de mes lèvres se fasse ruffian malgré moi? J'allais corrompre Catherine.—Je crois que je corromprais ma mère, si mon cerveau le prenait à tâche..." (IV, v, 428–434).

16. "Le vice a été pour moi un vêtement, maintenant il est collé à ma peau" (III, iii, 792–94).

17. "J'ai cru à la vertu, à la grandeur humaine, comme un martyr croit à son Dieu" (III, iii, 552–54).

18. "Ma jeunesse a été pure comme l'or. Pendant vingt ans de silence, la foudre s'est amoncelée dans ma poitrine; et il faut que je sois réellement une étincelle du tonnerre, car tout à coup, une certaine nuit que j'étais assis dans les ruines du Colisée antique, je ne sais pourquoi je me levai; je tendis vers le ciel mes bras trempés de rosée, et je jurai qu'un des tyrans de ma patrie mourrait de ma main. J'étais un étudiant paisible, je ne m'occupais alors que des arts et des sciences, et il m'est impossible de dire comment cet étrange serment s'est fait en moi. Peut-être est-ce là ce qu'on éprouve quand on devient amoureux.... J'étais heureux alors, j'avais le coeur et les mains tranquilles; mon nom m'appelait au trône, et je n'avais qu'à laisser le soleil se lever et se coucher pour voir fleurir autour de moi toutes les espérances humaines. Les hommes ne m'avaient fait ni bien ni mal, mais j'étais bon, et, pour mon malheur éternel, j'ai voulu être grand. Il faut que je l'avoue, si la Providence m'a poussé à la résolution de tuer un tyran, quel qu'il fût, l'orgueil m'y a poussé aussi. Que te dirais-je de plus? Tous les Césars du monde me faisaient penser à Brutus" (III, iii, 558–69, 574–83).

19. "Ah! vous avez vécu tout seul, Philippe. Pareil à un fanal éclatant, vous êtes resté immobile au bord de l'océan des hommes, et vous avez régardé dans les eaux la réflexion de votre propre lumière" (III, iii, 657–60).

20. "...la république, il nous faut ce mot-là. Et quand ce ne serait qu'un mot, c'est quelque chose, puisque les peuples se lévent quand il traverse l'air..." (II, i, 32–35).

21. "Mais si tu es honnête, quand tu auras délivré ta patrie, tu le redeviendras. Cela réjouit mon vieux coeur, Lorenzo, de penser que tu es honnête; alors tu

jetteras ce déguisement hideux qui te défigure, et tu redeviendras d'un métal aussi pur que les statues de bronze d'Harmodius et d'Aristogiton'' (III, iii, 774–80).

22. The gap between Philippe's romantic rhetoric and the violent act he supports can be usefully examined in the light of M. H. Abram's discussion of the relation between romanticism and revolution in "English Romanticism: The Spirit of the Age," in *Romanticism and Consciousness,* ed. Harold Bloom (New York: Norton, 1970), pp. 90–119; Abrams finds a shift from romantic advocacy of political revolution to a disillusionment with political violence that finds refuge in a vision of spiritual reformation. Philippe speaks as a reformer but advocates violence.

23. "Je te fais une gageure. Je vais tuer Alexandre; une fois mon coup fait, si les républicains se comportent comme ils le doivent, il leur sera facile d'établir une république, la plus belle qui ait jamais fleuri sur la terre. Qu'ils aient pour eux le peuple, et tout est dit.—Je te gage que ni eux ni le peuple ne feront rien" (III, iii, 815–20).

24. "Quand j'ai commencé à jouer mon rôle de Brutus moderne, je marchais dans mes habits neufs de la grande confrérie du vice, comme un enfant de dix ans dans l'armure d'un géant de la fable" (III, iii, 728–32).

25. Excerpted in Hegel, *Hegel on Tragedy,* ed. Anne and Henry Paolucci (1962; rpt., New York: Harper & Row, 1975), pp. 98–112.

26. On Lorenzo's worship of Plutarch's heroes, see I, vi, 1050–51 and II, iv, 580. He may incidentally share with the rebels of the Revolution a desire to prove himself part of a virtuous revolt by playing at being a Roman; on revolutionary rôle playing, see Harold Rosenberg, "Resurrected Romans," *Kenyon Review* 10 (Autumn, 1948): 602–20; Ronald Paulson, *Representations of Revolution (1789–1820)* (New Haven: Yale University Press, 1983), pp. 1–36.

27. Both Brutuses are mentioned in III, iii, 581–82, 796–98. Tarquin's Brutus is mentioned in II, iv, 580–95.

28. "Brutus a fait le fou pour tuer Tarquin, et ce qui m'étonne en lui, c'est qu'il n'y ait pas laissé sa raison" (III, iii, 796–98).

29. "Que les hommes me comprennent ou non, qu'ils agissent ou qu'ils n'agissent pas, j'aurait dit aussi ce que j'ai à dire.... Qu'ils m'appellent comme ils voudront, Brutus ou Érostrate, il ne me plaît pas qu'ils m'oublient. Ma vie entière est au bout de ma dague, et que la Providence retourne ou non la tête en m'entendant frapper...dans deux jours, les hommes comparaîtront devant le tribunal de ma volonté" (III, iii, 889–901).

30. "Suis-je le bras de Dieu? Y a-t-il une nuée au-dessus de ma tête? Quand j'entrerai dans cette chambre, et que je voudrai tirer mon épée du fourreau, j'ai peur de tirer l'épée flamboyante de l'archange, et de tomber en cendres sur ma proie" (IV, iii, 179–83).

31. "Tu me demandes pourquoi je tue Alexandre? Veux-tu donc que je m'empoisonne, ou que je saute dans l'Arno? veux-tu donc que je sois un spectre, et qu'en frappant sur ce squelette...(*Il frappe sa poitrine.*) il n'en sorte aucun son? Si je suis l'ombre de moi-même, veux-tu donc que je rompe le

seul fil qui rattache aujourd'hui mon coeur à quelques fibres de mon coeur d'autrefois! Songes-tu que ce meurtre, c'est tout ce qui me reste de ma vertu?" (III, iii, 855–64).

32. "Pauvre Catherine! tu mourrais cependant comme Louise Strozzi, ou tu te laisserais tomber comme tant d'autres dans l'éternel abîme, si je n'étais pas là" (IV, v, 451–53).

33. "Que la nuit est belle! Que l'air du ciel est pur! Respire, respire, coeur navré de joie!. . . Que le vent du soir est doux et embaumé! Comme les fleurs des prairies s'entr'ouvrent! Ô nature magnifique, ô éternel repos!" (IV, xi, 912–13, 918–20).

34. "Ô notre nouveau Brutus! je te crois et je t'embrasse.— La liberté est donc sauvée!. . . Le duc est mort!—ah! il n'y a pas de haine dans ma joie—il n'y a que l'amour le plus pur, le plus sacré pour la patrie, j'en prends Dieu à témoin" (V, ii, 260–61, 262–65).

35. This scene is printed by Dimoff as vi-a. There is some confusion about the numbering of the scenes in the final act and some question as to whether this scene was to be included.

36. See, for example, Sices, *Theater of Solitude*, pp. 123–25; and Haasan El Nouty, "Théâtre et anti-théâtre," pp. 604–12.

37. ". . . je porte les même habits, je marche toujours sur mes jambes, et je bâille avec ma bouche; il n'y a de changé en moi qu'une misère—c'est que je suis plus creux et plus vide qu'une statue de fer-blanc" (V, vi, 628–31).

38. "Au moment où j'allais tuer Clément VII, ma tête a été mise à prix à Rome. Il est naturel qu'elle le soit dans tout l'Italie, aujourd'hui que j'ai tué Alexandre. Si je sortais d'Italie, je serais bientôt sonné à son de trompe dans toute l'Europe, et à ma mort, le bon Dieu ne manquera pas de faire placarder ma condamnation éternelle dans tous les carrefours de l'immensité" (V, vi, 617–23).

39. "wir haben keine Zeit zu verlieren"; "Aber die Zeit verliert uns. Das ist sehr langweilig immer das Hemd zuerst und dann die Hosen drüber zu ziehen und des Abends in's Bett und Morgens wieder heraus zu kriechen und einen Fuss immer so vor den andern zu setzen, da ist gar kein Absehens wie es anders werden soll" (II, i).

The translation is that of Carl Richard Mueller in Georg Büchner, *Complete Plays and Prose* (New York: Hill and Wang, 1963). I will give translations with act and scene numbers in the text, the original in the notes: Georg Büchner, *Sämtliche Werke und Briefe,* ed. Werner R. Lehmann (Hamburg: Christian Wegner, 1967), 1.

My reading of Büchner is influenced by a number of earlier works, particularly Herbert Lindenberger, *Georg B*üchner (Carbondale: Southern Illinois University Press, 1964).

40. "Das Laster ist das Cainszeichen des Aristocratismus" (I, iii); "das Laster ist zu gewissen Zeiten Hochverrath" (I, vi).

41. "Die Revolution muss aufhören und die Republik mussanfangen" (I, i).

42. "Die Staatsform muss ein durchsichtiges Gewand seyn, das sich dicht an den Leib des Volkes schmiegt. Jedes Schwellen der Adern, jedes Spannen der

Muskeln, jedes Zucken der Sehnen muss sich darin abdrücken. Die Gestalt mag nun schön oder hasslich seyn, sie hat einmal das Recht zu seyn wie sie ist, wir sind nicht berechtigt ihr ein Röcklein nach Belieben zuzuschneiden" (I, i).

43. "Ist den nichts in dir, was dir nicht manchmal ganz leise, heimlich sagte, du lügst, du lügst!" (I, vi).
44. "Die Welt ist das Chaos. Das Nichts ist der zu gebärende Weltgott" (IV, v).
45. "Einander kennen? Wir müssten die Schädeldecken aufbrechen und die Gedanken einander aus den Hirnfasern zerren" (I, i).
46. "Wir haben nicht die Revolution, sondern die Revolution hat uns gemacht" (II, i).
47. "Willst du grausamer seyn als der Tod? Kannst du verhindern, dass unsere Köpfe sich auf dem Boden des Korbes küssen?" (IV, vii).
48. On time in Shakespeare's tragedies, see Frank Kermode, *The Sense of an Ending* (Oxford: Oxford University Press, 1967), pp. 67–89; see also, Herbert Lindenberger, *Historical Drama: The Relation of Literature and Reality* (Chicago: University of Chicago Press, 1975), esp. pp. 72–78.
49. Hugo seems to be discussing this type of characterization in his analysis of the sublime and grotesque. However, he tends to see them embodied in paired figures rather than in a single figure—though he does combine them in Lucrèce Borgia and Triboulet.
50. On the theme of art and the artist, see Affron, *Stage for Poets,* pp. 212–22; Robert Denommé, "The Motif of the 'Poète Maudit' in Musset's *Lorenzaccio,*" *Esprit Créateur* 5 (1965): 138–46; Gochberg, *Stage of Dreams,* pp. 109–99; Masson, *Musset,* pp. 211–21.
51. Sices, *Theater of Solitude,* pp. 161–68. He discusses the two scenes that Musset dropped, dealing with art, as well as the ones that remain. He argues that the final version of the play rejects art as a possible solution. He makes a key point in tying this rejected solution to the vision of *Fantasio* (pp. 164, 87–88); *Fantasio* and the comic plays in general outline a positive vision which is the counterpart of the tragic sense of life in *Lorenzaccio.*
52. See II, ii, where Tebaldeo not only praises the artist's ability to realize his dreams, but also argues that "Enthusiasm goes hand in hand with suffering" ("L'enthousiasme est frère de la souffrance"; l. 268; p. 30). When Lorenzo asks if he loves princes, Tebaldeo retreats into his art, saying he is an artist who loves his mother and his mistress (l. 336).
53. On the links between Musset's play and the July Revolution, see Lefebvre's *Musset dramaturge,* pp. 111–43.

CHAPTER 9: KLEIST'S *PRINCE FRIEDRICH OF HOMBURG:* THE TRAGEDY OF NON-TRAGIC MAN

1. See Hanna Hellman, "Kleists 'Prinz von Homburg' und Shakespeares 'Mass für Mass,' " *Germanish-romanische Monatsschrift* 2 (1923): 288-96; Sigurd Burkhardt, "*Egmont* and *Prinz Friedrich von Homburg:* Expostulation and

Reply," in his *The Drama of Language: Essays on Goethe and Kleist* (Baltimore: Johns Hopkins Press, 1970), pp. 94–100; Benjamin Bennett, *Modern Drama and German Classicism: Renaissance from Lessing to Brecht* (Ithaca: Cornell University Press, 1979), pp. 30–31 (on Kleist and *Tasso*); John C. Blankenagel, "Schiller's *Wallenstein* and Kleist's *Prinz Friedrich von Homburg*," *Germanic Review* 2 (1927): 1–11.

2. Blankenagel notes in his *"Wallenstein* and *Prinz Friedrich*," p. 11, that Kleist told his sister Ulrike not just to read *Wallenstein* but to learn it. See Kleist, *Sämtliche Werke und Briefe,* ed. Helmut Sembdner, 3rd ed. (1961; rpt., Munich: Carl Hanser, 1964), 2:517f.

3. Richard Samuel's edition of the play (*Jahresgabe der Kleist-Gessellschaft* 1963) lists in the notes more than twenty echoes from Schiller.

4. I will give the translation in the text; the translation is that of Peggy Meyer Sherry, in *Heinrich von Kleist: Plays,* ed. Walter Hinderer (New York: Continuum, 1982). Act, scene, and line numbers corresponding to the German original will be given: Heinrich von Kleist, *Sämtliche Werke und Briefe,* cited above, vol. 1. Except for brief passages, the German will be given in the notes.

5. Critics divide their sympathies between these two characters. Pro-Elector critics include V. C. Hubbs, "Heinrich von Kleist and the Symbol of the Wise Man," *Symposium* 16 (1962): 165–79; Charles Passage, "Introduction," *Prince Friedrich of Homburg* (Woodbury, NY: Barron's Educational Series, 1956); Benjamin Bennett, *German Classicism,* pp. 22–56. Pro-Prince critics include Gerhard Fricke, *Gefühl und Schicksal bei Heinrich von Kleist* (Berlin: Junker und Dünnhaupt, 1929), pp. 170–201; Arnold J. Henschel, "The Primacy of Free Will in the Mind of Kleist and in *The Prince of Hamburg*," *German Life and Letters* 17 (1963–1964): 97–115; and E. W. Herd "Form and Intention in Kleist's *Prinz Friedrich von Homburg*," *Seminar,* 2 (1966): 1–13. The best summaries of the criticism of the play are by J. M. Ellis: *Kleist's "Prinz Friedrich von Homburg": A Critical Study,* University of California Studies in Modern Philology, no. 97 (Berkeley: University Of California Press, 1970), pp. 3–10; "The Character of Kleist Criticism," in *Heinrich von Kleist: Studies in the Character and Meaning of His Writings,* University of North Carolina Studies in German Language and Literature, no. 99 (Chapel Hill: North Carolina University Press, 1979), pp. 143–64.

6. On these points, see Kleist's letters in the second volume of his *Sämtliche Werke und Briefe,* cited above; they are selectively translated in *An Abyss Deep Enough: Letters of Heinrich von Kleist with a Selection of Essays and Anecdotes,* ed. Phillip B. Miller (New York: E. P. Dutton, 1982). On his lifeplan, see, for example, his letters to Wilhelmine von Zenge of early 1800 and of 21 August 1800, where he speaks of keeping a journal to "improve and perfect my plan" (*Werke,* 2: 505–6, 527–31; *Abyss,* 33–35, 45–47); see also the letter to his sister Ulrike, 5 February 1808 (*Werke,* 2: 625–30; *Abyss,* pp. 89–93). In this last letter, we can already trace the beginnings of the "Kant Crisis" that becomes clearer in his letters of March 1801 (*Werke,* 2: 630–37; *Abyss,* 93–98). There has been much debate over this episode, much of it

sparked by Ernst Cassirer's "Heinrich von Kleist und die Kantische Philosophie," in *Idee und Gestalt* (Berlin: B. Cassirer, 1921). Robert Helbling, *The Major Works of Heinrich von Kleist* (New York: New Directions, 1975), has a compact chapter on the crisis (pp. 23–34).

7. The Prince was supposedly injured when thrown by his horse. This error about his role in the battle parallels the error about the Elector's "death" on his horse. On the importance of horses in the play, see Ilse Graham, *Heinrich von Kleist: Word into Flesh: A Poet's Quest for the Symbol* (Berlin: Walter de Gruyter, 1977), pp. 185–87.

8. Als ein Nachtwandler, schau, auf jener Bank,
Wohin, im Schlaf, wie du nie glauben wolltest,
Der Mondschein ihn gelockt, beschäftiget,
Sich träumend, seiner eignen Nachwelt gleich,
Den prächtgen Kranz des Ruhmes einzuwinden. (I, i, 24–28)

9. Und er, der Kürfurst, mit der Stirn des Zeus,
Hielt einen Kranz von Lorbeern in der Hand:
Er stellt sich dicht mir vor das Antlitz hin,
Und schlägt, mir ganz die Seele zu entzünden,
Den Schmuck darum, der ihm vom Nacken hängt,
Und reicht ihn, auf die Locken mir zu drücken
. . . .

Hoch auf, gleich einem Genius des Ruhms,
Hebt sie den Kranz, an dem die Kette schwankte,
Als ob sie einen Helden krönen wollte. (I, iv, 158–63, 172–74)

10. Du hast mir, Glück, die Locken schon gestreift:
Ein Pfand schon warfst du, im Vorüberschweben,
Aus deinem Füllhorn lächelnd mir herab:
Heut, Kind der Götter, such ich, flüchtiges,
Ich hasche dich im Feld der Schlacht und stürze
Ganz deinen Segen mir zu Füssen um:
Wärst du auch siebenfach, mit Eisenketten,
Am schwedschen Siegeswagen festgebunden! (I, vi, 358–65)

11. Wie könnt er doch vor diesen Tisch mich laden,
Von Richtern, herzlos, die den Eulen gleich,
Stets von der Kugel mir das Grablied singen,
Dächt er, mit einem heitern Herrscherspruch,
Nicht, als ein Gott in ihren Kreis zu treten?
Nein, Freund, er sammelt diese Nächt von Wolken
Nur um mein Haupt, um wie die Sonne mir,
Durch ihren Dunstkreis strahlend aufzugehn:
Und diese Lust, fürwahr, kann ich ihm gönnen! (III, i, 852–60)

12. The key work here is Fricke's *Gefühl und Schicksal*, cited above.

13. "Auf Ord'r! Ei, Kottwitz! Reitest du so langsam? / Hast du sie noch vom Herzen nicht empfangen?" (II, ii, 474–75).

14. In the debate between the Elector and his officers, Hohenzollern explains the Prince's actions in relation to his wish-fulfilling dream; since the Elector

staged that dream, Hohenzollern blames him for the Prince's failure to obey orders (V, v, 1623–1722).

15. See Hellmuth Kaiser, "Kleists *Prinz Friedrich von Homburg,"* *Imago* 17 (1930): 119–137; Heinz Politzer, "Kleists Trauerspiel von Traum: *Prinz Friedrich von Homburg,"* *Euphorion* 64 (1970): 200–20; Ellis, *Prinz Friedrich,* pp. 30–41, 83–99, and *Heinrich von Kleist,* pp. 89–114.

16. "Bei Gott, in mir nicht findet er den Sohn, / Der, unterm Beil des Henkers, ihn bewundre" (II, x, 782–83).

17.   . . . jetzt ist mir alles klar;
        Es stürzt der Antrag ins Verderben mich:
        An ihrer Weigrung, wisse, bin ich schuld,
        Weil mir sich die Prinzessin anverlobt! (III, i, 925–28)

18. Kleist, "On the Puppet Theater," in *Abyss,* cited above, p. 214.

19. Kleist's dislogists discuss a fencing bear as an unconscious animal capable of defeating self-reflexive man; puppets represent a man-made attempt to recapture such unconscious action: "Puppet Theater," pp. 215–16, 211–14.

20. Ibid., p. 216.

21.   Und der die Zukunft, auf des Lebens Gipfel,
        Heut, wie ein Feenreich, noch überschaut,
        Leigt in zwei engen Brettern duftend morgen,
        Und ein Gestein sagt dir von ihm: er war! (III, v, 989-92)

22.   Ich gebe jeden Anspruch auf an Glück.
        Nataliens, das vergiss nicht, ihm zu melden,
        Begehr ich gar nicht mehr. . . . (III, v, 1022–24)

23.   Ich will auf meine Güter gehn am Rhein,
        Da will ich bauen, will ich niederreissen,
        Dass mir der Schweiss herabtrieft, säen, ernten,
        Als wärs für Weib und Kind, allein geniessen,
        Und, wenn ich erntete, von neuem säen,
        Und in den Kreis herum das Leben jagen,
        Bis es am Abend niedeersinkt und stirbt. (III, v, 1030–36)

I have changed Sherry's translation to bring out the idea of circularity in the last two lines. Sherry has, "And thus pursue this life across the heavens, / Till sinking down at evening, it expires."

24.   Der Sieg ist glänzend dieses Tages,
        Und vor dem Altar morgen dank ich Gott.
        Doch wär er zehnmal grösser, das entschuldigt
        Den nicht, durch den der Zufall mir ihn schenkt:
        Mehr Schlachten noch, als die, hab ich zu kämpfen,
        Und will, dass dem Gesetz Gehorsam sei. (II, ix, 729–34)

25.   Den Sieg nicht mag ich, der, ein Kind des Zufalls,
        Mir von der Bank fällt; das Gesetz will ich,
        Die Mutter meiner Krone, aufrecht halten,
        Die ein Geschlecht von Siegen mir erzeugt! (V, v, 1566–69)

26.   Ich will ihn nicht für mich erhalten wissen—
      Mag er sich welchem Weib er will vermählen;
      Ich will nur, dass er da sei, lieber Onkel,
      Für sich, selbständig, frei und unabhängig,
      Wie eine Blume, die mir wohlgefällt. . . .(IV, i, 1085–89)

27.   Vielmehr, was du, im Lager auferzogen,
      Unordnung nennst, die Tat, den Spruch der Richter,
      In diesem Fall, willkürlich zu zerreissen,
      Erscheint mir als die schönste Ordnung erst:
      Das Kriegsgesetz, das weiss ich wohl, soll herrschen,
      Jedoch die lieblichen Gefühle auch.
      Das Vaterland, das du uns gründetest,
      Steht, eine feste Burg, mein edler Ohm:
      Das wird ganz andre Stürme noch ertragen,
      Fürwahr, als diesen unberufnen Sieg;
      Das wird sich ausbaun herrlich, in der Zukunft,
      Erweitern, unter Enkels Hand, verschönern,
      Mit Zinnen, üppig, feenhaft, zur Wonne
      Der Freunde, und zum Schrecken aller Feinde. . . .(IV, i, 1125–38)

28.   As would be expected, critics divide here between supporters of the Prince and defenders of the Elector; see n. 5 above.

29.   See IV, i, 1112–17 ("Were I a tyrant"; "Wär ich ein Tyrann") and V, ii, 1412–24 ("Were I the Dey of Tunis"; "Wenn ich der Dei von Tunis wäre").

30.   Ich will ihm, der so würdig vor mir steht,
      Nicht, ein Unwürdger, gegenüber stehn!
      Schuld ruht, bedeutende, mir auf der Brust,
      Wie ich es wohl erkenne; kann er mir
      Vergeben nur, wenn ich mit ihm drum streite,
      So mag ich nichts von seiner Gnade wissen. (IV, iv, 1380–85)

31.   Es ist mein unbeugsamer Wille!
      Ich will das heilige Gesetz des Kriegs,
      Das ich verletzt', im Angesicht des Heers,
      Durch einen freien Tod verherrlichen!
      Was kann der Sieg euch, meine Brüder, gelten,
      Der eine, dürftige, den ich vielleicht
      Dem Wrangel noch entreisse, dem Triumph
      Verglichen, über den verderblichsten
      Der Feind' in uns, den Trotz, den Übermut,
      Errungen glorreich morgen? (V, vii, 1749–58)

32.   Prinz Homburgs Braut sei sie . . .
      Der Fehrbellins halb, dem Gesetz verfiel,
      Und seinem Geist, tot vor den Fahnen, schreitend,
      Kämpf er auf dem Gefild der Schlacht, sie ab! (V, viii, 1790–94)

33.   Nun, o Unsterblichkeit, bist du ganz mein!
      Du strahlst mir, durch die Binde meiner Augen,
      Mir Glanz der tausendfachen Sonne zu!

> Es wachsen Flügel mir an beiden Schultern,
> Durch stille Ätherräume schwingt mein Geist;
> Und wie ein Schiff, vom Hauch des Winds entführt,
> Die muntre Hafenstadt versinken sieht,
> So geht mir dämmernd alles Leben unter:
> Jetzt unterscheid ich Farben noch und Formen,
> Und jetzt liegt Nebel alles unter mir. (V, x, 1830–39)

34. Schiller, *On the Aesthetic Education of Man in a Series of Letters,* trans. Reginald Snell (New York: Frederick Ungar, 1965), p. 137.

35. > Das Leben nennt der Derwisch eine Reise,
    > Und eine kurze. Freilich! Von zwei Spannen
    > Diesseits der Erde nach zwei Spannen drunter.
    > Ich will auf halbem Weg mich niederlassen! (IV, iii, 1286–89)

36. We clearly confront here again the tension between sympathy and judgment worked out in different ways in *The Cenci* and *Lorenzaccio.* Kleist's solution is to "theatricalize" both our sympathy and our judgment by playing with our reactions to the Prince and thus making us aware of how easy it is for the playwright to evoke and then revoke our sympathy for or judgment of a character.

37. Translated by Roy Campbell in *The Classic Theatre,* vol. 3: *Six Spanish Plays,* ed. Eric Bentley (Garden City, NY: Doubleday, 1959), 480.

38. Kleist's work can be usefully explored in relation to "romantic irony," a third key mode open to the romanticist along with the visionary and tragic ones. Bennett's reading in *Modern Drama and German Classicism,* pp. 22–56, explores the ironic self-consciousness of the play. On romantic irony, see Ingrid Strohschneider-Kohrs, *Die Romantische Ironie im Theorie und Gestaltung* (Tübingen: N. Neimeyer, 1960); David Simpson, *Irony and Authority in Romantic Poetry* (London: Macmillan, 1979); Anne K. Mellor, *English Romantic Irony* (Cambridge: Harvard University Press, 1980).

39. A few titles may help define this type of play: Martin Esslin, *Theatre of the Absurd,* rev. ed. (1961; rpt., Woodstock, NY: Overlook Press, 1963); Lionel Abel, *Metatheatre* (New York: Hill and Wang, 1963); Karl Guthke, *Modern Tragicomedy* (New York: Random House, 1966).

40. Eric Bentley reports a conversation in which Brecht spoke of the "tragic side" of Azdak in *Caucasian Chalk Circle;* Bentley suggests, "The tragedy of Azdak is that his life is a comedy": *Seven Plays by Bertolt Brecht* (New York: Grove Press, 1961), pp. xlviii-xlix.

41. Nietzsche, *The Birth of Tragedy and the Genealogy of Morals,* trans. Francis Golffing (New York: Anchor, 1956), pp. 19–24.

42. Ibid., pp. 65–66, 33.

43. Ibid., p. 34, where Nietzsche says, "As a moral diety, Apollo demands self-control from his people and, in order to observe self-control, a knowledge of self. And so we find that the esthetic necessity of beauty is accompanied by the imperatives, 'Know thyself,' and 'Nothing too much.' "

44. Ibid., p. 34.

45. Clearly, a full discussion of romanticism's impact upon modern drama would require another study as long as this one. For Ibsen's knowledge of Hugo, Byron, Goethe, and Kleist, and his production of Musset's *Un Caprice* in 1861, see Michael Meyer, *Ibsen: A Biography* (Garden City, NJ: Doubleday, 1971); see also, Errol Durbach, *"Ibsen the Romantic": Analogues of Paradise in the Later Plays* (Athens, GA: University of Georgia Press, 1982). On Strindberg and Byron, Goethe, and Schiller, see Elizabeth Sprigge, *The Strange Life of August Strindberg* (New York: Macmillan, 1949). Artaud's *The Cenci* has been translated by Simon Watson Taylor (New York: Grove Press, 1970). Sartre's version of Dumas's play is in *Kean, The Devil and the Good Lord and Two Other Plays* (New York: Random House, 1960). On Brecht and nineteenth-century drama, see Max Spalter, *Brecht's Tradition* (Baltimore: Johns Hopkins Press, 1967). On Shaw, see Martin Meisel, *Shaw and the Nineteenth-Century Theater* (Princeton: Princeton University Press, 1963). Herbert Lindenberger treats modern and traditional historical dramas in *Historical Drama: The Relation of Literature and Reality* (Chicago: University of Chicago Press, 1975). For more general speculations on romanticism and modern drama, see Bennett, *Modern Drama and German Classicism,* esp. pp. 229ff; W. D. Howarth, *Sublime and Grotesque: A Study of French Romantic Drama* (London: Harrap, 1975), pp. 399–409; Tom Driver, *Romantic Quest and Modern Query: A History of the Modern Theater* (New York: Delacorte Press, 1970).

SELECTED BIBLIOGRAPHY
OF CRITICAL WORKS

Abel, Lionel. *Metatheatre.* New York: Hill and Wang, 1963.

Abrams, M.H. *The Mirror and the Lamp.* New York: Oxford, 1953.

_____. *Natural Supernaturalism.* New York: Norton, 1972.

_____. "Wordsworth and Coleridge on Diction and Figures." In *English Institute Essays: 1952,* 171–201. New York: Columbia University Press, 1954.

Adam, Antoine. *Grandeur and Illusion: French Literature and Society 1600–1715.* Translated by Herbert Tint. London: Weidenfel and Nicolson, 1972.

Affron, Charles. *A Stage for Poets: Studies in the Theatre of Hugo and Musset.* Princeton: Princeton University Press, 1971.

Aikin, Judith. *German Baroque Drama.* Boston: Twayne, 1982.

Albrecht, W. P. *Hazlitt and the Creative Imagination.* Lawrence, KA: University Press of Kansas, 1965.

_____. *The Sublime Pleasures of Tragedy: A Study of Critical Theory from Dennis to Keats.* Lawrence, KA: University Press of Kansas, 1975.

Allem, Maurice. *Alfred de Musset.* Paris: Arthaud, 1948.

Allevy, M. A. *La Mise en scène en France dans la première moitié du XIXe siècle.* Paris: Droz, 1938.

Antal, Frederick. *Classicism and Romanticism with Other Studies in Art History.* New York: Basic Books, 1966.

Arvin, Neil Cole. *Eugène Scribe and the French Theater 1815–1860.* 1924. Reprint. New York: Benjamin Blom, 1967.

Ashton, Thomas. *"Marino Faliero:* Byron's 'Poetry of Politics.' " *Studies in Romanticism* 13 (1974): 1–13.

Atkins, Stuart. *Goethe's Faust: A Literary Analysis.* Cambridge: Harvard University Press, 1958.

_____. "Taught by Success—Kleist's Prince of Homburg." *German Quarterly* 50 (1977): 1–9.

Auerbach, Eric. *Mimesis.* Translated by Willard Trask. Princeton: Princeton University Press, 1953.

Ayrault, Roger. "Schiller et Rousseau: Sur la Genèse des *Brigands." Etudes Germaniques* 10 (1955): 97–104.

Bailey, Helen Phelps. *Hamlet in France from Voltaire to LaForge.* Geneva: Droz, 1964.

Baker, Carlos. *Shelley's Major Poetry.* Princeton: Princeton University Press, 1948.

Baldensperger, F. *Goethe en France.* Paris: Hachette, 1904.

Baldick, Robert. *The Life and Times of Frédérick Lemaître.* London: H. Hamilton, 1959.

Ball, Patricia M. *The Central Self: A Study in Romantic and Victorian Imagination.* London: Athelone Press, 1968.

Barrère, Jean-Bertrand. *Hugo: L'Homme et l'oeuvre.* Paris: Boivin, 1952.

Barton, Anne. " 'A Light to Lesson Ages': Byron's Political Plays." In *Byron: A Symposium,* edited by John Jump, 138–62. London: Macmillan, 1975.

Bassan, F. "Dumas Père et le drame romantique." *Esprit Créateur* 5 (1965): 174–78.

Bates, E. S. *A Study of Shelley's Drama 'The Cenci'.* New York: Columbia University Press, 1908.

Behler, Ernst. "The Reception of Calderon Among the German Romantics." *Studies in Romanticism* 20 (1981): 437–60.

Benjamin, Walter. *The Origin of German Tragic Drama.* Translated by John Osborne. London: NLB, 1977.

Benn, Maurice. *The Drama of Revolt: A Critical Study of George Büchner.* Anglica Germanica Series, no. 2. Cambridge: Cambridge University Press, 1976.

Bennett, Benjamin. "The Classical, the Romantic and the Tragic in Part Two of Goethe's *Faust.*" *Studies in Romanticism* 19 (1980): 529–50.

_____. "Interrupted Tragedy as the Structure of Goethe's Faust." *Mosaic* 11 (1977): 37–51.

_____. *Modern Drama and German Classicism: Renaissance from Lessing to Brecht.* Ithaca: Cornell University Press, 1979.

_____. " 'Vorspiel auf dem Theatre': The Ironic Basis of Goethe's *Faust.*" *German Quarterly* 49 (1976): 438–55.

Bentley, Eric. *The Life of the Drama.* New York: Atheneum, 1967.

Bingham, Alfred Jepson. *Marie-Joseph Chénier: Early Political Life and Ideas (1789–1794).* New York: Private Printing, 1939.

Bird, C. Wesley. *Alfred de Vigny's Chatterton: A Contribution to the Study of Its Genesis and Its Sources.* Los Angeles: Lyman House, 1941.

Blankenagel, John. *The Dramas of Heinrich von Kleist.* Chapel Hill: University of North Carolina Press, 1931.

_____. "Schiller's *Wallenstein* and Kleist's *Prinz Friedrich von Homburg.*" *Germanic Review* 2 (1927): 1–11.

Blöcker, Gunter. *Heinrich von Kleist oder das absolute Ich*. Berlin: Argon, 1960.

Bloom, Harold. *Shelley's Mythmaking*. 1959. Reprint. Ithaca: Cornell University Press, 1969.

_____. *The Visionary Company*. rev. ed. Ithaca: Cornell University Press, 1971.

_____, ed. *Romanticism and Consciousness*. New York: Norton, 1970.

Bloom, Harold and Frederich Hilles, eds. *From Sensibility to Romanticism*. Oxford: Oxford University Press, 1965.

Book-Senninger, Claude. *Théophile Gautier, Auteur dramatique*. Paris: A.-G. Nizet, 1972.

Booth, Michael. "A Defence of Nineteenth-Century English Drama." *Educational Theatre Journal* 26 (1974): 5–13.

_____. "East and West End: Class and Audience in Victorian London." *Theatre Research International* 2 (1977): 98-103.

_____. *English Melodrama*. London: Herbert Jenkins, 1965.

_____. *Prefaces to English Nineteenth-Century Theatre*. Manchester: Manchester University Press, 1980.

_____. "Theatre History and Literary Critic." *Yearbook of English Studies* 9 (1979): 15–27.

_____. *Victorian Spectacular Theatre 1850–1910*. Boston: Routledge & Kegan Paul, 1981.

Booth, Michael, et al., eds. *The Revels: A History of Drama in English*. Vol. 6, 1750–1880. London: Methuen, 1975.

Bornstein, George, ed. *Romantic and Modern: Revaluations of Literary Tradition*. Pittsburgh: University of Pittsburgh Press, 1977.

Bouvier-Ajam, Maurice. *Alexandre Dumas ou Cent Ans Après*. Paris: Les Editeurs Français Réunis, 1972.

Brandes, George. *Main Currents in Nineteenth-Century Literature*. 6 vols. New York: Macmillan, 1906.

Brereton, Geoffrey. *Principles of Tragedy*. Coral Gables, FL: University of Miami Press, 1968.

Brinkmann, Richard, et al. *Deutsche Literatur und Französische Revolution: Sieben Studien*. Göttingen: Vandenhoeck und Ruprecht, 1974.

Brinton, Crane. *The Political Ideas of the English Romanticists*. 1926. Reprint. Ann Arbor: University of Michigan Press, 1962.

Brion, Marcel. *L'Allemange Romantique*. Paris: Albin Michel, 1977.

Brombert, Victor, ed. *The Hero In Literature*. Greenwich, CT: Fawcett. 1969.

Bromfield, J. *De Lorenzino de Médicis à Lorenzaccio.* Paris: Didier, 1972.

Brooks, Peter. *The Melodramatic Imagination.* New Haven: Yale University Press, 1976.

Brown, Frederick. *Theater and Revolution: The Culture of the French Stage.* New York: Viking, 1980.

Brown, Laura. *English Dramatic Form, 1660–1760: An Essay in Generic History.* New Haven: Yale University Press, 1981.

Brown, Milton. *The Painting of the French Revolution.* New York: Critics Group, 1938.

Bruford, W. H. *Culture and Society in Classical Weimar 1775–1806.* Cambridge: Cambridge University Press, 1962.

_____. *Theatre, Drama and Audience in Goethe's Germany.* London: Routledge & Kegan Paul, 1950.

Brun, Auguste. *Deux Proses du Théâtre.* Aix-en-Provence: GAP, 1954.

Brustein, Robert. *The Theatre of Revolt.* Boston: Little, Brown, and Company, 1962.

Buck, Rudolf. *Rousseau und die deutsche Romantik.* Berlin: Junker und Dünnhaupt, 1939.

Burckhardt, Sigurd. *The Drama of Language: Essays on Goethe and Kleist.* Baltimore: Johns Hopkins Press, 1970.

Butler, E. M. *Byron and Goethe.* London: Bowes and Bowes, 1956.

_____. *The Tyranny of Greece over Germany.* 1935. Reprint. Boston: Beacon Press, 1958.

Cahine, S. *La Dramaturgie de V. Hugo (1816–1843).* Paris: A.-G. Nizet, 1971.

Calarco, N. Joseph. *Tragic Being.* Minneapolis: University of Minnesota, 1969.

Callen, A. "Dramatic Construction in Musset's *Lorenzaccio.*" *Forum for Modern Language Studies* 9 (1973): 182–89.

_____. "The Place of *Lorenzaccio* in Musset's Theater." *Forum for Modern Language Studies* 5 (1969): 225–31.

Calvert, William. *Byron, Romantic Paradox.* Chapel Hill: University of North Carolina Press, 1935.

Cameron, Kenneth, and Horst Frenz. "The Stage History of Shelley's *The Cenci.*" *PMLA* 60 (1945): 1080–1105.

Cantor, Paul. *Creature and Creator: Myth-Making and English Romanticism.* Cambridge: Cambridge University Press, 1984.

_____. " 'A Distorting Mirror': Shelley's *The Cenci* and Shakespearean Tragedy." In *Shakespeare: Aspects of Influence*. Edited by G. B. Evans, 91–108. Cambridge, MA: Harvard University Press, 1976.

Carhart, Margaret. *Life and Work of Joanna Baillie*. 1923. Reprint. New York: Archon, 1970.

Carlson, Marvin. *The French Stage in the Nineteenth Century*. Metuchen, NJ: Scarecrow Press, 1972.

———. *The German Stage in the Nineteenth Century*. Metuchen, NJ: Scarecrow Press, 1972.

———. *Goethe and the Weimar Theatre*. Ithaca: Cornell University Press, 1978.

———. *The Theatre of the French Revolution*. Ithaca: Cornell University Press, 1966.

Carr, Thomas J. "Byron's *Werner*: The Burden of Knowledge." *Studies in Romanticism* 24 (1985): 375–98.

Chevally, S. "Dumas et la Comédie-Française." *Europe* 490–91 (1970): 101–7.

Chew, Samuel C. Jr. *The Dramas of Lord Byron*. 1915. Reprint. London: Russell and Russell, 1964.

Christensen, Jerome. "*Marino Faliero* and the Fault of Byron's Satire." *Studies in Romanticism* 24 (1985): 313–33.

Clark, Kenneth. *The Gothic Revival: An Essay in the History of Taste*. rev. ed. New York: Scribners, 1950.

Clarke, M. L. *Greek Studies in England 1700–1830*. Cambridge: Cambridge University Press, 1945.

Clouard, Henri. *Alexandre Dumas*. Paris: Albin Michel, 1954.

Cobban, Alfred. *Edmund Burke and the Revolt Against the Eighteenth Century*. New York: Barnes and Noble, 1929.

Cohen, Ralph. "On the Interrelations of Eighteenth-Century Literary Forms." In *New Approaches to Eighteenth-Century Literature, Selected Papers from the English Institute*, edited by Phillip Harth, 33–78. New York: Columbia University Press, 1974.

Connoly, L.W. *The Censorship of the English Drama 1737–1824*. San Marino: The Huntington Library, 1976.

Cooke, Michael. *The Romantic Will*. New Haven: Yale University Press, 1976.

Cooper, Barbara T. "Canvas Walls and Cardboard Fortresses: Representation of Place in National Historical Dramas of Early Nineteenth-Century France." *Comparative Drama* 17 (1983–84): 327–47.

_____. "Master Plots: An Alternate Typology for French Historical Dramas of the Early Nineteenth Century." *Theatre Journal* 35 (1983): 23–31.

_____. "Staging a Revolution: Political Upheaval in *Lorenzaccio* and *Leo Burckart*." *Romance Notes* 24 (1983): 23–29.

Cottrel, Alan P. "*Faust* and the Redemption of Intellect." *Modern Language Quarterly* 43 (1982): 242–66.

_____. *Goethe's Faust: Seven Essays.* University of North Carolina Studies in German Language and Literature, no. 86. Chapel Hill: University of North Carolina Press, 1976.

Crosby, D. H., and George Schoolfield, eds. *Studies in the German Drama.* Chapel Hill: University of North Carolina Press, 1974.

Cross, Gilbert. *Next Week—"East Lynne": Domestic Drama in Performance 1820–1874.* Lewisburg: Bucknell University Press, 1977.

Cruickshank, John, ed. *French Literature and Its Background.* Vol. 4, *The Early Nineteenth Century.* Oxford: Oxford University Press, 1969.

Culler, A. Dwight. "Monodrama and the Dramatic Monologue." *PMLA* 90 (1975): 366–85.

Curran, Stuart. *Shelley's Annus Mirabilis: The Maturing of an Epic Vision.* San Marino: The Huntington Library, 1975.

_____. *Shelley's 'The Cenci': Scorpions Ringed with Fire.* Princeton: Princeton University Press, 1970.

Dale, R. C. "*Chatterton* is the essential Romantic Drama." *Esprit Créateur* 5 (1965): 131-37.

Damico, Helen. "The Stage History of *Werner*." *Nineteenth-Century Theatre Research* 3 (1975): 63–81.

Damrosch, Leopold, Jr. *Samuel Johnson and the Tragic Sense.* Princeton: Princeton University Press, 1972.

Daniels, Barry Vincent. "Victor Hugo on the Boulevard: *Lucrèce Borgia* at the Porte-Saint-Martin Theatre in 1833." *Theatre Journal* 32 (1980): 17–42.

Davies, Robertson. *The Mirror of Nature.* Toronto: University of Toronto Press, 1983.

Davies, R. T., and B. G. Beatty. *Literature of the Romantic Period 1750–1850.* Liverpool: Liverpool University Press, 1976.

Dédéyan, C. *Gérard de Nerval et l'Allemagne.* 3 vols. Paris: Société d'Enseignement Supérieur, 1957–1959.

Denis, Andrée. *La Fortune Littéraire et théâtral de Kotzebue en France.* 3 Vols. Paris: Honoré Champion, 1976.

Denommé, Robert. "French theater reform and Vigny's translation of

Othello in 1829." In *Symbolism and Modern Literature,* edited by Marcel Tetel, 81–102. Durham: Duke University Press, 1978.

_____. "The motif of the 'poète maudit' in Musset's *Lorenzaccio.*" *Esprit Créateur* 5 (1965): 138-46.

_____. *Nineteenth-Century French Romantic Poets.* Carbondale: Southern Illinois University Press, 1969.

Descotes, Maurice. *Le Drame romantique et ses grands créateurs.* Paris: Presses Universitaires de France, 1955.

_____. *Le Public de théâtre et son histoire.* Paris: Presses Universitaires de France, 1964.

Dobre, Bonamy. *Byron's Dramas.* London: University of Nottingham Press, 1962.

Dommanget, M. *Sylvain Maréchal: L'égalitaire, "l'homme sans Dieu": Sa vie, son oeuvre. 1750–1803.* Paris: Lefeuvre, 1950.

Donakowski, Conrad. *A Muse for the Masses: Ritual and Music in an Age of Democratic Revolution 1770–1870.* Chicago: University of Chicago Press. 1972.

Donohue, Joseph W., Jr. "Character, Genre and Ethos in Nineteenth-Century British Drama." *The Yearbook of English Studies* 9 (1979): 78–101.

_____. *Dramatic Character in the English Romantic Age.* Princeton: Princeton University Press, 1970.

_____. *Theatre in the Age of Kean.* Totowa: Rowman and Littlefield. 1975.

Dowd, David Lloyd. *Pageant-Master of the Republic: Jacques-Louis David and the French Revolution.* Lincoln: University of Nebraska Press, 1948.

Downer, Alan. "Players and the Painted Stage—Nineteenth-Century Acting." *PMLA* 61 (1946): 522–76.

Draper, F. W. M. *The Rise and Fall of French Romantic Drama, with Special Reference to the Influence of Shakespeare, Scott, and Byron.* London: Constable, 1923.

Driver, Tom. *Romantic Quest and Modern Query: A History of the Modern Theater.* New York: Delacorte Press, 1970.

Droz, Jacques. *L'Allemagne et la Révolution Française.* Paris: Presses Universitaires de France, 1949.

Durbach, Errol. *"Ibsen the Romantic": Analogues of Paradise in the Later Plays.* Athens, GA: University of Georgia Press, 1982.

Eastman, Arthur. *A Short History of Shakespearean Criticism.* New York: Random House, 1968.

Eggli, Edmond. *Schiller et le romantisme français*. Paris: J. Gamber, 1927.

Ehrmann, Jaques, ed. *Literature and Revolution*. Boston: Beacon Press, 1970.

Ehrstine, John. *The Metaphysics of Byron: A Reading of the Plays*. The Hague: Mouton, 1976.

Eichner, Hans. "The Eternal Feminine: an Aspect of Goethe's Ethics." *Transactions of the Royal Society of Canada,* Series 4, 9 (1971): 235–44.

_____. *Friedrich Schlegel*. New York: Twayne, 1970.

Ellis, J. M. *Heinrich von Kleist: Studies in the Character and Meaning of His Writings*. University of North Carolina Studies in Germanic Language and Literature, no. 99. Chapel Hill: University of North Carolina Press, 1979.

_____. *Kleist's 'Prinz Friedrich von Homburg': A Critical Study*. University of California Studies in Modern Philology, no. 97. Berkeley: University of California Press, 1970.

El Nouty, Hassan. "Théâtre et anti-théâtre au dix-neuvième siècle." *PMLA* 79 (1964): 604–612.

_____. *Théâtre et pre-cinéma: Essai sur la problematiqe du spectacle au XIXᵉ siècle*. Paris: A.-G. Nizet, 1978.

Emrich, Wilhelm. *Die symbolik von Faust II: Sinn und Vorformen*. Berlin: Junker und Dünnhaupt, 1943.

(The) Era of Goethe: Essays Presented to James Boyd. Oxford: Basil Blackwell, 1959.

Erdman, David. "Byron's Stage Fright: The History of his Ambition and Fear of Writing for the Stage." *ELH* 6 (1939): 219–43.

Esslin, Martin. *Theatre of the Absurd*. 1961. Reprint. Woodstock, NY: Overlook Press, 1963.

Estève, Edmund. *Alfred de Vigny, sa pensée et son art*. Paris: Bibliothèque d'histoire littéraire et de critique, 1923.

_____. *Byron et le romantisme français*. 2nd ed. Paris: Furne, 1929.

Evans, Bertrand. *Gothic Drama from Walpole to Shelley*. Berkeley: University of California Press, 1947.

Evans, David Owen. *Social Romanticism in France*. Oxford: Clarendon, 1951.

_____. *Le Théâtre pendant la période romantique (1827–1848)*. 1925. Reprint. Geneva: Slatkine, 1974.

Ewen, Frederic. *The Prestige of Schiller in England 1788–1859*. New York: Columbia University Press, 1932.

Falk, Eugene. "Musset's *Lorenzaccio.*" *Tulane Drama Review* 2 (1958); 32–37

Farrell, John P. *Revolution as Tragedy: The Dilemma of the Moderate from Scott to Arnold.* Ithaca: Cornell University Press, 1980.

Flag, John Sewell. *'Prometheus Unbound' and 'Hellas': An Approach to Shelley's Lyrical Dramas.* Salzburg: Institut für Englische Sprach und Literatur, 1972.

_____. "Shelley and Aristotle: Elements of the Poetics in Shelley's Theory of Poetry." *Studies in Romanticism* 9 (1970): 44–67.

Fletcher, Richard. *English Romantic Drama: 1795–1843.* New York: Exposition Press, 1966.

Fricke, Gerhard. *Gefühl und Schicksal bei Heinrich von Kleist.* Berlin: Junker und Dünnhaupt, 1929.

Frye, Northrop. *Anatomy of Criticism.* Princeton: Princeton University Press, 1957.

_____. *Fables of Identity.* New York: Harcourt, Brace, 1963.

_____. *Fearful Symmetry.* Princeton: Princeton University Press, 1947.

_____. *A Study of English Romanticism.* New York: Random House, 1968.

Frye, Prosser Hall. *Romance and Tragedy.* Lincoln: University of Nebraska Press, 1961.

Furst, Lillian R. *The Contours of European Romanticism.* Lincoln: University of Nebraska Press, 1979.

_____. *Counterparts: The Dynamics of Franco-German Literary Relationships 1779–1895.* Detroit: Wayne State University Press, 1977.

Gaiffe, Felix. *Le Drame en France au XVIIIe siècle.* 1910. Reprint. Paris: A Colin, 1971.

Gans, Eric. *Musset et le 'drame tragique'.* Paris: Jose Corti, 1974.

Garland, H. B. *Lessing, The Founder of Modern German Drama.* 2nd ed. London: Macmillan, 1962.

_____. *Schiller.* New York: Medill McBride, 1950.

_____. *Schiller, The Dramatic Writer.* Oxford: Clarendon, 1969.

_____. *Storm and Stress.* London: George C. Harrap, 1952.

Gassner, John. *Masters of the Drama.* New York: Dover, 1945.

Gaudon, Jean. *Victor Hugo dramaturge.* Paris: L'Arche, 1955.

Gaull, Marilyn. "Romantic Theatre." *Wordsworth Circle* 14 (1983): 255–63.

Geary, John. *Heinrich von Kleist: A Study in Tragedy and Anxiety.* Philadelphia: University of Pennsylvania Press, 1968.

Gerould, Daniel, ed. *Melodrama. New York Literary Forum*. no. 7 (1980).

Gilman, Margaret. *The Idea of Poetry in France from Houdor de La Motte to Baudelaire*. Cambridge: Harvard University Press, 1958.

Ginistry, Paul. *Le Mélodrame*. Paris: Louis-Michaud, 1910.

Girard, René. *Deceit, Desire, and the Novel*. Translated by Yvonne Freccero. Baltimore: Johns Hopkins Press, 1965.

Giraud, Jean. "Alfred de Musset et trois romantiques allemands." *Revue d'histoire littéraire de la France* 18 (1911): 297–334, 19 (1912): 341–75.

Glachant, P., and V. Glachant. *Un Labotoire dramaturgique, Essai critique sur le théâtre de Victor Hugo*. 2 vols. Paris: Hachette, 1902–1903.

Gleckner, Robert. *Byron and the Ruins of Paradise*. Baltimore: Johns Hopkins Press, 1967.

Gochberg, Herbert. *Stage of Dreams: The Dramatic Art of Alfred de Musset*. Geneva: Droz, 1967.

Goldstein, Stephen L. "Byron's *Cain* and the Painites." *Studies in Romanticism* 14 (1973): 391–410.

Gooch, G. P. *Germany and the French Revolution*. London: Longman, Green, 1920.

———. "Political Background of Goethe's Life." *Publications of the English Goethe Society,* n.s. 3 (1924–1926): 1–30.

Gottlieb, Erika. *Lost Angels of a Ruined Paradise: Themes of Cosmic Strife in Romantic Tragedy*. Victoria, Canada: Sono Nis Press, 1981.

Graham, Ilse. *Goethe and Lessing: The Wellsprings of Creation*. New York: Barnes and Noble, 1973.

———. *Goethe: Portrait of the Artist*. New York: Walter de Gruyter, 1977.

———. *Heinrich von Kleist: Word into Flesh: A Poet's Quest for the Symbol*. New York: Walter de Gruyter, 1977.

———. *Schiller: A Master of the Tragic Form: His Theory and His Practice*. Pittsburgh: Duquesne University Press, 1974.

———. *Schiller's Drama: Talent and Integrity*. New York: Barnes & Noble, 1974.

Granges, Charles-Marc Des. *Geoffroy et la critique dramatique sous le Consulat et l'Empire 1800–1814*. Paris: Hachette, 1895.

Grant, Richard. *The Perilous Quest: Image, Myth, and Prophecy in the Narratives of Victor Hugo*. Durham: Duke University Press, 1968.

———. *Théophile Gautier*. Boston: Twayne, 1975.

Gray, Ronald. *Goethe: A Critical Introduction*. Cambridge: Cambridge University Press, 1967.

Grimsley, Ronald. "The Character of Lorenzaccio." *French Studies* 2 (1957): 16–27.

Guthke, Karl. *Modern Tragicomedy*. New York: Random House, 1966.

Haile, H. G. *Invitation to Goethe's Faust*. University, AL: University of Alabama Press, 1978.

Hall, Jean. "The Socialized Imagination: Shelley's *The Cenci* and *Prometheus Unbound*." *Studies in Romanticism* 23 (1984): 339–50.

Hamburger, Michael. *Contraries: Studies in German Literature*. New York: E.P. Dutton, 1970.

Hamiche, Daniel. *Le Théâtre et la Révolution*. Paris: Union Génerale d'Editions, 1973.

Hammer, Carl. *Goethe and Rousseau: Resonances of the Mind*. Lexington, KY: University Press of Kentucky, 1973.

Harrington-Lueker, D. "Imagination versus Introspection: *The Cenci* and *Macbeth*." *Keats-Shelley Journal* 32 (1983): 172–89.

Hartman, Elwood. *French Romantics on Progress: Human and Aesthetic*. Madrid: Studia Humanitatis, 1983.

Hartman, Geoffrey. *Beyond Formalism*. New Haven: Yale University Press, 1970.

_____. *Wordsworth's Poetry 1787–1814*. Ithaca: Cornell University Press, 1971.

Hartog, W. G. *Guilbert de Pixérécourt, sa vie, son mélodrame, sa technique et son influence*. Paris: Champion, 1913.

Harvey, A. D. *English Poetry in a Changing Society 1780–1825*. London: Allison & Busby, 1980.

Hatfield, Henry. *Aesthetic Paganism in German Literature from Wincklemann to the Death of Goethe*. Cambridge: Harvard University Press, 1964.

_____. *Goethe: A Critical Introduction*. Cambridge: Harvard University Press, 1963.

Hauhart, William. *The Reception of Goethe's "Faust" in England in the First Half of the Nineteenth Century*. 1909. Reprint. New York: AMS, 1966.

Hauser, Arnold. *The Social History of Art*. 4 vols. Translated by S. Godman. New York: Random House, 1951.

Hauser, Ronald. *Georg Büchner*. New York: Twayne, 1974.

Hawkins, Frederick. *The French Stage of the Eighteenth Century*. 2 vols. 1888. Reprint. Grosse Pointe: Scholarly Press, 1888.

Haym, R. *Die romantische Schule*. Berlin: R. Gaertner, 1870.

Hayman, Ronald, ed. *The German Theater: A Symposium*. New York: Barnes and Noble, 1975.

Hayter, Alethea. "Coleridge, Maturin's *Bertram*, and Drury Lane." In *New Approaches to Coleridge. Biographical and Critical Essays*, edited by Donald Sultana, 17–37. London: Vision Press, 1981.

Heilman, Robert. *Tragedy and Melodrama: Versions of Experience*. Seattle: University of Washington Press, 1968.

Heitner, R. R. *German Tragedy in the Age of Enlightenment*. Berkeley: University of California Press, 1963.

Helbling, Robert E. *The Major Works of Heinrich von Kleist*. New York: New Directions, 1975.

Heller, Erich. *The Artist's Journey into the Interior and Other Essays*. New York: Vintage, 1968.

———. *The Disinherited Mind*. 1952. Reprint. New York: Farrar, Straus, and Cudahy, 1959.

Hellman, Hanna. "Kleists 'Prinz von Homburg' und Shakespeares 'Mass für Mass.' " *Germanisch-romanische Monatsschrift* 2 (1923): 288–96.

Henschel, Arnold. "The Primacy of Free Will in the Mind of Kleist and in the *Prince of Homburg*." *German Life and Letters* 17 (1963–1964): 97–115.

Herbert, Robert. *David, Voltaire, "Brutus" and the French Revolution: An Essay in Art and Politics*. New York: Viking Press, 1972.

Herd, E. W. "Form and Intention in Kleist's *Prinz Friedrich von Homburg*." *Seminar* 2 (1966): 1–13.

Hobson, Harold. *French Theatre Since 1830*. London: John Calder, 1978.

Hoffmeister, Gerhart. "Goethe's *Faust* and the *Theatrum Mundi*—Tradition in European Romanticiam." *Journal of European Studies* 13 (1983): 42–55.

Holmes, Richard. *Shelley: The Pursuit*. London: Weidenfeld and Nicholson, 1974.

Holzmann, Albert. *Family Relationship in the Dramas of August von Kotzebue*. Princeton: Princeton University Press, 1935.

Houston, John Porter. *Demonic Imagination: Style and Theme in French Romantic Poetry*. Baton Rouge: Louisiana State University Press, 1969.

———. *Victor Hugo*. New York: Twayne, 1974.

Howarth, W. D. *Sublime and Grotesque: A Study of French Romantic Drama*. London: Harrap, 1975.

Howe, Irving. *Politics and the Novel*. New York: Horizon Press, 1957.

_____. *Shakespeare und das deutsche Theater.* Stuttgart : W. Kohlhammer, 1947.

Staiger, Emil. *Friedrich Schiller.* Zurich: Atlantis, 1967.

_____. *Goethe.* 3 vols. Zurich: Atlantis, 1957.

Starobinski, Jean. *1789: The Emblems of Reason.* Translated by Barbara Bray. Charlottesville: University of Virginia Press, 1982.

States, Bert, Jr. "Addendum: The Stage History of Shelley's *The Cenci.*" *PMLA* 72 (1957): 633–44.

Steffan, Truman Guy. *Lord Byron's 'Cain': Twelve Essays and a Text.* Austin: University of Texas Press, 1968.

Steiner, George. *The Death of Tragedy.* London: Faber & Faber, 1961.

Stern, J. P. *Reinterpretations.* New York: Basic Books, 1964.

Stock, Frithjof. *Kotzebue im literarischen Leben der Goethezeit: Polemik-Kritik-Publikum.* Dusseldorf: Bertelsmann, 1971.

Stockley, V. *German Literature as Known in England 1750–1830.* London: Routledge, 1929.

Stokoe, F. W. *German Influence in the English Romantic Period 1788–1818.* New York: Russell & Russell, 1963.

Stower, Richard. *Alexandre Dumas Père.* Boston: Twayne, 1976

Strich, Fritz. *Goethe and World Literature.* Translated by C. A. M. Sym. 1949. Reprint. London: Kennikat Press, 1972.

Strohschnieder-Kohrs, I. *Die romantische Ironie im Theorie und Gestaltung.* Tübingen: N. Neimeyer, 1960.

Sturzl, Erwin A., and James Hogg. *Byron: Poetry and Politics.* Salzburg: Institut für Englische Sprach und Literatur, 1981.

Taborski, Boleslaw. *Byron and the Theatre.* Salzburg: Institut für Englische Sprach und Literatur, 1972.

Tandon, B. G. *The Imagery of Lord Byron's Plays.* Salzburg: Institut für Englische Sprach und Literatur, 1976.

Taylor, John Russell. *The Rise and Fall of the Well-Made Play.* New York: Hill and Wang, 1967.

Thibaudet, Albert. *French Literature from 1795 to Our Era.* Translated by Charles L. Morkmann. New York: Funk and Wagnalls, 1967.

Thompson, Bruce. *Franz Grillparzer.* Boston: Twayne, 1981.

Thompson, L. F. *Kotzebue: A Survey of His Progress in France and England.* Paris: Champion, 1928.

Thompson, G. R., ed. *The Gothic Imagination: Essays in Dark Romanticism.* [Pullman]: Washington State University Press, 1974.

Howell, Margaret J. *Byron Tonight: A Poet's Plays on the Nineteenth-Century Stage.* Windlesham, Surrey: Springwood Books, 1982.

Hubbs, V. C. "Heinrich von Kleist and the Symbol of the Wise Man." *Symposium* 16 (1962): 165–79.

Huebert, Catherine. "The Quest for Evil: Lorenzaccio and Caligula." *Romance Notes* 18 (1977): 66–67.

Huet, Marie-Hélène. *Rehearsing the Revolution: The Staging of Marat's Death 1793–1797.* Translated by Robert Hurley. Berkeley: University of California Press, 1982.

Hunt, Herbert. *Le Socialisme et le romantisme en France.* Oxford: Clarendon Press, 1935.

Irwin, Joseph. *M. G. "Monk" Lewis.* Boston: Twayne, 1976.

Jacobus, Mary. " 'That Great Stage Where Senators Perform': *Macbeth* and the Politics of Romantic Theatre." *Studies in Romanticism* 22 (1983): 353–87.

Jacqot, Jean, ed. *Le Théâtre Tragique.* Paris: Editions du Centre National de la Recherche Scientifique, 1962.

James, Louis. "Was Jerrold's Black Ey'd Susan more popular than Wordsworth's Lucy?" In *Performance and politics in popular drama: Aspects of popular entertainment in theatre, film and television 1800–1976,* edited by David Bradby, Louis James, and Bernard Sharratt, 3–16. Cambridge: Cambridge University Press, 1980.

Jones, John. *On Aristotle and Greek Tragedy.* London: Chatto and Windus, 1962.

Jourdain, Eleanor. *Dramatic Theory and Practice in France, 1690–1808.* London: Longmans, Green, and Company, 1921.

Jusserand, J. J. *Shakespeare en France.* Paris: Colin, 1898.

Kahn, Robert. "Kotzebue's Treatment of Social Problems." *Studies in Philology* 49 (1952): 631–42

Kaiser, H. "Kleist's *Prinz Friederich von Homburg.*" Imago 17 (1930): 119–37.

Kauffmann, F. W. *German Dramatists of the Nineteenth Century.* Los Angeles: Lyman House, 1940.

Kaufmann, Walter. *Tragedy and Philosophy.* 1968. Reprint. New York: Doubleday, 1969.

Kermode, Frank. *The Sense of an Ending.* Oxford: Oxford University Press, 1967.

Kistler, Mark. *Drama of the Storm and Stress.* New York: Twayne, 1969.

Klapper, Roxana. *The German Literary Influence on Byron.* Salzburg: Institut für Englische Sprach und Literatur, 1974.

_____. *The German Literary Influence on Shelley.* Salzburg: Institut für Englische Sprach und Literatur, 1975.

Knight, G. Wilson. *Byron and Shakespeare.* New York: Barnes and Noble, 1966.

_____. *Byron's Dramatic Prose.* Nottingham: Nottingham University Press, 1953.

_____. *The Golden Labyrinth.* London: Phoenix House, 1962.

Kohlschmidt, Werner. *A History of German Literature 1760–1805.* Translated by Ian Hilton. New York: Holmes & Meier, 1975.

Koone, Helene, and Richard Switzer. *Eugène Scribe.* Boston: Twayne, 1980.

Korff, H. A. *Geist der Goethezeit.* 5 vols. Leipzig: Koehler & Amelang, 1923–1954.

Kramer, Dale. *Charles Robert Maturin.* New York: Twayne, 1973.

Krieger, Murray. *The Tragic Vision: The Confrontation of Extremity.* 1960. Reprint. Baltimore: Johns Hopkins Press, 1973.

Krook, Dorothea. *The Elements of Tragedy.* New Haven: Yale University Press, 1969.

Kushner, E. "Histoire et théâtre chez Vigny." *Esprit Créateur* 5 (1965): 147–61.

Lafoscade, L. *Le Théâtre d'Alfred Musset.* 1901. Reprint. Paris: Nizet, 1966.

Lamport, F. J. *Lessing and the Drama.* Oxford: Clarendon, 1981.

Lancaster, H. Carrington. *A History of French dramatic literature in the seventeenth century.* 4 vols. Baltimore: Johns Hopkins Press, 1929–1942.

_____. *French Tragedy in the Reign of Louis XVI and the Early Years of the French Revolution.* Baltimore: Johns Hopkins Press, 1953.

_____. *French Tragedy in the Time of Louis XV and Voltaire.* Baltimore: Johns Hopkins Press, 1950.

Langbaum, Robert. *The Modern Spirit.* New York: Oxford University Press, 1970.

_____. *Mysteries of Identity.* New York: Oxford University Press, 1977.

_____. *Poetry of Experience.* 1957. Reprint. New York: Norton, 1971.

Lange, Victor, ed. *Goethe: A Collection of Critical Essays.* Englewood Cliffs: Prentice-Hall, 1968.

Larabee, S. A. "The 'Closet' and the 'Stage' in 1759." *Modern Language Notes* 56 (1941): 282–84.

Leacroft, R. *The Development of the English Playhouse.* Ithaca: Cornell University Press, 1973

Lebois, R. *Vues sur le théâtre de Musset*. Paris: Droz, 1966.

Le Breton, André. *Le théâtre romantique*. Paris: Bibliothèque de la Revue des cours et conferences, 1924.

Lefebvre, Henri. *Alfred de Musset dramaturge*. Paris: L'Arche, 1955.

Legouvé, Ernest. *Eugène Scribe*. Paris: Didier, 1874.

Liebz, Adolphe. *Etude sur le théâtre de M.-J. Chénier*. 1901. Reprint. Geneva: Slatkine, 1971.

Lindenberger, Herbert. *Georg Büchner*. Carbondale: Southern Illinois Press, 1964.

_____. *Historical Drama: The Relation of Literature and Reality*. Chicago: University of Chicago Press, 1975.

Lioure, M. *Le Drame de Diderot à Ionesco*. Paris: A. Colin, 1973.

Lob, Ladislaus. *From Lessing to Hauptmann*. London: University Tutorial Press, 1974.

Loftis, John. *Sheridan and the Drama of Georgian England*. Oxford: Basil Blackwell, 1976.

Lote, G. *En preface à Hernani*. Paris: J. Gamber, 1930.

Lough, J. *Paris Theatre Audiences in the Seventeenth and Eighteenth Centuries*. London: Oxford University Press, 1957.

Lougy, Robert. *Charles Robert Maturin*. London: Associated University Presses, 1975.

Lovejoy, A. J. *Essays in the History of Ideas*. Baltimore: Johns Hopkins Press, 1948.

Lovell, Ernest J., Jr. *Byron: The Record of a Quest*. Austin: University of Texas Press, 1949.

Lowin, Joseph. "The Frames of *Lorenzaccio*." *French Review* 53 (1979–1980): 190–98.

Lukács, Georg. *Deutsche Realisten des 19. Jahrhunderts*. Bern: A. Drancke, 1951.

_____. *Goethe and His Age*. Translated by Robert Anchor. 1968. Reprint. New York: Grosset and Dunlap, 1969.

_____. *The Historical Novel*. Translated by Hannah and Stanley Mitchell. Boston: Beacon Press, 1962.

Maas, Joachim. *Kleist: A Biography*. Translated by Ralph Manheim. New York: Farrar, Straus and Giroux, 1983.

Mackintosh, Iain. *The Georgian Playhouse: Actors, Artists, Audiences and Architecture 1730–1830*. London: Arts Council of Great Britain, 1975.

Mainland, W. F. *Schiller and the Changing Past*. Melbourne: W. Heinemann, 1957.

Man, Paul de. *Allegories of Reading: Figural Language in Rousseau, Nietzsche, Rilke, and Proust.* New Haven: Yale University Press, 1979.

———. "The Rhetoric of Temporality." In *Interpretation: Theory and Practice,* edited by Charles S. Singleton. Baltimore: Johns Hopkins Press, 1969.

Manifold, Gay. *George Sand's Theatre Career.* Theatre and Dramatic Studies, no. 28. Ann Arbor: UMI Research Press, 1983.

Mann, Otto. *Geschichte des deutschen Dramas.* Stuttgard: Alfred Kroner, 1960.

Mann, Thomas. *Essays of Three Decades.* Translated by H. T. Lowe-Porter. New York: Alfred A. Knopf, 1947.

Manning, Peter. *Byron and His Fictions.* Detroit: Wayne State University Press, 1978.

Mantzius, Karl. *A History of Theatrical Art in Ancient and Modern Times.* Translated by C. Archer. New York: Peter Smith, 1937.

Marchand, Leslie. *Byron: A Biography.* 3 vols. New York: Knopf, 1957.

Marsan, J. "Le Mélodrame et Guilbert de Pixérécourt." *Reveu d'histoire littéraire de la France* 7 (1900): 196–220.

———. "Le Théâtre historique et le romantisme." *Revue d'histoire littéraire de la France* 17 (1910): 1–33.

Marshall, William. *The Structure of Byron's Major Poems.* Philadelphia: University of Pennsylvania Press, 1962.

Mason, Eudo. *Goethe's Faust: Its Genesis and Purport.* Berkeley: University of California Press, 1967.

———. "In My Beginning Is My End." *German Language and Literature* 31 (1978): 135–44.

Mason, James Frederick. *Melodrama in France from the Revolution to the Beginning of Romantic Drama (1791–1830).* Baltimore: J.H. Furst, 1912.

Masson, Bernard. *Lorenzaccio ou la difficulté d'être. Lettres Modernes* 46 (1962).

———. *Musset et le théâtre interieur.* Paris: A. Colin, 1974.

Matthews, Brander. *French Dramatists of the Nineteenth Century.* New York: Charles Scribner, 1905.

Maurois, André. *Olympio: The Life of Victor Hugo.* Translated by Gerald Hopkins. New York: Harper, 1956.

McGann, Jerome. *Fiery Dust.* Chicago: University of Chicago Press, 1968.

McGlathery, James M. *Desire's Destiny: The Plays and Stories of Heinrich von Kleist.* Detroit: Wayne State University Press, 1983.

McIntyre, Clara F. "The Later Career of the Elizabethan Villain-Hero." *PMLA* 40 (1925): 874–80.

_____. "Were the 'Gothic Novels' Really Gothic?" *PMLA* 36 (1921): 664–67.

McKel, Kenneth. "Voltaire's Brutus during the French Revolution." *Modern Language Notes* 56 (1941): 100–106.

McKenna, Wayne. *Charles Lamb and the Theatre.* New York: Barnes & Noble, 1978.

McVeigh, Daniel M. " 'In Cainnes Cynne': Byron and the Mark of Cain." *Modern Language Quarterly* 43 (1982): 337–51.

Meeks, Leslie Howard. *Sheridan Knowles and the Theatre of His Time.* Bloomington, IN: Principia Press, 1933.

Meisel, Martin. *Shaw and the Nineteenth-Century Theatre.* Princeton: Princeton University Press, 1963.

Mellor, Anne. *English Romantic Irony.* Cambridge: Harvard University Press, 1980.

Mennehet, 0. *Order and Freedom: Literature and Society in Germany from 1720 to 1805.* London: Weidenfel and Nicolson, 1973.

Meyer, Michael. *Ibsen: A Biography.* Garden City, NJ: Doubleday, 1971.

Milatchitch, D. Z. *Le Théâtre de Honoré de Balzac, d'après des documents nouveaux et inédits.* Paris: Hatchette, 1930.

Miles, Josephine. *Eras and Modes in English Poetry.* 2nd ed. Berkeley: University of California Press, 1964.

Milne, F. "Shelley's *The Cenci:* The Ice Motif and the Ninth Circle of Dante's Hell." *Tennessee Studies in Literature* 22 (1977): 117–32

Minor, Lucian. "French Melodrama, That Social Climber." *Journal of Popular Culture* 10 (1977): 760–65.

Moland, Louis Emile Dieudonné. *Théâtre de la Révolution.* 1877. Reprint. Geneva: Slatkine Reprints, 1971.

Montgomery, Marshall. *Studies in the Age of Goethe.* Oxford: Oxford University Press, 1931.

Moore, John David. "Coleridge and the 'Modern Jacobinical Drama': Osorio, Remorse, and the Development of Coleridge's Critique of the Stage, 1797–1816." *Bulletin of Research in the Humanities* 85 (1982): 443–64.

Moser, Walter. "*Lorenzaccio:* Le carnival et le cardinal." *Romantisme* 19 (1975): 94–108

Moureau, Pierre "L'Ironie de Musset." *Revue des Sciences Humaines* 108 (1962): 501–14.

Moynet, M. J. *L'Envers du théâtre.* Paris: Hachette, 1873.

Murphy, John. *The Dark Angel: Gothic Elements in Shelley's Works.* London: Associated University Presses, 1975.

Nebout, Pierre. *Le Drame romantique.* 1895. Reprint. Geneva: Slatkine, 1970.

Nemoianu, Virgil. *The Taming of Romanticism: European Literature and the Age of Biedermeier.* Cambridge: Harvard University Press, 1984.

Nicholson, Watson. *The Struggle for a Free Stage in London.* 1906. Reprint. New York: Benjamin Blom, 1966.

Nicoll, Allardyce. *A History of English Drama 1660–1900.* 5 vols. Cambridge: Cambridge University Press, 1960.

Nordon, Pierre. "Alfred de Musset et Angleterre." *Les Lettres Romanes* 21 (1967): 245–50.

Odoul, Pierre. *Le drame intime d'Alfred de Musset.* Paris: La Presse Universelle, 1976.

Otten, Terry. *After Innocence: Visions of the Fall in Modern Literature.* Pittsburgh: University of Pittsburgh Press, 1982.

_____. *The Deserted Stage: The Search for Dramatic Form in Nineteenth-Century England.* Athens, OH: Ohio University Press, 1972.

Parnell, Paul E. "The Sentimental Mask." *PMLA* 78 (1963): 529–35

Partridge, Eric. *The French Romantics' Knowledge of English Literature.* Paris: E. Champion, 1924.

Pascal, Roy. *The German Sturm und Drang.* Manchester: Manchester University, 1953

Paulson, Ronald. *Representations of Revolution (1789–1820).* New Haven: Yale University Press, 1983.

Peacock, Ronald. *Goethe's Major Plays.* New York: Hill and Wang, 1959.

_____. *The Poet in the Theatre.* New York: Hill and Wang, 1960.

Peck, Louis. *A Life of Matthew G. Lewis.* Cambridge: Harvard University Press, 1961.

Peckham, Morse. *Beyond the Tragic Vision.* New York: George Braziller, 1962.

Peyre, Henri. *Shelley et la France.* Paris: Droz, 1935.

_____. *Victor Hugo: Philosophy and Poetry.* Translated by Roda Roberts. University, AL: University of Alabama Press, 1980.

_____. *What is Romanticism?* Translated by Roda Roberts. University, AL: University of Alabama Press, 1977.

Pitou, Alexis. "Les Origines du mélodrame français à la fin du XVIIIᵉ siècle." *Revue d'histoire littéraire de la France* 18 (1911): 256–96.

Poggioli, Renato. *Theory of the Avant-Garde*. Translated by Gerald Fitzgerald. Cambridge: Bellknap Press, 1968.

Politzer, Heinz. "Kleists Trauerspiel von Traum: *Prinz Friederich von Homburg.*" *Euphorion* 64 (1970): 200–220.

Pommier, J. *Varietés sur Alfred de Musset et son théâtre*. Paris: Nizet, 1966.

Poulet, Georges. *The Interior Distance*. Translated by Elliot Coleman. Baltimore: Johns Hopkins Press, 1959.

Prawer, Siegbert. *Romantic Period in Germany*. New York: Schocken Books, 1970.

Prior, Moody. *The Language of Tragedy*. Gloucester, MA: Peter Smith, 1964.

Prudhoe, John. *The Theatre of Goethe and Schiller*. Oxford: Basil Blackwell, 1973.

Rahill, Frank. *The World of Melodrama*. University Park, PA: The Pennsylvania State University Press, 1967.

Rajan, Tilottama. *Dark Interpreter: The Discourse of Romanticism*. Ithaca: Cornell University Press, 1980.

Ralli, Augustus. *A History of Shakespearean Criticism*. 2 vols. London: Oxford University Press, 1932.

Reed, T. J. *The Classical Centre: Goethe and Weimar 1775–1832*. New York: Barnes & Noble, 1980.

Rees, J. "Shelley's Orsino: Evil in *The Cenci.*" *Keats-Shelley Memorial Association Bulletin* 12 (1961): 3–6.

Rees, Margaret. *Alfred de Musset*. New York: Twayne, 1971.

———. "Imagery in the Plays of Alfred de Musset." *French Review* 36 (1963): 245–54.

Revue des Sciences Humaines, n.s. 108 (1962): Musset issue.

Richards, Kenneth, and Peter Thompson, eds. *Essays on Nineteenth-Century British Theatre*. London: Methuen, 1971.

Richer, Jean. "Nerval et ses deux *Leo Burkhart.*" *Mercure de France* 307 (1949): 645–78.

Rickert, Heinrich. *Goethe's Faust: Die Dramatisch einheit der Dichtung*. Tubingen: Mohr, 1932.

Ridenour, George. *The Style of Don Juan*. New Haven: Yale University Press, 1960.

Ridge, George Ross. "The Anti-Hero in Musset's Drama." *French Review* 32 (1959): 428–34.

———. *The Hero in French Romantic Literature*. Athens, GA: University of Georgia Press, 1959.

Rieger, James. *The Mutiny Within: The Heresies of Percy Bysshe Shelley.* New York: George Braziller, 1967.

Robinson, Charles E. *Shelley and Byron: The Snake and Eagle Wreathed in Fight.* Baltimore: Johns Hopkins Press, 1976.

Romantisme et Politique 1815–1851: Colloque d'histoire littéraire. Paris: A. Colin, 1969.

Root-Berstein, Michèle. *Boulevard Theatre and Revolution in Eighteenth-Century Paris.* Theatre and Dramatic Studies, no. 22. Ann Arbor: UMI Research Press, 1984.

Rose, William, ed. *Essays on Goethe.* London: Cassel, 1949.

Rosenberg, Harold. "The Resurrected Romans." *Kenyon Review* 10 (1948): 602–20.

Rosenblum, Robert. *Transformations in Late Eighteenth-Century Art.* Princeton: Princeton University Press, 1967.

Rosenfield, Sybil. *A Short History of Scenic Design in Great Britain.* Oxford: Basil Blackwell, 1973.

Rosenthal, M. L. "Ezra Pound: The Poet as Hero." In *Modern American Poetry: Essays in Criticism,* edited by Jerome Mazzaro. New York: David McKay, Inc., 1970.

Roston, Murray. *Biblical Drama in England.* Evanston, IL: Northwestern University Press, 1968.

Rowell, George. *The Victorian Theatre: A Survey.* 1956. Reprint. Oxford: Clarendon Press, 1967.

Russel, Olga. *Etude historique et critique des Burgraves de Victor Hugo, avec variantes inédites et lettres inédites.* Paris: A.-G. Nizet, 1962.

Schamber, Ellie Nower. *The Artist as Politician: The Relationship between the Art and the Politics of the French Romantics.* New York: University Press of America, 1984.

Schladenhauffen, Alfred. *L'Univers existentiel de Kleist dans le 'Prince de Homburg.'* Paris: Les Belles Lettres, 1953.

Schneider, Elizabeth. *The Aesthetics of William Hazlitt; A Study of the Philosophical Basis of his Criticism.* Philadelphia: University of Pennsylvania Press, 1933.

Scholl, Margaret. *The Bildungsdrama of the Age of Goethe.* Frankfurt: Peter Lang, 1976.

Séché, Leon. "Le Baron Taylor et le 'Léonidas' de Michel Pichat en 1825." *Les Annales Romantiques* 5 (1909): 241–72.

Seidlin, Oskar. "Goethe's Iphigenia—'verteufelt human?' " In *Von Goethe zu Thomas Mann. Zwölf Versuche.* Göttingen: Vanderhoeck und Ruprecht, 1963.

Serrano, Lucienne. *Jeux de Masques: Essai sur le travesti dérisoire dans la littérature.* Paris: A.-G. Nizet, 1977.

Sessely, A. *L'Influence de Shakespeare sur A. de Vigny.* Berne: Chandelier, 1928.

Sewall, R. B. *The Vision of Tragedy.* New Haven: Yale University Press, 1959.

Sharpe, Lesley. *Schiller and the Historical Character: Presentation and Interpretation in the Historiographic Works and in the Historical Dramas.* Oxford: Oxford University Press, 1982.

Sherbo, A. *English Sentimental Drama.* East Lansing, MI: Michigan State University Press, 1957.

Shroder, Maurice. *Icarus: The Image of the Artist in French Romanticism.* Cambridge: Harvard University Press, 1961.

Sices, David. *Theatre of Solitude: The Drama of Alfred de Musset.* Hanover, NH: University Press of New England, 1974.

Silz, Walter. *Early German Romanticism.* Cambridge: Harvard University Press, 1929.

————. *Heinrich von Kleist.* Philadelphia: University of Pennsylvania Press, 1961.

————. *Heinrich von Kleist's Conception of the Tragic.* Baltimore: Johns Hopkins Press, 1923.

Simpson, David. *Irony and Authority in Romantic Poetry.* London: Macmillan, 1979.

Sims-Gunzenhauser, William D. "Conflict of the Inner Life in Goethe's *Iphigenia* and Shelley's *Cenci.*" *Neophilogus* 63 (1979): 95–107.

Singh, Sheila Uttam. *Shelley and Dramatic Form.* Salzburg: Institut für Englische Sprach und Literatur, 1972.

Skerry, Philip J. "Concentric Structures in *Marino Faliero.*" *Keats-Shelley Journal* 32 (1983): 81–107.

Smith, James. *Melodrama.* London: Methuen, 1973.

Smith, Paul. "Restless Casuistry: Shelley's Composition of *The Cenci.*" *Keats-Shelley Journal* 13 (1968): 77–85.

Sontag, Susan. *Against Interpretation and Other Essays.* New York: Farrar, Straus & Giroux, 1961.

Spalter, Max. *Brecht's Tradition.* Baltimore: Johns Hopkins Press, 1967.

Sprigge, Elizabeth. *The Strange Life of August Strindberg.* New York: Macmillan, 1949.

Stahl, E. L. *Friedrich Schiller's Dramas.* Oxford: Clarendon, 1954.

————. *Heinrich von Kleist's Dramas.* Oxford: Basil Blackwell, 1961.

Thorburn, David, and Geoffrey Hartman, eds. *Romanticism: Vistas. Instances, Continuities.* Ithaca: Cornell University Press, 1973.

Thorn, Arline. "Shelley's *The Cenci* as Tragedy." *Costerus* 1 (1973): 219–28.

Thorslev, Peter L., Jr. *The Byronic Hero.* Minneapolis: University of Minnesota Press, 1962.

_____. "Wordsworth's *Borderers* and the Romantic Villain Hero." *Studies in Romanticism* 5 (1966): 84–103.

Trevelyan, Humphrey. *Goethe and the Greeks.* 1941. Reprint. New York: Octagon Books, 1972.

Trotain, M. *Les Scènes historiques: études du théâtre livresque à la veille du drame romantique.* Paris: Champion, 1923.

Ubersfeld, A. "Désordre et génie." *Europe* 490–91 (1970): 107–18.

Valency, Maurice. *The Flower and the Castle.* New York: Grosset & Dunlap, 1966.

Van Tieghem. R. P. *Musset, l'homme et l'oeuvre.* Paris: Boivin, 1944.

Veen, Jan van der. *Le Mélodrame nusical de Rousseau au romantisme, ses aspects historiques et stylistiques.* The Hague: M. Nijhoff, 1955.

Vietor, Karl. *Goethe the Poet.* Translated by Bayard Morgan. Cambridge: Harvard University Press, 1949.

_____. *Goethe the Thinker.* Translated by Moses Hadas. Cambridge: Harvard University Press, 1950.

Walter, Gerard. *Hébert et le Père Duchesne.* Paris: Janin, 1946.

Walzel, Oskar. *German Romanticism.* Translated by A. E. Lussky. New York: G. P. Putnam's Sons, 1932.

Wasserman, Earl. "Shakespeare and the English Romantic Movement." In *The Persistence of Shakespeare Idolatry*, edited by Herbert Schueller, 77–103. Detroit: Wayne State University Press, 1964.

_____. *Shelley: A Critical Reading.* Baltimore: Johns Hopkins Press, 1971.

Watkins, Daniel. "Violence, Class Consciousness, and Ideology in Byron's History Plays." *ELH* 48 (1981): 799–816.

Watson, Ernest Bradlee. *Sheridan to Robertson: A Study of the Nineteenth-Century London Stage.* Cambridge: Harvard University Press, 1926.

Watson, Melvin. "Shelley and Tragedy: The Case of Beatric Cenci." *Keats–Shelley Journal* 7 (1958): 13–21.

Webb, Timothy. *English Romantic Hellenism 1700–1824.* New York: Barnes & Noble, 1982.

Weitz, Morris. *Hamlet and the Philosophy of Literary Criticism*. Chicago: University of Chicago Press, 1964.

Wellek, René. *History of Modern Criticism: 1750–1950*. Vols. 1 and 2. New Haven: Yale University Press, 1955.

Wells, Stanley. "Introduction." *Nineteenth–Century Shakespeare Burlesques*. Vol. 1. London: Diploma Press, 1977.

Welschinger, Henri. *Le Théâtre de la Révolution*. 1880. Reprint. Geneva: Slatkine, 1968.

Wessel, Leonard. "Schiller and the Genesis of German Romanticism." *Studies in Romanticism* 10 (1971): 176–98.

Wetzels, Walter D., ed. *Myth and Reason: A Symposium*. Austin: University of Texas Press, 1973.

Whitman, Robert. "Beatrice's 'Pernicious Mistake' in *The Cenci*." *PMLA* 74 (1959): 120–35.

Wicks, C. B., ed. *The Parisian Stage*. Part 2, *(1816–1830)*. University, AL: University of Alabama Press, 1961.

_____, ed. *The Parisian Stage*. Part 3, *(1831–1850)*. University, AL: University of Alabama Press, 1960.

Wiese, Benno von. *Die deutsch Tragödie von Lessing bis Hebbel*. Homburg: Hoffman und Campe, 1948.

_____, ed. *Deutsche Dramaturgie vom Barock bis zur Klassik*. 2 vols. Tubingen: N. Niemeyer, 1956.

Williams, Raymond. *Modern Tragedy*. Stanford: Stanford University Press, 1966.

Wilson, A. Leslie, ed. *A Schiller Symposium*. Austin: Department of Germanic Languages, University of Texas, 1960.

Wilson, James D. *The Romantic Heroic Ideal*. Baton Rouge: Louisiana State University Press, 1982.

Wilson, Milton. *Shelley's Later Poetry*. New York: Columbia University Press, 1959.

Winner, Anthony. "Richardson's Lovelace: Character and Prediction." *Texas Studies in Language and Literature* 14 (1972): 45–60.

Winter, Marian Hannah. *The Theatre of Marvels*. Translated by Charles Meldon. New York: Benjamin Blom, 1964.

Witowski, F. *The German Drama of the Nineteenth Century*. Translated by I. E. Hurning. New York: Henry Holt, 1909.

Woodring, Carl. *Politics in English Romantic Poetry*. Cambridge: Harvard University Press, 1970.

Yarrow, P.J. "Three Plays of 1829 or Doubts about 1830." *Symposium* 23 (1969): 373–83.

Yates, W. E. *Grillparzer: A Critical Introduction*. Cambridge: Cambridge University Press, 1972.

Zeydel, E. H. *Ludwig Tieck, The German Romanticist: A Critical Study*. 1935. Reprint. New York: G. Olms, 1971.

INDEX

Abrams, M.H., 19, 257 n.22, 284 n.6, 291 n.22

Addison, Joseph, 30

Aeschylus, x, 4, 35, 36; *Agamemnon*, 8; *Oresteia*, 6, 7, 9, 10, 11, 81, 82, 205, 210; *Prometheus Bound*, 6, 8, 9, 37

Affron, Charles, xi, 192

Alfieri, Vittorio, ix, 34, 35, 127

Andrews, Miles Peter (with Frederick Reynolds): *The Mysteries of the Castle*, 114

Antal, Frederick, 37

Ancelot, François: *Fiesque*, 286; *Louis IX*, 178

Arnault, Antoine-Vincent, 179; *Germanicus* 170

Arnim, Achim von, 39

Arnold, Matthew, 279 n.42

Art or imagination, theme of, xiii, 2, 3, 15, 16, 18-19, 20, 21, 93, 95, 102, 106-7, 136, 152, 159, 160, 167-68, 194-95, 205-6, 222-23, 281 n.41, 293 n.51

Artaud, Antonin, x, 254; *The Cenci*, 155

Audience, 30, 34, 38, 43, 46, 47, 55, 58, 82, 84, 109, 110, 111, 163-64, 170, 175, 179, 243

Baillie, Joanna, 110, 120, 121, 126, 127, 137; *De Monfort*, 118-19, 123; *Orra*, 118; *A Series of Plays*, 43-44, 117-19

Baker, Carlos, 143

Baldick, Robert, 287 n.29

Ballanche, Pierre-Simon, 185

Balzac, Honoré de, ix, x, 182, 183; *Père Goriot*, 208-9

Bardolatry, 14, 31, 148

Baroque, 30, 55

Bates, E.S., 156

Battine, William: *Another Cain*, 279, n.37

Beaumont and Fletcher, 251, 255 n.10

"Beautiful soul," 71, 79, 87, 152, 205, 206, 229, 232-33, 235, 236

Beckett, Samuel, 251

Beddoes, Thomas Lovell, ix, 31, 32, 110, 139, 280 n.1

Benda, Georg: (with Jean Christian Brandes) *Ariadne auf Naxos*, 261 n.29; *Medea*, 262 n.29

Benjamin, Walter, 256 n.12

Bennett, Benjamin, xi, 166, 268 n.9, 269 n.20, 271 n.43, 298 n.38

Bentley, Eric, 251

Bernhardt, Sarah, 38

Blake, William, ix, 16, 18, 19, 21, 84, 106, 135, 151, 168, 204, 223, 236

Blankenagel, John C., 294 n.2

Bloom, Harold, 106, 136, 257 n.22

Boaden, James, 111; *Fountainville Forest*, 114; *Secret Tribunal*, 110, 112

Booth, Michael, xi, 27, 40, 259 n.1

Bradley, A.C., 45

Brecht, Bertolt, x, 39, 73, 254; *Mother Courage*, 251

Brentano, Clemens, 39

Brereton, Geoffrey, xi

Brooks, Peter, x, 4, 47, 283 n.34, 287 n.37

Browning, Robert, ix, x, 120-21; *Stafford*, 45

Bruford, W.H., 58

Büchner, Georg, ix, 56; *Danton's Death*, 172, 217-20, 222, 250

Buckstone, John: *Luke the Laborer*, 50

Bulwer-Lytton, Edward (Lord Lytton), 110

Burletta, 27, 38

Butler, E.M., 270 n.33

Byron, George Gordon (Lord Byron), ix, x, 13, 25, 28, 31, 39, 49, 51, 67, 76, 77, 83, 102, 107, 109, 110, 123, 127-37, 139, 140, 148, 162,